WRIT IN THE STONES

A new history of Brechin Cathedral

Roderick J Grahame

ISBN: **978-1-5272-0842-1**

Published by the Society of Friends of Brechin Cathedral

6 Church Street, Brechin, DD9 6EU

www.brechincathedral.org.uk

First Published: June 2017

Photography by Douglas Whyte and also some archive photos by Ted Drahony

Other photographs are in the public domain on the web.

Medieval plan of Brechin and 1867 plan of Brechin Cathedral courtesy of Angus Council collections managed by ANGUSalive Museums,Galleries and Archives. Used with permission.

Printed by City Press of Brechin.

To Emily and David –

may their life stories be as exciting as this story

Over the years and the centuries the Cathedral flourished

and the Cathedral declined

\- Ian Henderson

THE ROOND TOO'R

(Discovered in a Brechin Almanac by J.C., in the style of
McGonagall)

High, hoary, venerable too'r,
Wi' form as firm at thy first hour,
Confrontin' calmly storm and shoo'r
An' ither ill –
A silent witness to the power o' Pictish skill.

Upon the brink o' Michael's Den
Thou'st stood for more than centuries ten,
But for what end? Inquiry's vain,
As a' can see,
To trace the purpose o' the men that set up thee.

Perhaps 'twas some religious hope
Inspired them wi' the work to cope;
Perhaps 'twas danger made them stop
Their common toil,
Until they raised thee to the top attack to foil.

But whether hope, or faith, or fear
Was moving cause that placed thee here,
Thou hast been lang an object queer,
By many found,
And fouk in hundreds year by year aft view thee round.

Could thou man's history true relate,
Since first it cam' to be thy fate,
To look sae patient and sedate,
The ages o'er
Thou'd throw a licht on Church and state ne'er seen before.

Strong, sturdy stalk o' stane and lime,
That tak'st nae note o' want or crime,
Though standin' far ayont thy time
Thou need'st nae pity,
The object stateliest, most sublime in a' the city.

CONTENTS

FOREWORD

A familiar but baneful response to history is to configure the past as comfortingly different from the present day. Previous societies are caricatured as less sophisticated, more primitive, cruder, alien. Such attitudes reveal nothing so much as a collective desire to reassure the modern observer by demeaning the experience of the past...All historical investigations remain contingent on surviving evidence. One of the regular temptations seducing historians and their audience is to imagine knowledge of the past. Most has been lost, by nature, accident or design. The muddle of existence is simplified both by the historians' craft, which is at the root of selection, and by gaps in the evidence.[1]

All history is provisional. That does not mean that the events themselves are provisional, they are indeed *Writ in Stone* (as my title suggests), unalterable, unchangeable. Yet, every history is open to revision. Partly because new evidence from a long forgotten document or an archaeological find may shed new light on events. Partly because each age must re-interpret, re-evaluate its history in its own way, according to its own values and methodology. That is why this book is a "new history" of Brechin Cathedral. I have no doubt that in 200 years at the millennium celebrations of the Cathedral building some other scholar will come along and dissect my work, creating new interpretations; rightly so too!

I make no apology therefore that, as well as primary sources, I have sought guidance from those who came before me. Dr Coats' *Short History of Brechin Cathedral* (1902) proved a valuable skeleton, fleshed out by much of D.H. Edwards' material, David Adams perceptive scholarship and the many articles in the Society of Friends publications. Like the eighteenth century weavers of the town, my task was to weave all these strands together into a new tapestry. In some cases, I have offered new interpretations on old events, while still giving the reader the option of other viewpoints (fervently hoping, of course, that the reader would opt for my solution to an historical conundrum!) Elsewhere I have simply presented the facts and let the reader decide.

This work is prepared for a two-fold celebration: 2017, which marks the 70th anniversary of the Society of Friends of Brechin Cathedral, inaugurated by Rev James Anderson in 1947, and 2020, the eight hundredth anniversary of when most scholars suggest the current building received its foundation stone at the West door. So we get two bites at the anniversary cherry!

---

[1] Christopher Tyerman, *God's War: A new history of the Crusades* (London: Penguin Books, 2007) xiv

When I came to Brechin in autumn 2010 I was unaware that my family too had played its part in the history of the city. My great grandmother, Isabella Farquharson Mearns Buist, had died at Brechin Infirmary in April, 1953. Centuries before, George Ferrier, another ancestor, had been the coachman on the Brechin to Dundee mail coach. He may well be buried somewhere in the Cathedral graveyard, not far from my own Manse.

I also have become aware during my years here that many "locals" are only sketchily (if at all) aware of the rich, vibrant history of the little city in which we live and work. As Henderson stated, "The history of Scotland is writ in the stones of Brechin Cathedral."[2] It is so Brechiners might learn more of their own past, and to my "adoptive" niece and nephew, Emily and David, that this work is dedicated.

Roderick J Grahame, Lent 2017

---

[2] I.A.N. Henderson "Bringing the gospel to Brechin" in *Scots Magazine*, 1996, 242

ACKNOWLEDGEMENTS

Since I myself have carefully investigated everything from the beginning, it seemed good to me also, most excellent Theophilus, to write an orderly account for you too

-   St. Luke 1:3

Any historical account is built on the scholarship of previous generations in which old threads are woven into a new pattern. This book is unashamedly no exception! So I wish firstly to record a debt of gratitude to those whose own research I have begged or borrowed. These include W.W. Coats, whose own little book *A short history of Brechin Cathedral* (published at the time of the Cathedral's restoration in 1902) provided me with a substantial skeleton. To the former Session Clerks: D.B. Thoms and William Low whose own passion for the Cathedral's history shines through and to D.H. Edwards' many historical works and his wonderful little snippets in the Brechin Almanacs. A full bibliography for those wishing to read more on particular eras is provided at the end of the book.

I thank too all those whom I interviewed for my D Min thesis and whose reminiscences helped me flesh out many of the bones; to Elizabeth, our Society of Friends' archivist, and to Pam, the Secretary, for answering all my questions and pointing me to the right sources. A great debt is also owed to the extremely patient and helpful staff in Brechin Library who never found any of my many requests too onerous; to Alison, who was again my second pair of eyes, pointing out mistakes, offering advice on better phrasing and ensuring in covering controversial episodes that I remained the objective historian rather than passionate theologian! To the congregation for their forbearance and encouragement as I pursued my passion for history and, last, but no means least, my long suffering mother, Margaret, who has put up with my long periods of disappearing into the study or library for research and writing and my two Labradors, Butey and Smokey, who sat so patiently at my feet throughout. To you all, I offer my heartfelt gratitude.

NOTE: Throughout the text the dates given for various clergy refer to their tenure at Brechin Cathedral and not their living dates.

CHAPTER ONE

Misty Beginnings

"Let's start at the very beginning, a very good place to start"[1]

- *The Sound of Music*

As the song suggests, the best place to begin any account is at the beginning. Yet, in the case of the historical story of Brechin Cathedral that proves problematical, for we must ask: where does that story really commence? Should we begin in January 1929, when Rev Dr Walter William Coats received by post a Roman coin of probable 5th century origins, reputedly dug up during the Restoration of the Cathedral in 1901? Does this mean that there were inhabitants on the site of the Cathedral as early as the 400s? We certainly know of a Roman fort near present day Stracathro[2] Church that dated from Agricola's campaigns of AD83/84[3]. Or, should we side with the Rev James Landreth who strongly believed that the Cathedral site had been a centre of Druidical practices long before Christian missionaries came to these shores? Landreth declared that: "If Druidism ever flourished on the site of our present Cathedral, then the cry of a tortured victim has rent the air, and the green hill has run red with human blood, when the flames rose high, and when priestly blades were sheathed in palpitating bosoms."[4] Heady stuff!

---

1 From the song Do-Re-Me

[2] From Gaelic *Strath Cathrach* or strath of the city.

[3] My thanks to Dr James Bruhn for supplying research on the Stracathro Roman encampments; the fort was probably abandoned by AD87.

[4] James Landreth, *Brechin Cathedral: its history, with a survey of the religious bodies that have worshipped on the site.* (Brechin, 1883)p. 8 M.E. Leicester Addis is also of the view that Brechin was a major seat of Druidism north of the Forth. However, many Celtic scholars urge caution regarding the Druids, for aside from scant references to them by Greek and Roman writers, there is little archaeological nor textual evidence to support their existence. Julius Caesar refers to them in his *Commentarii de Bello Gallico* as being concerned with divine worship and questions of ritual practice.

It is certainly the case that the site on which the Cathedral stands would have been ideal for the Druidical religion; water nearby at the Skinner's burn, a wood and a hill. It is also very likely that any Christian missionaries would tend to utilise and "Christianise" former sites of pagan worship. We know too of the Iron Age hill forts of the Brown and White Caterthuns[5] nearby, which tends to suggest that the area was well settled for several centuries before the Roman incursions of the first century. In June 1907 a Bronze Age funeral urn was unearthed during ploughing of Stracathro Hill; the urn contained several human bones,[6] thus indicating the area was inhabited from prehistoric times.

---

[5] From the Gaelic *Caithir Dun* or City Hill; Ptolemy writing in the mid-2nd century assigns to the Venicontes tribe of Angus and the Mearns merely one city, Orrea. There may of course have been others.
[6] 1908 Brechin Almanac

Or, another alternative theory is to go with the legend of Brychan, son of Anlach, son of Coronoc, an Irish king, and Marchell, daughter of Tewdrig, king of Garthmadrun. Brychan (whom legend states had a staggering eleven sons and twenty five daughters!) was reputedly martyred for his Christian faith down by the inch of river South Esk in the mid-late 5th century[7]. We could, of course, start even later in the late 10th century when King Cinaed Mac Mael Coluim II (r.971-995) dedicated the great monastery of Brechin to the Lord.

However, while all of these theories and starting points are possible, I am going to begin my account with a Pict called Dubhoc who lived circa 650 and who founded a small Pictish Christian community at, or near, the site of the present Cathedral. According to Archibald Scott[8], Dubhoc (not to be confused with Duthoc of Tain) probably came from the parent monastery of Monifod (present day Monifieth) in the mid seventh century. We know that Monifod was founded in circa 578 therefore it seems entirely plausible that, within seventy years, that monastic community was sending out monks within the neighbouring areas to convert the populace. What we cannot be certain of is whether these Monifod monks were off-shoots of the Columban mission (563 – 97) or that of Ninian (394 - 432). Bradley, for one, cautions against any legends or claims we might have regarding a visit

---

[7] A manuscript was found amongst the Cottonian manuscripts in the British Museum in which this Brychan is mentioned.

[8] Archibald B. Scott *The Pictish Nation – its people and its Church*. (Edinburgh: TN Foulis, 1918) p.345

to Brechin by the great Columba; reminding us that much of the saint's life was actually spent in prayer and meditation on Iona, so he could not possibly have made as many visits as he is supposed to have! According to Scott, Christianity is brought to Angus much earlier in c. 480 by Buidhe, an Irish Pict.[9] Buidhe, Scott states, was a follower of Ninian and built upon and extended his legacy.[10] Bringing sixty workers as part of his *muinntir*[11], amongst them ten brothers and ten virgins, Buidhe established a fortified community at Caer-Buddhe, present day Kirkbuddo. This is close to Dunnichen and leads to an intriguing possibility.

With the defeat of King Ecgfrith's Northumbrian army by Bridei's Picts in 685 at the battle of Dun Nechtain,[12] did the political situation stabilise sufficiently for a distinctly Christian *Pictish* mission to take place in the locality of Brechin? Bede certainly suggests that the battle resulted in the stalling of the Roman influence within Pictland.[13] Bede records that following the Northumbrian defeat, the fortunes of the "Anglian kingdom began to ebb and fall away" within Pictland; so much so that the Roman bishop, Trumwine, withdrew his monks from the monastery at Abercorn in West Lothian. It is therefore highly possible that into this ecclesiastical vacuum, the Pictish Church began its own mission, of whom Dubhoc was one such protégé.

Dubhoc himself probably lived in a small circular cell like hut, but, in time, a Church or *Dairteach,*[14] probably a structure of oak logs with a stone foundation would be built. While the Picts did prefer round structures (the devil couldn't hide in corners!), the possibility is that this first

---

[9] Buidhe Mac Bronach of the family of Tadhg occupied Kiannaght in Ulster.

[10] We must, of course, realise that converting the staunchly pagan Picts to a new faith was an ongoing, rather than one-off task. While Buidhe (and Ninian) may have been moderately successful in their day, by later centuries the Picts may have lapsed back to their old ways.

[11] Religious communities founded along the lines of the Pictish/Celtic clan system and possibility initiated by Martin of Tours and then Ninian.

[12] Or Nechtansmere as the battle is sometimes called.

[13] Bede *Ecclesiastical History of England* p.293.

[14] Literally "oak house"

Church in Brechin was a rectangular structure. It may even have had attached a round wooden watch tower, from which the Round Tower would evolve. The location of the original Pictish Church was probably where today's **West door of the Cathedral** lies, since this would have been the central point.

David Adams suggests that this wooden church was surrounded by a protective earth bank called a *rath* (Gaelic) or *vallum* (Latin).[15] In the midst of this semi-circular banking, with the burn on its southern flank, would have been a number of turf or wooden dwelling huts, perhaps some subsidiary chapels or oratories and a burial ground. Ceremonial standing crosses (at this stage most likely of wood) guarded the west and northern entrances of this enclosure. A body of itinerant priests would have served this early Christian settlement, as well as any outlying preaching stations.[16]

Sadly, we know little else of Dubhoc. His disciple may have been St. Drostan Dairthaighe (Drostan of the oak house cell) who lived "in the heights of Brechin" (probably Glen Esk) and died in 719. Drostan's ministry lasted some thirteen years during the reign of Nechtan (706 – 724). Given that Drostan's ministry occurs a mere twenty years after the battle of Dun Nechtain, and if we accept that Dubhoc's ministry began shortly after the battle, we can see that there is a strong likelihood that not only were they contemporaries, but perhaps Drostan may indeed have been Dubhoc's "apprentice" in the faith.

As is often the case in this early period, the records then go dark until in the late eighth/early ninth century emerge the Culdee monks, who found a monastery on the site of Dubhoc's earlier Church. Yet Dubhoc's influence was to persist. Within the mediaeval Cathedral there was a side altar dedicated to his memory and the Pictish missal of the blessed Marnoc (a fellow Pict) was still being used within Cathedral worship as late as 1348.[17] The Culdees (or Cele Dei[18]) originated in Ireland under Maelran in Tallaght in 774.[19] They were, in essence, a reforming movement of ascetics, separated from the

---

[15] See David Adams *Brechin – the Ancient City*, edt. Gillian Zealander. To be found as an unpublished manuscript in the Brechin Public Library.

[16] The Brechin Cathedral clergy were probably not fully resident until the early 12th century with the Cele Dei.

[17] See Cosmo Innes *Registrum Episcopatus Brechinensis*.

[18] Literally "servants of God".

[19] See William Reeves *The Culdees of the British Isles* (Felinfach: Llanerch Publications,Small paper reprint, 1994)

general faithful, who lived under a specific rule and within a collegium or community[20]. The earliest reference to the Cele Dei in Scotland comes from 843 when Bridei, King of the Picts, gave the "island of Loch Leven to God omnipotent, to S. Servanus and to the Keledei hermits living there."[21] We may perhaps speculate that following Nechtan's acceptance of the Roman date for Easter in 712, and his subsequent expulsion of the Columban clergy in 717, the route was open for a new ecclesial movement to fill the void, namely the Cele Dei, passionate reformers themselves.

At this point in our tale it is worth pausing to consider another, rather intriguing, suggestion by Norman Atkinson. Following the expulsion by Nechtan of the Columban clergy, the King seems to have decided to be (re?) baptised by bona fide clergy with allegiance to Rome, rather than Iona. Atkinson suggests that Curetan (697-717) , bishop of the Picts under King Brude in 697, is none other than Boniface, a name change expressing his new found loyalty to Rome[22]. Hector Boece records that:

> Boniface was carried in a boat into the River Tay and landed near the mouth of a little river which separates the district of Gowrie from Angus. Here he built a Church and dedicated it to St. Peter. From there he set off to preach at the village of Tellein and founded a second Church, some three miles distant. He founded a third church at Restenneth..."[23]

The Venerable Bede records that following Nechtan's adoption of the Roman date for Easter: "the nation thus reformed, rejoiced, as being newly put under the guidance of Peter, the most blessed chief of the Apostles, and committed to his protection."[24] Thus in the light of Nechtan's decision to throw his lot in with Rome (rather than Iona) it would seem that several churches in Angus were built and received dedications to St. Peter.

Linked to this is a reference within the *Aberdeen Breviary* which recounts:

> ...that Nechtan the King of the Picts, when the sign was seen, had come to this place with his army. Seeing such a great multitude of strangers he was not a little affected by admiring amazement. But suddenly inspired by the grace of the Holy Spirit, in that hour, he, with all his elders and ministers, received the sacrament of baptism in the name of our Lord Jesus Christ at the hands of blessed Boniface and his bishops. Indeed, the king of whose God fearing men handed over and delivered blessed Boniface *the place of baptistery in the Name of the Holy*

---

[20] The college of the Culdees was situated in the College yards, what is now near the Cathedral allotments.
[21] *Registrum Prior St. Andrew's* (H.S., C.E.D. ii 147)
[22] Possibly in honour of Boniface V (575-625) A Pictish bishop was present at a Council in Rome in 721.
[23] Hector Boece The Chronicles of Scotland (Paris, 1527) Vol.1
[24] Bede's Ecclesiastical History of England, 364

Trinity. In this place well nigh innumerable people were signed by him (Boniface) with the holy unction of the Christian faith, and he employed himself with the example of his completely holy life even into his old age in the construction of churches and other places of devotion with the purpose of imbuing people with his faith.[25]

Atkinson's contention is that it was Brechin, rather than the traditional Restenneth, that was the sight of Nechtan's baptism. He bases this view on two main factors. Firstly, that no other church in Angus received a dedication to the Trinity. Second, the St. Mary Stone (which we will return to later) is eighth century and consequently: "such a slab being produced in Brechin in the early 8th century is strong supporting evidence for the Holy Trinity dedication at Brechin indicating the church of Nechtan's baptism."[26] While I agree with Atkinson in that the story of a church in Brechin starts much earlier than the donation of Cinead II in the 10th century, I am more cautious as to Atkinson's reasoning on Nechtan's baptism. For one thing, giving over the place of baptistery in the name of the Holy Trinity does not necessarily mean a church dedication. Any gift to the Church at this time (whether land, property or goods) would be made in the name of the Triune God. It would also seem odd that having dedicated all his previous churches in honour of Peter (and thus to the Pope in Rome) Boniface would suddenly change tact in favour of the Trinity in the single case of Brechin. Furthermore, just because the St. Mary slab may be 8th century in origin need not mean it was *produced* in Brechin. If Atkinson is correct in the Byzantine influence, it may indeed have been made in that far off Empire and brought to these shores in later centuries. I am also rather more cautious than Atkinson in moving away from the pedigree of Restenneth which, by strong local tradition, is considered Boniface's Church of St. Peter.

Where the evidence does support Atkinson is that clearly Brechin was a Church of some significance even as far back as 712; it may have been natural therefore for King Nechtan to seek baptism at such a holy sight. We may simply say then that we do not know if Nechtan was baptised at Brechin or not; the jury is still out.

So what of the Cele Dei? The structure of governance of the Cele Dei was very similar to the *muinntirs* of the Picts, and this may have helped pave their way amongst the native Pictish population. Within the Cele Dei community the Abbot or Ab (a priest) was senior to the bishop who, while still part of the community, had a particular function as "the prime evangelist".[27] Thus was the monastery independent of any diocesan

---

[25] Aberdeen Breviary (Edinburgh: Walter Chepman and Andrew Millar, 1510) lectio octaua, transl. R.K. Mackenzie
[26] Norman Atkinson "The coming of Christianity to Angus" in Soc. Paper no.43, 14
[27] John Finney Recovering the past – Celtic and Roman mission 55

control. Indeed, in a tribal society, the idea of a bishop's see had not yet arisen. Dowden reminds us that the bishop still had sacerdotal authority, in that only he could confer holy orders, but jurisdictional authority lay with the Abbot. The bishop often lived a solitary life as a hermit, separate from the community life, yet still a key part of it.[28] The community itself was eremitical in nature; that is to say that the monks lived in separate cells within a walled enclosure, the Church being the central building within the structures. Given Adams' description earlier of the Pictish community, it is easy to see that they were not so dissimilar.

As to their ethos and lifestyle, Peter O'Dwyer describes their focus as "total self-abandonment to the loving providence of God."[29] Their reforming zeal addressed the desire for possessions and lack of charity amongst the existing clergy, the lack of celibacy and the ignorance of the laity of basic Christian tenets. Penance for sin was encouraged, but not excessive mortification; the preference being to seek to inculcate virtue amongst the lapsed. There was a stress on the Anam cara (soul friend) as the proper means of confession:

> It is right to refuse the confession of a person who does not perform penance according to the soul friend, unless there happens to be a soul friend near whom he considers more learned in the Rules, in the ways of Scripture, and in the rules of the saints…and let him afterwards be enjoined penance according to the rules of frequent confession. [30]

According to Jocelyn in his twelfth century *Life of St. Kentigern,* the Cele Dei were well known for their practices of fasting, sacred vigils, prayers and meditation on the Divine Law. They carried out manual labours such as growing crops and sewing clothes and were sparring in both dress and diet, much of their Rule being concerned with dietary matters. For example: "New skimmed milk is allowed if there be no other kind of milk, and one fourth part of water mixed with it."[31] The tone of the community is summed up thus: "Silence and fervour, tranquillity without guile, without murmur, without contention, is due everyone."[32] Interestingly, this tenor of peaceable Christian life will re-appear in several guises in the Cathedral's later history. Thus a small monastic settlement of Cele Dei along these lines existed in Brechin, probably in the early-mid ninth century.

---

[28] John Dowden *The Celtic Church in Scotland* (London, SPCK, 1894)

[29] Peter O'Dwyer "Celtic monks and Culdee reform" in *An Introduction to Celtic Christianity*, edt. James Mackey 144

[30] Reeves, 90

[31] Reeves, 86

[32] Reeves, 83

Yet the ninth century was also to bring a new menace from the north, Vikings! The Norse invaders had already harried Iona in 795 and again in 802. In 806 a large number of monks were slaughtered at Martyr's Bay and by 851 Iona had been abandoned altogether. In 839 the Vikings devastated the Pictish kingdom of Fortrenn, slaughtering the king and his nobles, laying waste to the land and reducing many of the Pictish monastic communities (along with their precious libraries) to ashes. It seems highly probable, given the national picture of destruction by the terror of the Vikings, that Brechin was not immune and that it too was attacked in this period. It was not the last such attack – as we shall see. But in a way it marked the death knell of the purely Pictish Church for, following the defeat of 839, there arose a new king, a monarch of both Picts and Scots, Cinead I or Kenneth MacAlpin as he is better known (842-58)[33].

Cinead was determined to reform the Pictish Church along Scotic lines, thus bringing in Scotic clergy to the Pictish monastic settlements. Brechin was one Pictish centre that held out longest, probably due to its geographical isolation, for it was not until the twelfth century that final vestiges of the Pictish model vanished altogether; as Scott observes: Brechin, Deer, Abernethy, St. Andrew's and other Pictish areas "were sometimes cut off from one another, and from the world, by blockading wedges of Viking colonists."[34] The trouble with isolation is that while protecting the long established traditions, it also finally results in extinguishment for no new blood or ideas can permeate from further afield. Brechin's resistance to Cinead's reforms and the hostile Viking settlements nearby resulted in the clergy being insulated from the great theological continental thinkers that began to arise in this period. Under Charlemagne's governance men such as John Scotus Eriugena (c.815 – c.877) put forward their Neoplatonist ideas. Yet it is likely that Brechin, disconnected from new thoughts, continued to think and worship according to a Pelagianist form of Christian belief.[35]

Cinead's attempts at reform were strongly resisted by the Pictish Church. For one thing, it meant that the crown now had much more power over the Church, rather than it being bound more to clan ties. This assertion of monarch over Church resulted in one great clash: the appointment of the Abbot of the *muinntir*. The tradition was that on the

---

[33] Dr. Alex Woolf of St.Andrew's University holds that Cinead I should more properly be considered as one of the last Pictish kings rather than the first king of Scots. When we refer to Scots in this context we mean those of Irish extraction. Cinead's dynasty was certainly the first royal dynasty of Scotland and he did unite the peoples in a way as never before.

[34] Scott, 471

[35] Pelagius (c.360 – 418) was an Irish born theologian who opposed the idea of predestination and asserted the doctrine of human free will. There has been much debate about his influence on the churches of Britain pre-Norman period. I tend to agree that the Pictish and Celtic churches may have been strongly Pelagian.

death of the Abbot, his successor was sought amongst either his family or the family of the founder who had started the community. Clan ties were paramount. Cinead soon realised that this meant trouble for his reforming agenda: "Pict would succeed Pict; and the Scoticizing designs of Kenneth and his dynasty would be obstructed or defeated"[36]. Cinead and his advisors came up with an ingenious solution; the Abbot could be replaced along the old Pictish lines but a new appointment of Vicar (naturally a Scot) would control the spiritual work of the community, the education of the young and (crucially) the dispensing of the sacraments.

We should not think though that this transforming of the Pictish Church into a Scottish model took place in one reign, it was to take centuries and probably only reached its apogee in 906 when King Constantin and Bishop Kellach met at Moot Hill near Scone to bind Church and State into a social contract.

---

[36] Scott, 473

CHAPTER TWO
Medieval Flowering

"Hic est qui tribuit magnam civitatem Brechne Domino"

- ***From the Pictish Chronicle***

With these few brief words from the Pictish Chronicle, Brechin Cathedral finally enters written history proper. For it was probably early in the reign of Cinead II[1] (971 – 995) that the king "gave the great *civitas* of Brechin to the Lord." As Douglas Simpson has correctly pointed out, we should understand *civitas* not in the sense of a city but rather a principal monastic house which had chapels, preaching stations and perhaps even daughter houses associated with it and connected to it.[2] The very fact that it is recorded as a "great monastery" tends to suggest that it had already been in existence for several hundred years, thus confirming the claim of Dubhoc as originator and founder. Pictish churches did not receive dedications to saints in the same way that churches allied to Rome did, thus the dedication to the Holy Trinity[3] also may have been a "gift" from the King. It is likely also that at this time, or possibly even a little before it, that the Round Tower came to be built.[4]

What were Cinead II's motivations therefore in granting this monastery at Brechin royal patronage? These were probably twofold. On the one hand it was likely to have been a continuation of the Scotic influence upon the Pictish Church started by Cinead I. In granting lands, titles and wealth to the monastery there can be little doubt that this came at a price; Cinead placed his own Scotic-Irish clergy within the Church. However, the proud Picts were not so easily humbled or brushed aside by these upstart newcomers. The native clergy held onto their "college" or *muinntir* as well as a remnant of the old lands. They also continued to minister to the local people and it was not until

---

[1] Often called King Kenneth MacMalcolm

[2] Simpson Book 1 of Society, 4

[3] Strictly Brechin Cathedral is the Cathedral Church of the Holy Trinity.

[4] My guess is that the Round Tower was built c. 950 during the reign of Mael Coluim I, Cinead II's father. Cinead, having been passed over for the kingship by another branch of the family was thus to continue what his father had begun.

the twelfth century, with the further Roman reforms of Queen Margaret, that the final vestiges of the Pictish college of the Cele Dei finally died out.[5]

The second reason for Cinead II's gift to Brechin was much more political and worldly. For many years the Mormaers (or Earls) of Angus and the Mearns had been powerful nobles, governing their territory almost as pseudo-kings. One can imagine the blood ties to the clergy in the monastery of Brechin that had strengthened this local northern power base. With the centralizing tendencies of Cinead Mac Alpin and his successors, this power began to be threatened. When Cinead II came to the throne in 971 he acted quickly to establish his unrivalled authority by several raids; first into Strathclyde, then into England. By 973, he was attending a conference of Kings at Chester where Edgar the Peaceable (959 – 975) recognised Cinead's claims and secured the frontier between the two kingdoms. By 977, Cinead had eliminated his near rival for the throne, Olafr mac Castantin, and his position as King was secure. Now, Cinead turned his attention to the rebellious Mormaer of Angus and the Mearns, Cunthar. He stripped Cunthar of several lands and it was these the King then endowed to the monastery at Brechin. The point was clear: while the King could not rely on the loyalty of the Mormaer Cunthar, he could rely upon the fealty of a Church which he himself had gifted. We may then surmise that the gifting of the "great monastery of Brechin" by Cinead II took place c. 978, shortly after he had safeguarded his throne.

Yet, Cinead's treatment of the Pictish clergy and Cunthar, the local noble, was to prove his undoing. In 995 he was invited on a pretext to Fotherkern (present day Fettercairn) where "by treachery"[6] he was slain by his own subjects on the orders of Finella (or Finvela), daughter of Cunthar, whose only son Cinead had killed by his own hand at Dunsinnan. John of Fordun tells us:

> This wily woman (Finella), therefore, ardently longing for the king's death, caused to be made, in an out of the way little cottage, a kind of trap, such as had never before been seen. For the trap had, attached to it on all sides crossbows always kept bent by their several strings, and fitted with very sharp arrows; and in the middle thereof stood a statue, fashioned like a boy, and cunningly attached to the crossbows: so that if anyone were to touch it, and move it ever so little, the bowstrings would suddenly give way, and the arrows would straightway be shot forth and pierce him through. Having thus completed the preparations for perpetrating the crime, the wretched woman, always presenting a cheerful

---

[5] Though as noted in Chapter One, the missal of the blessed Marnoc, a Pict, was still in use as late as 1348.
[6] Ulster Annals

countenance to the king, at length beguiled him by flattery and treacherous words.[7]

Naturally enough, the king's curiosity was aroused concerning the mysterious statue inside the cottage and Finella, suggesting that by examining the statue's head a joke would be found, enticed the king to touch it. Thus he did and Cinead II perished as the crossbows unleashed their deadly arrows. Revenge was a dish best served cold! S. Berchan confirms these details saying that Cinead died on the moorland at the foot of the Mounth.[8] The king's companions upon finding his body searched for Finella but, failing to find her, set fire to Fettercairn as vengeance upon Cunthar's daughter.

Brechin's next mention is in 1012, when the monastery was laid waste by the Norsemen. Sweyn Forkbeard, King of Denmark, England and Norway sought to bring Scotland too under his control and despatched the legendary Danish captain, Camus, to bring back the Stone of Destiny. Having failed to land in the Firth of Forth, Camus landed at present day Lunan Bay and marched forth to Brechin; besieging the Citadel "which nature as well as art had fortified, but finding that its capture would too long delay them" they proceeded to take revenge on the inhabitants.[9] On this occasion the "city" was consumed by fire and only the Round Tower remained. Hector Boece records that the "ancient Pictish town of Brechin" was besieged by the Norsemen whose leader failed to capture the citadel. In retribution he destroyed the citadel by fire, from which it never recovered its former glory, save for the Round Tower, which was built by great

skill.[10] It was not to be the end of the Viking incursions for they were to return in 1034, though this time we have no knowledge of the damage they inflicted.

In or around this time, possibly shortly after the Normans conquered England, work began on the first purely stone Church. This may have been part of the re-building

[7] Fordun Book IV, Chapter 32
[8] Chronicle of the Picts and Scots, 96
[9] James Wylie (1886) 421f.
[10] I paraphrase here the Latin of Hector Boece *Scotorum Historiae*, lib. Xi (fol. 242 b, Paris 1575)

following the Viking destructions, but it was also undoubtedly part of a process of Church reform at this time. Richard Fawcett, Emeritus Professor at St. Andrew's University, has dated the base of a pillar within the current Cathedral (near to the Vestry) to the early part of the twelfth century.

Further, during John Honeyman's 1901 Restoration, remains were found in the west wall of the south aisle as well as at the Chancel which revealed an early Norman Church. Thus vestiges remain of what was likely to have been a small but beautiful Romanesque Church, probably completed in the early part of the 1100s. In particular, an ornate archway (c.1130-80) was unearthed near the West door, which probably originally formed the entrance to the Chancel.

This construction of a Church of stone properly marks the first Cathedral, since the Church now became the *Cathedra* or see of the bishop of Brechin. For at this time too, Queen Margaret[11], wife of Mael Coluim III (Malcolm Canmore), began her reforms of the Scotic-Pictish Church along Roman lines. On arrival in Scotland Margaret had been horrified by the laxity and irregularities of the Church and set about correcting these with passion. Although Margaret never lived to see her reforms completed, she passed on the torch of reform to her son, David I (reg. 1124 – 53)[12]. It was David (the so called "sair sanct for the crown") who re-introduced dioceses to Scotland, including the new bishopric of Brechin c.1150. When David came to the throne there were only four or five dioceses already functioning and to these he added five others, including Brechin and Dunblane. This was the list: Glasgow, Whithorn[13], St.Andrew's, Dunkeld, Aberdeen, Moray, Ross, Caithness, Brechin and Dunblane. Within the Cathedral vestry is therefore a stained glass window showing Bishop Samson administering Communion to King David.

---

[11] Margaret of Wessex (1045-93) was the sister of Edgar Aetheling, the last uncrowned Anglo-Saxon king. Born in exile in Hungary but returning to England in 1057, Margaret fled to Scotland following the Norman invasion of 1066. She married Malcolm Canmore in 1070 and was to become mother to three future kings of Scotland.

[12] King David has particular resonance for our family. Legend goes that the Graham line was started by William de Graham, an illustrious Anglo-Norman knight who accompanied David on his return to Scotland for his coronation in 1124. William was granted lands in Dalkeith and Abercorn.

[13] Whithorn chose to be subject to the Archbishop of York. Scottish ecclesial independence was finally recognised in a bull *Cum universi* by Pope Celestine III in 1192 and the Church in Scotland became "a daughter of Rome" by a special dispensation and subject to the Pope.

Whether this event actually took place or not is doubtful; for one thing David was to die at Carlisle in May 1153 after a lingering illness of some months, while Samson (previously the Abbot) did not become bishop until c. 1158. We know that Leot or Leod[14], Abbot of Brechin, witnessed to a charter given by David to the Church at Deer in 1132. The link between David and Brechin only becomes explicit in another charter from the reign of William the Lion and is dated c. 1165-71. The charter reads:

> William rex Scotie sciatis me concessisse et carta mea confirmasse Episcopis et Keldeis de ecclesia de Brechin donationem illam quam dedit illis rex David avus meus per cartam suam de foro imperpetuum habituro in villa per dies dominicos adeo libere sicut Episcopus Sanctiandree forum habet.[15]

The charter re-confirms a charter from the reign of King David in which the Bishop and Cele Dei of Brechin are granted a donation and permitted in perpetuity to hold a market on Sundays. A Sunday market was a rather unusual choice of timing, and we may perhaps suppose that other local markets on weekdays forced Brechin to hold one on Sundays.[16]

It is also of interest that the Cele Dei formed the nucleus of the new Chapter in Brechin. As Thoms comments: "David I showed himself rather severe and high handed in the treatment of the old Culdee clergy at some of his new episcopal sees, but at Brechin he retained the Culdees as the nucleus of the cathedral chapter."[17] Quite why the king is so lenient here is unclear, but we must recall that Brechin was an old centre of Pictish rule, so perhaps there were harbouring resentments against the new Norman overlords. In any case, we see during this period the gradual supplanting of the Cele Dei by Roman clergy. Samson (1158 – 78) is usually referred to as the first bishop of Brechin[18] and was probably the last of the Cele Dei bishops, having previously been Abbot. Samson's son Dovendalus (or Domnall) was to succeed his father as Abbot (the common Cele Dei practice) but not as bishop. Turpin, the first non-Cele Dei bishop and a personal friend of King William the Lion (r. 1165 – 1214), was possibly a Norman. Elected in 1178, Turpin was consecrated in 1180. During Bishop Turpin's time (1178 – 1198) we find not only Dovendalus as Abbot but Bricius as prior, thus revealing that the community of Cele Dei were still in existence under a prior. In 1219 John, son of

---

[14] Cosmo Innes has Leot as father of Samson; Reeves however is more cautious as to this family relationship. I too share Reeves' caution.

[15] Reeves, 119

[16] In 1466 Market day was changed to a Monday at "the instigation of the baillies and citizens of Brechin", though no reason was given for the alteration. In 1647, during the Cromwellian period, the Market day was then moved to a Tuesday to prevent "necessary preparations from infringing upon the Lord's day".

[17] D.B. Thoms "The Cathedral Kirk of Brechin" in *Book 11 of the Society of Friends*, (1958), 17

[18] Though another bishop, known only as "T" precedes Samson.

Malistus, appears as Abbot of Brechin in a mention of a grant to the monastic house at Aberbrothoc (Arbroath). John appears to have been succeeded as Abbot by his son, Murgundus, who was very likely the last of the Cele Dei Abbots. With the arrival of Gregory as archdeacon and Andrew as chaplain, the rule of the old Cele Dei had come to an end. By 1218, the Cele Dei are distinct from the Cathedral chapter and by 1248, they have disappeared altogether in favour of Dean and Chapter.

The Romanizing of the Church at Brechin was not accomplished overnight; begun at the instigation of Queen Margaret it was only a century or so after her death that it was finally accomplished. Attempts by King David and the radically anti-Celtic bishop Robert of St. Andrew's to absorb the diocese of Brechin were to fail however, for Samson was to outlive them both. Adams adds the comment: "It may be that the proprietorial interests of the abbatical family and Cele Dei were too entrenched even for the Crown to intervene."[19] The King may too have recalled the fate of Cinead II, slain at the hand of Finella of Angus and the Mearns! The side-lining of Brechin was thus partly due to the rise of St.Andrew's but also because the new Anglo-Norman monarchy feared the strength of old Pictish affiliations. Brechin too lacked any saintly relics, a key to ecclesiastical status in the Medieval world.

Thus while Dundee, Glen Isla and Strachan on Deeside remained part of Brechin's diocese, Menmuir and Fern were taken by Dunkeld; Edzell, Aldbar, Dun and Aberlemno by St. Andrew's. This gives the reader an idea of the very patchwork quilt affair that was land holdings in the Medieval diocesan structures.

James Landreth contends that the Church was ripe for reform, that the Cele Dei had become "erratic, greedy and pleasure loving", a "worldly minded and secularised priesthood."[20] We certainly know that the Cele Dei at St. Andrew's had not only wives but concubines also. While they had begun life as an ascetic movement, dedicated to reform, they ended corrupted by the worldliness that surrounded them. Yes, for a while their arcane rituals continued amongst the local people (for example, the missal of the blessed Marnoc, a Pict, was still in use as late as 1348) until they too vanished into history. The ending of the Cele Dei is a melancholy moment in the Cathedral's story but it was to lead to a great Medieval flowering.

---

[19] Adams, 11
[20] Landreth, 13f.

THE GREAT SEAL OF THE CATHEDRAL CHAPTER

At some point in the early thirteenth century it was decided that a new, larger Church should be built. Quite why is not clear, though we may speculate. In the early part of the reign of William the Lion (r. 1165 – 1214) the charter to the Cathedral from David I is re-confirmed (see text above). This may have been part of a continuation of the Romanizing policies of the Crown. It is also possible that the earlier Norman Romanesque Church had rather shallow foundations, a fact suggested by the excavation work of Honeyman,[21] and this may have resulted in structural problems. Coats in his *Short History of Brechin Cathedral* tells us that "Somewhere about 1220 the ancient Norman Church appears to have been deliberately pulled down, and the top of the knoll to have been levelled eastward of the Round Tower in order to make room for a larger building."[22] Interestingly, a recent structural survey undertaken by Nicoll Russell studios of Dundee concurs with this assessment regarding somewhat shaky foundations: "During the condition survey, excavations to the west of the Square Tower revealed very shallow foundations built of what appeared to the foundations of a previous structure."[23] Photographs taken appear to show the Square Tower, for example, resting on varying sized boulders[24]. I would thus

---

[21] Coats, 9 suggests that the foundations were only four to five feet in depth.

[22] Coats, 9

[23] Nicoll Russell studios, Condition report on Brechin Cathedral, 23

[24] Ibid. Appendix 2

concur with Coats and date the foundation of the present building to c.1220 (rather than the hitherto earlier date of 1150).

Bishop Turpin (1178 – 1202), who had attended the Third Lateran Council in Rome in March 1179, was succeeded by **Rodolph or Ralph (1202 – 14)**, formerly Abbot of Melrose and royal chaplain. Elected in 1199, Rodolph[25] was finally consecrated in 1202. **Bishop Hugo or Hugh (1214 – 18)**, who was probably from a native family who previously had provided the Cele Dei abbots of Brechin, then followed. It is very likely that it is Rodolph and Hugo who were involved with the initial architectural designs for the new Cathedral. The original plans were very likely to have been much grander than what was eventually built, and we can only guess at how magnificent that Cathedral might have been[26]. The reason for this change in the designs may very well have been the Papal interdict (Feb 1217 – Feb 1218) that was placed upon the Kingdom of Scotland by Pope Honorius III (1150 – 1227). The trouble, naturally enough, had a political rather than ecclesiastical cause! Alexander had sided with the English barons against the abuses of John of England (1166 – 1216) and wanted Louis, Dauphin of France, to inherit the English throne. Unfortunately, upon John's death, both the Pope and the English nobles changed sides, now supporting the nine year old Henry III (1216 – 72), John's son. This change left Alexander and the Scots facing a dilemma: support the young English King and abandon the alliance with France or stick with France and face the ire of the Pope. While Alexander considered, Guala Bicchieri, cardinal and papal legate instituted an interdict against the Scots. It was probably prepared at Bristol in November 1216 though was not made fully effective until 1217. Alexander himself was pronounced excommunicate in July 1217.[27] Of course, Alexander could not hope to hold out long against the mighty spiritual and political power of Honorius III and by November 1218, Honorius had issued a bull *Filia specialis* in which he re-asserted the special place of the Scottish Church to Rome.

For Brechin though, this papal interdict had come at the worst possible time. No services would be held in this period and the doors of the Cathedral would remain closed: no burials, baptisms or weddings officiated by clergy; the people would live and die without the rites or comforts of Holy Mother Church. Yes, the monastic offices would proceed, but Mass would only be celebrated privately by the clergy, not in public for the

---

[25] The appearance of Anglo-Norman names does not necessarily imply that these were interlopers, for such names became fashionable amongst the local families; Gregory, for example, may be an Anglicisation of the Pictish Giric.

[26] It might be argued however that it was the relative plainness of the Cathedral that saved it from total destruction at the time of the Reformation – a fate that was to befall its near neighbour, St. Andrew's Cathedral.

[27] For a good analysis of this incident see Richard Oram's *Alexander II: King of Scots 1214 - 49*

people. For the Cathedral authorities this also had a financial impact, for the revenues for burials, marriages and baptisms were also lost for more than a year. This may have meant that from being a prosperous diocese able to afford a new elaborate building it suddenly became an impoverished one, one in which the grandiose plans had to be severely curtailed. Although peace was reached in the autumn of 1217 between Alexander, Henry, Louis and the Pope, the damage had been done. Even when building work re-commenced in 1219 "the heart would be taken out of the people."[28] Any modern visitor to the Cathedral always remarks on how the pillars on the south are of inferior workmanship to the north – the papal interdict of 1217 may very well be the reason. It might also be conjectured that Hugo, who was relatively short-lived as bishop, may have been replaced by Gregory, precisely because Hugo had supported King against Pope during the interdict. It is merely a possibility, but given the timings, and the fact that Hugo was close to Alexander II as a royal clerk, a rather intriguing one!

Added to the loss of impetus in building the new Cathedral caused by the papal interdict, a further pressure to complete the building was added, for, according to Coats, in 1237, Lady Margaret, a (probably illegitimate) sister of Alexander II, was married at the Cathedral to a local noble[29]. Perhaps the nave had to be completed hurriedly for this marriage ceremony? Or maybe a cheaper design and inferior workmen were used? There is certainly a noticeable difference in quality between the work of the earlier masons and the later ones. Was this because of cost, the demands of the Royal wedding or did the Church authorities suddenly find other priorities on time and money? We simply do not know. Normally, medieval Cathedrals took a long time to be built, very often work stopping and starting as men, money and materials became available; a point well made by Frances and Joseph Gies in their illuminating *Life in a Medieval City*. They comment that "as work on a cathedral halts, resumes, progresses, halts again, several master builders may in charge at different periods, which among other things leads to stylistic alterations and inconsistencies."[30] Given normal practice, Brechin therefore seems to have been force finished within a comparatively short time of less than twenty years.

This new Cathedral would have consisted of an aisled nave, which served as the Parish Church, and an un-aisled Choir, hidden behind the rood screen where the clergy performed the daily offices. Into this space was also placed no less than seventeen

---

[28] Coats, 11

[29] Very Rev Dr James Cooper, Regius Professor of Ecclesiastical History at the University of Glasgow (1899-1922) has Lady Mariona, sister to Alexander II, marrying Gilbert, Earl of Pembroke and Lord Marshal of England, in Brechin in 1234. However, it seems unlikely to be this Royal wedding. Records show this took place at Berwick, which georgraphically is much more convenient for the Royal house. See Richard Oram's *Alexander II* (Birlinn, 2013)

[30] Frances Gies and Joseph Gies *Life in a Medieval City* (Harper Collins e-book reprint, 2016) loc.1751

Altarages and side-chapels (see text box below), though some Altarages served a double dedication. The Medieval Chancel or Choir would have been much longer than today's,

consisting of nine lancet windows on each side (three for each of the Trinity) along with hooded choir stalls for the various dignitaries and prebends of the Cathedral. With the painted statues of the saints and the ornate altars, it must have been a very colourful if rather outlandish site.

THE CHAPTER HOUSE (Now the Vestry)

By the time of Bishop Gregory (1218 – 46/7) we are onto firmer historical footing and we know a great deal more about him than his predecessors. Gregory first appears in a charter (c.1189 – 98) stating that he was Archdeacon of Brechin. Gregory was consecrated bishop on 15th December, 1218 and we have confirmation of Gregory's status in the following charter:

> Gregory, bishop of Brechin by the grace of God, bid eternal greetings in the Lord to the faithful of the Son and holy Mother Church. We, having good memory of Rodolph and Hugo, our well beloved predecessors, and seeking to follow in their footsteps, and with a view to charity, and with the consent of the chapter, have granted and by this charter so confirm to the Abbot and convent of St. Thomas the martyr…[31]

---

[31] Registrum Episcopatus Brechinesis, 261

It is extremely likely that, as bishop, Gregory was the person who was the motivator and

driving force behind the building of the new Cathedral. He too was to oversee the beginnings of the absorption of the Cele Dei's college into the new Medieval chapter. By the time of Gregory's death in 1246/47, the old Pictish-Celtic Abbot family had been transformed into secular Scottish nobles, the MacNabs.[32] Gregory is also named as a papal judge-delegate on several occasions and was present at the Royal Council at Forfar in 1225 and Dundee in 1230.

Gregory was succeeded by the short-lived Gilbert, who barely survived a few months and was never formally consecrated. Albin or Alwin (1247/46 – 69?) is the first of our more interesting bishops of Brechin. Originally Precentor within the Chapter, he was elected by them following Gilbert's untimely and sudden death. Yet there was a barrier to Albin's consecration; he was illegitimate and this was apparently widely known. There is even the suggestion that he may have been the bastard son of Henry de Brechin, who was himself the illegitimate offspring of Earl David of Huntingdon, younger brother to King William the Lion, in which case, although born on the wrong side of the sheet, Albin was of royal blood. University educated with the title *Magister*, Albin was described as "careful, discreet and prudent both in spiritual and temporal matters, born of unmarried parents."[33] The Papal Legate, Otto of Tonengo, bishop of Porto, thought that, despite his illegitimacy, Albin had the necessary qualities and gifts to be bishop. Thus, having been commended by the Legate for his "life, manners and learning",[34] the Pope commands the bishops of St. Andrew's, Glasgow and Dunkeld to proceed to consecration, providing Albin takes the usual oath of fidelity. This Papal Bull from Lyon is dated 19th July, 1247, which greatly assists our timeline, for it shows that sometime in early 1247 Albin was formally consecrated.

Following the death of King Alexander II of fever in 1249, Scotland was plunged into the minority kingship of the boy king Alexander III, a seven year old. Two factions arose, one based around Walter Comyn, Earl of Menteith and the other around Alan Durward, Justiciar. Although there is no concrete evidence to suggest that Albin allied himself with either faction, the late Prof. Donald Watt of St. Andrew's has suggested that he may have had a bias to the Durward faction. This did not prevent Albin, along with Bishop David of St. Andrew's, from writing a letter of protest in 1250 against the Durward led government erosion of church liberties, presumably due to the translation of St. Margaret's to Dunfermline that summer.

---

[32] From fillus Abbe, or Mac in Abbe, sons of the Abbot.
[33] Registrum 388
[34] Ibid.

Bishop Albin seems to have been well thought of by the Papacy of the day as there are several records of him acting as papal mandatory in various ecclesiastical and secular disputes. Chief amongst these was an investigation into Alan Durward's claim to the Earldom of Mar in 1257. At various points during his episcopate Albin seems to have been carrying out various papal mandate duties in Durham. However, in 1264 allegations were made of nepotism against Albin himself in that he had appointed a relative, one Adam, as Archdeacon at Brechin. Unfortunately, we know no more and the outcome of the case is unrecorded.

In the spring of 1267, Albin witnessed the charter of William de Brechin which gifted the hospital of Maison Dieu to the Cathedral for "the souls of William and Alexander, kings of Scotland." According to the Melrose Chronicle, Albin was to die in 1269 at an unknown location. There is some dispute however as to the exact date of his death, Coats placing it nine years earlier in 1260 at Brechin. Given the record of the gifting of Maison Dieu in 1267 which mentions Albin by name this earlier date seems unlikely however. Albin's episcopate is significant too in that by 1250 the Cele Dei were fully incorporated into the Cathedral Chapter. A bull by Pope Innocent IV of February 1250 records that: "The brethren at Brechin who were called Cele Dei are now by change of name styled canons." Albin's period as bishop can therefore be truly considered as a medieval episcopate as the final vestiges of the old Pictish model disappear.

There is following Albin some confusion as to his successor. Part of the reason for the uncertainty is that two Williams feature in our lists. The first of these is probably William de Crachin who was Dean at Brechin. According to some sources he was elected by the Chapter as Bishop but the papal legate, Ottobone, refused to consecrate him. He was said to be a fine character but with a "harsh voice" that was unpleasant to the ear. It seems likely that he appealed against the papal legate's decision but died in 1274 during the Second Council of Lyons.

Our second William may very well be William de Kilconcath, who was rector of the Dominican friars at Perth. However, unlike the other William, he was never elected by the Chapter and in fact declined the see of Brechin because the revenues were too small – an indication that this was one of the poorest Scottish sees.

At this point some sources include one Urwardus or Edward, a monk at Coupar Angus who was "a man very zealous in his calling; for it is testified of him that he went on foot through the whole kingdom with one Eustathius, Abbot of Aberbrothock (Arbroath), preaching the gospel wherever he came." His dates however seem to be the 1260s, during the episcopacy of Albin. Other sources, notably D.H. Edwards, state that Edward was a monk of the Red Friars or Trinity Friars from Coupar Angus who set up a Convent of

Friars in Brechin in 1260. About the same time a Hospitium of the Knights Templar was also founded, now the site of the Dalhousie Hotel and bar[35]. I suspect that the itinerant Edward was never bishop, yet he did have a significant influence within Brechin.

My own view is that due to various factors, not least the refusal of the papal legate to consecrate William de Crachin, the see may have lain vacant for several years until finally in 1284 Robert, Archdeacon, was consecrated as bishop. His episcopacy was short-lived and by 1286 yet another William, bishop of Brechin, is recorded as receiving an indulgence at Durham. The reign of Alexander III (r. 1249 – 86) was a period of great prosperity for Scotland; trade with Europe increased, the Norsemen were finally brought to heel at the battle of Largs in 1263 and the churches, monasteries and abbeys grew and flourished. For Brechin Cathedral this too must have been the period of a great medieval flowering. The library of the bishop of Brechin was reputedly well known throughout the kingdom and further afield. During the archaeological excavations at the Cathedral Hall in the summer 2009/10, one find of particular interest was the fragment of the fin of a glass goblet dating to the mid-late C13th, probably from the Low Countries[36]. We also know that by the mid C13th there was a wall around the Channonry and that many of the clergy associated with the offices of the Cathedral lived within its bounds. All of this suggests a wealth and opulence within the Cathedral in this period. Yet, on the night of 18th March, 1286, suddenly all that changed: Alexander III died tragically in a riding accident while travelling from Edinburgh to visit his new queen, Yolande de Dreux in Fife, whose birthday was the next day. His heir was a three year old grand-daughter, Margaret, Maid of Norway. The medieval flowering was about to wilt in uncertainty, revolt and war.

---

[35] Norman Atkinson in a recent talk at the Forfar and District Historical Society on the Knights Templar suggested that there were possible three Templar properties in and around Brechin: Templewood House at Keithock, Dalgety Farm on the South Bank of the River Esk near Kinnaird Castle and the Dalhousie Bar. In the case of the latter, it is described as Saddler's land in Charterrow. All of these would have been private gifts of land to the Order, none connected with the Cathedral Chapter.

[36] "Excavations in Bishop's Close" H K Murray and J C Murray, 48

ADDITIONAL INFORMATION – Section 1

THE ROUND TOWER OF BRECHIN

The original function of the Round Tower was threefold: as a *cloicteach* or bell tower to summon worshippers to prayer, as a treasury and library housing the important manuscripts and liturgical vestments and vessels, and as a refuge, particularly during the Viking incursions. In a *Short Account of the Town of Brechin* there is suggestion of a fourth possible usage: a place where penitents were confined until restored to the bosom of Mother Church.[37] While this is entirely possible, there is no concrete evidence in support of that theory.

A handbell rung from the top of the tower was used to summon the clergy to worship for the daily offices of matins (prayers during the night), lauds (before dawn), prime (6am), terce (9am), sext (noon), nones (3pm), vespers (about 6pm) and compline (the final office of the day).

There are two figures on the side of the Tower, one with a Celtic crozier, probably the Abbot or Bishop and the other with a Tau-crozier who represents either the Prior or the Ferlaiginn, the head of the clerical school or college. These figures may alternatively be apostles on either side of the Crucified Jesus, possibly Peter and Paul. There are two animals also depicted: a lamb and a lion. It is also likely that originally the insignia of the Trinity was also upon the Tower.

What of its construction date? Adams, with Edwards and this author, dates it to c. 950, it may have been inspired by Cinead's queen who came from the banks of the Liffey in Ireland and was thus likely familiar with these distinct structures. James Cooper, Regius

---

[37] See *Short Account of the Town of Brechin*, publ. T Colquhoun, Edinburgh, 1828

Professor of Ecclesiastical History at Glasgow University (1899 – 1922) concurs, suggesting that its inspiration is Irish while the skill of the Picts in its architecture is clearly shown.[38] Some art historians (notably Petrie) date the Tower to c. 1020, or later, on the grounds that Christ is tunic clad in the crucifixion depiction, whereas earlier depictions of Christ crucified show Him "reigning from a tree" in merely a loin cloth. However, this assumes that the development of religious art history moved at a uniform pace throughout Christendom, which it did not. Given that one of the Round Tower's functions was defensive, this later dating seems highly improbable, for the majority of Viking incursions had ceased by this date.

In support of an earlier dating for the Tower, we may also consider that when Cinead II gifted the *magnum civitas* to the Lord in the later C10th, several notable structures were likely already on the site, probably including the Round Tower. The evidence also points to the fact that it alone survived the burning of Brechin by the Viking Danes in 1012. There is one other piece of the jigsaw we must not overlook: relations between Ireland and Scotland had been very strong for several centuries and reached their apogee with Mughron Ua Nioc, Abbot of Tuam. After his death in 1032, and the arrival of the Normans in England in 1066, Scottish Kings began to look more to the south and east rather than the west for alliances. Thus the construction of an Irish tower on Scottish soil any time after the early C11th seems therefore highly improbable.

The round "cap" on top of the tower is of likely C15th origin and famously blew off in the great storm of 1683.

THE GREAT BRIG O' BRECHIN

The earliest record of a bridge at Brechin over the Esk comes from C13th when in 1220 Stephen of Kinnardsley granted disposition to Bishop Gregory to build one. The charter reads:

> (for) the sustenance of the Brechin Bridge, and the maintenance of the chaplains praying for the dead, his (Stephen's) lands of Drunsleed, with all the pertinents peculiarly enumerated.

This first bridge would have been wooden. Prior to this folk would have crossed the bridge further upstream at the fording point, a highly dangerous or even impossible act

---

[38] See *Scottish Church Society volume* in memory of James Cooper.

when the river was in spate[39]. By the 1470s a stone bridge was in place; the south arch being completed during the time of Bishop David Crannach (1436-59).

In 1684 considerable repairs were required to the Bridge and on 19th January £31.13s Scots was collected to "help repair the bridge of Brechin" though by 1686 these repairs had still not been carried out and the bridge was in an "ill and dangerous condition".

The north arch was rebuilt in 1787 by Alexander Stevens (1730-96) who also designed the Bridge of Dun. It was at the Brig that Jonat Coupar was reputedly bit on the neck by the devil. The sight of the Duke of Cumberland's troops marching over the Brig on their way to Culloden in 1746 was said to be a "splendid sight". Until 1796 it was the only bridge over the South Esk.

CATHEDRAL ALTARAGES

The seventeen[40] altarages in the Medieval Cathedral consisted of the following dedications:

| Our Lady the Virgin Mary | Early (mentioned Aug 1348), possibly founded by David Barclay, a friend of Robert the Bruce. Also endowed by Walter Stewart, Earl of Atholl, husband of Margaret Barclay, heiress of Brechin in 15th century; Enriched too by Erskines of | Supported by rents of properties in Brechin, Montrose and Dundee; Mass said daily each morning at the ringing of the second bell (lauds) for the souls of the Earl, his wife and successors. |

---

[39] There are numerous C19th and early C20th sources telling of the drowning of children at this point in the river.

[40] There may have been eighteen, if we include a very late one, that of St. Mary Magdalene, founded by James VI which was endowed by the lands of Arrat, which ran along what we call now Montrose St.

	Dun.	
Holy Cross formerly Nomine Jesu?	Nomine Jesu almost certainly the earliest; Endowed further June 1541 Holy Cross mentioned Aug 1348	May have received an endowment during the Crusades.
St. Katherine, blessed Virgin	Founded by Robert Hill, citizen of Brechin in Dec 1447	Endowed by houses and gardens towards its support. The Earl of Crawford also gave 20s ont of the lands of Drumcairn in Lethnot.
All Saints	Founded by William Meldrum, archdean of Dunkeld, c.1525	Endowed by Henry Quhit or White, prebendary at Finavon, left rents of a house and toft. Mass to be said with lighted tapers on the Sunday after All Saints Day annually. The house of Chaplains of this altarage was on the west side of the city.
St. Thomas the martyr	Possibly Thomas a' Becket? Archbishop of Canterbury, Martyred 1170, reputedly on the orders of King Henry of England.	Founded by Sir John Wishart, July 1442
St. Christopher the martyr	Literally "Christ-bearer". If he ever existed, may have been martyred under Emperor Decius in 251.Patron of Travellers. No longer on the official Roman Catholic List of Saints.	Founded by John Smart, citizen of Brechin, April 1458
St. Nicholas	4th century bishop of Myra in Asia Minor (now Turkey). Patron of Children and repentant thieves.	Both these altars were endowed in April 1512 by Gilbert Strachan, Canon of Brechin, but the likelihood is they may well have existed before this time due to popular demand.
St. Sebastian, the martyr	Martyred under Diocletian	See above

	c. 288. Reputedly a Praetorian guard to the Emperor himself. Popular saint amongst males, Patron of soldiers and athletes. In modern times has become something of an icon for the Gay movement due to rumours over his sexuality.	
St. Lawrence	One of the seven deacons of Rome under Pope Sixtus II, Martyred c. 258 under Emperor Valerian Patron of students, cooks and the poor.	
St. James	Brother of Jesus	This altar seems to have been on the same site as that of St.Anne
St. Anne	Mother of Mary	See above
St. Matthew	The Apostle	
St. John the Baptist	Founded 1429 by Atholl family to say low mass on ordinary days as opposed to High Mass at the main altar on feast days	Endowed further 1533
St. Andrew	Patron of Scotland	Probably founded by Robert Erskine, July 1525 Further endowed March 1537
St. Ninian First mentioned Jan 1451	Not a very important altarage, perhaps suggesting that Ninian's link with Brechin was fairly tenuous.	
St. Dubhoc or Duthac	Founder of a Church in Brechin	Endowed Nov 1485 by Malcolm Guthrie, citizen of Brechin.
All Souls	May have been same altar as All Saints.	

With all these side altars, the Cathedral must often have been a rather crowded and busy place. We should note that some Altarages may have had double dedications. Priests or later Choral Chaplains were employed simply to sing masses at these altars for the souls of their benefactors that they might lessen the soul's time in Purgatory. They were often referred to as "chantries" because of the singing that went on – often at great speed!

CHAPTER THREE
Siege and Sanctity

EDWARD I.

"Scots, wha hae wi' Wallace bled,

Scots, wham Bruce has aften led,

Welcome to your gory bed, or to victorie.

Now's the day, and now's the hour;

See the front of battle lour!

See approach proud Edward's power – chains and slaverie!

-   Robert Burns,
"Scots wha hae"

William, bishop of Brechin (1286 – 90) was obviously a man of some importance for he is recorded as being one of the Scottish clergy who addressed Edward I of England with a view to the marriage between Margaret, Maid of Norway, and his son, Prince Edward of Caernarvon. Sadly, poor little Margaret died of complications caused by seasickness in the Orkney isles in September 1290; the history of the whole of Britain would have been very different had she lived and the crowns of Scotland and England had been joined in matrimony.

With the Maid of Norway's death, the magnates of Scotland invited Edward I to adjudicate on who amongst the claimants was rightful King of Scots. Thus begins a period of great uncertainty in Scotland. There were initially fourteen claimants to the throne of Scotland, though realistically only four: John Balliol, Robert de Brus, Baron Hastings and John Comyn had any chance of success. This large field of possible kings was further complicated by Edward of England, who insisted that he was overlord of Scotland and the throne of Scotland was a feudal dependency of England. Significantly, Edward produced no evidence in support of his claims and the Scots magnates asserted that only a King of Scots could affirm this; they had no authority to affirm or deny Edward's assertion. Even all these centuries later, the rival claimants still provoke much controversy. John Balliol's claim was probably the strongest, for he was a legitimate great-grandson of David of Huntington, brother to King William the Lion. But Robert de Brus was of similar line, being son of Isabel, David's second daughter. Eventually in November 1292, Edward ruled in Balliol's favour with Edward Balliol, John's son as heir designate.

Unfortunately, John Balliol only ruled Scotland with Edward's consent and increasingly Edward undermined the Scottish throne, with a list of demands that became more and more outlandish, until in summer 1294 Edward demanded that, as Scotland's overlord, the Scottish king and nobles perform military service for him in his ongoing war against France. This was a step too far! By the summer of 1295 the Scottish nobles had had enough of Edward and his puppet king. They appointed a Council of Twelve, or Guardians, to rule instead. In response, in spring 1296, Edward invaded, sacking the chief port of Berwick. Balliol summoned an army but failed to lead them – indeed the Scots cavalry were badly beaten at Dunbar in April, 1296 by the earl of Surrey, Balliol's

THE ARMS OF THE BALLIOVN

own father-in-law! John fled to Montrose where he was captured by Edward's forces. In July 1296, John was ceremonially taken to the churchyard at Stracathro where he was ritually stripped of his royal vestments, earning him forever the nickname "Toom Tabard", the empty sur-coat. A few days later, at Brechin Castle, John formally abdicated his crown into Edward's hands in the shape of Edward's proxy, the Bishop of Durham. The record records:

In the cemetery of Stracathro (Stronkatherach) at the hour of vespers – John, King of Scotland, renounced his league with France, and confessed his sins against his liege lord the King, desiring to be reconciled with him…

…The said King John of his own free will resigned his kingdom, his royal dignity, his lands and goods, homage and all rights, saving only incarceration, in the hands of Edward, King of England, together with his royal seal in a purse under his privy seal.[1]

Edward's vengeance upon the rebellion was vindictive as he removed both the Stone of Scone and all the Scottish government records to London.

So what of Brechin in this period? According to the archaeological evidence[2] it seems that there was a great conflagration of fire in the late C13th. It would be natural to link this to Edward's invasions, though it is unclear whether it was the one of 1296 or 1303. Certainly, it seems that during these years many of the records and charters are lost and the bishop's great library destroyed – whether this was by the fire or removal of the manuscripts to London is impossible to conjecture. What we do know is that Edward destroyed all the Scottish prayer books in the Cathedral and re-constituted the Cathedral Chapter along the liturgy of Sarum (or Salisbury)[3]. Because our records are scanty from this time it is difficult to know who was bishop, but one bishop **Nicholas (1296-98)** makes a fleeting appearance. A papal document in his favour was sent from Pope Boniface VIII to John Balliol in January 1296 and Nicholas was consecrated shortly afterwards. By June 1298 however Nicholas was dead and **John de Kininmund or Kinninmunth (1298 – 1328)** was bishop. Did Nicholas perish in the fire that destroyed much of the bishop's palace and surroundings? Or was he to lose his bishopric with the abdication of John Balliol, his champion? We simply do not know of his fate.

John de Kinninmund was himself of an ancient and noble Fife family and was to be a great friend of Robert the Bruce, one of the clerics at his side during the decisive battle of Bannockburn in 1314. Kinninmund appears to have been appointed bishop of Brechin shortly after William Wallace gained the Guardianship of Scotland in September 1297, though whether his appointment was political in nature we cannot be sure. He was a former archdeacon and makes several appearances in the records. He is certainly elected according to canonical practice by the Chapter and consecrated by Matthew Aquasparta, cardinal bishop of Portus. In April and October 1304 he is at Brechin as bishop but in the winter of 1304/05 seems to be resident at St. Andrew's. In 1309 he is one of the bishops of Scotland who recognise Robert the Bruce's title to the crown, and in 1311 his seal is affixed to an agreement between the monasteries of Cambuskenneth and Coupar. In July 1321, John is at attendance at Parliament when King Robert

---

[1] Joseph Bain *Calendar of Documents relating to Scotland*, ii, 194; preserved in HM Record Office. These events occurred on 7th and 10th July, 1296 respectively.

[2] See H K and J C Murray

[3] See panel

confirms the right of Brechin to hold a Sunday market. His final appearance is in 1323 as he witnesses a gift of King Robert to the monastery at Aberbrothock (Arbroath).

Unfortunately, Brechin had not seen the last of Edward, *Malleus Scotorum*, for he returns in the summer of 1303. Sir Thomas Maule, younger brother of Sir William of Panmure and custodian of Brechin Castle, held it for the Scots. Edward's army laid siege to the castle, probably between the river and Butterkill, on the south side. Edward brought to bear his great siege engine, War Wolf or *Lupi Guerre*, stripping lead from the roof of the Cathedral to act as counter-weight. Fortunately, Edward's Christian conscience troubled him enough to send a payment of gold, fifty loads of lead and twelve oaks via his Chamberlain on 31st March 1305 to "J. Breghinsei espiscopo" that the Cathedral roof should be made good again! A number of stone coffins from earlier periods were discovered in the C19th century in a nearby field, and Jervise surmises that these were probably some of the missiles used by the English forces. Thomas Maule held out for twenty days, frequently seen dusting the battlements of the castle where English missiles had fallen. But Maule could not last indefinitely and finally an English missile hit him upon the breast. The little force in the Castle held out until the next day before throwing the gates open to the enemy. The castle was then completely destroyed for, in August 1303, a payment of 3s is made that sulphur may be purchased "for burning the castle at Breghyn"[4]. Care was taken however of the documents; they were placed in a wooden coffer at the cost of 2s 6d.

Other than John de Kinninmund being at the battle of Bannockburn in 1314, Brechin Cathedral vanishes once more into the mists of time, although we may presume

---

[4] Jervise, 126

that following a fire at the bishop's palace and the stripping of the roof lead from the Church some repairs and urgent reconstruction took place.

Adam of Moravia (1328-50)[5] was to succeed John as bishop. Adam had been in attendance at Avignon[6], along with James Bene, Archdeacon of St. Andrew's, as proctors to progress the case of King Robert the Bruce, who was still under sentence of excommunication by the Papacy. Robert had offered the Papacy £2000 to achieve this aim and clearly negotiations were at a delicate stage. News arrived at Avignon that the sees of both Brechin and St. Andrew's were vacant and Pope John XXII (who seems to have taken a liking to both Adam and James) advanced both of them to the episcopacy. It seems that at this time the see of Brechin was no longer to be filled by the election of a bishop within the Chapter, but that Pope John reserved the see to his own provision (*ea vice*). Adam was consecrated on papal order by William, bishop of Sabina, on 31st October, 1328 at Avignon. Some days before (20th) the Pope had already granted Adam the degree of doctor of Canon Law, all this papal preferment in spite of his illegitimate birth (as earlier with Bishop Albin).

Adam appears to have been favoured not only by the Pope but also by the Scottish Royal house[7]. He is auditor of the Exchequer (originally clerk to the Lord High Treasurer) in 1329, 1340 and 1342 and Ambassador to England in 1335-36. He was plenipotentiary again to the Royal court of England in 1341-42, having been granted safe conduct by the English crown in treaty negotiations. Adam was amongst the Scottish ambassadors who sought the liberation of King David II from English captivity in 1348.[8]

Adam also appears at the Scottish Parliament at Scone in September of 1341. We might therefore assume (given how well regarded Adam was by Pope, King Robert and King Edward III alike) that Adam of Moravia was a man of great skill, presence and personal charm. He was clearly a diplomat of considerable expertise and Brechin in this period must have been a real powerhouse with Adam at the helm. We know that he did visit Brechin on more than one occasion (e.g. August 1348) and that the likelihood is that Adam died in Brechin in the winter of 1348-49. It was also in this period (1347-50) that a

---

[5] Sometimes referred to as Adam of Moray, the confusion may arise because Adam was present with the bishop of Moray at Avignon when advanced to the see at Brechin.
[6] The Avignon exile of the Papacy from Rome was to last from 1309 (Clement V) until 1377 (Gregory XI). It's cause was the conflict between the Papacy and the French crown.
[7] Adam also appears to have been greatly favoured by Edward III of England who bore his expenses while he was in that country.
[8] David II had been taken into English captivity after his defeat at the battle of Neville's cross in 1346.

great plague was to strike Scotland[9], as John of Fordun records in his *Chronicle of the Scottish nation*:

> In the year 1350, there was, in the kingdom of Scotland, so great a pestilence and plague among men (which also prevailed for a great many years before and after, in divers parts of the world – nay, all over the whole earth), as, from the beginning of the world even unto modern times, had never been heard of by man, nor is found in books…nearly a third of mankind were thereby to pay the debt of nature. Moreover, by God's will, this evil led to a strange and unwonted kind of death, insomuch that the flesh of the sick was somehow puffed out and swollen, and they dragged out their earthly life for barely two days. Now this everywhere attacked especially the meaner sort and common people – seldom the magnates. Men shrunk from it so much that, through fear of contagion, sons fleeing as from the face of leprosy or from an adder, durst not go and see their parents in the throes of death.[10]

Whether Adam of Moravia (and indeed other clerics within the Cathedral compound) were victims of this plague is impossible to say, though it strikes me as somewhat of a co-incidence that Adam died during the time the plague held sway.

Philip Wilde (1350-51) was the Dean of the Chapter and was to succeed Adam as bishop. However, the succession was not without controversy. The Chapter duly elected Philip as bishop, as in past practice, and sent the necessary paperwork off to Avignon. However, we recall that John XXII (1316-34) had previously reserved this see as being appointed by the Papacy (perhaps a sign of its importance by the mid-fourteenth century). Clement VI (1342-52) pronounced the election null and void as being contrary to his wishes. Philip thus travels to Avignon to lay the facts before the Pope in Consistory. Philip's plea was that his election had not been out of disobedience to the Holy Father, but simply a case of plain ignorance; the Chapter being unaware of the papal reservation. Philip seems to have impressed Pope Clement for he is shortly after named as "Clement's man" and duly consecrated sometime in February 1350. His episcopacy was sadly short-lived; he was dead by the late summer of 1351.

Philip's successor was to be one of the more interesting characters in the history of the Cathedral. **Patrick de Lochrys or Leuchars (1351-83)** was named by Clement VI in an epistle from Avignon on 17th November, 1351. As with Philip before him, Patrick,

---

[9] This was the Second Great Pandemic. Recent research suggests that the "Black Death" may in fact not have been bubonic plague (as often thought) but some sort of mutated viral infection spread person-to-person. If so, this might explain the sheer speed of the process that caused infection to death in a matter of days. See Karen Jillings *Scotland's Black Death* (Tempus, 2003)

[10] John of Fordun CLXVII

a canon of St. Andrew's and a priest, had been elected by the Chapter at Brechin, having received permission to stand as a candidate by his superior, the Prior of St.Andrew's. Again, Clement VI asserts his rights to the see, declaring the election null and void. Yet, clearly Clement VI was mindful of the case of Bishop Philip and by December of 1351, Patrick has been consecrated by Bertrand, bishop of Sabina. The local candidate again received Papal approval.

We know a little of Patrick's career before his consecration. In June 1344, Clement VI received a request from King David II (1324-71) and Queen Joan to confirm Patrick as Dean of Haddington and rector of Tynyngham. By the time of his episcopal consecration to Brechin, Patrick held the benefice of Tannadice in the diocese of St. Andrew's and was a canon of that Chapter. His patronage by the royal house was to be continued for by 26th September, 1357, Patrick has reached the giddy heights of Chancellor of Scotland, a position he held until 1370.

It was during Patrick de Locrys tenure as bishop that the work began on the Square Tower. There has been some debate over this, some scholars suggesting that it was merely the "little cap" that was added to the Round Tower at this time, but Andrew Jervise is firmly of the view that it was the Square Tower, even if additions of style were made to it in later centuries. It seems that the architect was Sir William Disschington or Dishington (who may also have designed the steeple in Dundee). This William was the son of the original Sir William and his wife, Elizabeth Bruce, daughter of King Robert the Bruce, so clearly the family had important royal connections. The younger William was *seneschal* or steward at the court of David II, as well as being Master of the Fabric of several royally endowed churches. In 1366 he received a grant of lands from David of a mill at Aberlemno plus lands at Tillywhandland and Balgassie; Jervise conjectures this was for architectural work on the Square Tower. It also seems likely that one Alan Dorward was master mason. We know too that between 1354-84, in part payment of an ecclesiastical due, Henry Lechton, Vicar at Lethnot, delivered to Patrick "a large white horse and a cart to lead stones for the building of the belfry of the Church of Brechin."[11] Apparently, according to legend, the white horse was used to a better life than dragging a cartful of stones and proceeded to kick the builders! Perhaps as part of this exchange the prebendary at Lethnot was to become a canon of the Cathedral in 1384. We may thus date the construction of the Square Tower to the 1360s.

Patrick was also the driving force behind the *Declaratio* of 1372 in which the constitution of the Cathedral chapter was finally laid down in some detail:

---

[11] Edwards 16

There are eleven benefices of old erected into canonries in the Cathedral, of which four are dignitaries, namely Dean, Precentor, Chancellor and Treasurer; the fifth, the office of Archdeacon; all five incompatible with other benefices.[12] The other six benefices, namely those of the Vicar, the Pensioner, the sub-Dean with the prebends of Kilmoir, Butirgill and Guthrie we find to be simple prebends, and compatible with any other benefice, even with cure; and it is expressly declared that albeit two of the prebendaries of the latter class are commonly named Vicar and sub-Dean, yet they have no cure nor prerogative of dignity nor office nor administration within the Cathedral nor without.[13]

Perhaps unusually, Patrick was to resign the see in 1383 due to "old age and infirmity"[14] into the hands of the cardinal bishop of St.Mark's in Venice. Such was the esteem in which he was held by the Papacy that he was granted a pension of 100 merks sterling from the revenues of Brechin, was permitted to exercise pontifical rights and to be buried *in pontificalibus,* i.e. in his full episcopal vestments as befitted his station.

Stephen de Cellerio was to succeed to the see of Brechin in June 1383. Stephen it seems had become Archdeacon of Brechin in 1369, having previously been canon at Dunkeld Cathedral. We may therefore assume that he was very much Patrick's natural successor and carried on much of the work of his former mentor. It was during Stephen's episcopacy that Lethnot was added to the Chapter of the Cathedral.

There then appears a little confusion. Bishop Stephen appears to have died at some point in the winter/spring of 1405, for by Whitsun 1405 the see was declared vacant. According to some scholars the next bishop, Walter, was in post by early 1401 yet other records show that the see lay vacant until 1407 and that Walter was not consecrated until May 1410. The reason for this confusion may well be the Western schism (1378-1417) where for a time there were no less than three Popes vying for control of the Church.[15] In the midst of such confusing times it is little wonder that episcopal sees were not filled quickly. In 1407-8 a Council of clergy was held at Perth[16], at which a trial for heresy was instituted against James Resby, an Englishman and a

---

[12] This was to change after only a short while, leading to absentee prebends from parishes who also held offices in the Cathedral Chapter.

[13] Registrum Epicopatus Brechinensis, vol.I, xvif. Although the Declaratio lays down the constitution of the Cathedral Chapter the likelihood is that it had been in existence for some considerable time before this. D.B. Thoms makes the point that 14 documents of the Chapter pre-date 1372, only 6 ante-date it.

[14] Dowden 183

[15] The three rivals were Benedict XIII (1394-1423) based in Avignon; Gregory XII (1406-1415) the Roman claimant; John XXIII (1410-1415) the Pisan claimant.

[16] Held at the Dominican Church in Perth, it was probably a provincial rather than national council of clergy.

supporter of Wycliffe. The Inquisitor was the theologian Laurence de Lindores[17]; the outcome was a forgone conclusion and Resby was duly burnt at the stake, the first heretic in Scotland to be so. However, it may well have been during this Council that the Scottish clergy re-affirmed their support for the Avignon pope, Benedict XIII and that **Walter Forrester**'s appointment to Brechin was secured from the Papal court. Part of Benedict's hesitation in appointing Walter to the see may have been Forrester's previous antipathy to the Avignon Pope. Indeed bishops Wardlaw of St.Andrew's and MacCaelein of Dunblane were asked to investigate Walter's suitability. However no barrier to his appointment appears to have been found, and by May 11th 1410 Bishop Walter was consecrated.

So what do we know of him? Walter Forrester was likely born in Angus c. 1355 and his family, while of English origin, had risen to prominence in the local area. His brother, Patrick, was a burgess in Dundee and another kinsman, John, was Archdeacon of Teviotdale. Walter began his career as an agent of the Scottish Crown, serving as Depute Clerk of the Wardrobe (late 1370s) and Keeper of the Privy Seal (1386). Indeed he is described in several sources as a "royal clerk". As early as 1384, he is described as being a canon at Aberdeen Cathedral and holding the prebendary of Mortlach[18] in 1392. In 1386 he is named as Archdeacon of Lothian, a fairly prestigious position. During this period he was also studying in Europe, graduating Batchelor of Arts from the University of Paris in 1375 and studying canon law at the University of Orleans (1375-79). And in the early 1390s, Walter appears to have returned to Europe (at the Scottish Crown's expense) to continue further study. He graduates MA (Paris) 1394 and Batchelor of degrees, 1398. During this period he also served as university rector (late 1395) and was representative or *proctor* for (interestingly) the "English nation"[19] at the second council of Paris (1396) and the Third Council in 1398. This Third Council is of particular significance for one of its aims was to end the Western Schism that so divided the Papacy. The Third Council distanced itself from Benedict XIII, a position Forrester appears to have enthusiastically endorsed, perhaps explaining Benedict's later reticence in promoting him to bishop!

None of this was particularly unusual for an ambitious young man in late Medieval Europe, yet Walter had still to decide whether to serve Crown or Cross. The crunch seems to have come in March 1391 when he relinquished his land held at

---

[17] Laurence de Lindores was a scholastic philosopher of European reputation. He became a dominant figure at St. Andrew's University and was to be a fervent opponent of the Lollards, insisting on an anti-Lollard oath for graduands.

[18] Now Dufftown.

[19] We should bear in mind however that his family were originally of English stock.

Inverdovat at Forgan, Fife, to other members of his family, a clear signal that he was now set on an ecclesiastical path. Yet Walter was to continue to serve the Scottish King, first as ambassador to England and second, from 1403, as Clerk of the Rolls, a position he retained until his death. By the early part of the 15th century, Walter was sub-dean at Brechin Cathedral and his meteoric rise through the ranks thus takes him to bishop in 1410.

Rather surprisingly perhaps, we know rather less about his time at Brechin! Indeed, as D.E. R. Watt observes "though he (Forrester) did visit Brechin from time to time and did take some interest in the organisation and property of his see, it did not add up to much."[20] Walter continued to act in a diplomatic capacity for the Crown (1412-13) and in 1423 he was in Rome and Flanders in 1424. He certainly was in Brechin in 1410, for several charters are witnessed by him at the Cathedral Chapter. He also appears in 1412-13 to have pursued, via the Sheriff of Angus, crown revenues due to the Cathedral and his own see. In July 1419, Walter once more was at a provincial Synod at Perth. By the spring of 1425, Walter Forrester was dead. A new incumbent at Brechin was to be a very different character, yet was to fall foul of the Forrester family of which Walter had been a key part.

John de Crannoch (Carnoth or Crannog) is arguably the most colourful and saintly of all Brechin's Medieval clergy. He came to Brechin as its bishop with considerable expertise and experience. Probably born around 1385 possibly in Banffshire,[21] his father may well have been Laurence de Crannoch, a prominent burgess of Aberdeen. His uncle, Adam, was a prominent Augustinian who became Abbot of Scone. We also know of at least three brothers: William (an Augustinian and Abbot of Inchaffray), David (sub dean of Dunkeld and later Dean of Brechin) and Robert (precentor at Brechin and Dean of Dunblane). Given this notable family from which John emerged, it was perhaps inevitable that the Crannoch family would clash with the Forresters.

Educated at the University of Paris, John emerged with a BA in 1405 and an MA in 1406. He later taught at the University of Paris and was part of the university representatives who denounced the teachings of Jean Petit[22] at an ecclesial council in Paris in 1413. John was to gain a Batchelor of Theology by late 1416 and by the early part of 1418 he had left Paris for the Papal court which was currently at the council of

---

[20] Watt Biographical Dictionary, p.200
[21] The de Crannoch may relate either to the parish of Grange or Marnoch in this shire.
[22] Jean Petit was a theological Professor at the University of Paris who had argued that political assassination or tyranncide was justified according to Scripture.

Constance[23]. It was while at Constance that he began to become valuable to Pope Martin V, the Scottish King James I and the French Dauphin, Charles, to whom he acted as both diplomat and counsellor.[24] In particular he sought to act as one of the diplomatic team trying to secure the ransom of James I of Scotland from the English court, where he was to spend eighteen years as prisoner/guest (1406-24). John is recorded at the funeral of Charles VI of France in October 1422 and his service to the Papacy was rewarded in the December of the same year by Martin V granting him the see of Caithness. However, despite John being named bishop of Caithness, the Crannoch family were unable to secure the necessary money to pay for the Papal bulls, even in spite of an extension for payment. In any case, events took over, and by June 1426, John had been translated to the see of Brechin by the Pope. It is doubtful that he ever set foot in Caithness and remained forever the unconsecrated bishop of that diocese.

James I had sent John Crannoch, along with Thomas Mirton, Dean of Glasgow, on a diplomatic charm offensive to Rome in the summer of 1426. James wanted to appoint John Cameron, his Chancellor, as bishop of Glasgow. The Pope however stood in the way, for the benefice was a reserved Papal appointment. Crannoch clearly impressed Martin V by his diplomatic efforts on behalf of the Scottish crown and it was while in Rome he received the translation to Brechin. Again, money was to be a problem, for it was only after certain payments, including one for the Papal bull of appointment, that a bishop could proceed to consecration. He was still in arrears as late as 1430[25] but it would appear that by 1429 his consecration had taken place. However, this was only the beginning of John Crannoch's problems at Brechin. He was almost immediately opposed by Gilbert Forrester, Archdeacon and nephew to the former bishop, Walter. Gilbert almost certainly believed that the see should have been his after his uncle's death and had even attempted to appropriate to his own pocket some of the revenues of the see. This was to be the beginning of a long and bitter feud between the two clerics – as we shall soon learn!

---

[23] This was the Church council that ended the Western Schism, deposing the Spaniard Benedict XIII (whom Scotland recognised) and electing Martin V.

[24] It is noticeable that John Crannoch served the Scottish-French alliance while the Forrester family were much more pro-English in their sentiments. Political differences may thus also be one reason for the antipathy between them.

[25] Crannoch appears to have paid 16 florins, 33 shillings and 4 pence for his "common and little services" in August, 1426. On July 1st, 1430, he paid a further 125 florins and this payment regularises his position as bishop.

During his time in Brechin for his consecration, John secured the support and patronage of Walter Stewart, Earl of Atholl[26], who made a grant of £40 Scots in 1429 for a Sang Schule in the Cathedral. This was to be unique, the only Sang Schule of its kind in Scotland. It consisted of two chaplains and six boys who were to perform divine services in the choir and (later) to sing masses for the Earl and his family. The boys were to be taught music and grammar, were given a haircut, a strict code of behaviour and a coat or tabard of purple or white (presumably to make them quite distinctive amongst other youngsters). The boys were also to be accompanied at all times by one of their chaplains and were to refrain from going into the fields – to stop them getting into mischief! This did not always work and one story records them raiding the bishop's famous orchard by dead of night. Foolishly, they were easily spotted and identified in their colourful uniforms! The College or Sang Schule was operational by 1433, and by the March of that year, Crannoch was again resident in his diocese. Crannoch's stress on education might very well, under different circumstances, have resulted in the second of Scotland's universities being at Brechin, rather than Aberdeen. There is some evidence that Crannoch's plans for a Papal Bull for a university in Brechin were quite well advanced when he died suddenly in 1453.[27] Sadly, for Brechin, the proposal died with him.

In the earlier part of his episcopate, John Crannoch was frequently absent from his see. He appears there in 1429, intermittently 1433-36[28] and finally settles there in 1445. In 1435 he accompanies the eleven year old Princess Margaret, daughter of James I, to be married to the thirteen year old Dauphin, later Louis XI of France at La Rochelle. Sadly, the union was to be an unhappy one and Margaret died in 1445, apparently of fever. It was during one of his intermittent visits to Brechin in the 1430s that one of the most notorious events occurred. In the winter of 1438[29], John Crannoch's nemesis, Gilbert Forrester, is alleged to have physically assaulted the bishop within the Cathedral itself. The Chapter on 27th February, 1438 immediately imposed a sentence of excommunication upon the Archdeacon. However the background to this violent incident is itself illuminating. The battle began almost as soon as Bishop John had been consecrated. The Chancellor, Gaufridus of Arbroath, had alleged that Gilbert had demanded precedence over him, possibly even at the service of consecration itself.

---

[26] Walter Steward was also the founder of the Altar of our Lady in the Cathedral. He was grandson of Robert II and regarded by many as rightful king of Scotland. Rumour had it amongst his enemies that he had tried to procure said crown by despatching his own relatives. This was never proved but he was eventually brought to the scaffold for complicity in the murder of James I in February 1437, which he confessed to after three days of excruciating torture.

[27] Bear in mind that St. Andrew's (Brechin's great ecclesiastical rival) founded a university in 1413. Aberdeen university was not founded by Bishop Elphinstone until 1495.

[28] In this period Crannoch appears to have been seeking to secure property and revenues for the see.

[29] This date is uncertain. Certain sources cite 1435, but the chronology favours the 1438 date.

Further, it was alleged that Gilbert had refused to give up a breviary to one of the choral vicars, that he had failed to provide a living and suitable accommodation to the vicar who did the work of his parish at Strachan and that he omitted to pay the salary of the staller who supplied his place in the choir. All in all, Gilbert seems to have been drawing the revenues from his parish at Strachan but failing to utilise them in paying for spiritual services for his parishioners. By 1435 the conflict had intensified as Bishop and Archdeacon now quarrelled over respective jurisdictions. Gilbert, as Archdeacon, sought to be responsible for the discipline of faults of both laymen and clerics, even within the Cathedral precincts themselves. The case went to arbitration at the chapel of St. Paul the apostle in Perth in March 1435. The arbiters duly ruled in favour of the bishop. This did not satisfy Gilbert Forrester and by June 1436 he was in Rome seeking to be considered as a papal acolyte which would have removed him from Bishop John's jurisdiction. He did receive Papal permission to read the canonical hours according to Roman custom and rule and, since Brechin used the Rule and Liturgy of Sarum, "Gilbert's privilege was bound to bring him into conflict with the Bishop on liturgical as well as disciplinary matters, if he should attempt to exercise his immunities at home."[30] It is ironic that the dispute reached a peak during worship when, Crannoch alleges the Archdeacon "prodigal of his state and tarnishing the dignity of the Divine majesty, has disturbed the peace and liberty of the Church of Brechin, laying violent hands on the Bishop when he was saying divine hours in his Cathedral."[31] The Chapter had no choice for a sentence of excommunication was automatic.

In 1437 John Crannach suffered another blow with the murder of his friend, James I. The loss of his patron, combined with the execution of his other patron Walter Steward for the King's murder, was a major dent in Crannoch's fortunes. Indeed, Bishop John was never again to be involved in diplomacy on behalf of the Scottish Crown. He does make a few brief appearances at the Parliaments of June 1445 and January/May 1450 when matters ecclesiastical were being discussed[32] but other than this plays a fairly low key political role. More than that, not for the first time, the Cathedral was to find itself at the epicentre of political and ecclesiastical schism. Not only did the minority of James II create political instability, but in 1439 the Council of Basle deposed Pope Eugene IV and elected Duke Amadeus of Savoy in his stead as Pope Felix V.[33] Churchmen took different sides in this Papal controversy, with Stephen Angus, the

---

[30] Soc of Friends, Book 6, 23
[31] Reg Supp, 347, 116
[32] In particular the Bishop's right of testament was confirmed by the Crown.
[33] This was part of the struggle between the authority of the Papacy and that of the Conciliar movement which sought to assert the power of ecclesiastical councils, i.e. Basle. Eventually the Papacy was to be triumphant.

Treasurer of the Cathedral as an adherent of the power of the Council and even Bishop John's brother, David, having to clear his own name.

In the meantime Bishop John sought to enhance his power over the Cathedral Chapter by taking six of the benefices that he might appoint folk of his own choice. An allegation of nepotism might however be levelled against Bishop John as he sought to give one brother, Robert, the precentorship (1440 – 53) (Robert having failed in an earlier bid to become Dean), while his other brother David became Dean (1438- 40). In addition, the Crannach family finally sought to oust Forrester as Archdeacon by replacing him with William Fetchet, John's nephew. None of these moves, save that of Robert, was to be terribly fruitful. By 1440, both John and David had gone to Rome to fight their corner, leaving Robert as Vicar General. David had an allegation of schismatic activities dropped against him, including that of being a supporter of the Council of Basle. In exchange, John de Lichton, a member of another notable local family and part of the Forrester faction, took the Dean's benefice.[34] David Crannach and Duncan de Lichton both retained canonries, Bishop John got the rectory of Kilmany, along with its much needed revenues, but William Fetchet was dropped. The result was therefore a stalemate between the Crannochs and Forrester, power was still evenly balanced.

In 1446, Gilbert Forrester (whose star was rising with the young King James II) was sent to Rome as the Crown's proctor at the Curia. John Crannach sensed his opportunity. He re-published the sentence of excommunication upon Forrester and, in addition, attacked abuses in the Chapter itself. Most notably instructing the Dean, John de Lichton, to remove his concubine from his house and to abstain from cohabitation or "suspect conversation" with her[35] or face a fine of £40 Scots. Lichton's response is not recorded! Just months later, Crannach is again at war with his Dean, this time for failing to impose a tax upon the canons for repairs to the hoods in the Choir stalls. Crannach also at this time appoints his brother David as Chancellor of the Cathedral, but David was to enter a legal struggle with his predecessor, Richard Wylie, to secure this position. Meantime, Forrester had returned from a successful trip to Rome flouting special letters of exemption from the Pope. Crannach was unlikely to take this insult lying down and in March 1451 he set in motion the necessary legal formalities, Forrester having contumaciously refused to pay a debt of £10 Scots the previous October. In May 1452 civil war broke out in Angus between King James II and an alliance of nobles affiliated to the Black Douglases; ecclesiastical conflict was put on hold.

---

[34] John de Licton's brother, Duncan, had held it (1437 – 40) until being usurped by David Crannach.
[35] In fact it is unclear whether concubine is singular or plural. Other sources suggest Lichton may have had two!

44

By 1453 Forrester was again back in Rome prosecuting his case and both Bishop John and his brother David were dead, probably of plague. Some sources suggest that they died in France either on their way to or return from business in Rome, so in a way, the Forrester controversy finally killed John Crannach; as Annie Dunlop rightly says "Like life itself, John Crannoch's career is an unfinished story."[36]

So how may we assess John Crannach, as one of the most colourful of all Brechin's Medieval bishops? The Auchinleck Chronicler for one describes Crannach as "a gud, actif and vertuis man and all his tyme wele gouvernand."[37] Adams reminds us of his legacy, not only in founding Brechin Brig but also building the gatehouse tower (Carnock's tower[38]) and causing necessary repairs to the Cathedral to be carried out. Most of all, ecclesiastically, Crannoch was responsible for much "reform, revival and refurbishment."[39] He ensured that proper vestments, furnishings and vessels were used during the liturgies, gifting to the Chapter in 1434 six silver cups in a case of red leather as well as a silver gilt cup with the rays of the sun upon it in a cover of leather. This latter cup particularly was only for the use of the Dean and canons in worship and not for any common usages. In addition, he ensured that preaching was revitalised within the Cathedral for the common folk, who probably had not heard a sermon or even homily for nearly fifty years! Of course, one of Crannach's greatest achievements was the foundation of the Sang Schule, and his interest in education extended to the supervision of the school in Dundee. He dearly desired to have an educated clergy and "evidently wished to replace the aged and infirm or illiterate members of his Chapter with younger and better educated men."[40] In all these ways John Crannoch was a prototype Reformer, a century ahead of his time. And yet…we are still left with a very sour taste over the quarrels he had, particularly with Gilbert Forrester, and indeed the nepotism he displayed in making Chapter appointments. Certainly Crannoch was not entirely at fault; he was facing some fairly intransigent and long established local families. Annie Dunlop observed: "his own hands were not free from the evils which he attacked; perhaps he had no alternative and deemed that the end would justify the means."[41]

George de Schoriswod or Shereswood (1454 – 63) was rector of Culter and Chancellor of Dunkeld prior to appointment to Brechin. He was also secretary and confessor to James II and held office as Chancellor of Scotland from 1455 until the

---

[36] Soc. Of Friends, Book 6, 26
[37] Black, 309
[38] The remains of which is still visible on the High Street into Bishop's Close.
[39] David Adams *Brechin the Ancient City* (unpublished), 36
[40] Dunlop, 20
[41] Ibid., 27

King's death in 1460.[42] Bishop George seems to have been of English speaking origin of the family of Bedshiel (or Bettsshiell) in Berwickshire. At some stage in his clerical career he also seems to have been vicar of Haddington from whence he came to Brechin, being consecrated in April 1454. Little else is known of Schoriswod's episcopacy other than he was appointed papal nuncio for Scotland in 1456.

The crest of Bishop Shereswood (1454 – 63) can still be seen within the Cathedral

He was also given safe conduct by the English crown to go on pilgrimage to Durham with forty attendants in 1459, so was clearly well regarded on both sides of the border. What is interesting is that this successor to the reformist Crannach was reputed to have had several illegitimate children, so it would seem that the moral rectitude of the previous bishop had been overturned!

By Whitsun 1463 it appears that Bishop George had died and the mantle of bishop fell upon a member of the Scottish Royal house, Patrick Graham, nephew to James I by his mother, Lady Mary Stewart, daughter of Robert III. His father was himself also a Scottish noble. **Patrick (1463-65)** was to be Bishop of Brechin only briefly. He had held the parish of Kinnell in the diocese of St.Andrew's and was translated to St.Andrew's from Brechin in 1466 where he was the very first Archbishop of that diocese. What seems particularly scandalous in our modern eyes is that Patrick was guilty of simony, paying both for his appointment to Brechin (ratified by Pope Pius III) and over three thousand gold florins for the see of St.Andrew's (ratified by Pope Paul

---

[42] James II died aged only thirty when a cannon exploded, killing him instantly during the siege of Roxburgh Castle.

II).[43] Though, it must be added, that this was quite common practice in pre-Reformation times.

John Balfour (1465 – 88) was vicar of Linlithgow and rector of Conveth (now Laurencekirk) when he was advanced to the see of Brechin and was appointed by Pope Paul II in a bull from Rome dated 29th November, 1465. He was granted dispensation by the Pope to retain Conveth after episcopal consecration and was consecrated bishop on 8th December, 1465 by Mark, bishop of Vicenza, Athanasius, bishop of Gerace and John's own predecessor at Brechin, Patrick Graham, now bishop of St.Andrews. Despite a fairly lengthy episcopate of eighteen years little else is known about Bishop John. He was in attendance at the Scottish Parliament in October 1467 and several times thereafter. What is perhaps most interesting is how his successor was appointed. We find in June 1488 that Walter Monypeny, prior at St. Serf's in Loch Leven pays 200 lbs. of Flemish *grossi* to a Florentine merchant for Papal bulls to expedite William Meldrum, vicar of Brechin, to succeed to the see when it becomes vacant by "the resignation or death of the reverend Father in Christ, John Balfour, now bishop of Brechin."[44] It seems that John Balfour resigned in the July of 1488 (possibly due to age) and was dead a few months later.

In any case by January 1489, **William Meldrum**, formerly vicar of Brechin had been elected bishop. He seems to have been consecrated sometime between January and July of that year, for by the summer he was clearly signing charters as bishop. William appears to have been one of the Meldrum family of Seggie and it seems bishop William engaged in some nepotism, advancing his family to key posts within the Chapter. Henry Meldrum was Precentor in July 1489 and was succeeded by another Meldrum, William, in May 1500. James Meldrum became sub-dean in October 1490 followed by one Thomas Meldrum in December 1504 (later promoted to Chancellor in 1510). John Meldrum was also given the benefice of Butergill. Clearly a case of jobs for the boys! Bishop William, as with his predecessor, had a long episcopate of twenty seven years, dying in March 1516.

By now the Medieval flowering of the Cathedral had long waned. Corruption, nepotism (as we have noted!), immorality and financial irregularities were rife. We find

---

[43] Sixtus IV was to elevate the bishopric of St.Andrew's to Archepiscopal status in 1472. Sadly, Patrick's end was to be quite tragic. In 1476, Sixtus IV instructed John Huseman, Dean of St. Patroclus in the diocese of Cologne, to investigate allegations against Archbishop Patrick. He was deposed in January 1478, apparently suffering some form of insanity, and condemned to perpetual confinement in a monastery or "other place". Confined at Inchcolm, then Dunfermline, he died at Loch Leven castle in late 1478.
[44] Registrum Episcopatus Brechinensis, vol.II, p.124

ourselves on the very eve of the Reformation for on the eve of All Saints, 1517, a monk and scholar called Martin Luther nailed his Ninety-Five Theses (or propositions) to the door of his Church at Wittenberg. It was to be the spark that would set Europe alight in the Protestant Reformation. It was Brechin's misfortune that its very last pre-Reformation bishop was to be a staunch adherent of the Roman Church.

ADDITIONAL INFORMATION – Section 2

THE SARUM LITURGY AND PRACTICE

Prior to Edward I's institution of the liturgy of Sarum in Brechin, it would seem likely that the Cathedral was using partly old Pictish (which survived until 1348) and Gallican liturgies. The liturgy of Sarum was favoured by the Normans and was built upon the work of Osmund, bishop of Salisbury, who had been appointed by William the Conqueror in 1078. The rites of worship involved fairly elaborate rituals and the greater use of priestly vestments. In addition, there was a greater stress on feast days and on several robed clergy participating in the Mass. Although the Mass was only celebrated in one kind (bread), it is likely that rinsed yet un-consecrated wine was used and the Priest when elevating the host would hold out his arms outstretched in a cruciform shape, as in the Eastern monastic tradition. It seems likely that Brechin was probably an amalgam of the liturgies of both Sarum and Lincoln.

Before the practices of Sarum were introduced by Edward I, it is likely that the Cathedral clergy may have lived under a common rule of life and lived in community, sharing equally wealth and possessions, as did their Cele Dei predecessors. This rule may well have had its origins in the Picto-Celtic Church (as we saw in Chapter One).

However, Sarum introduced secular canons to the Cathedral Chapter; i.e. canons who were not members of a common religious order or particular religious rule (e.g. Benedictine rule). These secular canons could hold their own property and reside in the Manse appropriate to their office within the Cathedral Chapter. Although not keeping to a religious rule, these canons would be expected to keep the Cathedral statutes. As well as drawing upon their own benefices from the parishes they held as Prebends, each Chapter member would receive a proportion each year of the *capitular mensa* (the common income for the Cathedral from lands, rents and revenues). This was a kind of early form of shareholders' benefits! In addition, if resident in the Chanonry they were entitled to a weekly subsistence allowance, the *communa*. It is easy to see how in the latter Medieval period these incomes were exploited with some canons holding several offices in different dioceses as well as multiple benefices.

The Cathedral Chapter was the administrative body that governed the Cathedral. Within Brechin's Cathedral Chapter the four main offices were:

DEAN (decanus) – a position of veneration and distinction. He headed the Chapter and presided over its meetings. He was elected by the Chapter but once chosen held in great respect. The Dean was responsible for administering the Chapter's affairs including the discipline and morality of the other clergy. The bishop, while pre-eminent in diocesan matters was inferior to the Dean in matters relating to the Cathedral itself. Choir stall on the south side nearest the altar.

PRECENTOR (cantor or chanter) – was responsible for the Cathedral's worship and music. Later he would take on the running of the "Sang School", supervising both the music and the boy choristers. Choir stall on the north side nearest the altar.

CHANCELLOR (cancellarius) – keeper of the documents and the Cathedral's great seal. He would deal with the correspondence and charters, as well as the supervision of the Bishop's Library and Grammar School. Kept and recorded the minutes of the Chapter meetings. Choir stall on the north side nearest the Nave.

TREASURER (thesaurarius) – responsible for the upkeep of the Cathedral including its fabric, furnishings, vestments, ornaments and treasures. Choir stall on the south side nearest the Nave.

Other offices included the SUB-DEAN, SUB-CHANTER, ARCHDEACON (the Bishop's chief administrative officer), VICAR (the Bishop's parochial deputy) and the PENSIONER (so-called because this canon was maintained by a fixed sum drawn from land rents of Redgorton in Perthshire and the teinds and offerings of the parish of Panbride.).

Brechin was unique in Scotland in that, contrary to usual practice, the Bishop had a seat in the Chapter as an ordinary canon. For not only was he Bishop of the diocese but also the local parish priest or prebend, the Rector of Brechin. He could thus both attend and influence decisions in Chapter. So the Cathedral was also the Burgh Kirk for the town – a position which was to save it come the Reformation. Thus the **Canon Vicar** was peculiar to Brechin, often acting as depute to the bishop in his absence. The **Rector** of Brechin by contrast was the priest charged to represent the Bishop in the cure of souls. At times the two roles became confused!

The offices held benefices; that is to say that their holders were also the priests or prebends of parishes out with Brechin and drew the revenues from there. These were Dean (Farnell), Chanter or Precentor (Stracathro), Chancellor (Navar) and Treasurer (Glenbervie – until 1422 when the priest there became a canon in his own right). In addition there were originally the prebends of Kilmoir, Buttergill and Guthrie. To these were added Lethnot (1384), Glenbervie (1422), Finavon (1474) and Strachan (date unknown). Thus did the number of canons increase from six (1274) to eleven (1372) and finally to fifteen (1422). Of course, many of those holding both Cathedral administrative Offices and parochial charges could not function as both meaning that substitute pastors or Vicars were appointed in the parish to carry out the priestly functions. Chief amongst these being the Vicar of Brechin, depute to the Bishop, for the Bishop was often away on papal or national business. The Rectors who held the benefice were entitled to the first teind (grain offerings) whilst the Vicar had the second teind (animals). The Archdeacon (though later Strachan), Sub-Dean (though later Cuikston) and Vicar did not therefore hold benefices or cures yet were Chapter members and this was to be challenged in the lay courts. In time, it gave rise to priests who were absentees and thus was a contributory cause to the Reformation.

BISHOP'S CLOSE,

Close to the Bishop's Palace, it shows Crannog or Crannoch's Tower dating from the time of Bishop John Crannoch (1426-53)

In additon to the secular canons and prebends there were increasingly in the later Medieval period CHORAL VICARS (or in Brechin, chaplains to the Choir). These were not all priests but some lay clerks whose job it was to sing at the Masses and seven daily offices in the place of the priests, deputising for the Canons in the Cathedral services. The Choral Vicars were also responsible for singing at the various altarages (or side chapels) within the Cathedral building. Probably there were seventeen Choral Vicars plus ten or so choristers of the "Sang School" thus by the end of the Cathedral's Medieval life the community associated with it may well have numbered some fifty or so souls.

In addition to their benefices, each canon was entitled to a prebendal manse and these were clustered around the Cathedral in an area called The Chanonry (see 1550 map in Appendix). Between the West Port and Chanonry Wynd there stood the Manse and garden of the Canon Vicar along with the College and its adjacent gardens (hence today's name of College Yards for the allotments). Chanonry Wynd had on the south side (west to east) the Canon Pensionary, the Dean and the Canon Prebend of Kilmoir. Their gardens ran down to Skinner's burn (formerly College burn). On the north (again west to east) Manses of Precentor, Chancellor, Archdeacon and Subdean whose Manse adjoined present Church Lane. In this case the gardens were generally in front of the properties rather than at the rear. Finally in Kirk gate (now Bishop's Close) we find the Treasurer's Manse on the site of the Cathedral Hall and the Bishop's palace in the area of the old stables and garages. The old Parish Manse, on the south side of Bishop's Close, was the site of the Bishop's gardens and his famous orchard. There were probably too some manses for the Choral Vicars, that they might easily conduct Cathedral services. The Parochial Vicars carried out the parish duties in each prebend (their Manses would be located in the parish) whilst the Cathedral officers drew on the revenues of the parishes, paying the Parochial Vicars directly.

CHAPTER FOUR
Reform and Revolution

"…the coming of the Reformation was to offer one solution to the dilemma of belonging – The myth of a revived and purified nation bound together in a single congregation under God"

- **Scotland Reformed, Frank D Bardgett**

John Hepburn (1516 – 1557?) was one of the younger sons of Sir Patrick Hepburn,1st Earl of Bothwell and Margaret, daughter of George Gordon, 2nd Earl of Huntly and, as one of the younger sons of nobility, would undoubtedly have been expected to go into the Church. He was probably born in East Lothian around 1500 and this would explain why, although appointed by Pope Leo X in March 1516, as a result of a "defect of age" (presumably his youth) he was not consecrated as bishop until sometime between June 1522 and February 1523, the evidence being somewhat complex and contradictory. John Hepburn thus comes to the bishopric with virtually no worldly experience and certainly no pedigree resulting from earlier ecclesiastical appointments. Yet, by 1524, he was to make his first appearance in the Scottish Parliament.

Hepburn was a close friend and confidant of Cardinal David Beaton Archbishop of St. Andrew's (1539-46) and was just as vociferous as Beaton in opposing reform and was present at both the trial and execution of Patrick Hamilton in St. Andrew's in 1528[1]. William Arth, a friar, preached in Dundee against the moral laxity of the clergy, including Hepburn, as well as denouncing the abuse of excommunication and miracles. It is recorded that Hepburn "having placed his placeboes (parasites) and jackmen (armed retainers) in the town, buffeted the Friar and called him Heretic." With Hepburn's men out to arrest him, Arth fled to St. Andrew's where his fiery denunciations received a more sympathetic hearing from Master John Major, Provost of St. Salvator's College. Another friar, Alexander Dick, was protected by the burgesses of Dundee from

---

[1] Hamilton was tried by a council of bishops and clerics headed by James Beaton, uncle of David and Archbishop of St. Andrew's. He faced thirteen charges, seven related to doctrines proposed by Lutheran Phillip Melancthon. He was burned at the stake outside St. Salvator's College and it is said that the "reek of Master Hamilton infected as many as it blew upon." In other words, his martyrdom was the Launchpad for the Scottish Reformation.

Hepburn's wrath in 1532. Another so-called heretic was forcibly rescued from the Cathedral's cells and Hepburn appealed to the Privy Council for their support. However in 1538 George Wishart was wise enough to flee Montrose when (as the burgh schoolmaster) his teaching the New Testament in Greek came to Hepburn's attentions! Any opposition to tradition, even if it meant traditional ecclesial abuses, was seen as heresy by Hepburn. Slowly and steadily by a sermon here, a bible study there, the Reformation began to take root in the soil of Angus and the Mearns. Generally, it was to receive a sympathetic audience from many of the local landowners. But Bishop Hepburn held out to the last, dying on the eve of the Reformation in the early summer of 1557. For forty years, Hepburn had been a thorn in the side of the Reformers. Thus Bardgett sums up Hepburn's episcopacy in these terms: "he remained a barrier against the reform of the institutions of the Church from within: his diehard opposition to change in the long run helped to drive those seeking spiritual renewal to seek it outside of the Roman Church."[2]

Moral laxity in his own house was to be reflected in the birth of no less than four illegitimate sons, one of whom, also John Hepburn, moved from being Treasurer in the Chapter (1552-60) to the first Protestant minister of the Cathedral (1560-98). During Bishop Hepburn's tenure too the buildings reached a very poor state of repair; the Cathedral lacked a roof and the bishop's palace was dilapidated[3]. Funds meant for building repairs had been siphoned off into the pockets of many of the Cathedral officials and it was only as late as 1557/8 that Bishop Hepburn sought to feu land to raise much needed cash. In a way, the poor state of the Cathedral building was to be an advantage when the Reformation "proper" dawned; unlike St. Andrew's Cathedral it was neither ransacked nor destroyed but quietly adapted into its new function as the Parish Kirk, monies being provided from taxing parishioners for the purpose.

After Hepburn's death, **Donald Campbell**, Abbot of Cupar and Keeper of the Privy Seal, received a nomination to Brechin's see by Mary of Guise, the Regent. However, events were to overtake them. Just a few short months after Bishop Hepburn's death a group of Scottish nobles and landowners met in December 1557 to sign a "covenant" in which they self-styled themselves as "the faithful congregation of Christ Jesus in Scotland". These "Lords of the Congregation" included local man John Erskine of Dun as well as the Earls of Argyll, Glencairn and Morton. They were opposed to Mary

---

[2] Bardgett, 20

[3] In fact the old bishop's palace continued in use as a Manse for the first charge as late as the time of Rev David Blair. It is recorded that the palace was still in a habitable state in 1690 and it was not until 1770 that £250 sterling was granted by the Barons of Exchequer to build a new house in the old bishop's orchard. We now refer to that as the "old Manse" – the current modern Manse being constructed in 1996.

Queen of Scots marriage to the Dauphin of France as well as the increasing French (thus Catholic) influence at Court. With the subsequent death of the Regent Mary of Guise[4] in June 1560 (followed soon after in the December by that of Mary Queen of Scots' husband, Francis II of France) the Protestant lords seized their opportunity to make Scotland a Protestant nation. Following the Treaty of Edinburgh in July 1560, the Parliament of Scotland ratified that Scotland was Protestant in the August of the same year.

Of course, it was hardly as simple as that! Different localities reacted in different ways to this sea-change of religious and also political allegiance; Scotland now saw England as its Protestant partner, rather than the "auld alliance" with France. As Henderson records "There was much to be done before the Church could indeed be called Reformed."[5] For one thing, preaching of the Word of God had not been heard in the Cathedral for possibly several generations, nor had the reading of the Bible in the vernacular; prayers for the dead[6] along with the Latin Mass and the authority of the Pope were abolished. The Book of Common Order became the rule of worship in 1564[7], psalm singing and family worship were encouraged and the Scots Confession was adopted in 1560 as "wholesome and sound doctrine grounded upon the infallible truth of God's word."[8] Daily prayers, once the preserve of the clergy through the offices, were now said and parishioners' participation encouraged. Within the Cathedral itself the Choir (now the Chancel area) was allowed to fall into ruin with the nave retained as the Parish Kirk; at the great West door a niche contained a statue of the Virgin Mary which was removed and destroyed, as were the side Altarages and chapels endowed by many notables. John Bisset, minister of the first charge (1769-98) records in the First Statistical Account of Scotland that the reformers themselves demolished "that part of the Cathedral where the grossest acts of idolatrous worship had been performed."[9] Presumably Bisset means the Choir area, the very fact that this area was associated with the saying of the old Mass may have resulted in a superstition that it was defiled and thus unsuitable for worship. So the Chancel Arch was built sealing it off from the nave and the pulpit moved to the south side of the nave. The fact it became a parish Kirk in the Reformed Church saved the Cathedral from the doom of many of its sister Cathedrals in Scotland.

---

[4] Mary of Guise was wife to King James V of Scotland and consequently mother of Mary Queen of Scots. She died of dropsy, though some alleged she had been poisoned by the Scottish Protestant nobles.
[5] G.D. Henderson, The Church of Scotland, 51
[6] An "Exhortation of the Word" was permitted at funerals, from whence probably our modern eulogy arose.
[7] Sometimes called John Knox's liturgy, a copy, printed in 1635, is held by the Cathedral in its archives.
[8] Ibid. 51
[9] Stat. account, 88

So was there opposition within Brechin to the new Reformed faith? Certainly in December 1559 a writ was issued from the Privy Council discharging the jurisdiction of the Commissary courts[10] of Brechin, the Council having been informed that "certain wicked persons within the city of Brechin, malevolent members of the Antichrist" had opposed an earlier general edict. These malevolent persons are not named though it is possible that it may have been John Cockburn, prebendary of Kilmoir[11] and long-time associate of Bishop Hepburn. A member of the "old guard", he had acted as commissary in recent years. Or it may have been Sir James Robertson, clerk to the chapter in 1553 and commissar in 1555. We know too that Sir Robert Abercromby, prebend of Burghill (or Butterkill)[12] failed to conform and was accused of "wicked papistrie". He did however hold on to his benefice as late as 1587 and was reportedly abroad with the Jesuit order in 1571, at which point he was deprived of the revenues of the benefice of Caputh; he may also have been party later to the burning down of Reformed ministers' manses in Angus!

Very little now remains of the site of the Church at Burghill.[13]

---

[10] The Commissary or Consistorial courts of the Medieval period were under the bishop's jurisdiction and heard cases relating to executry, matrimony and bastardy.

[11] Kilmoir Church was likely to be on the site of the Dalhousie Estate Offices.

[12] Rather interestingly, there may actually have been grassroots support amongst the laity in Kilmoir and Butterkill for the Catholic cause; the Reformed Church in rationalising parishes combined them with Brechin. These were the only ones of the old Medieval chapter to be rationalised, perhaps suggesting that the Protestants wanted to get rid of any prospect of opposition on the ground.

[13] With thanks to Dalhousie Estate and George Mitchell for their valuable assistance in locating this site.

Abercromby had been in dispute with John Hepburn and thus likely too young John Hepburn, first Reformed minister, and later records suggest that he was sympathetic to the reforms of the Council of Trent[14]. He must have been a comparatively young man at the time of the Reformation, unlike those others who were old and for whom it was too late to change allegiances. David Lindsay, prebend at Finavon, for example, was also anti-Reform, but he was deceased by 1560. We know too that when Bishop Campbell asked the Town Council in May 1580 to levy a special tax on citizens to convert the Cathedral for Protestant use, this was opposed by one David Dempster, a member of the Council; whether because he opposed the Reformed faith or simply because he thought the amount of extra tax excessive is not clear, though one might suppose he wasn't passionate enough for the new faith to impact upon his purse! The Burgh Court minutes record:

> My Lord Bishop of Brechin and Council has ordainit ane taxation to be liftit of the citiners extending to ane hundred merks, whereof twenty merks to be applyet to the reparation of the Tolbooth and four score merks to the reparation of the Kirk, and this to be gadderit and collectit with all diligence.[15]

A few days later

> David Dempster, being ane of the Counsell, dissentit to the act of ane taxation of ane hundred merks grantit for the reparation of the Kirk and Tolbooth.[16]

Generally though both Chapter and landowners were sympathetic to the Reformed Church; Dean, arch-deacon, chanter, canon-vicar and prebend of Glenbervie were all kin to lairds who accepted the Reformation. In many cases the Reformation aided the canons financially. By now, most canons were secular and non-resident yet the Privy Council permitted them to retain their revenues from their former benefices (though they had to subscribe to the Protestant cause at a ceremony in St. Andrew's in February 1560). The arch-deacon appears to have actually profited from resigning his benefice, retaining his lands and manse. So too it was with George Hepburn, the Chancellor, who demolished his manse but later in 1580 feu-ed the waste land where once it had stood. These rents and revenues from the former see were considerable. John Bisset records: "£410.5s Scots, 138 capons, 208 fowls, 18 geese, 1 chalder[17], 2 bolls of corn for horses, 3 barrels of salmon; in teinds - £24.6.8 Scots, 11 bolls wheat, 14

---

[14] The Council of Trent was held between 1545 – 63 as the Catholic response to the Reformation.
[15] Minute Book of the Hammermen's Incorporation, 29, 16th May, 1580
[16] Ibid., 31, 24th May, 1580
[17] A Chalder is an ancient Scottish measure of dry grain, so too a boll.

chalders, 6 bolls of bear (a type of barley), 25 chalders, 5 bolls of meal."[18] As Frank Bardgett reminds us, virtually all the canons of the Medieval Cathedral were secular men with a head, not for spiritual matters, but business affairs. So Bardgett states:

> The elderly canons of Brechin Cathedral, men like Mr. Robert Erskine[19] whose careers had followed conventional paths to the crisis of 1560, they were as unfitted for the Jesuit Order as they were for the Protestant Kirk. The need for reform was accepted by all: with different degrees of reluctance and enthusiasm, with quarrels over theology and church discipline. These were matters for which the canons of Brechin were not trained. At the Reformation they were content to retain two-thirds of their stipends and to retire…The chapter of Brechin continued the work with which it was most familiar, the administration of the business affairs, the lands and revenues of the Cathedral.[20]

Reform of the Church was thus the task of the younger breed. Amongst these two individuals must be singled out. The first, John Hepburn, was the illegitimate son of the former bishop; born c. 1530, John was clearly acknowledged as blood by his father, for by 1541 he was described as a "scholar, by 1543 he was given the perpetual vicarage of Montrose and by 1549 he was treasurer of the chapter, second only to Dean Cunningham within the Chapter. Unlike his diehard Dad, Hepburn clearly saw the need and benefits of Church reform and was appointed by the Assembly in December of 1560 as the first Protestant minister of Brechin, though he appears to have been fulfilling that function as early as 1558 after his father's death. In 1563, Hepburn was one of the first commissioners to the General Assembly with authority to plant Protestant churches in Moray and the north.

The second figure of great note was John Erskine of Dun (1509 – 91) who Bardgett claims has greater claim to the title "Father of our National Church" than Knox himself. He was certainly a more moderate influence and often acted as mediator in the disputes between the Catholics and Protestants (and between the Reformers themselves!) during the reign of Mary Queen of Scots. Mary herself described Erskine as "a mild sweet natured man with true honesty and uprightness." Having fled to Europe in 1530 because of an accident in which a priest died, young Erskine came under the influence of the new learning of the Renaissance. He was friends both to George Wishart and John Knox and in such esteem was he held that he was the only layman appointed as superintendent of the new Reformed Kirk (though by 1561 he had been ordained as a

---

[18] Stat. Account of Scotland.
[19] Robert Erskine was the longest serving canon of the Cathedral at the time of the Reformation, having been given the benefice of Glenbervie by James V in 1525.
[20] Book of Society of Friends, 39, p.12f.

minister and went on to be Moderator of the General Assembly on no less than four occasions.) Erskine was to become one of the co-authors of the Second Book of Discipline in 1588. Brechin gave a grant to John Erskine for his work in "the suppression of superstition, papistrie, idolatrie and the advancement and propagation of the evangel of Jesus Christ."[21] Yet Erskine was not universally popular; he had difficulty within Angus and the Mearns finding men of calibre as ministers and readers and was accused by some of appointing ignorant readers, "popish" vicars and ministers who were either absentees or of doubtful morals; though the job of these superintendents in these early years must have been nigh impossible. Was indeed John Erskine a fully formed Presbyterian? In 1572 at the Leith convention he supported James Douglas, 4th Earl of Morton, in proposing a modified form of episcopacy. This concordat allowed bishoprics to remain until James VI reached his majority and for Cathedral chapters to continue until their members died out. In practice this meant that only one third of the revenues from the former benefices went to the Reformed Kirk, while the remaining two-thirds went towards provision for the incumbents, along with a life rent of vicarages. It was a generous settlement yet one that was exploited by the landowners and the Crown who siphoned off much of the rich pickings. We see this in the case of Brechin Cathedral itself where the "boy" bishop Alexander Campbell (1566 – 1607) gave over virtually all the historic revenues of the diocese to his patron, the Earl of Argyll.

On 5th July, 1572, we see from an incident that although the town appeared to have "sailed with the tide of the Reformation"[22], violence was still associated with the change from Catholic to Reformed faith. Catholic Queen Mary had been forced to abdicate in favour of her one year old son James (who was controlled by the Protestant lords) in July 1567, yet many nobles were still sympathetic to the Queen. Amongst these was Sir Adam Gordon of Auchindown who came upon a group of the King's party in Brechin in July, 1572 and slaughtered each man in turn. The fact that the King's party had lodged in Brechin perhaps gives another indicator that Brechin was far more favourable to reform than Queen Mary. Such was the horror of this incident that it was a story still being told in the 1790s by Rev. John Bisset.

So what had happened to the bishop of Brechin in the midst of all this change and flux? While Donald Campbell, Abbot of Cupar, had received royal nomination on Bishop Hepburn's death, he did not prove acceptable to Rome on account of Campbell's pro-

---

[21] D.H. Edwards, 94
[22] Edwards, 94

Reform tendencies.[23] By early 1563, Campbell himself was dead. **John Sinclair, Dean of Restalrig,** was nominated by Queen Mary to the bishopric of Brechin (possibly as early as 1562) and clearly was a great favourite of the Queen, having officiated at her marriage to Henry Stewart, Lord Darnley at Holyrood in July 1565. Sinclair was of noble birth being of the house of Roslyn (his brother, Henry was bishop of Ross) and it is said that he was blind in one eye. He was also a very learned lawyer in both civil and canon law and became President of the Lords of Session. What is of most significance in our story however is that he was an ardent opponent of reform, urging the Queen to adopt extreme measures against the Reformers. If Sinclair had been successful in shaping Mary's ecclesiastical policy, Scotland might have found itself in an even worse situation than England did under "bloody Mary". Yet Sinclair's attempts to gain Brechin's bishopric proved fruitless; pro-reform Lord Argyll would not surrender the properties and, by all accounts, Sinclair (like Campbell before him) was never consecrated. He died in Edinburgh in April 1566 having contracted a fever. Sinclair was to be the last Papal nominee as Bishop of Brechin.

It was now seven or more years since there had been in reality a bishop of Brechin and we may imagine that in this time young John Hepburn, the first Protestant minister of the charge, had become well accepted and established. Yet the bishopric persisted at least in name. Queen Mary had used royal prerogative during the vacancy to gift David Murray a pension of 500 merks annually for life. This left little "of the temporal revenues of this see once this pension had been extracted."[24] In 1566, while he was still a minor, the formidable Earl of Argyll, put forward **Alexander Campbell (1566 – 1607)** as "the boy bishop". A son of the house of Arkinglass, Campbell had a rather varied education: he enjoyed the company of the great Reformer, Andrew Melville, yet is also recorded as having attended the Jesuit College in Paris. Records show that in 1574 he was studying in Geneva with his tutor, Andrew Polwart. He was an excellent example of what Knox referred to disparagingly as a "tulchan bishop"[25]; this was certainly the case for in May 1566, the Privy Council endorsed an outrageous measure for boy bishop Campbell: "cum potestate sibi, dare et disponsere singular beneficia, tam spiritualitatis

---

[23] Donald Campbell abandoned monastic habit, banned mass from his monastery and destroyed altars and icons at Cupar in 1559. He also sat in the Reform Parliament of 1560 which abolished the authority of the Papacy. These actions were hardly likely to endear him to Rome!

[24] Bardgett 122

[25] A **Tulchan** (from the Scottish Gaelic, tulachan) was in Scotland a man appointed as **bishop** after the Reformation, who was a **bishop** in name only and whose revenue was drawn by his patron. The term originally referred to a calfskin stuffed with straw, and presented to a cow, as if living to induce her to give milk.

quam temporalitatis dignatatis, aut alia, infra diocesan Brechinen, nun vacan, aut quando eadem vacare contigerit, quae prius donation episcoporum Brechinen, pertinuerunt" (a rough translation being: with the power to give and dispose of singular benefits, both spiritual and temporal in dignity or others, within the diocese of Brechin now vacant, or when it becomes vacant, these prime donations belonging to the bishops Brechin.) What this meant in practice is that Campbell happily off loaded virtually all the lands, titles and tithes to the Earl of Argyll, his patron, reserving "to himself and his successors scarce so much as was moderate competency for a minister at Brechin."[26] As early as December in 1566, a mere six months after the measure was passed, Campbell grants to Argyll the lands of Farnell and the office of bailie for life. Yet Campbell's lavish generosity with the revenues of the see finally caught up with him and in 1575, his studies apparently over, John Erskine of Dun was sent by the Assembly to remind him of the duties befitting a bishop. In November 1580 the Assembly at Dundee ordered John Hepburn, the minister, to summon Campbell to give his submission. And in October 1582 the Presbytery of Mearns brought charges against him for "non-preaching and (failing) in ministration of the sacraments, of negligence in doctrine or discipline, haunting or frequenting the company of excommunicated persons, wasting of the patrimony of the Kirk, setting of tacts against the Acts of the Kirk, giving collation of benefices against the said acts, and finally of giving sclander (sic) in life and conversation."[27] How far any of these charges were specific to Campbell is not known for he is lumped together with other bishops by the Assembly; any records of these charges coming to trial are, sadly, lost to us.

Campbell continued to attend many parliaments, Assemblies and meetings of the Privy Council, though while attending a meeting of the Privy Council in Brechin in April 1602 he was denounced as a traitor. He resigned shortly afterwards in spring 1607, retiring to his estates at Carco, and by February 1608 was dead. One more thing must be noted of our "boy bishop" – he married, twice! For now, of course, there was no Papal insistence on celibacy governing clergy conduct. His first wife was Margaret Bethune and his second, who survived him, Helen Clephane; she bore him two daughters and a son.

By the beginning of the seventeenth century our first Reformed minister John Hepburn himself had died and was succeeded by **John Mershell (or Marshell) 1600-08** of whom we know relatively little. An M.A. graduate of Edinburgh University, King James had appointed him sub-dean of the almost defunct Chapter in 1602; he was in fact the last individual to hold this post. He appears to have been translated from Brechin to another parish in 1608 and by 1635 had died. His widow, Marjory Smith, received

---

[26] See David D Black, 315
[27] Coats, 28

charitable support from the parish of Mid Calder in 1647 and was again recommended by the General Assembly for further financial provision in 1657 as she was "on the point of starving". Marjory appears to have still been living in 1659, perhaps suggesting that John had died at a comparatively young age.

In 1603, James VI of Scotland gained the throne of England becoming James I. The King was now determined to restore episcopacy to Scotland in its fullest sense. So in April 1607, a bishop returned to Brechin in the shape of **Andrew Lamb (1607-19)**. He had been ordained minister at Burntisland in 1593, was translated to Arbroath in 1596 and South Leith in 1600. A great favourite of King James, he supported the re-introduction of episcopal governance and the rituals and ceremonies of the English Church. Lamb, however, was a moderate man and a conciliator. On 20th October, 1610, Lamb was consecrated in England by three English bishops, though he did not need to undergo re-ordination as deacon and priest. On his return to Scotland, he, along with two other bishops consecrated according to the English rite, duly consecrated the Bishops of both Aberdeen and Caithness at the Cathedral in the winter of 1610/11. It is said that Andrew Lamb enjoyed the good things of life and was averse to a life of poverty; thus arose a schoolboy's rhyme about him! For a time Lamb held the benefices not simply of bishop but minister of the charge and also Domine[28]; recalling the famous orchard of the medieval bishops, the schoolboys sang:

The Minister, the Domine and Maister Andrew Lamb,
Gaed into the garden where three pears hang –
Tho' ilka he took ane, twa still hang![29]

There is still within the Cathedral a rather splendid brass chandelier or hearse[30] donated by Andrew Lamb himself in 1615, probably of Flemish or Dutch origin and undoubtedly made before the date of its donation, possibly in the 1550s. Lamb translated to Galloway diocese in 1619 and died at Leith, apparently blind, in 1634.

---

[28] Scots for schoolmaster.

[29] See Edwards *Pocket History*, 22

[30] From the Medieval Latin *hercia*; originally the meaning of hearse was as a flat framework for candles hung over a coffin (late C13th). It was later extended in meaning to cover the means of transportation of the dead person to the grave.

Alexander Bisset (1608-44), an M.A. graduate of King's College in Aberdeen, was proposed by Bishop Lamb to the parsonage and vicarage of Kilmoir[31] in the Cathedral Kirk of Brechin in 1608. Notably, Lamb held on to most of the benefice of the charge until his translation to Galloway in 1619; Bisset was very much his vicar and deputy. Shortly after Bisset's arrival in Brechin a significant event for future historians took place – the Kirk Session was founded and in 1615 began to keep minutes![32] I have quoted the original Acts and Ordinances from the first Minute book here to give the Reader a flavour of the times.

FOR SANCTIFICATION OF THE SABBATH

Imprimis. It is statute and ordained that the haill citiners and landward shall sanctify the Lord's Day and repair to the hearing of God's Word and whosoever shall be found absent without a lawful and weighty excuse shall pay five shillings for the first fault and so toties quoties doubling, together with their repentance.

AGAINST MERCHANTS AND CRAFTSMEN IN TIME OF PREACHING

Item. It is statute that no merchant, tradesman or craftsman be found exercising their ordinary calling upon the day aforesaid under the penalty of twenty shillings, according to the Act of Parliament, and repentance.

AGAINST LANDWARD MEN BREAKERS OF THE SABBATH

Item. Whosoever in landward, husbandman or cottar, by themselves or servants, shall be found in the break of the Sabbath shall be punished, as said is, according to the Act of Parliament, or at the discretion of the Session according to their estate, together with their repentance, and the masters to relieve the servants.

AGAINST MILNERS AND BAXTERS;   THESE WHOSE STUFF THEY WORK

Item. It is statute and ordained, because of the great abuse that is within the said parish by the milners and baxters, that none of them from sun to sun grind or bake, and the contravener pay forty shillings, and likewise the persons that give their stuff to be ground or baked, and ilk one of them make their repentance.

FOR KEEPING OF KIRK ON WORK DAYS

---

[31] It is of interest that Bisset was appointed to a prebendary that had been abolished at the Reformation. A clear sign perhaps that Andrew Lamb saw him as an understudy rather than an equal.

[32] The Kirk Session Minutes of Brechin Cathedral begin in 1615 and are more or less continuous to the present day. There are one or two breaks:

Item. It is stature and ordained that the haill inhabitants of this city shall repair to the hearing of the Word on Tuesday and Thursday in time of preaching and exercise, dispensing only with the servants' absence, and whosoever, man or wife, be found absent shall pay forty pennies.

FOR KEEPING THE SESSION BY THE ELDERS THEMSELVES

Item. It is statute and ordained by the hall consent of the elders and deacons themselves that they weekly keep the ordinary time of Session on Tuesday after preaching and whosoever by absent without a lawful excuse shall pay two shillings toties quoties; providing always that the landward elders shall be free, if one of the out of every quarter shall be weekly present (successive).

FOR COLLECTION OF ALMS

Item. It is statute and ordained that the most zealous and honest within the town and landward shall collect to the poor on Sunday and Tuesday and make count thereof before the Session weekly.

FOR THE VISITATION OF THE TOWN

Item. It is statute and ordained that those who collect the alms shalt the next Sabbath following visit the whole town and bairns thereof as well afternoon as beforenoon, and that they presently imprison or cause warn to the Session such as they find absent from the kirk, and suspicion is that people have closed themselves within their houses, they shall make patent doors or the visitors to ding them up.

VISITATION ON TUESDAY

Item. It is stature and ordained that the collector of the alms on Tuesday shall go through the town in time of sermon and remark what masters in trade or craft they sit in their booths, and likewise when they find any drinking the said time, and finally that the crave support to the poor of all whom they find whether stranger or other.

DISTRIBUTION OF ALMS AND PENALTIES

Item. It is statute and ordained that the whole alms collected of penalties received shall be distributed at the sight of the Session without all partiality and respect of persons. Except the necessity of any person be so great that they may not abide the day of the Session, which shall be referred to the discretion of the Minister, collector and one or two elders or deacons with them and they think necessary to give, which shall be as sufficient in that respect as if it had been by common consent of the whole Session.

FOR KEEPING OF THE EXAMINATION

Item. It is statute and ordained for the better repairing to the examination at the hours and times appointed thereto that every person absent at their appointed time, man or woman, whether in burgh or landward, shall pay as follows; that is to say, the master or mistress of the house – four shillings, the bairns or servant – two shillings and the cottar siclike – two shillings; providing always if any of the aforesaid persons be thrice cited and warned to the examination, as said is, they shall compear before the Session to acknowledge their contempt and triple the said penalty; and if the stay of the bairns or servants be in the parents or masters, then in that case the parent or master shall relieve them of their said penalties.

FOR TRIAL OF FAULTS AND VAGABONDS

Item. It is statute and ordained that every elder in town and landward shall carefully attend what enormities fall out in their quarters and weekly report the same to the Session; and also that they acquaint the Session if any vagabonds or strangers be received within the foresaid quarters.

FOR SETTING OF HOUSES TO STRANGERS OR RECEIVING THEM IN SERVICE

Item. It is statute and ordained that no person within the town having void houses set them to any stranger without sufficient testimonial received by them from the said strangers of their life and conversation from the minister or magistrates of the parish where they have remained before and produced the same before the Session; neither receive any stranger in service without the like testification under the pain of ten pounds, as also whatsoever persons set to any codrow wife, one or more, a dwelling house without he obtain licence shall pay as said is.

ACT AGAINST ADULTERERS

Item. It is statute and ordained that all persons convicted in adultery shall be committed to ward fourteen days on bread and water besides their public satisfaction, and this their warding to be nowise relieved but by payment of eight pounds by ilk person, and having kept the time of their ward, to be taken thereafter to the Market Cross and their heads to be shaven, and in case the foresaid penalty be paid, they to be relieved of the said ward. But their public shaving at the Cross not to be overpassed unless they relive by such a penalty as the Session shall think expedient, always exceeding the penalty of eight pounds.

ACTS AGAINST FORNICATORS

Item. It is statute and ordained that ilk person convicted of fornication be committed to ward from the Session day till the next Sunday, or else to relieve themselves by the penalty of six pounds, thereof the man paying four pounds, the woman forty shillings; and so oft as the said persons shall happen to fall, their penalty to be doubles with their public repentance.

ACT AGAINST PERSONS HAVING COPULATION BETWIXT CONTRACT AND MARRIAGE

Item. It is statute that if any persons contracting in marriage shall before the solemnization of their marriage have carnal copulation, whether it come to light or not, before the said solemnization, shall pay the penalty of fornicators.

CONTRACTS FOR MARRIAGE

Item. It is ordained that all persons contracting for marriage shall come to the Session the day before their proclamation and shall give up their names and then ratify their civil contract, and every one of the said parties shall find caution for abstinence from carnal copulation and performance of their promise within forty days under the penalty of ten pounds, and shall pay to the Clerk of the Session for inserting their names in the Session Book twelve shillings.

ACT AGAINST CURSERS AND SWEARERS IN THE MARKETS ON THE STREETS

Item. It is statute and ordained that every elder and deacon as well in the burgh as landward shall carefully observe and remark whatsoever persons they find on the market day or otherwise swearing, cursing, banning or speaking filthy or profane speeches; to exact of them four pennies toties quoties, and if they be such as citiners in the aforesaid sins, to be delated to the Session and punished as public offenders.

ACT AGAINST DRUNKARDS

Item. It is statute and ordained for the avoiding of the great abuse of drinking that whatsoever person, man or woman, shall be found drunk to be cited before the Session there to acknowledge their offence and punished by their repentance and purse at the discretion of the Session according to the estate of their person and offence.

ACTS AGAINST SLANDERERS

Item. It is statute and ordained that all slanderers of their neighbours, either privately or publicly, the slander being sufficiently proved by witnesses, shall be put on the market day in the jougs or gives there to stand or sit from ten hours before noon until twelve, or to be relieved therefrom by the payment of four pounds the Sunday thereafter after the sermon before noon come before the pulpit and acknowledge the offence.

FOR WARNING OF SLANDERERS

Item. That the beadle in nowise warn any party slanderer at the suit of any complaint without special direction given by the Minister thereto and consignation of six shillings eight pennies be made by the complainer in the hand of the Minister, whereof he shall be countable and redeliver to the complainer if the slander be proven, otherwise to be put in the box.

MARRIAGE AND BAPTISM

Item. It is statute and ordained that all persons that would receive the benefit of marriage to themselves and baptism to their bairns shall give count of Lord's Prayer, Belief, Ten Commands and Catechism; otherwise marriage or baptism to be refused or to pay in penalty as the Session shall think expedient according to the quality of the person.

REGISTER OF MARRIAGES AND BAPTISMS

Item. It is appointed that there be a register of all baptisms and marriages and burials within the congregation by the reader as he shall be answerable to the Session.

BAPTISMS AND MARRIAGES

Item. It is ordained that for every baptism shall be paid to the beadles forty pennies, for every marriage six shillings and eight pennies or more according to the quality of the persons. And if any persons shall desire solemnization of their marriage to be without the parish, in that case they shall pay the aforesaid six shillings and eight pennies.

BURIAL IN THE KIRKYARD

Item. It is statute that for every person who is buried in kirkyard without a kist shall be paid six shillings and eight pennies; and for such as shall be buried there having a kist thirteen shillings and four pennies; as also for such as shall be buried with the kirk twenty-six shillings eight pennies or more according to the quality of the person.

RINGING THE BELL AT BURIAL

Item. It is ordained that the great bell be only knelled, a space intervening betwixt every knell with a dead sound, and that the little bells be nowise rung under the pain of deposition of the beadles from their offices.

FOR THE BEADLES TO KEEP THE CHURCH

Item. It is ordained that the beadles shall be present in the kirk in the time of the preaching, and that one of them attend morning and evening in time of prayer under the pain of deposition.

FOR GOING WRONG OF THE KNOCK

Item. It is statute that whensoever the knock shall be found out of order by the sloth and negligence of him who has the charge thereof, he shall be warded twenty-four hours or relieved therefrom by the penalty of ten shillings.

AGAINST ABUSING THE CHURCHYARD

Item. It is ordained that the beadles carefully attend that the kirkyard be nowise polluted or defiled either by excrement of man or beast, and whatsoever persons be found in that offence shall pay forty shillings with their repentance and the owner of every beast ten shillings toties quoties.

BURIAL IN THE KIRK

Item. The Session ratifies with their hale consent the act of the visitation enjoining ten pounds to be paid for every burial of those that are past bairnhood within the kirk, and that every one be covered in the body of the kirk with a stone at their expense, and that no caution be taken for the said ten pounds but before the yeird be broken to be paid.

FOR CATECHISING ON SUNDAY

Item. The Session ordains that a scholar every Sabbath day answer to the Catechism, the reader speiring at him at morning prayers and at the second bell to the aforenoon's sermon for instruction of the people.

It should be obvious, even to a casual reader, how organised and regulated religious life in Reformed Scotland had become; long gone were the lengthy ornate masses with their (latterly) chaotic shambles of worship. The first minute from 9th May, 1615 just starts abruptly with little prelude:

9 May 1615

After the invocation on the name of God,

the elders and deacons present

Collected on Sunday last and this Tuesday by Gilbert Ochterlownie and James Rait: three pounds fifteen shillings and nine pennies.

The which day compeared William Ramsay, fornicator with Isobel Burn, confessed his fault and, because he had a wife, his is ordained to bring a testimonial from the minister where his wife died, and is ordained to have it ready against the next Session day; and the woman likewise is ordained to be present.

The which day anent a bill of slander given in by James Read in Pittendreich against Alexander Gardyne. He being cited compeared not, is ordained to be summoned pro secundo.

The which day Alexander Clerk is ordained to give to John Campbell, a poor man, a coat cost 40 shs.; to give to Walter Dun, a poor sick man, 6 shs.

The which day compeared George Woll, cordiner, and Elspit Barclay, in this parish, contracted for marriage; cautioner for the man John Woll his father, for the woman

Mr Thomas Ramsay, both for abstinence and completing of marriage, under the pain of £10 within forty days.

The which day delated to the Session, Agnes Ramsay, servitrix to Elspit Kynninmont, being with child. She is ordained to be summoned against the next Session day.

Within two years this fairly regulated form of Reformed religion was to undergo a significant challenge from the King himself. James VI returned to his Scottish homeland in 1617 determined to introduce the form of episcopal worship he had encountered in England. This was to bring him into direct conflict with the Reformed Kirk. The King, manipulated by the Earl of Arran (a diehard anti-Reformer) had already forbidden Presbyteries in his "Black Acts" of 1584, though not Sessions or Synods. In 1606, the General Assembly had been manipulated by James to approve bishops as perpetual moderators The first salvo in this new war with the Kirk was an instruction by the King prior to his arrival to install images in his private chapel at Holyrood. Andrew Lamb, mindful of public opinion, was one of the bishops who wrote to James urging him to rethink. James "the wisest fool in Christendom" was not however always good at heeding advice. The next innovation from James was the so-called "Five Articles" to be debated at Perth in 1618. These articles set out to re-introduce old practices, namely: Communion to be taken kneeling, the allowance of private Communion for the sick as well as private Baptism in houses of necessity, confirmation for children of eight years or older and the celebration of Christmas, Holy Week, Easter, Ascension, Pentecost and other notable festivals. To our modern ears, these ideas sound quite moderate, but in the Scotland of the early seventeenth century many of them were anathema to the Reformers.

68

At the Perth Assembly in 1618, eighty-six voted to obey the King in these ecclesial matters, forty-nine (mostly ministers) voted against. In practice it proved almost impossible to impose the King's will upon the Church; it wasn't until 1621 that the Scottish Parliament ratified them and by 1625 James was dead. His son, Charles, was not to learn from his father's experiences in Scotland and his interference in ecclesiastical affairs would lead not just to revolt but ultimately revolution.

Before leaving James we must note his visit to Brechin on 27th May, 1617. In preparation for the royal visit, Bishop Lamb ordered that any statues or images be removed: "The haill deacons of the crafts being present in the Session are ordained to take away off the seats and lofts all figures of men's bodies, lest they be offensive to his Majesty at his here-coming."[33] Whether Lamb was trying to make a point about his own opposition to images, or whether it was because James had argued that the Scots Kirk was inconsistent in allowing images of devils, dragons and other mythical beasts but not statues of the saints, is impossible to determine. In any case, the emblems of the various trades were removed from their lofts and any remaining statues from before the Reformation were also disposed of. The Beadle, James Gordon, was given 20 merks to purchase a new blue joup[34] for his livery and new pewter badges were issued to the resident beggars who hung about the Kirk door for alms. We have no evidence that James actually ever visited the Cathedral at this time[35] though the Court was resident in Kinnaird Castle. Amongst the courtiers was one William Laud (not yet a bishop) whose liturgy twenty years hence was to be the spark that ignited a revolution.

David Lindsay (1619 – 34) succeeded Andrew Lamb as Bishop. Brother to Colonel John Lindsay, laird of Edzell, he was a doctor of divinity and a man of great learning. He was consecrated at St. Andrew's on 23rd November, 1619 and on the accession of Charles I proved a great ally in the King's drive for a much more ornate worship in the Kirk, largely as a result of Lindsay's book *Resolutions for kneeling at the Sacrament.* Indeed it was he who crowned Charles King at Holyrood in June 1633. He was then rewarded for his loyalty by being transferred to the bishopric of Edinburgh in 1634 following Bishop Forbes' death. However, Lindsay's tenure at St. Giles' was short-lived; he suffered the vengeance of the Edinburgh mob when the Dean of St.Giles' tried to read Laud's liturgy on Sunday 23rd July, 1637 prompting Jenny Geddes' stool and

---

[33] Coats, 32

[34] Wide coat

[35] There is some suggestion that the King had been in Brechin in June 1580 to make the Earl of Mar a burgess, see Black, 46.

famous remark: "De'il gie you colic, the wame o' ye, fause thief; daur ye say Mass in my lug?"[36] Lindsay was deposed and excommunicated by the General Assembly in 1638.

Meantime, at Brechin, Alexander Bisset continued faithfully as minister. In 1619 we have the first references to a problem that was going to convulse the Scottish Church in years to come: witchcraft. Marion Marnow is recorded in March 1619 as being "a witch that was burnt" and in the October of the same year the local smith, David Finlason, brought unsubstantiated allegations against one Bessie Logan for the same offence. It was also during Alexander Bisset's tenure that the Town and Landward Sessions were separated in June 1624 due to the length of the meetings![37] In 1630 an interesting incident took place in which Bisset went to the docks in Dundee and negotiated with a skipper there to take the great (or "muckle") bell of the Cathedral to Holland for it to be re-cast as it was badly riven[38].

Thomas Sydserf (1634 – 35) was the new Bishop of Brechin after Lindsay's translation to St.Giles'. He too was a royalist, pro-Episcopacy and a supporter of

Arminianism[39], which, in Sydserf's case led to accusations of being a papist (he is alleged to have worn a crucifix). The anti-Catholic party within Brechin was now very much in the ascendancy; in 1632 one Robert Cowie had been brought before the Session on charges of "seeming to show himself a papist." Sydserf, perhaps because of his High Anglicanism, did not last long in Brechin. He was translated to Galloway the following year. It is an interesting footnote that Sydserf was the only Bishop still living (and duly re-instated as bishop of Orkney) in 1660 on the Restoration of Charles II.

---

[36] A rough translation into English would be "The Devil give you colic in your stomach, false thief, for saying Mass in my ear". Even without the translation, Geddes' displeasure is evident!

[37] Rev John Willison eventually re-united the two sessions in 1708, though not without some difficulty and resistance!

[38] One James Pieres gave a donation of £100 Scots towards the cost of the re-casting. The bell was subsequently recast again in 1780, possibly as a result of some vigorous ringing by local youths. In this case the cost was offset by public subscription.

[39] Based on theological ideas of the Dutch Reformed theologian Jacobus Arminius (1560–1609) and his historic supporters known as the Remonstrants, in the English context the opposition to Arminianism was often related to ritual and was headed by the Puritan party. Laud's liturgy was part of the pro-Arminian settlement.

Walter Whiteford (or Whitford) (1635 – 38) succeeded Sydserf as bishop but was to last only a little longer than his predecessor in that office! Originally minister at Monkland and sub-dean of Glasgow (an office he continued to hold in commendam), he was rector of Moffat when appointed to the episcopacy.

By 1637, the conflict between King and Protestants was reaching its apogee. In July 1637, Whiteford sought to introduce Laud's liturgical innovations, including the much detested Prayer Book (see above for Jenny Geddes' reaction in Edinburgh). In Brechin, the response was no less hostile; the Town Council had already protested to the Privy Council in Edinburgh about Charles' "High Kirk" practices. But Whiteford, as chief magistrate, was not so easily deterred, stressing he would serve the King unlike other "feeble cowards". Going early to the Cathedral that Sunday morning in July, there were only a few of the congregation in attendance. With two primed pistols ready in the pulpit should the congregation revolt, Whiteford read Laud's liturgy.

 Apparently, his wife and servants also had pistols about their persons just in case things got ugly! At the end of worship, Whiteford was mobbed and fled home for his life. He persisted in his use of Laud's Prayer Book despite the folk urging him otherwise until, finally in November 1637, the exasperated congregation rose against him. His residence was ransacked and he fled Brechin for the relative safety of Edinburgh then England. The General Assembly in Glasgow of December 1638 abolished episcopacy[40], thus depriving Whiteford of his living. He was also accused of "drunkenness, incontinence and the use of masse crucifixes in his chamber." Whether there was any truth in this is uncertain, though Whiteford, unlike some other Scottish bishops of the time, was certainly pro-Royalist and was certainly keen on high liturgical practice. He was eventually presented by the King to the living of Waldegrave in Northamptonshire where he died in 1643. As an interesting footnote to his tale, his third son, Adam, died amongst the Royalist troop in the siege of Oxford in 1647 aged twenty-three.

---

[40] The exact words were: "all episcopacy different from that of Pastor over a particular flock was abjured in the Kirk and to be removed out of it." Burleigh, 220 The controversial Five Articles of Perth were also pronounced contrary to Reformed religion.

During summer 1640 into the spring of the following year we find few Session meetings taking place as the now sole remaining clergy, the minister, Alexander Bisset, was often at Edinburgh attending various assemblies as the crisis in Church and State deepened.

On 28th February, 1638, the National Covenant was signed at Greyfriars Kirk in Edinburgh and copies sent throughout Scotland for signing. Although the Covenant professed loyalty to the Crown it called on all the liturgical and ecclesiastical innovations since 1580 to be withdrawn. It is not known what the reaction was in Brechin to these extraordinary events but, given that Brechin became a main rendezvous point for the Covenanters in 1644 and 1645, we might suppose that the town joined in signing. In September 1638 the duplicitous Charles finally agreed to withdraw the Canons and Prayer Book, but by now momentum was gathering against the King. By August 1643, Bisset was again in Edinburgh at Assembly seeking to prepare a new directory for Public worship to replace Laud's Prayer Book. At this time the Solemn League and Covenant was also signed; effectively a treaty between the English Puritans and Scottish Covenanters, it demanded the preservation of Reformed religion in Scotland as well as the reform of religion down south with the abolition of popery and prelacy. Suddenly however, as events moved towards their cataclysmic conclusion and armies began approaching the town itself, Alexander Bisset died early in the morning of 30th January, 1644. He was fifty nine years of age and one of his final acts as minister had been to gift in 1643 a silver Communion cup. In the midst of all the vicissitudes of this turbulent period, Bisset had remained ever faithful to his flock and his Reformed Kirk.

Following Bisset's death, Brechin became the very frontline between the Covenanters and the Royalists being occupied by one army or another no less than five times in the course of the year 1644-45. In April 1644 the Session failed to meet because of many strangers passing through the town to the army in the north – presumably the townsfolk were afraid to leave their properties unattended for too long. Presbytery fared little better, their minute records that:

> …from April 1644 to May 1645, by reason of the troubles, Brechin being plundered by the common enemy, this Presbytery book was taken away by the rebels together with the scrolls containing the proceedings of the Presbytery from April 1644 till the first of May 1645, which scrolls wholly perished, notwithstanding that the book being carried away out of the shire was afterwards regained.[41]

There were neither services nor collections held at Brechin from 17th September until 19th November 1644 and it was not until 3rd December, 1644 that William Rait, MA, (1644 – 62) minister at Aberluthnot was inducted to the charge of Brechin in the very midst of the War of the Three Kingdoms.

In September 1644 first the Marquis of Montrose had arrived with the Royalist troop on 10th followed a week later by the Marquis of Argyll and the Covenanters. But it was Montrose the town feared the most and news in early October that his was on back with his army provoked mass panic, so much so that many inhabitants fled and the town was almost deserted. In the November, Argyll's men returned, now in a rather more sorry state after their failure to capture Montrose at the battle of Fyvie. In March 1645 again the Session failed to meet "for fear of the merciless enemy" and the Treasurer, one John Cargill, hid the collection of £5.10s Scots which, to this day, has never been recovered.[42] March 23rd, 1645 proved a disastrous day for Brechin as Montrose's army returned, plundering and setting fire to the town; it seems that fifty or sixty houses were burned to the ground and the Castle plundered. Given that Brechin in that time was only a few streets, the misery and devastation caused by the Royalist troop was long-lasting and far-reaching. There were neither services nor meetings of the Session for nearly a fortnight and on 4th April the second part of Montrose's army along with most of his baggage train arrived in Brechin. The mort cloth[43], Sunday collections and the Landward Session records were all lost at this time; the entire town was in chaos. Spalding records that "the

---

[41] Presbytery of Brechin minutes, vol. I, April 1644

[42] Whether the collection still lies buried or was found and removed by Montrose's troops is unclear.

[43] This was a special cloth, hired by bereaved families from the Cathedral and used to cover the coffin. Generally speaking it was either of black or purple material.

townspeople hid their goods in the castle thereof and kirk steeples, and fled themselves, which flight enraged the soldiers; they herried their goods, plundered the castle and hail town, and burned about sixty houses."[44] For a few short months, Brechin sought to recover. But in July 1645, for about a fortnight, Montrose's troops returned. Yet things had settled well enough in the August for poor Rev. William Rait to at last celebrate Communion with his folk; their prayers that Montrose would never return must have been fervent ones. In September, 1645, Montrose was defeated by Sir David Leslie's Covenanting army at Philiphaugh, but Brechin had not yet seen the last of the Marquis! In November Ludovic Lindsay, 16th Earl of Crawford, a friend of Montrose drew near the town and William Rait, the minister, finally fled.

From 30th June 1646 – mid August 1646, again all Cathedral services were held at Brechin Castle "for fear of the enemies being in the field." This time the fear proved greater than the reality and while on August 11th, Montrose and his now depleted troop were again in the town, this was the last Brechin would see of him. A few weeks later he sailed into exile in Norway. It is perhaps little wonder that on 22nd May, 1650, the day after Montrose's execution at the Mercat cross in Edinburgh, that the citizens of Brechin held a service of thanksgiving in the Cathedral. Such had been the appalling misery that the Marquis and his men had inflicted upon Brechin over several years. Yet there were some who clearly supported Montrose within the town. In November 1646 the newly returned William Rait was instructed by the General Assembly to investigate his elders, some of whom, it was alleged, had drunk the good health of the Marquis. The penalty was for them to be debarred from Communion until public confession of their sins. Although they all denied these allegations, and the investigation proved fruitless, later pro-Jacobite sympathies re-surfacing in 1715 suggest that perhaps a few folk in Brechin were sympathetic to the Royalist cause.

In January 1647 the Scottish Parliament finally granted Brechin exemption from quartering troops and paying the tax levy of £80 Scots per month. It was a measure designed to alleviate at least some of the suffering that the townsfolk had undergone at the hands of the Marquis of Montrose. In March 1647 this time it was Argyll's men who were in the town. Although they were received more favourably and behaved more respectfully, this army brought another misery to Brechin: plague. From 7th April – 8th December an "infecting sickness" prevented any Session meetings as the "Moderator and remnant members thereof were afraid to convene under one roof." The Presbytery met outside the city at Buttergill Hill (Burghill) recording that there had been "no meeting since the first of April till this time because of the pestilence in Brechin."[45] The plague was to diminish slightly over the winter of 1647-48 but by August 1648 it had returned;

---

[44] David D. Black, 68
[45] Presbytery of Brechin minutes, vol. I, 25th July, 1647

there was no preaching in the Kirk and in mid-September the minister "went from the town". It is impossible to guess either the nature of the plague in modern medical terms, nor indeed the number of casualties. Most scholars estimate that of a population of one thousand, six hundred or two thirds of the people perished (and not just the young and the elderly). One contributory factor may have been the very bad snows and ice that occurred in the spring times of the 1640s. But the strong likelihood is that Argyll's soldiers were the carriers, though the people of the time saw it very much as punishment for sin by God and the Session sought to root out the sinners in their midst. Strangers were shunned,

and those of drunken habits or a lewd life banished. Purity had to be maintained.

The later memorial plaque[46] reads:

> *Luna quarter crescens*
> *Sexcentos peste peremptos –*
> *Disce mori – vidit.*
> *Pulvis et umbra sumus.*[47]

It would seem that at least the local citizens who survived realised the need for cleansing. Many

---

[46] The original plaque is now on display within the Cathedral. There is a copy (rather faded) in the graveyard. Most of the victims of the plague were buried in a common pit which, according to Edwards, was opposite the porch door of the Cathedral. This larger pit was eventually opened in 1846 but "no bad consequence ensued" (Edwards). Some folk however were interred near the Bishop's gate on the western side; these graves still remain sealed. The "legend" was that a bluish mist or vapour was seen hovering over the plague pit and that, if opened, will escape from the contaminated graves and spread throughout the town.

[47] A rough translation being that at the quarter moon six hundred died of plague, learn to die, we are but dust and shadow!

people took up residence in huts in the fields around Trinity while their homes within the town itself were burnt by "the cleansers". Some folk, of course, already had the plague when they moved to the huts; if they died in the huts, the structures were simply pulled down on top of them and became their graves. The magistrates also supervised either the boiling or destruction of clothes and bed-linen, believing that the plague was contained within the dirt and squalor. We do not have full records of exactly what happened in Brechin but, if similar to other plague outbreaks in the sixteenth and seventeenth centuries, we can imagine that carts rumbled through the streets with the mournful Mort bell ringing and the cry "Bring out your dead!" Some folk, having contracted the plague, were so concerned at no-one being left to bury them that they literally sewed themselves into their own shrouds. The body-bearers were feared, not simply as possible plague carriers, but because they were the scum of society: brigands, cut-throats and thieves; often they removed not just the dead person from their home, but their valuables too. The hospitals outside the city walls (such as Maison Dieu) was not somewhere the sick would eagerly go to; entry therein was a death sentence as windows and doors were sealed, supposedly to keep disease out but in actual fact sealing the plague in a confined space within.

Despite the undoubted loss of people and money to the Cathedral authorities, it is noteworthy that they often gave funds to those who had lost all their possessions because of the fire cleansings caused by the plague. An extraordinary example is that of the "poor woman in the Craigend of Auldbar, who lost all her gear by cleansing at the time of the infection"[48] and was given £20 Scots to start up again! So too in January 1650, Brechin had recovered sufficiently to gift £42 14s 2d Scots to the inhabitants of Montrose in their own time of pestilence.[49] Similarly in 1652, £93.6s.8d Scots was collected for the town of Glasgow after "a great part of the town was burnt by a sudden and violent fire."[50] The folk of Brechin, who had suffered so badly from war and plague, were very sympathetic to citizens of other places who also suffered.

Despite Charles I's execution at Whitehall in January 1649, armies once again returned to perplex Brechin. Lair's regiment paused briefly in the town in late February resulting in Session failing to meet. In the November, 1649, the Kirk Session minutes record:

> No preaching, neither collection this Wednesday by reason the town was in fear that the Laird of Echt and his troop should invade and trouble the town; And that because a trooper was killed in the night on market day – unknown by whom it was done.[51]

---

[48] Kirk Session minutes, 1st March, 1648
[49] Accounts of Brechin Cathedral, 15th January, 1650.
[50] Kirk Session minutes, 15th September, 1652
[51] Ibid. 28th November, 1649

One can almost detect the fear and anxiety in these few short words. Greater anxiety followed shortly afterwards, for we find by 1650 that the seventeenth century witch-hunts had arrived in the locality. In December 1649, first at Aberbrothoc (Arbroath) then Montrose, William Rait, the minister, was absent by reason of attending the Committee for witches. In the March of 1650 Alastair Gormach and William Smyth were both paid £4 Scots for "watching those women who were imprisoned as witches."[52] Gormach and Smyth were probably the beadles and £4 seems to have been much higher than their usual rate for guarding prisoners! The women were imprisoned on the first floor of the Square Tower at the Cathedral. Amongst them almost certainly was Jonat Coupar of Brechin. We know a considerable amount about Coupar's case; nine witnesses appeared against her at her trial. James Da stated that a "branded dog" had met her upon the Brig of Brechin, the dog had licked her but he was unsure if she had kissed the dog or not. Helen Ker said she saw Jonat hail the dog upon the Brig, while Marat Johnstoun and John Allardes said that they had seen the dog at Jonat's home and heard her promise it that if would get a master that very afternoon. Another witness said that she had refused to give Jonat butter and she was then unable to make more butter that season. Jonat's fate was sealed from the moment the trial began. As D.H. Edwards comments: "any singularity in word or look exhibited by an old crone was sufficient to brand her a witch and subject her to the most inhumane treatment."[53] Coupar was sentenced to be executed. We cannot know exactly what tortures she endured; sleep deprivation was standard – perhaps accounting for Gormach and Smyth's fees. Before the end, perhaps to frighten the authorities and incriminate others, Jonat confessed to being a witch. She stated that it was "about fur (four) year since she was

---

[52] Ibid. 6th March, 1650
[53] Edwards Pocket history, 119

acquainted with the Divell…and that the Divell had caused her to renounce her baptism and take the name Nikki Clerk."[54] Furthermore, the fault lay with Catherine Skair and Catherine Walker who led her to the Devil. She saw them talking together on the "watter syd the wast (west) mill". Jonat's ultimate fate is unrecorded though it is likely that, as by Scots tradition, she was first garrotted then burnt in a barrel of tar. In any case, Edwards records that in the nineteenth century, in a hollow near the gas works, ashes and charred bones were found, including an ankle bone still attached to an iron manacle. In 1972, further charred skeletons were found in Witchden Road during roadworks. Were these remains those of Jonat Coupar, as well as Elspit Gray of Balwyllo and Marat Marchant of Menmuir (who were tried by the Session for witchcraft in 1649)? Yet rumours of witches persisted well into the nineteenth century: Nelly Low, who kept a load of cats, was considered by many locals to be the last of the witches. She died aged ninety in 1846 and "by the bairns she was a well-known and much dreaded character."[55] A witch's branks or scold's bridle was often used to prevent suspected witches from putting a curse upon folk.

The Scold's Bridle

IN mediæval times, the scold's bridle was used in parts of England and Scotland as an instrument of punishment for women whose harsh chiding was a source of annoyance to family or neighborhood. The bridle was fastened upon the head and, having an iron part that fitted into the mouth, rendered speech impossible.

Another significant event in the Cathedral's story occurred on 24th May, 1650 when **Laurence Skinner (1650-90)** was inducted as minister of the "second charge".[56] He was not the first choice; as far back as 1641, the Provost and Town Council had sought to have a local man, one John Fyffe as second to Alexander Bisset. Presbytery had concurred but, for some unknown reason, Fyffe was not as expected ordained and inducted. Certainly he

[54] William Sievwright, *Brechin in Olden and Modern times*, 45 (1902), 45
[55] Edwards, 120
[56] David Carnegy was the first minister of the second charge (1631-33) followed by William Marshall (1633-39), who also held the post of schoolmaster. Similarly Robert Norie (1639-42) was schoolmaster and minister of the second charge. The second charge was often seen as a stepping stone to a charge of your own. Laurence Skinner, formerly minister at Navar, was the first to move from second to first charge. A full list of clergy is in the Appendices.

covered some of the preaching tasks after Bisset's death during the vacancy (and even sat in Session) but as D.B. Thoms puts it "of his projected ordination and induction to the second charge at Brechin there is no word."[57] It is not until 1648 that things become a little clearer. The Town Council renewed its call to Fyffe but he prevaricated; firstly he states that he has not the confidence, then that it was not "a fair and hearty call"[58] and the stipend is not competent. Eventually, the real reason for Fyffe's refusal of the second charge appears to be his health; he seems to have suffered some sort of disability that had grown worse with the passage of the years[59]. With Fyffe's refusal, the way was open for Skinner, minister at Navar to be accepted. Skinner was to be very much the "toon's man" and though Brechin did not know it at the time his son, John, was to become a veritable thorn in the side of the Presbytery many years later.

By the summer of 1651, Cromwell's forces were moving north. Charles II had already been in Scotland, indeed, a (now lost) landward Session minute records that on 30th June, 1650 minister William Raitt had preached before the King at Kinnaird Castle. In July, 1651 Cromwell's ships were sighted off Aberbrothoc (Arbroath) and in late August, his troops were at the ports (gates) of Dundee. It was only a matter of time before Brechin was once again in the line of action. Dundee fell on 1st September and by the end of the month Monck's army had entered Brechin; Session meetings and even worship services themselves were suspended until mid-October. A Session minute from November 1651 records that "No Session or sermon this Wednesday by reason twelve hundred Englishes were in the town Tuesday all night and on

---

[57] Thoms, Kirk of Brechin, 111

[58] Presbytery of Brechin Minutes, Vol.I, 11th October, 1649

[59] Ironically, John Fyffe was ordained to Navar in September 1650 following Skinner's translation. He did not serve long, dying in May or June 1658

Wednesday till the time of the divine service was past."[60]

For the next seven years Commonwealth troops came and went within Brechin and, while at first folk tended to stay indoors when troops were stationed in the town, gradually the population got used to them. Indeed, in the early years we find the townsfolk ministering to hurt soldiers both on the Scots side and also Cromwell's own troopers. Collections too were often made for soldiers who had been captured at home or abroad. The English troops, if anything, enhanced the spiritual life of the community, for they were generally well-disciplined and regular in attending divine services. This was welcome news for the Cathedral authorities who seem to have had a cordial relationship with the army. One incident particularly stands out in August 1658: Captain William Hellen denounced one of his own men for fornication with Lilas Gentleman after being asked to do so by the Kirk Session. Other troops even married local lasses; John Bowden "a free English youth" was contracted in marriage to Agnes Young of the parish in September, 1657, for example.[61]

The winter of 1653/54 was a particularly harsh one with the result that the horses from Cromwell's Cavalry were stabled inside the Cathedral and services took place in the Tolbooth. There is no suggestion however that this arrangement was anything other than by mutual agreement. By late 1658, following Cromwell's death in the September, Monck withdrew his men. The stage was set for the return of Charles II and with him episcopacy to the Cathedral.

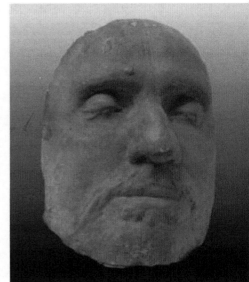

Cromwell's death mask

---

[60] Kirk Session minutes 19th November, 1651
[61] Ibid. 23rd September, 1657

ADDITIONAL INFORMATION – Section 3

WITCHES AND TRIALS

"…we find it really difficult to believe that Presbyteries and Commissions appointed by the General Assembly should have been able to sit in solemn conclave to discuss and adjudicate upon manifold charges of witchcraft, so grossly and mournfully absurd, and so foul and offensive: and by their outrageous decisions subjecting the poor unfortunate creatures to the most inhuman treatment by many acts of barbarity and savage cruelty, at the very name of which we now shrink with horror."

- **William Sievwright, *Brechin in Olden Times* (1902)**

The first record in the Presbytery of Brechin Minutes concerning old superstitions occurs in September 1639 when one **Janet Lovie of Maryton** "confessed that she brak ane roik over ane person long sick, being informed that it suld mak him either ament or die shortlie."[1] By the 1640s we find Presbytery in their superintendence of parishes not only ascertaining the correct preaching of Reformed doctrine, but also rooting out "Papistrie or witchcraft"; it is noticeable that the fear of one often led to suspicion of the other. One of the earliest records of a trial for witchcraft concerns three individuals from St. Andrew's found guilty in 1542 of witchcraft *and apostasy*. The first witch trial itself took place in Aberdeen in 1536 of one **Agnes Scot**; though a pure witchcraft trial (without background politics, as with **Lady Glamis** in 1537) was very unusual pre-Reformation.

It was only with the death of the Regent, Mary of Guise, in 1560 that the Reformation launched in Scotland and with it came the Witchcraft Act of 1563. It read:

> In as much as the Queen's Majesty and the three Estates in the present Parliament are informed that the heavy and abominable superstition employed by divers subjects of this realm, by using witchcrafts, sorcery and necromancy…it is decreed and ordained…that no manner of person or persons of whatever station, rank or condition they may be, take upon hand at any time hereafter to use any kind of witchcraft, sorcery or necromancy…

An earlier draft of the Act by John Knox included Catholicism alongside sorcery but this was withdrawn after Mary Queen of Scots refused to sign the Act. It was quite clear though that in the mind of some of the Reformed ministers Catholicism = witchcraft!

---

[1] *Extracts from the records of the Presbytery of Brechin 1639-1660*, W.M. Ogilvie (Wm. Kidd, Dundee; 1877)
September 12th, 1639

Note that the penalty for not only being a witch but using or consulting one, or even having knowledge of the forbidden craft, was death. In Scotland this usually involved being garrotted on a pole and then having your remains burned in a barrel of tar and your ashes scattered to the wind (to prevent Resurrection on the Last Day). It could be an expensive business; the average cost of executing a witch was £38 Scots, more than it cost to hire a domestic servant for an entire year!

Locally, the first mention of witches occurs in 1568 when the bailies of Arbroath put forty people on trial for sorcery, including one from Brechin. In 1619, John Duncanson, a baxter from Brechin, applies to have an act of slander over the suggestion that he was connected to **Marion Marnow of Menmuir** "a witch that was burnt".[2] The accusation of someone being a witch could rebound as in the case of **Bessie Logan**. Accused by David Finlason of witchcraft, he could produce no substantiated evidence whereupon Finlason himself was imprisoned and fined.[3] In 1621 the Privy Council in Edinburgh granted a commission to examine accused witches in Brechin; regrettably we have no more details.

But the real peak of the witch trials occurred from 1640 – 1690 for a number of reasons: there was plague, climate change with the little Ice Age, civil war, the great Fire in London in 1666 and the death of Cromwell in 1658. All this led religious folk to ask whether the end of the world was indeed nigh and to speculate on demonic forces being abroad. In Scotland particularly the witch fires were particularly stoked by the publication of King James VI book *Daemonologie* in 1597.[4]

Within Brechin Presbytery the rural areas were often hotbeds of witchcraft! So, for example, **Jon Donaldson of Lochlie** admitted in 1649 of being a "charmer" and of "casting the Shemfur."[5] What is of interest is that Donaldson states that "many others in Glenesk besides him used to cast the Shemfur…"[6]

In January, 1650, **Marat Merchant** was accused of witchcraft by David Crystie on his death bed. It seems to have all started as a fall out between neighbours when, at the end of their feeing time, Merchant and her husband James Clark had left their house and moved next door. Crystie was given their former house and Marat seemed to resent this. She blew in Crystie's face, causing his illness and shouted curses at him. Other accusations began to surface. It was said that she used a special cloth to turn ewe's milk bloody. Another accused Merchant of killing David Low with a sore back and cursing John Mertin for striking Merchant's daughter. Finally, on the 19th March, 1650 Marat Merchant made the following confession:

---

[2] Kirk Session minutes, 2nd March, 1619

[3] Ibid., 19th October, 1619

[4] James believed that he had been subject to attack by the North Berwick witches in 1589 when he returned home with his new bride, Princess Anne of Denmark, and the ships were caught in severe storms.

[5] It is not clear from the records if this is a particular form of divination involving shears and a sieve or summoning a particular spirit, possibly a werewolf.

[6] *Extracts from the Presbytery of Brechin*, Ogilvie, 1649.

1st. She confessed...that at a certyn tym, when shee was going to the toun of
Brechin with thrie chopins of milk, she met with the Divell in the
common muir...at the Lucifers Logh, and that he lay with her thair.
2nd. Confessed that the Divell bade her meet him there again.
3rd...that he caused her renounce her baptisme, and called her by
name Jonat Archbald.
4th...that the Divell promised that at the naming of Peter and Paul
milk should come from other Kye to her Kowe's Edder.
5th...that shee practised the same by taking away John Archbald
and Thomas Trotter's kye's milk, both in the muir of Balrounie;
nixt, John Mertin and John Brand's key's milk, both in Dykehead.
6th...that shee was David Crystie's death by spitting in his face;
and when shee was askd what evil that would doe, shee answerd
much ill if ye knew it.

What became of Marat Merchant we do not know, though it seems likely she paid with her life for these many accusations against her.

The next case begins in February, 1650 when **Elspit Gray of Balwyllo** was suspected of witchcraft. Once again the accusations focus upon a mixture of acting oddly (setting four fires and casting salt on them) and that neighbourly discord led to illness or even death. Janet Arcle, wife of William Menmuir, testified that after her husband had suddenly left her employ to work for the Laird of Dun, William had taken hot and cold flushes "from harvest until Martinmas"[7]; he was assured that this was a sure sign of the witch roasting his image over the fire.

For some the mere threat of being classified as a witch was enough. A witch called **Finlayson** lived at Auchmull in Glen Esk. A Mearns man, named Robert Bruce, suspected that fatalities in his cattle were caused by her. He threatened that he would have her burnt as a witch and somewhat co-incidentally there were no more deaths recorded in his herd! Isobel Reany of Magdalen Chapel admits taking south running water to **Marat Forbes**, but denies that she sought "any secret thing from her".[8] On 11th April 1650, Thomas Humball of Navar was cited for consulting the witch **Marat Gold** in order to charm his animals. He was ordered to appear in the kirks of Navar and Lethnot clothed in sackcloth. Isobel Fordell also consulted the same witch and was commanded to appear before Presbytery.
Probably the most famous "witch" of Brechin was **Jonat Coupar**. Rather interestingly she brings herself to the notice of the authorities in November 1649 "complaining that

[7] *Extracts from the Presbytery of Brechin*, 21st February, 1650. Roughly from mid-August to late September; a period when colds would naturally be at their height.
[8] Ibid. April, 1650

some had scandalized her by calling her a witch."[9] Needless-to-say various witnessed are called and the evidence begins to build against Jonat. Isoble Kid, spouse of Thomas Dounie, claimed that Jonat had come to her house three years ago on Holy Rood Day (the old Celtic Beltane) and made her ill through a ritual which involved stroking her thigh. When Isoble Murison had her side stroked by the accused, her new born infant lived only a further eight days. Catherine Davidson's ale went sour and she had to throw it out, and Bessie Stiel's milk turned bloody. Another neighbour refused her butter and the neighbour could make no more butter that season.A new mother stated Jonat had spoiled her breasts and the baby would not feed. As D.H. Edwards states: "Any singularity in word or look exhibited by an old crone was sufficient to brand her a witch and subject her to the most inhumane treatment"[10]

James Da saw a branded dog meet Jonat Coupar while she was going along the bridge of Brechin; the dog lapped upon her, but the witness could not tell if Jonat kissed the Dog or not. Helen Kerr also saw Janet with the dog in the same place, and heard Janet ask the beast "What now, gossop?" When Janet was asked who owned the dog, she replied cryptically, "He would get a maister afternoone."[11]

The likelihood is that Jonat was imprisoned in the Cathedral's Square Tower, probably deprived of sleep, for several days. The Session minutes record that Alastair Gormach and William Smyth were both paid £4 for "watching those women who were imprisoned as witches."[12] Clearly, given the perceived spiritual and

---

[9] Ibid. 25th November, 1649
[10] Pocket History of Brechin, Edwards, 119
[11] Ibid.
[12] Kirk Session minutes, 6th March, 1650

physical risk, the authorities had to make it worth the beadles' effort! But even with Jonat imprisoned, still the town did not feel safe. A soldier, Duncan Campbell, claims that, even though she was without candle or fire, he saw fire coming out of the prison window. Shortly afterwards Helen Bowman claims to have seen the same phenomena and that very night a soldier was killed.[13]

By now, exhausted through lack of sleep and seeking to end her torment at the hands of her accusers, Jonat would confess to anything. And we have a detailed confession from her lips. Jonat claimed that she had known the Devil for around four years. Her first meeting with him happened when she was on her way to the mill. Catherine Skair and Catherine Walker told her to go down a certain lane, where she saw Satan and lay with him. She then went on to the mill, and on her return journey had sex with the Devil again in the same place. She affirmed that the great hound on Brechin Bridge was actually Satan in disguise. On one occasion it followed her home and slept with her, in the guise of a man. The Devil caused her to renounce her baptism and call herself Nikkie Clerk and that he had bit her upon her neck.

All of these are classic elements in any confession from that time: having sexual relations with the Devil, being given a new name instead of the one given at Baptism and a "devil's mark", having a familiar (often in the form of an animal) and dancing naked with the devil and other witches. All these are common elements. Various theories have been offered over the years as to why these confessions were given by these women. Was it, as some suggested recently, that the Medieval sleep pattern allowed for a state of semi-wakefulness in the middle of the night when these activities were imagined to occur[14]? Or were these visions drug induced by some herbal potion? Was it simply that these women lacked love and excitement in their lives and were drawn into a web to spice things up, a web that finally caused their deaths? Whatever the truth, others were "named" as witches by the confessing witch.

So, following Jonat's confession, a process begins against **Catherine Skair and Catherine Walker** whom Jonat Coupar claimed "she saw them and the Divell (sic) together upon the watter syd besid the wast mill."[15] It was heard that after Skair had an argument with William Young, his son died. She had cast some water from a well on a field at Careston for some, presumably magical purpose. When David Daikens shot his gun over the head of one of Catherine's sons in October some sixteen years previously, she informed him that it would be a 'dair stroke to him'. He soon became ill. A woman she also bewitched became sick on the eve of the Holy Rood whereupon Robert Skair

---

[13] This may relate to the same incident recorded on 28th November, 1649
[14] See, for example, A. Roger Ekrich's *At Day's close: a history of nighttime* (Phoenix, London, 2006)
[15] Confession of Jonat Coupar, *Extracts of Brechin Presbytery.*

(Catherine's brother) sent for a "Skeelfull woman" of Brechin who laid something upon the sick woman's breast and said some strange words; the ill woman soon recovered.

In **Catherine Skair's** confession she said that her familiar spirit appeared to her as a big, round-headed cat. At first she 'boasted it away'. But the creature told her, 'Let me be, ye shall not be the worse of me.' Afterwards this spirits was sometime a cat and sometimes a black dog. One night as she was making her bed it appeared, 'and bade her mak that bed weill, and I and ye must lye in it this night'. But a soldier came to the house and the spirit disappeared for three or four nights. When she eventually slept with the demon she found him very cold. She stated that she kissed this demon and fed it in her kitchen with bread and drops of milk.
When an ex-soldier, John Tullo, stayed in the house and lent Catherine and her husband £100, they refused to pay it back when Tullo asked for it. The familiar spirit appeared and instructed her to kill the man with 'plumb Damouses' and sugar. Tullo died and the couple kept his money, less the £10 it cost to bury him. The obliging demon also provided Catherine with money and victuals or instructed her to borrow from certain individuals who dared not deny her. Catherine had consulted the demon over a sick servant lass and the girl sufficiently recovered to eat her supper that very same night. In her confession, Catherine implicated several other "wyse folk" including Marat Gold of Navar and John Young of the watterhead.

Catherine Walker too was investigated. It was recorded that she had kicked a man named William Steill in the groin and he afterwards died. Another man received similar treatment, a child and some cattle of George Stewart also perished. Catherine Allan too had quarrelled with Catherine Walker whereupon "Catharin Allane's barin fell seik in ane extraordinary diseas, sweld in the extreme parts as the day aross, but not in the bellie, and was cold in the morning but sweld at night."[16] While she was held in prison, a guard stated that she had stared into a corner of her cell and muttered a spell: 'Here I cast a compass, there I cast a compass.' The Devil appeared to her there and lulled her gently to sleep.
John Kinkel made deposition before the Brechin Kirk Session that Catherine Walker had the Devil's mark upon her person. John Lyon, a burgess of Brechin, directed his second son, John, to School well because his eldest son was dangerously ill and needed cold water. There the young lad met Catherine Walker who, he claimed, put her feet in the water of the well. When he came home and gave the water to his brother, the brother lost his senses, was paralysed from the waist down and ten weeks later was dead.

Catherine knew that a confession meant her death and she vowed to her friends that she would never give one. She swore that, if she was executed, some of the "great people in Brechin" would suffer two days later. She remarked that some of the men of the town who were now accusing her of witchcraft were like swine and should be locked up in

---

[16] Process against Catherine Walker, *Extracts of Brechin Presbytery*

prison with her. Several witnesses swore that her prayers brought an infection to the town. One man spoke vaguely that he had seen Satan with her, shaped either like a cat or a dog.

Many of the witnesses claimed that Catherine had various marks of the Devil about her person and one begins to suspect, given these men's intimate knowledge of her body that she may in fact have acted as a local prostitute; now the wives were out for revenge! The deciding factor in her fate was probably that she confessed before the ministers that she had killed two of her own children, whether deliberately or by accident is not clear from her testament.

Our final recorded witch from this period is **Catherine Lyall** whose supposed crimes generally follow the pattern of the others. She caused the death of Marat Hackett from the pox after thirty-six weeks in December 1649 after a quarrel over the sale of meal. A woman named Isobel Simpson saw Catherine on the winter day when Thomas Scott's ship left port. She was sitting within the tidemark - a notorious supernatural border region, being neither land nor sea - and she was staring hard at the waves. When Isobel and her companion Barbara Petrie enquired what she was doing, Catherine said that she was keeping sheep. This bizarre statement takes a while to comprehend, and is not otherwise explained in the testimony. What could Catherine have meant? There is no recorded Scottish supernatural tradition explaining why sheep should be living in the sea. But there is a tantalising connection, further down the coast past Dundee, where the famous and prophetic *Goors of Gowrie*, standing stones which somehow ended up in the River Tay at Invergowrie, had the alternative name of the *Yowes* - Ewes - of Gowrie. Tradition said that these stones got nearer to land each year.

Catherine was seen again on the shore when a crowd had gathered to watch Alexander Reid bring back Thomas Scott's new ship. Asked what she was doing, Catherine commented, to their confusion, *that she was keeping sheep*. Shortly afterwards, the ship foundered, drowning everyone on board. Catherine confessed that she had sunk the ship, and said that Satan, the 'Foull Thief', visited her. He gripped her body unkindly, causing her to pull away from his embrace. When she was asked by officials how a human and a spirit could co-join, she answered that she was strong in nature.

Marat Bruce claimed that Lyall had injured and ultimately killed her horse. Elspit Soutar stated that jealousy of her milk cow led Catherine Lyall to curse it and consequently the cow rebelled when milked. James Scott, a maltman, replaced Lyall's son as a labourer with the Laird of Craig, whereupon he fell sick for three quarters of 1642. He wad sweats and chills and "Elspit Neddrie in the tym of his seikness haunted his hous."[17] Alexander Coullie and Alexander Machir both claimed that Catherine quarrelled with the master of the Mill of Dun over an overpayment and cursed the Mill. The Mill shortly afterwards caught fire. Jon Grym's ship (or bark) had sunk at the estuary in 1627. Grym claimed that Lyall was behind the loss of his cargo.

In her confession before Thomas Coupar, minister at Montrose and James Granger, minister at Kineff, Catherine admits to causing the death of Marat Hackett, as well as the

---

[17] Articles of Information against Catherine Lyall, witch; *Extracts of Brechin Presbytery*

burning of the mill, slaying of the horse and the cow giving no milk. But she will not admit to the loss of Alexander Reid and the ship. She also confessed that the Devil had appeared to her as a man, in her own house when she was alone, between nine and ten in the morning. The Devil embraced in his arms and kissed her and would have lain with her, but she resisted. Before meeting her fate, Catherine Lyall implicated Thomas Cramond and Elspit Law as other witches.

It is highly likely that most, if not all of these women were tortured and killed, though several others examined sometimes survived. One woman, named Janet Sym, had her case examined by a committee who reported that the evidence against her was insufficient. None of the Glen Esk charmers seem to have suffered the ultimate penalty.

All of these events were, of course, occurring when plague, conflict and warring armies were invading Brechin. Strangers too could invoke suspicion, as in the case of Margaret Grub, a young woman who appeared before Session in February 1651[18] having escaped from the enemy when Edinburgh fell to Cromwell's troops in December 1650. At least she avoided the fate of being labelled a witch.

The final two local cases concern the schoolmaster at Inchbrayock who, as late as 1667, was sharply rebuked by Presbytery for using the casting of stones to seek to recover stolen goods. Such superstitious practices were seen as unlawful. Agnes Mackie of Oathlaw was also rebuked for the art of charming and disobedience to Church discipline. It seems that she heeded the advice for, if she had acted unlawfully again, she would be "holden to be a witch."

Why did these witch-hunts finally cease? Part because the case of **Janet Cornfoot** of Pittenweem who was killed by a lynch mob in 1704 after being incited by Patrick Cowper, the local minister. This event so shocked communities throughout Scotland that the appetite for seeking out witches waned. Part too because following the coming to the throne of William and Mary and the religious settlement of 1690, Scotland entered into a much more stable political period. Theologically too, Calvinism (with its stress on the depravity of Man) became more moderate in tone while Catholicism (often associated with superstition) was pushed to the geographical margins. Yet, as late as 1767, a heifer was sacrificed on Mull to drive disease from the rest of the Cattle. So too Victoria Helen McCrae Duncan (1897-1956) was prosecuted during the Second World War under the 1735 Witchcraft Act for using sorcery to discover details of the sinking of HMS Barnham in November 1941.[19] The Witchcraft Act was only repealed in 1951.

---

[18] Brechin Kirk Session minutes, 12th February, 1651
[19] It later turned out she had inside knowledge from someone in the Admiralty!

A seventeenth century Witch trial in progress.

CHAPTER FIVE
New kids on the block – the rise of Presbyterianism

During the transition period from 1560 to 1688, which included the alternate ascendancy and decline of Presbyterianism, the inhabitants of the Ancient City were being quietly and slowly leavened with the Presbyterian spirit

- ***D.H. Edwards***

-

Although Charles II had technically been monarch of Scotland from 30th January 1649 to the establishment of military government in September 1651[1], the King was really only able to begin to reign properly after his restoration in May 1660. In terms of ecclesiastical policy this meant that Charles (who abhorred the Covenanters and had defeated them at Dunbar in September 1650) re-introduced episcopacy to the Scottish Church. So from a day of thanksgiving "for the King's safe return to his dominions and throne"[2] we find a few years later that "all Sessions are discharged 'til a way be made and granted hereafter for using and exercising discipline."[3]

The change was not to affect William Raitt. He had already been invited as far back as May 1651 to be Principal at King's College, Aberdeen[4]. At the time, the Kirk Session had resisted this move and appealed against it successfully at both Presbytery and Commission of Assembly. However, with this change in the ecclesiastical weather due to episcopacy, Raitt left Brechin for King's College in the summer of 1661. Perhaps it was not what he expected, for he stayed only a year before taking up an appointment at St. Paul's in Dundee where he died in 1679.

In the meantime, **David Strachan (1662 – 1671)** was appointed as the new bishop of Brechin and preached in the Cathedral for the first time on 3rd August, 1662. Strachan came from the Mearns and had been Minister at Fettercairn since 1630 and was

---

[1] Charles was crowned at Scone on 1st January 1651
[2] Kirk Session minutes 2nd June, 1660
[3] Ibid. 29th January, 1662
[4] In August, 1647, commissioners from the Presbytery and Town Council of Edinburgh had appeared at Brechin seeking to have Raitt as their minister. However, in the midst of the plague, the Presbytery refused. Raitt himself seems also to have been unwilling to move.

clearly familiar with the area. He was also extremely loyal to the house of Stuart and this won him Royal patronage. In the case of the second episcopacy, the bishops were much more "hands on", effectively being the minister of the first charge (Laurence Skinner remaining minister of the second). When available, the bishops acted as moderator of the Kirk Session. Although some of these later bishops retained their former charges (notably Robert Laurie, who remained Dean of Edinburgh) they would appoint "conjunct ministers" or chaplains, to carry out many of the day to day tasks. Some of these "conjunct ministers" are not named in the Session minutes though we do know of **John Dempster (1665 – 75)**, who went on in January 1676 to be inducted to the Kirk of Monifieth, and **Henry Lindsay (1676 – 82)** who went thereafter to Farnell and shortly afterwards to Dunnichen.

David Strachan in 1665 gifted the Kirk a clock for the steeple or, as the mortifications board inside the Cathedral describes it "the orlodg". It seems likely that this was the first of several clocks to grace the Steeple face. Strachan was to be opposed however in his episcopal status; a minute from 1662 records that Laurence Dundas, John Kinnear and John Guthrie went to "another kirk" for Communion, clearly dissatisfied with the King's ecclesiastical settlement.[5] A few years later, in 1667, John Mill, a merchant of the town, is summoned to appear before the bishop for going to Bridgend to hear "outed" preachers.[6] We are fortunate in having a full record of Mill's dispute with Bishop Strachan. He replied that the bishop was mistaken in stating that he (the bishop) was building upon an old foundation. By mid-October, Mill re-appears:

> He (Mill) only wished that the Bishop might not strike at the root, and wished that he might not leave the old foundation, and upbraided the Bishop in the face of the Session for saying he attested the Lord, that he did not process John Mill out of envy or a desire for revenge.[7]

Clearly exasperated, Strachan sends Mill for trial before Presbytery. The outcome was a compromise; Mill promised not to hear any more outed ministers and craves pardon to the Bishop for any offence to him or the elders, for his part, Strachan pardons Mill and takes no further action against him, indeed the minute suggests the Bishop showed great charity and forbearance. Mill never re-appears before Session, so we must assume he kept his side of the bargain. The incident does perhaps suggest though that Strachan was not so well supported as some of his predecessors had been before the War of the Three

---

[5] Ibid. 15th August, 1662

[6] These were preachers who had refused to accept the settlement of Charles II and preached at conventicles. They were especially prevalent in south west Scotland. See Kirk Session minutes 28th August, 1667.

[7] Ibid. 16th October, 1667

Kingdoms; even the Presbytery seeks a compromise rather than disciplining Mill forcibly. Strachan died in the autumn of 1671, apparently fairly suddenly, for he preached on 27th September and died a week or so later. He was buried on 12th October, 1671 before the Cathedral pulpit..

Two other matters should be noted before we leave this period. Firstly, there was a little Ice Age which for several years from 1669-75 saw unseasonably cold weather in the spring with a consequent impact upon the later harvests. Secondly, Strachan laid down some kind of regulation about baptisms and weddings. Baptisms were to be administered on Sundays, Wednesdays or Saturdays after morning or evening prayers and at no other time, unless the child was not expected to live. Marriages could not take place on either a Tuesday[8] or Thursday and they must be between 10 am and 2 pm; fees were set.

With Bishop Strachan's death, **Robert Laurie (1672-78)** succeeded as bishop. Laurie had originally been a minister in Perth (where he succeeded his father in 1641) but with episcopacy restored (and being the only minister in Edinburgh to conform) was appointed as Dean of Edinburgh and preacher at Holy Trinity in Edinburgh; these appointments were held concurrent with the episcopal office of Brechin from 1672, partly because the benefice from Brechin was so small. Laurie was thus much more of an absentee than Strachan had been, for he still held his pastoral ministry in Edinburgh. He did of course rely heavily upon John Dempster and later Henry Lindsay as his conjunct ministers or chaplains. Laurie is described by the historian Keith as "a celebrated preacher and man of moderation".[9] He was consecrated as bishop of Brechin at Edinburgh in July 1672. Prior to Bishop Laurie preaching for the first time on 9th October, 1672, two events of note occurred. Firstly, in early March, a great fire broke out in the town; the minutes record that the inhabitants busied themselves "in quenching the great flame that was in the town on the Sabbath which was tempestuous by the wind."[10] As a result both worship and Session were suspended that day. The Presbytery record gives a little more detail as to the fire:

> The magistrates of the burgh of Brechin appeared presenting the sad and deplorable condition of the distressed people in the town through great loss by a devouring fire on the 3rd (of March) between one and two after midnight, whereby their dwelling houses, inside furnishings, corn in barns and barnyards

---

[8] Possibly because it was Market day and the town would have been already rowdy enough!
[9] Black, 318
[10] Kirk Session minutes, 7th March, 1672

were destroyed, and supplicated a recommendation to several Kirks within the Presbytery for charitable support, which was granted…[11]

Secondly, in the May, a dispute arose between one Robert Strachan, the Kirk Officer and David Mill, who had charge of the bells and new clock. It seems to have centred on the removal of seats from the Cathedral. The trouble with Strachan rumbled on into the summer of 1675 and the minister, Laurence Skinner, seems to have sided with Strachan. Bishop Laurie on the other hand wanted Strachan deposed and James Liddell appointed in his stead. Skinner did give way to the bishop's wishes but then Strachan appealed to no less than the Privy Council in Edinburgh and was duly re-appointed! Laurie seems to have spent most of his time in Edinburgh and it is there he died in March, 1678.

George Haliburton (1678 – 82) as the third bishop of the second episcopacy was a far more energetic man, whom D.B. Thoms describes as a man "with a lively sense of the duties and prerogatives of office."[12] Educated at St. Salvator's College in St. Andrew's where he obtained an M.A. in 1652, he was to be made a Doctor of Divinity by the University in 1673. He came to Brechin having been minister at Coupar Angus from 1659 (a post he continued to hold during his four years in Brechin) as well as Archdeacon of Dunkeld (1663) and Moderator of the Presbytery of Meigle (1678). Consecrated in June 1678, he preached at the Communion service and had his first Session meeting in late September. At this meeting, he indicated that under his episcopacy the elders would have a consultative rather than determinative role; they must restrict their activities in his absence to rooting out scandal and the care of the poor. He insisted that he be presented with the Cathedral keys, the Session minutes and the Accounts, making a thorough inspection of everything. He also indicated that come the December he would seek a revision of the elders' roll. Haliburton also took on a civic role as Provost, appointing in September, 1681 David Donaldson, the younger, as his Baillie for the ensuing year. Perhaps unfortunately for Brechin this highly motivated bishop served only a short time, being translated to the see of Aberdeen in 1682. One notable footnote regarding Haliburton is that he was an avid Jacobite; he lived long enough to witness the raising of the standard of the Old Pretender (James VIII) at Feteresso in September 1715.

The final three bishops can be dealt with fairly speedily. **Robert Douglas (1682 – 84)** had been educated at King's College, Aberdeen and was first the minister at Laurencekirk before going on to Bothwell, Renfrew and Hamilton. It was during his time

---

[11] Presbytery of Brechin Minutes, Vol. II, 25th March, 1672
[12] Thoms, Kirk of Brechin in the Seventeenth Century, 119

as Dean of Glasgow that Douglas received his preferment to Brechin. He preached in the Cathedral on only four occasions: twice in October, 1683, before being translated to the bishopric of Dunblane. He died in Dundee in September 1716 at the grand age of ninety two years!

Alexander Cairncross (June or August – December 1684) was bishop for only a few months yet his story is of some interest. Though originally of an ancient family, Cairncross' circumstances had fallen so low that he began life as a Dyer in the Canongate of Edinburgh, a job he held for many years. Afterwards he was appointed minister at Dumfries from where the Duke of Queensberry recommended him to the see at Brechin. He preached only once in the Cathedral on 1st October, 1684, taking as his text Acts 20:28 "Keep watch over yourselves and all the flock of which the Holy Spirit has made you overseers (or bishops)". Unfortunately, his period of oversight was cut very short when in December, 1684 he was translated to the vacant see of Glasgow. Deprived of his episcopal status in the revolution of 1687-88, King William nevertheless appointed him bishop of Raphoe in Ireland in 1693 and he thus became the only Scottish bishop to be appointed back to episcopal status after the abolition of episcopacy in Scotland. He died at Raphoe in May 1701.

James Drummond (1684-88) was to have the dubious distinction of being the last bishop to hold the Cathedral. Son of Rev. James Drummond, minister of Foulis in Perthshire, he began his ecclesial career as minister of Auchterarder in 1650 before being translated to Muthill in 1655. He was consecrated as bishop of Brechin at Holyroodhouse by Archbishop Rose on Christmas Day, 1684. It is not until September, 1685 that we have a definite record of Bishop Drummond at Brechin, though he was clearly expected in the Spring of that year. He preached on 1st October, 1685. Keith records that "no man was more stedfast in the Protestant religion than he, and both by his preaching and otherways, he gave ground to believe, he would have been as stanch as any man against the opening a door to let in Popry…"[13] But it was not Popery but Presbyterianism that was the rising star within Scotland. By December 1688, the Roman Catholic King, James VII of Scotland, had fled to France to be succeeded by his daughter, Mary and her Dutch husband, William of Orange.

James Drummond preached in the Cathedral for the last time as bishop on 18th April, 1689 and by the July, the Scottish Parliament had seized its chance and abolished episcopacy for good. Like the rest of his brethren, Drummond was deprived of his office and went quietly into retirement as the guest of John Hay, 12th Earl of Errol. He died of dropsy, unmarried, aged sixty-six at Slaines Castle on 13th April 1695.

---

[13] Black, 321

Just a few weeks after Drummond's departure, Laurence Skinner, minister of the second charge, preached a sermon of thanksgiving from Popery on 16th May, 1689; his text being I Peter 2:7 "to you who believe, this stone is precious." However, Skinner, who now claimed the title "Minister of the First Charge" from the exiled bishop was not to enjoy his prize for long. This long-serving minister, who had seen so many changes over nearly forty years (from Cromwell to the restoration of episcopacy to a King fleeing into exile again), died in August 1691. A great preacher in his time, it seems apt that it was Laurence Skinner who gifted the great Pulpit Bible to the Cathedral in 1655. With his death, a time of great change fell upon Scotland and upon Brechin. We must now re-introduce a character who has been patiently waiting in the wings, one John Skinner, son of Laurence, for it is his turbulent story we must now enter.

John Skinner was born in January 1662 and, aged twenty one, seemed to wish to follow in his father's footsteps and so was admitted to his probationary trials in 1683. By 1685 he had been ordained by Bishop James Drummond and was appointed by him as "conjunct minister" or assistant in 1687. John Skinner was however to prove to be historically unfortunate; for one thing he was an avid Episcopalian in an age which was about to see the rapid establishment of Presbyterianism. For another he was literally "last man standing" in Brechin; with the abolition of episcopacy and then death of his father in 1691, it fell to John to become the only "minister" within the town. Further, with the "Glorious Revolution" the pieces on the ecclesiastical chessboard had radically shifted and it was not yet immediately obvious what the new situation would be. However, John continued to fill his father's shoes (and pulpit!) and was well supported in his ministry both by the Town Council, the heritors and the local inhabitants. As far as the heads of families were concerned they had "chosen" John Skinner as the toon's minister. At least so it seemed until the old bishop, James Drummond, died in April 1695. Some months passed until in April 1696 a petition from eighteen persons of Presbyterian persuasion came before the United Presbyteries[14] asking for the vacant first charge to be supplied. Mr. Abercrombie, minister at Lauder, duly arrived in May with a commission from the Presbytery of Dundee. However, he was prevented by the Town Council from entering the Cathedral and was forced to declare the "first charge" vacant (technically that of the late bishop) from the Kirkyard! A letter of apology was to follow from Council to Presbytery and various Presbyterian ministers thereafter began to provide supply for the morning diet of worship. Skinner however lived with this change, reverting to his old role of minister of the "second charge" and conducting the afternoon service. We may also presume that at this stage John Skinner was also providing most of the pastoral care for the town. Again, the situation settled until 1697 when another commission from the

---

[14] These were the Presbyteries of Angus, Mearns and Dundee.

Presbytery of Dundee arrived, this time in the form of Ninian Lumie, minister at Preston. He declared the "second charge" vacant and those providing pulpit supply in the morning stayed in the pulpit until the time of the afternoon diet.

The engraving by John Sleze below shows Brechin as it was in 1695

This left John Skinner in a somewhat awkward position, a minister without a charge. The issue was that both in 1693 and 1695, clergy were required by Act of Parliament to take an oath of allegiance and assurance to William and Mary as rightful sovereigns[15]. This

---

[15] These were as follows:

The Oath of Allegiance:I, A. B. do sincerely promise and swear that I will be faithful and bear true allegiance to their majesties King William and Queen Mary, so help me God.

The Assurance:

I, A. B. do in the sincerity of my heart assert, acknowledge and declare that their majesties King William and Queen Mary are the only lawful, undoubted sovereigns of this realm as well *de jure*, that is, of right, king and queen, as *de facto*, that is, in the possession and exercise of the government, and therefore I do sincerely and faithfully promise and engage that I will with heart and hand, life and goods maintain and defend their majesties' title and government against the late King James and his adherents, and all other

was to declare that they were not only King and Queen *de facto*, but also *de jure*. We cannot, of course, know exactly what was in John Skinner's heart in his refusal but it seems that it was the Assurance more than the allegiance that troubled him, for he declared that he would not take the Assurance since assurance was not attainable in this life – a good theological reply! Since Skinner had refused the Oath, Presbytery made the assumption he had abandoned the charge and this was verified by Commission of Assembly on 1st August, 1697. But Skinner was still in the area, still in possession of the Kirk records[16] and still moderating the Landward Session. In fact, Skinner waited until the afternoon service was complete and then proceeded to enter the Kirk and conduct a *third* service. The Town Session having gone into abeyance, during the month of August eight new elders (including Provost Alexander Young) were admitted by the United Presbyteries forming a new Town Session. A leet of four ministers was also handed to the Town Council to consider for filling the vacancy. However, local loyalty to Skinner and the memory of his late father was strong and the Council resorted to delaying tactics, including a "Testificate and Declaration by the magistrates and inhabitants and Town Council of Brechin in favour of Mr. John Skinner, present minister there."[17] As D.B. Thoms observed however, what had been exposed was "a whole complex of emotions, of personal loyalties and animosities in conflict with political and church attachments, which like dangerous cross-currents had lain unsuspected or disregarded beneath the placid surface of life in Brechin."[18] A very similar situation would arise three hundred years later during the ministry of Robin Mackenzie.

The situation rumbled on for the next few years, there is even a suggestion that the populace of Brechin wanted to apply to the Privy Council to have Skinner settled as their minister. By 1701, the newly formed Presbytery of Fordoun, Brechin and Aberbrothoc had successfully filled five pulpits originally held by episcopally-friendly clerics,[19] yet Brechin still eluded their grasp. So, finally, steps began to be taken in view of the "long desolate condition of the parish of Brechin."[20] Yet again Presbytery decided to offer a leet of four ministers to the Parish otherwise Presbytery itself would make the

---

enemies who either by open or secret attempts shall disturb or disquiet their majesties in the possession and exercise thereof.

[16] No Town Session records exist from May 1697 – 1703, presumably either lost or never handed over by John Skinner himself!
[17] Thoms, 128
[18] Ibid, 128
[19] These were Fern, Menmuir, Craigo, Montrose and Stracathro.
[20] Thoms, 129

appointment. Yet a complex web of emotions and personal loyalties to the Skinner family were still very much at work in the town, and so Presbytery's advice went unheeded and its authority was ignored. Whereupon the Presbytery tried to enlist the support of the Town Council but Provost Doig, mindful of the interplay of personalities involved, stated that there was no stipend for the first charge, since the revenues of the bishopric now went straight to the Exchequer. This was a canny move by the wily Provost, for it avoided either himself or the Council coming down on either side.

By December 1702 Presbytery was becoming exasperated and sought guidance from Commission of Assembly. They suggested a meeting of heritors and magistrates, however this attempt proved fruitless. Presbytery was reluctant to flex its ecclesial muscle and impose a minister, but clearly the impasse could not be allowed to continue indefinitely. The new Provost, David Gray, and John Spence (hospital master) attempted the break the deadlock at a Presbytery meeting by suggesting that the Kirk Session be enlarged. Six elders from the 1697 intake were still surviving and, surprisingly perhaps, fifteen further names were suggested by the congregation. This would allow the local congregation some measure of control over who was appointed as minister, and also hopefully usher in a more collaborative relationship between Presbytery and town. The edict was duly served and all was in readiness for the ordination but on the Sunday in March 1703 not one single possible elder appeared. Perhaps these men had been intimidated or perhaps it was just the unpopularity of the established Presbyterian Kirk within the town; in any case, that very Sunday afternoon John Skinner, who for the last six years had not interfered but simply conducted a third late afternoon service, decided to assert himself. He "entered the Kirk and violently intruded upon and at his own hand repossessed himself of the afternoon's diet at the Church in Brechin"[21] even though the pulpit supply minister appointed by Presbytery was already within the building. As a result of John Skinner's dramatic action a complaint was sent to the Privy Council in Edinburgh.

In the April of 1703, Presbytery made one last attempt to get the heritors and magistrates to call a minister. Once again the plea fell on deaf ears and so in September, 1703, the designated committee from Synod gave a call to **John Willison (1703-16)**, probationer within the Mearns. Willison himself had been educated in Glasgow and came from Stirling, where he was licensed in 1701. Vogan suggests that Willison's move to the Mearns was prompted by the 1698 General Assembly's attempt to get twenty

---

[21] Thoms 130

probationers from the south into the north, where a Presbyterian presence was much sparser[22]. The Presbytery minute records:

THE REV. JOHN WILLISON
Minister at the First Charge of Brechin (1703-1716)
and at the Third Charge, Dundee (1716-1750).
(Reproduced from vol. i. of "The Whole Works of the Reverend and
Learned Mr John Willison", published in four vols. at Edinburgh, 1816)

At Brechin upon Friday the third day of December, 1703, after sermon by Mr. William Arrot, Minister of the Gospel at Montrose…Mr. John Willison was by solemn prayer and the imposition of the hands of Presbytery in conjunction with the Committee of the Synod appointed for that end ordained and set apart to be Minister of the Gospel at Brechin and the Moderator and the rest of the Brethern gave to him the right hand of fellowship.[23]

Brechin had a new minister but what welcome would he receive from the townsfolk?

Willison's first priority was to establish a new session. At first a special committee of Presbytery's own members assisted but, finally, seven of the former fifteen men who had been invited to be elders came forward. Three had been ordained in 1697, one had been an elder in Dundee and a further three were duly ordained. Twenty others were invited but only three were prepared to pledge allegiance to the new regime. This new Session duly met for the first time on 19th January, 1704 with Andrew Doig, a local merchant as interim Clerk. James Millar, shoemaker and former Deacon Convener, was ordained in February 1704 and duly appointed as Treasurer. Opposition to this new Session from the townsfolk is evident in that the Town Council referred to "Mr. John Willison and his pretended Session."[24]

Three urgent matters now had to be dealt with. Firstly, the first charge manse had to be repossessed and put into good order. Since this had originally been the bishop's residence and since the Exchequer were benefitting from the revenues, the expense of re-fitting the Manse fell to them! Secondly, the financial accounts of the congregation had to be investigated. Thanks however to the good offices of John Wood (Oct 1696 – Jan

---

[22] Matthew Vogan "The Origins of John Willison's emphasis on the Lord's Supper" in *Scottish Reformation Society Historical Journal*, 7, (2017) 108

[23] Ibid. 130

[24] Black, 116

1698) and John Shiress (July 1698 – Jan 1704) the accounts proved to be in surprisingly good order.

The third issue was to be more intractable: what were they going to do about John Skinner? Not only did Skinner still possess many of the Session records and archives, but he was also conducting marriages, baptisms, funerals, giving testimonials and preaching regularly! "Ferment and disorder" as Thoms puts it was rife in the town as a result. In March 1704, Skinner was summoned to appear before Presbytery. He admitted that he was preaching on a Sunday afternoon[25] and that "he always owned himself as Minister of Brechin and therefore had still along exercised the other parts of the ministerial function as much as he was capable."[26] However, he relinquished control of the Session to Willison and claimed only the second charge. Presbytery however would not agree to this, whereupon Skinner threw down his paper and appealed to the Privy Council.

Astonishingly perhaps to our minds, the Lord Advocate was seen to be more accommodating towards Skinner, urging Presbytery to show forbearance and to try to reach some kind of *modus operandi* with Skinner. We must remember, of course, the political background against which these events were unfolding. Skinner represented the old episcopal settlement and Jacobitism was strong in the corridors of power. Negotiations had just begun in the reign of Queen Anne with a view towards the union of the Parliaments of England and Scotland, so sensitivities of English views on Scottish matters were uppermost. Sir James Stewart (the Lord Advocate from 1692 – 1709) was keen not to rock the boat.

On 11th April 1704 the ministers who were supplying the Sunday afternoon service reported to Presbytery that "a violent and unruly mob, occasioned by Mr. Skinner and his friends"[27] had caused a great disturbance. This occurred again in the May and Willison was thus instructed by Presbytery to supply the afternoon service himself. He reported however that this was impossible as he could not gain access to the Cathedral or pulpit. Indeed, Skinner basically threatened mob violence again Willison should he attempt to conduct the afternoon worship. Meanwhile it seems that the Town Council and magistrates sat on their hands and offered Willison no support.

---

[25] Skinner stated Presbytery could consider it the second or third service as it pleased. In practice, Skinner had actually conducted a third service from 1697 until the Spring of 1703 when he had taken back control of the second service.
[26] Thoms, 132
[27] Thoms, 133

Meanwhile, at the continued urging of Sir James Stewart, Synod attempted to reach an accommodation with Skinner, rather generously offering him an equal division of town and landward parishes[28]. Skinner felt himself though to be in the ascendancy and refusing to meet the delegation en masse, promptly refused saying "he would exercise all the parts of his ministry to any through the whole parish that desired, being presented and collated to the whole charge."[29] It is possibly now that residual sympathy towards Skinner begins to wane. He was showing a stubborn intransigence and no attempt whatsoever at a reconciled solution.

So this state of ecclesiastical paralysis rumbled slowly on for a further five years. Willison took the morning diet of worship and Skinner the afternoon. It is impossible to guess the strain that must have been felt by John Willison. He was an ardent Presbyterian but personal animosity to him grew to such an extent that he faced social ostracism. It is said that when he and his family finally did translate to a Dundee parish in 1716 so abhorred was he in Brechin that he could not find a local carter to move his possessions![30] As D.B. Thoms suggests: "The Established Church had gained a foothold in Brechin and had brought the first charge under its wing, but it had failed to discredit Episcopalianism or dislodge its representative."[31]

Brechin still hankered after its bishop.

This unfortunate set of circumstances was neither Willison's fault nor, initially at least, Skinner's. The feeling of the town was that this Presbyterian minister had been imposed upon them[32] and that "Willison's Presbyterian principles were not in accordance with the feelings of the people of Brechin…he was persecuted in every way by the inhabitants, especially by those of the higher ranks, most of whom were violent Jacobites and Episcopalians."[33] Yes, perhaps Presbytery might have sought to be more flexible, but so ought to have John Skinner. His father, Laurence had been a well-beloved and faithful servant of the Church; it is a huge pity that John used his family name ultimately for a power-struggle rather than the Gospel of peace.

---

[28] It is an interesting quirk of history that had this happened, Brechin might have had two parish churches over a hundred years before it finally did.

[29] Thoms, 133

[30] Black, 119

[31] Thoms, 134

[32] An accusation, interestingly, that would later be made against Rev. Dr. Robin Mackenzie.

[33] Black, 119

ADDITIONAL INFORMATION – Section 4

OLD CUSTOMS CONCERNING RITES OF PASSAGE

BABIES

To combat the "evil eye" as well as the wiles of the fairy folk, a newborn would be washed three times (for the Trinity) in saltwater. A string of coral (as a charm) was also put round the baby's neck. Swaddling bands were wrapped round the child, arms close to the side, encasing it "mummy-like" in linen. The "merry meat", a pot of flour, bread, ale and sugar, was put on the fire for friends and relatives who called to see the baby. This was combined with a toast in a "hot brew" – a potent brew of ale, brandy and sugar with a little bread.

No baby was called by its name until the baptism; that was considered very unlucky. On the way to church a small parcel of bread and cheese was pinned to the baby's shawl. This was offered as a gift from the baby to the first stranger encountered on the road. On entering a house for the first time, a little salt or sugar was put in the baby's mouth for luck.

Particularly during the Victorian period the practice grew up of babies being baptised at home, rather than in Church (possibly out of fear they might die suddenly, in an era of high infant mortality). This continued in many areas until after the union of 1929 when the Church of Scotland renewed the old Reformed policy of a child being "baptised in the face of the congregation." Several old Cathedral members I interviewed were baptised at home by Dr Coats or Tait Hutchison. James Anderson introduced the practice of baptisms taking place after the morning service at 12.30pm and Peter Gordon pursued the model of baptism during normal worship times – which continues today.

MARRIAGES

These were usually celebrated on Fridays (the day dedicated to Friga, the norse goddess of happiness). May was a month to be avoided, being the season of ancestor worship (Beltane, the old Celtic festival, falling on 1st May) when the wrath of the hidden powers might be provoked by merry-making.

Despite the discouragement of the Reformed Kirk (who sought to abolish them in 1645) "Penny weddings" or "Penny bridals" were very popular amongst the poorer folk in Scotland. In these weddings the guests each brought some food and drink and contributed some money (between a penny and never more than a shilling) to defray any expense to the newlyweds. Guests might also offer to sing, or play a musical instrument, thus contributing to the festivities that could often go on for several days. Any money left was given over to the couple as a wedding gift from the community. The bride and groom would lead the first reel (or dance) and if the groom had older brothers or sisters they had to join in the dancing – without their shoes! From this emerged the modern "wedding reception" – a rather posher affair today! Unfortunately, as the years passed penny weddings became rather rowdy affairs.

The day before a wedding, the bride's possessions (often including a new spinning wheel along with a kist[34] of bed and other linen) was transported to the new home. The bride was given a new bonnet and braw plaid while the groom was given a beaver hat and a blue coat – these were to serve the couple at formal functions for the rest of their lives. A liberal sprinkling of sea-salt was scattered throughout the new home for luck.

On the wedding day itself the bride's female friends would arrive at the bride's home in the morning (accompanied by their male partners) while the groom's friends would assemble at the couple's soon to be new home. The groom's party then proceeded to the bride's family home (or later some hall) where most marriages took place. This made the merry-making easier. There the groom's mother would break (or "heckle") a cake or biscuit over the bride's head – the forerunner of confetti! The unmarried members of the wedding party were given pieces of the broken biscuit to place under their pillows and dream of their yet to come suitors. The bride was then gifted either an apron or, in rural areas, more likely a poker and tongs as symbols of her new office and duty. Pistols were often fired as part of the wedding festivities! The first wedding in a Presbyterian Church in Brechin took place on 16th April, 1885; the bride was Alice Foote, younger daughter of Rev. Alexander Foote. The first wedding in the restored Cathedral took place on 5th November, 1902 between Dr Sinclair (medical officer for the Burgh) and Miss Annie Hume.

The "banns" were called on three successive Sundays (the cheapest way) or simply on one Sunday, which was considerably more expensive. In Brechin these fees ranged from 5 shillings to 10 shillings and 6 pence. It was considered unlucky for a couple to hear their own banns read.

After their marriage ceremony, the newly-weds would not go off on honeymoon as they do today, instead they along with their married friends would attend Church on the Sabbath following to be "kirked".

---

[34] Or chest, usually linen made over several years previously by the bride's mother.

DEATHS AND FUNERALS

One of the very first things a newly married woman was expected to do was buy "deid claes" for herself and her husband to be laid out in, and to put aside money for their burial.

Various traditions were associated with the approach of death: a dog moaning in the night, or a candle suddenly spurting when lifted by someone. After the death itself, clocks were stopped in the deceased's home and mirrors covered with white cloths. Cats and dogs were frequently excluded from the house until after the funeral out of fear that they might leap over the corpse giving the Devil power over it.

It was fear of the Devil that resulted in "lyewakes" where relatives took turns to sit with the deceased (usually in the best room or parlour.) So too a bowl of salt was placed on the chest of the corpse to keep the Devil at bay. There was a great fear of the undead (nowadays we would call them zombies) who could be used as the Devil's creatures for nefarious ends.

Because many people could not read it fell to a deputation of the undertaker or wright, along with a family friend (sombrely dressed in black), to go round inviting family, friends and neighbours to the wake and funeral. Funerals often took place on Sundays – being more convenient for people to attend. Weekday funerals were less popular as folk simply turned up in their working clothes with aprons and caps.

CHAPTER SIX
Repairs, Riots & Revolts

"considering a mob has raged in this place for some days past...and that a spirit of rancour and malice, clamour and evil speaking too visibly prevails in the place, they for their parts found themselves exceedingly straightened to proceed to the solemnization of that ordinance which supposes Christian love and charity in its highest exercise amongst all that would worthily partake in it..."

- ***Kirk Session Minutes of Brechin Cathedral, 28th March, 1741***

Whilst the troubles with Skinner rumbled on, the Session had nevertheless work to do. Poor relief had largely fallen by the wayside and in early spring 1704 applications from needy souls were invited that a new Poor Roll might be drawn up. This was to prove difficult to fund as, while the Sunday collections were being gathered in and there were fees payable for pastoral services (not least the tolling of the church bell at funerals), the local landowners refused to make contribution in the light of the Presbyterian settlement. The Landward elders refused to collect for the Kirk and, notably, James Maule, the 4th Earl of Panmure was withholding charity for the poor because of his Jacobite leanings. All this meant that the majority of the Cathedral's income was being spent on Poor relief and consequently urgent fabric repairs to the building could not be funded. Nevertheless in summer 1705 the South Aisle, which had had a thatched roof, was finally slated at a cost of £328.18s.8d Scots, part of which was paid out of current income and part paid some three years later. The Town Council though was particularly obstructive and as a result the tradesmen employed largely came from Montrose, though the slater, Peter Reid was local and an elder. The builders who did do the work were even accused by a local laird of horning[1] and their wages arrested. Thanks to the intervention of Provost Doig in Edinburgh, the charges were suspended and the men duly paid. However, this certainly marked a low point in relations between Town Session and country.

This also raised an intriguing possibility as to how to take away part of Skinner's powerbase. Since 1624, the Landward (or rural) Session had been separate from the Town Session, largely because the rural elders objected to the length and tedium of the

---

[1] In other words, failing to pay their debts; the name originating from the three horn blasts that preceeded the letters of accusation being issued. A person so accused was said to be "put to the horn".

meetings and because they could not "conveniently attend the town Session weekly by reason of the distance of place and their urgent and necessary labour and affairs at home."[2] Thus a practice grew up whereby the Landward Session met before the Sunday afternoon diet of worship. As a result, almost by default, Willison had become identified with the Town Session and Skinner with the Landward. Skinner too had held on to the Register of Minutes as well as the Baptismal registers – arguing that many parents sought to have him (one so well kent by generations of the family) administer the child's entry to the Faith. So Willison, in a stroke of political genius, sought to re-unite the two Sessions which had first been separated in 1624. Thus in May 1708, the General Assembly, after consultation with the Lord Advocate, resolved "that in time coming there be but one Kirk Session in the town and Parish of Brechin."[3] In practice, as Thoms notes "it would be more correct to say that the Landward Session had been suppressed for its lack of co-operation with the Established Church."[4] It was to be seven years before anyone from the Landward area came forward to offer to serve as an elder.

Meantime, another attempt was made by Provost Doig to get Skinner to relinquish the records he held. Finally, in January 1709, he released the baptismal records from August 1612 – December 1689 and January 1690 – December 1705, though it would not be until December 1718 that he finally relinquished the Session minutes.[5] The Town Council had also withheld several items belonging to the Session, including four silver Communion cups (retrieved from Skinner in 1704). It was only after a threat of legal action by Session against the Council that Bailie Spence (later to be a leading Jacobite) finally handed them over.

In 1705 Willison decided that contracts of marriage would be prohibited on Saturdays. This probably sounds decidedly odd to our ears but it was to prevent excessive partying (and consequently drunkenness) on the night before the Sabbath. Sore heads on a Sunday did not lead to good attendance at Kirk! In 1707, Willison intimated that he desired to celebrate Communion which, extraordinarily, had not been observed

---

[2] Thoms, 138
[3] Ibid., 139
[4] Ibid.
[5] These included: Town minutes 1615 – 77 and 78 – 97; Register of marriages 1700-04 and register of dead 1630-86; Landward minutes 1701-04, which sadly have since disappeared. Two other volumes of Landward Session minutes have also vanished: one being taken by Montrose's army in March, 1645 when the town was sacked and the other lost (though it was recorded as returned to the Town Session by the Lairds of Keithock and Ardovie in 1706). The only extant volume is that of 1644 – 70, written by Patrick Brocas, Clerk to both Sessions.

for the last thirteen years.[6] Skinner, not to be outdone, and fearing that this would indicate some deficiency in his ministry, promptly indicated he would do likewise! Indeed, Skinner did all he could to impede the success of Willison's celebration. In particular, by giving out testimonials, he sought to divert folk into communicating at Edzell, Careston and Kinnaird[7] – anywhere but Brechin! However, for reasons unclear, Skinner postponed his Communion and Willison duly celebrated on 3rd August, 1707. Though we cannot be certain of the number of communicants, £41.12s.6d was collected which, as Thoms points out, compares reasonably favourably with the average of £67 collected in 1675-89. Skinner himself celebrated Communion at Easter 1708 which raised £38.2s.6d. Again, although these financial figures cannot give a reliable guide to numbers attending services, they do tend to suggest that Willison may have had more support than hitherto supposed and Skinner perhaps a little less. The tide may have been beginning to turn in Presbyterianism's favour. One factor too in Willison's support may have been the Act of Union, which formally came into being in May 1707. Although the Parliament of Scotland was now dissolved, it did mean politically that Protestantism, particularly anti-papal Protestantism, was in the ascendancy.

Presbytery had held back in summer 1708 from pursuing action against Skinner due to the threat of war with France[8] but, with invasion now receding, Presbytery summoned the seven intruder ministers[9] within its bounds to appear before it at the December meeting. Skinner however refused to appear either in December or January 1709, saying Presbytery was not competent to try him! In the February, despite a church officer being sent to his home, Skinner appealed to the General Assembly and it was not until the August that the General Assembly's Commission reported back that Skinner's objection of competency was unfounded and thus dismissed. Finally, on 31st August, 1709, Skinner appeared before Presbytery and (despite misgivings from the court) Skinner was allowed to read out a written statement of answers to the four counts against him.

---

[6] This fact actually counts against Skinner since, not being truly ordained, the Sacrament of Communion probably did not feature much in his training or experience. Willison himself celebrated Communion six times during his period in Brechin, annually from 1711 (by which time Skinner had been expelled from the bounds by the Lords Justiciary). For a detailed study on this see Ian MacLeod *The sacramental theology and practice of the Reverend John Willison 1680-1750* (University of Glasgow, 1994)

[7] Pulpits all filled by those, like Skinner, who were "intruders" and did not support the Established Church.

[8] The day before Presbytery met the Old Pretender (vis. James VIII) had sailed from Dunkirk with the French fleet and 6000 men at arms. It reached the Firth of Forth but the English fleet compelled it to withdraw.

[9] Aside from Skinner, these were John Grub at Oathlaw, John Ochterlony at Aberlemno, Francis Rait at Kinnaird, Robert Lindsay at Edzell, Robert Thomson at Lethnot and Alexander Lindsay at Careston, former Episcopal incumbent at Cortachy, who was conducting services and performing liturgies according to the practice of the English Church.

On the first count of parish intrusion, Skinner claimed that although he had never taken the Oath of Allegiance to William and Mary he had prayed for their Majesties and this was equivalent to the Oath. Skinner also claimed that his right to the second charge had been established by the deed of presentation, given by the late bishop James Drummond. In 1704 when he was sentenced, he stated he had been on the verge of complying with Presbytery's requirements! These claims and the whole 1687 procedure were dismissed by Presbytery as being "wholly illegal, clandestine and contrived."

On the second count of being unfit for the office and work of Holy ministry, this charge was based upon a Pasch (Easter) Sunday sermon he had given in 1708. Skinner sought either to distance himself from these or show that he had been misrepresented and that "ordinary hearers every Lord's Day…give an ample testimony of their satisfaction with my ministry."[10]

The final two counts related to Skinner's attempts to obstruct John Willison from holding Communion and Skinner's own attempts to do so. Presbytery itself presented evidence that Skinner's supporters had brought influence to bear on the heritor's factors who, in turn, had influenced many tenants to boycott Willison's Communion service. The ruling was given that he must submit to a catechetical trial in September.

On 14th September, 1709, Skinner arrived accompanied by Provost Young, members of the Town Council and citizenry and the lairds of Keithock and Findowrie. His supporters presented a Declaration and Representation arguing, basically, that they were satisfied with his qualifications as a minister and Presbytery had no business putting him to the test. When Skinner himself refused to undergo a catechetical trial, Presbytery passed sentence and deposed him from office. He appealed to Synod, though this too failed. With all legal avenues exhausted, Skinner and his supporters resorted to force once more and again Skinner seized the pulpit on the afternoon service two Sabbaths after Synod had met. The preacher who had been scheduled to preach was chased by schoolboys and pelted with stones. Now Presbytery did not hesitate; it raised a criminal action against Skinner and in January 1710 the Lords Justiciary sentenced him to be banished and expelled from the bounds of the Presbytery of Brechin. Skinner himself was imprisoned until he gave a solemn undertaking to the Lords that he would desist from engaging in ministerial functions. For the moment, the Skinner tale had come to an end[11].

---

[10] Thoms, 146

[11] It was not until November, 1710 that Skinner vacated the manse of the second charge.

With Skinner's deposition and expulsion the way was now clear for a minister to be called to the second charge. A meeting was called for 30th March to discuss the matter but on the day no-one turned up and Provost John Doig refused to help in any way. Presbytery thus sought to impose a minister on the second charge and called William Trail, one of its own probationers. Not long afterwards Presbytery learnt that a petition had been raised, opposing Trail because of his voice and seeking instead **John Johnston (1710 – 32)** from Dundee who had preached his trials in Brechin the previous December with a view to going to Edzell. With Trail himself rejecting the call on account of the parish's petition, Presbytery were eager to settle a new minister in the second charge and accordingly Johnston was ordained and inducted on 18th May 1710.

Johnston had been educated at Marischal College in Aberdeen and licensed in March 1706 by the Presbytery of Stirling. For the next five years, he and Willison began to exercise fruitful ministries in Brechin. Pews were installed in the Cathedral, George Carney, a glover who had gone to live in London, left £60 to the poor of the parish whilst Isabel Mathie donated her house and garden at the South Port. Communion was now celebrated annually and, as Thoms points out, the rise in the Communion givings from £48.17s.6d in 1711 to £57.4s.2 d in 1715 would tend to suggest that things were settling down and attendance was increasing. It was merely the calm before the storm…

In 1712 under the Act of Toleration an Episcopal meeting house was set up in Brechin led by one Gideon Guthrie. This was permitted providing that the Episcopal priest took the oath of allegiance to Queen Anne and prayed for her; Guthrie however refused to take the oath. Episcopalians were also permitted to conduct both marriages and baptisms but Guthrie went further and started exercising church discipline, a right reserved to the Established Church. The matter came to a head in 1713 when two cases of fornication (one involving William Mather and Janet Laing and another involving Thomas Anderson and Agnes Leitch) refused to appear before the Cathedral Session on the grounds that their cases had already been heard and processed by Guthrie. Willison and Johnston took the matter before Presbytery and in February 1715, it took steps to prosecute Guthrie before the Court of Session. In August, Guthrie was fined 100 marks, prohibited from preaching or ministering in Brechin under penalty of a further 500 marks and banned from holding any charge in Scotland for seven years. However, political events were soon to render such judgement obsolete.

In August of 1714 the last of the Protestant Stewart monarchs, Queen Anne, died suddenly and the Whig government in London proclaimed the Elector of Hanover, King George I. This was certain to rile the Jacobites and in September 1715 John Erskine, the

22nd Earl of Mar[12] raised the standard of James VIII at Braemar. A few days later the Earl of Panmure declared for the Jacobites at Brechin's cross and was joined by the Earl of South Esk. The final Session minute of 31st August, 1715 reads:

> In the month of September following broke out the Earl of Mar's rebellion against our most gracious Sovereign King George and the Protestant succession in his family and in favour of a popish pretender whom they called King James VIII. That which rebellion continued until the month of February thereafter; and this is the reason why there was no meeting of the Session from foresaid 31st August to 29th February thereafter.[13]

It was only come February 1716, when the fog of rebellion lifted, that it became clear what events had unfolded in the interim. Once again, John Skinner had re-appeared in the town this time in cahoots with Gideon Guthrie[14] of the Episcopalian meeting house. It would also seem that on this occasion Skinner had usurped the role of minister of the first charge. James VIII had in fact stayed at Brechin Castle for two days in the very early days of the New Year and in early February the Jacobite army had entered Brechin for a short time. It was however but a short lived rebellion and by 4th February James VIII had gone scurrying back to France leaving others to face the consequences. John Doig of Unthank, who was currently Provost, had been imprisoned by the Jacobites and Bailie Spence (long a suspected Jacobite supporter) had:

> usurped a most tyrannical power over men's bodies and consciences and threatened and forced people to hear the foresaid rebellious intruders (viz. the clergy Skinner and Guthrie), drink disloyal healths and otherwise countenance the said rebellion; and particularly did wickedly impose a base and traitorous oath upon the people called the Test, in which, besides other absurdities and contradictions, they did swear to the popish pretender as King and renounce our only lawful Sovereign King George as a foreign prince. With which wicked impositions and base oaths a great number of the people and even several of the elders have complied, either out of ignorance or slavish fear or desire to shun suffering.[15]

---

[12] Mar had gone to London to curry favour with the new king, only to be rebuffed in the attempt.

[13] Kirk Session minutes, 31st August, 1715

[14] Gideon Guthrie was born on 24th May, 1663 at Castltoun in the Mearns, son of Harry of Halkertoun and Margaret Sibbald of Kair. After his trial in July 1715, he was banished from Brechin and forbidden to carry out ministerial functions. When the Earl of Panmure declared for the Jacobites on 19th September 1715, Skinner and Guthrie seized control of the Cathedral on Sunday 25th September, remaining until January 1716. Guthrie was appointed bishop of Brechin by James VIII (the Old Pretender). After the 1715 rebellion failed, he fled to Montrose and in October 1716 was forced to flee again to Edinburgh when Hanoverian soldiers searched the house in which he was staying. Guthrie died in Edinburgh in 1732.

[15] Black 129, Thoms 153, Kirk Session minutes 4th March, 1716

It is ironic for those of us several hundred years later to see how George is regarded as rightful Sovereign and James VIII as a foreign prince, when in fact both came from Europe! And to note also that while the Whigs insisted on an Oath of Allegiance, the Jacobite Test was seen in a less favourable light. Some of those who had been rebels were dealt with privately by Willison and Johnston but four elders were dismissed, including the Treasurer James Miller and the Church Officer Alexander Allardyce. Seventy five men in all were to appear before the Session in connection with the 1716 rebellion, of which twenty five were weavers.[16] Amongst the rebels was John Petrie, master of the Grammar School, who had until now managed to keep secret his Jacobite allegiances. It became clear that he had in fact been acting as Treasurer and Clerk to the Episcopalian meeting house, which Petrie argued he was free to do. However, when Thomas Paul (the doctor at the School) along with the janitor, accused Petrie of haranguing the students with Jacobite propaganda, he was instantly dismissed.[17]

In July 1716, perhaps with his last vestiges of dignity and self-respect in tatters following the Rebellion, Willison had had enough of Brechin and accepted a call to Dundee. Both the Presbytery and Provost Doig begged him to stay and build on the foundations he had built[18], but his mind was made up and in the September he moved to the second charge of Dundee, albeit with the help of John Guthrie of Kincraig, having failed to find a local carter willing to assist! Willison went on to become a prolific writer of Presbyterian works including the *Afflicted Man's Companion* and *The Mother's Catechism*. He died in Dundee in May 1750, aged seventy. In assessment of Willison, Thoms writes:

> …upon Willison was focussed the personal animosity of the whole parish. Willison during those early years in Brechin had to endure a hostility and measure of social ostracism that seem incredible to a more tolerant age. But beneath the aversion from the Presbyterianism that Willison represented and the attachment to Episcopalianism championed by Skinner there lay other emotions that found their outlet in dislike of the incomer…the rift in Brechin was not without political element"[19]

---

[16] Thoms, 153, gives a full breakdown of figures as: weavers 25, shoemakers 15, hammermen 9, gunsmiths 5, tailors 5, merchants 5, glovers 4, fleshers 4, baxters 2 and one maltman.

[17] As indeed were the schoolmasters of both Montrose and Dun.

[18] Ian Macleod in his PhD Thesis *The sacramental theology and practice of the Rev John Willison (1680-1750),* (Glasgow University, 1994) draws attention to the fact that Willison may have had experience of resistance in the transition from Episcopalianism to Presbyterianism from his Stirling roots. In which case, he might have left Brechin earlier had that experience not strengthened him.

[19] Thoms, 134

With Willison's departure and the end of the Jacobites, at least for now, "Brechin became perfectly quiet after the insurrection was quelled."[20] Presbytery considered moving John Johnston from the second to the first charge but the matter was badly dealt with in committee and the plan was shelved. In January 1717, Thomas Paul, now schoolmaster following Petrie's disgrace, represented to Presbytery the "ruinous case of the Kirk of Brechin".[21] In April, a call was presented to Robert Gray of Edzell, who had gone to the charge three years earlier amidst great opposition from congregation and heritors alike. Thomas Paul opposed the call saying that "no honest man would sign or subscribe a call to Mr. Gray"[22] but nevertheless **Robert Gray (1717 – 1738)** was duly inducted on 8th May, 1717. Gray had been born c.1685 and was licensed by the Presbytery of Aberdeen in 1710. Thereafter he went to Cabrach (1711) and Edzell (1714). His son, Alexander, became a famous surgeon on the island of Sumatra.

Gray's principal focus was the fabric of the Church and in July 1718 it was said to be in a ruinous state with urgent work required on the north aisle, the Steeple and the glass windows. The records suggest that Willison's relationship with the heritors had been somewhat terse and at times tempestuous, whereas Gray approaches them in a "friendly way"[23]. At first it appears the heritors are willing to pay for the repairs, the total cost being estimated at £380 Scots. However we find by June 1719 that many of the heritors have not paid and, while the Session has purchased the materials, the repairs to the Steeple and north aisle are still outstanding. Grudgingly, the heritors finally allowed repairs in 1720 to the Steeple and the slating of the two aisles. A seat was also put up at the back of the pulpit. But they still were not keen to part with money and in May 1722 the process of extracting funds from the heritors had dragged on, becoming bogged down in the legal process. The clock was repaired in September 1727 by William Robb of Montrose and in November 1731 workmen repaired the great bell. In July, 1725, the congregation raised £26 Scots for the Scots Presbyterian Church in the city of New York.[24]

It was not simply the physical structure of the Kirk that required attention; the spiritual state of the people did too. Thanks to the Rebellion of 1716 many years had elapsed since Communion had been celebrated. Gray sought to put this on a more regular

---

[20] Black, 131

[21] Kirk Session minutes, 9th January, 1717

[22] Thoms, 155

[23] Kirk Session minutes, 30 July, 1717

[24] Over two centuries later in the 1960s, the New York Scots Presbyterian Church contacted all the churches who had initially supported them and the Cathedral sent a stone, dating from Medieval times, that had been left over in the 1902 restoration.

footing and so the first Sunday in March was set as Communion season or "Holy Fair"[25]. In late December 1718, John Skinner, so often a thorn in the side of the Presbyterian establishment, had his last contact with Brechin when he handed over the final registers to the Session.[26] He died in Edinburgh in 1725.

Gray sought too to bring some order to Brechin! Marriages were sometimes a rather unruly affair where multiple ceremonies took place at once in the Kirk and couples were desperate to be "first out" as superstition held this to be a lucky omen. This came to a head in the winter of 1725/6 when it seems there was "great disorder…contrary to the Apostle's rule"[27]. Gray was determined to stamp this out. It was a marriage in July 1732 that indicated that once again the spectre of Jacobitism was raising its head. Andrew Scott and Isobell Jack were to be married but before the banns[28] could be read, testimonials had to be produced for both of them. Unfortunately Andrew Scott's testimonial came from an Episcopal minister and Gray declared this invalid. Nevertheless, Thomas Thomson, the town officer, proclaimed the banns on 2nd and 9th July "in a most irregular manner and contrary to all law intruding into the Church at Brechin, and before the pulpit foot, in the very time of ringing of the last bell, immediately after ten o'clock of the forenoon, to the occasioning of great disorder and confusion in the congregation."[29] The Session sought to have the town officer discharged but the problem was he was employed by the Town Council, who were beginning anew to show pro-Jacobite sympathies. As to the poor couple, they were married by Mr. Ogilvie, minister at the Episcopalian meeting house.

The deaths of the two ministers occurred in the 1730s. John Johnston died on 3rd November, 1732, leaving a legacy of £1000 to establish a school at Pitpollux at the west end of the parish. The school was later moved to Little Brechin. Robert Gray then died on 12th July, 1738[30]. Their untimely deaths were to pave the way for another interesting character in the Cathedral's story: **Rev. David Blair (1733 – 38; 1738 – 69)**.

---

[25] This practice, though discouraged by the General Assembly, saw a week's long series of events; Thursday was fast day; Friday the local men gave their interpretation of Bible verses; Saturday was Preparation Day. Sunday saw several Communion services, sometimes beginning as early as 8 am. These often took place in the open air and were attended by vast crowds and led by neighbouring ministers "imported" for the Fair. Monday concluded with a service of Thanksgiving.

[26] These included: Town Session minutes 1615-77 and 1678 – 97; Landward Session 1701-04; Register of marriages 1700-04 and Register of dead 1630 – 86.

[27] Kirk Session minutes, 14th December, 1725

[28] Usually the banns were read THREE times (the cheapest way) or ONCE (the most expensive).

[29] Kirk Session minutes, 10th July, 1732

[30] William Hall was paid £1.10s for putting up new mourning cloths on the pulpit following the death of Robert Gray in September, 1739.

David Blair was born in 1701 and graduated with an M.A. from St. Andrew's in 1719. He appears to have been chaplain to Colonel Patrick Ogilvie before being licensed by Dundee Presbytery in March 1728 and then ordained to Lochee in September, 1729[31]. In June, 1733, following the death of John Johnston, he became minister of the second charge and then was presented by George II to the first charge in August 1738, being inducted in the October. He married Christina Doig, daughter of Provost Doig of Cookston, who was also an ardent Hanoverian and imprisoned by the Jacobite sympathisers on the Council. Clearly Blair too was loyal to the Hanoverian settlement and is described as "a staunch, if overbearing, Hanoverian."[32] Yet, he was to be the right man when the 1745 rebellion broke out.

One of Blair's first considerations was the Cathedral's finances. In July 1740, the Poor Fund was almost exhausted. There were two reasons for this: firstly, there was a "scarcity of victual"[33] which was forcing more folk below the breadline and increasing the number of poor in the parish with consequent demands upon the limited funds; secondly, the weekly contributions had fallen year on year. Despite misgivings by some of the Session, Blair borrowed £20 Scots from John Low, a councillor and local merchant, and £100 Scots from John Dunbar, the aged minister in the parish of Menmuir. But it was not enough to alleviate the misery and by Christmas 1740 we find that:

> The Session taking under their serious consideration the very straightening circumstances of the poor in this place through the scarcity and high prices of victual and the stormings and inclemency of the season, and at the same time

---

[31] It was also in 1729 that the Muir of Brechin was feued by the Town Council to John Ogilvy who created Little Brechin.

[32] Adams, *Brechin the Ancient City*, 54

[33] Kirk Session minutes, 8th July, 1740; Possibly a famine caused by the very long and severe winter of 1739/40. 1740 was actually one of the coldest years in Britain's history and the circumstances of the poor must have been dreadful.

their utter inability to supply them as their necessities demand, the weekly contributions being very inconsiderable, their funds being a great deal exhausted already and what remains not answering for the present…a voluntary contribution to be made at the Church door on Sunday 4th January for supplying the necessities of the poor…"[34]

The desperation of the feelings of the Session in the minute are obvious and in the January of 1741 the pew rent was introduced to raise much needed capital. Things improved a little following the special offering for £54.14s.10d Scots was collected and later that winter Blair purchases 40 – 50 bolls[35] of meal at £8 Scots per boll.

With David Blair's translation from the second to the first charge, a vacancy now had to be filled. At first, it looked as if a Mr. Gellatly was going to be called but by June 1739, **William Shank or Shanks (1740 – 44)** was nominated as minister of the second charge and ordained on 16th January, 1740. Born in June 1714, the son of Alexander Shank, minister at Drumoak, he was educated at Aberdeen University gaining an MA in 1730. Sadly, his ministry was to be cut short prematurely for he died at Brechin on 11th April 1744, aged thirty nine and left £66.13s.4d to the school at Pitpollux, founded by his predecessor, John Johnston.

In the spring of 1741, the Session minutes record that a riot by weavers had occurred in the town. As a result Revs Blair and Shanks decided to delay the June celebration of the sacrament of Communion.

---

[34] Kirk Session minutes, 24th December, 1740

[35] A boll was a measure, which varied from locality to locality, but in case of meal was usually around 140lb. Meal in Scotland was normally oatmeal, the staple diet of the working man.

The Moderator (David Blair) signified to the Session that his colleague (William Shank) and he had been talking in private anent the administration of the sacrament of the Lord's Supper which the Session…had agreed should be set about sometime in June next, and that considering a mob has raged in this place for some days past, in which not a few whom better things might have been expected have been in some way or other engaged, and that a spirit of rancour and malice, clamour and evil speaking too visibly prevails in this place…that therefore they had called the Session to advise with them, whether it would not be more expedient to delay setting about this work for sometime and till we see the Lord in his mercy bring us to a better frame and disposition of mind…[36]

Unfortunately, none of the records give us the cause of the riot but, given the stress on meeting the needs of the poor, hunger and poverty may well have been contributory factors. Indeed, a later minute in 1742 and 1743 records that Peter Duncan, weaver, applied to be admitted to Communion and Charles Kinneir for the baptism of his child; both were refused on the grounds that the two men had taken part in the Spring riots of 1741 and they had gone "through the country taking people's victuals from their hands."[37] Desperation had clearly resulted in lawlessness, which the Kirk could not sanction.

It was about this time that a new Manse[38] was built for Mr. Shanks, the cost of which was offset by offering the old yard to the Council for £250 Scots. It is also in these years that one of the most colourful episodes took place concerning a Session Clerk[39]. On

22nd May, 1744, Mr. Philip, the Clerk[40], had gotten drunk in the house of William Finlay, the local vintner or wine merchant. He had then gotten into a fight with Alexander Grim and Finlay had put Philip to bed in an upstairs room. However, Philip had woken up and escaped through an attic window. He was naked and proceeded to run down the High Street to the "consternation of the ladies of the vicinity."[41] The

---

[36] Kirk Session minutes, 28th March, 1741
[37] Ibid., 29th September, 1742 and 6th February, 1743
[38] This Manse was demolished in 1803.
[39] In this time the Clerk also had the function of being the Precentor who led the praise in Church.
[40] It must be noted, in defence of Philip, that in those days the Clerk was generally a young man who was engaged in studies and sought to make some money from being Clerk and Precentor. He was not therefore the first drunk or naked young student!
[41] Kirk Session minutes, 31st May, 1744

matter was referred to Presbytery and Philip was duly deposed on 10th June.

With the sudden death of William Shank in April 1744, the choice of his successor lay between Alexander Spence of Glasgow or William Gourlay of Dundee. In the end the Crown appointed[42] the relatively obscure **James Fordyce (1745 – 53) as** minister of the second charge. Fordyce was born in 1720, the third son of George Fordyce, merchant and Provost of Aberdeen. Given that his father sired no less than twenty children, young James was not short of siblings! His appointment to Brechin caused some controversy because he was a Crown appointee and the townsfolk held out for free election of the "toon's minister". Fordyce did not get on well with David Blair and in 1753 translated to Alloa having gained his MA from Aberdeen. He went on to gain a doctorate from Glasgow University and became a prolific theological writer and popular preacher at a Presbyterian Kirk at Monkwell Street in London, where he associated with the famous writer Samuel Johnson. When the congregation declined after a rift and due to poor health, Fordyce retired to Bath where he died of complications caused by syncope and asthma in October 1796.

1745 saw, of course, another Jacobite rebellion, this time led by James VIII's son, the

young Pretender, Bonnie Prince Charlie.

This was less of an affair in Brechin, which seemed to have learnt from the disruption caused by the 1716 rebellion. Certainly there is a break in the Session minutes from 21st June 1745 – 28th November 1746 and the Town Council elections were abandoned for two consecutive years. The likelihood is that the common folk were for the Prince, as were some of the councillors

---

[42] Crown patronage was very much in vogue for clergy appointments. It was to become the live "hot potato" of the 19th century in the Kirk, leading to the Disruption of 1843.

and magistrates, though on this occasion loyalty ran mainly to words, not active rebellion. A later Presbytery minute from March 1748, in which Blair and Fordyce speak of the rebellion, records that six of the thirteen councillors were professed rebels, including the Provost and one bailie. Some of them kept guard on the prisoners from the *Hazard*[43], while others harboured goods for the rebels or drank toasts to "the King across the seas"[44]. David Blair, of course, was an ardent Hanoverian and prayed for King George even when threatened by armed rebels in the pulpit! The story goes that some soldiers of Prince Charlie entered the Cathedral during divine service and threatened to shoot David Blair if he prayed for "the Hanoverian usurper". Blair was clearly not a man to be easily intimidated and, despite the fact the soldiers sat in the gallery facing the pulpit with pistols primed, Blair carried on as if they had not been there. Having done what he considered right in praying for "his godly Majesty, King George", the soldiers caused no disturbance and left the Church rather sheepishly. As D.H. Edwards puts it "we can still appreciate the worthy pastor's care for his people's souls while he sternly denounced their politics."[45] Blair considered it his spiritual duty in sermons to warn his parishioners of the errors of the Jacobites in religious practice and belief, as well as the civil consequences of provoking the "displeasure of the Government." It seems that when a daughter of Baillie Allardice sang "scurrilous songs" in the streets in contempt of George II and the Duke of Cumberland, Blair took grave exception. The Presbytery record goes on to say that:

> Mr Blair, one of the ministers in Brechin, took notice of these wicked and treasonable practices from the pulpit on a Lord's day, and warned the people against them, as things extremely evil in themselves, and which, if continued, behoved to draw down the displeasure of the Government upon the place…so far as the ministers know, the magistrates of the place bestow no care to discourage the spirit of disaffection which rages here, or to give check to the non-jurant (non Kirk) ministers, or so much as to inquire into their conduct and seditious practices…they (the magistrates) attend public worship in the Established Church themselves, yet none of them have ever brought their wives or any of their children…the wives and daughters are among the most zealous friends of the non-jurant preachers…his Majesty's most zealous friends who have persisted in attending worship where King George was prayed for, when both ministers and people were in greatest danger from armed rebels in the church, have been insulted and beat upon in the streets by disaffected persons, and such as bore arms

---

[43] *HMS Hazard* was a sloop captured by Jacobite forces in Montrose harbour in November 1745 and sailed to Dunkirk where she was renamed *Le Prince Charles*. Hanoverian forces later re-captured her in March 1746 en route to Inverness.

[44] James VIII

[45] D.H. Edwards "A Staunch Hanoverian minister" in Brechin Almanac

in the rebellion, without receiving the smallest redress from the magistrates of the place, who ought to protect the king's lieges by the execution of the laws.[46]

Despite David Blair's protestations there is no record of any Government action against the magistrates.

John Strachan was sent to Tilbury Fort on the Thames for treason but later released. Alexander Low, host of the *Swan Inn* was a well kent Jacobite before the rebellion; he too was arrested (probably on information supplied by Blair himself) and held for nearly a year but eventually turned King's evidence and released. Blair, in a clear swipe at Low, states in his Presbytery speech that the lenient treatment Low received was because his brother-in-law, Mollison, had recently been elected town councillor! This antagonism between minister and landlord continued afterward; in one famous incident some years later, Low and Blair were both at a party and recounted that they had been in London at the same time in 1746. The party host expressed surprise that the two men had not met during their time there, whereupon Low quipped "Sir, I was sick and in prison and he visited me not!" Blair quickly left the party and never again mentioned his London visit! Low became a famous wit at parties in Angus and storyteller of Jacobite times. He was said to have encouraged the wearing of white rosettes (the Jacobite symbol) in bonnets, though always maintained he did not permit bonnets to be worn at his Inn, thus avoiding the charge of public Jacobite sympathies. It was to be a long time before the Jacobites of Brechin forgave David Blair for his "betrayal" of them to the authorities.

Two rebel ministers were active during the rebellion, including James Lyall of Carcary who sought to minister in the parish of Farnell "instilling bad principles into the minds of deluded votaries and baptizing children."[47] In early February 1746 the Jacobite army, led by Lord George Murray, came to the town causing terror in their wake. These uncultivated men seized the Town Hall as their base, breaking up benches and burning records for fuel. Yet, they were, an eyewitness of the time reports, the toast of the lassies who adored the pretty Highland lads in their kilts! They "were no ways scrupulous in helping themselves to anything which struck their fancy…(and) were chiefly noted for their predilection for gingerbread."[48]

The Duke of Cumberland's Hanoverian troops arrived a few weeks later. They were much better disciplined but did not enter the city proper, crossing the Brechin Brig where they rested and took refreshments. Yet they would not accept any hospitality from

---

[46] Black, 151f.
[47] Ibid. 151
[48] Black, 142

the townsfolk[49]; Cumberland insisted they ate only their provided rations and they drank water from the South Esk. Going on their way they took the East Mill road and passed Pitforthie on their way to Aberdeen.

The battle of Culloden took place on 16th April, 1746 and several Brechin men were present. Very few returned to give an account of the battle and those who did were reticent to speak. One man who joined the Prince (though significantly he never stated *which* Prince, Charlie or Cumberland) spoke of the determination of the Highlanders. The battle itself was in some ways inconclusive, but Prince Charlie failed to take the military initiative and, like his father before him in 1716, slunk back to France. On his return to Brechin following the battle, Cumberland's troops, apparently egged on by David Blair, tore up the benches of the Episcopal meeting house, burning the woodwork and prayer books. Yet, perhaps surprisingly, the meeting house was spared, Blair requesting its use by the Cathedral for the Wednesday service – the Cathedral being too large and too cold. As far as known, it was never used by the Kirk but later became the church for the United Presbyterians.

With Prince Charlie defeated "every cool thinking Jacobite saw the sun of their hopes had set on the field of Culloden."[50] Yes, songs, stories, even toasts would persist for some years but the advantages of political union between Scotland and England began to be perceived. In 1759, the Town Council tore down the walls and ports of the old city; invasion was no longer to be feared. Whatever issues the Cathedral would face in the future would be generated by ecclesiastical rather than national events.

---

[49] One local brewer who lived at the end of the Bridge, whether out of fear or loyalty, laid out tables offering the army pitchers of beer and small loaves. So too Baillie David Mathers offered wine and cake to the officers but these were all refused; the speculation is that (following local Jacobite sympathizers in the 1715) Cumberland did not trust the Brechiners!

[50] Black, 153

CHAPTER SEVEN
Decay and Disruption

It was a sad day for the auld Kirk as the doors remained locked. A portion of the outgoing congregation remaining loyal to the outgoing ministers had stayed at home whilst many others had attended the Secession churches.

- 2nd June, 1843, Town Clerk of Brechin's minute book

We cannot leave the ministry of David Blair on a purely negative note. Although one of Blair's successors, Walter William Coats, would later describe him as "singularly destitute of humour and sweet reasonableness"[1] Blair nevertheless ought to also be remembered as a man who in 1760 began the first Sabbath evening school in Scotland for weavers and their families. In April 1752, the Session sought to re-institute the old penalties for fornication and adultery. Although some incidents of discipline against offenders are recorded in the later minutes, society itself had begun to move on and we find the frequency of such cases before the Session greatly diminishing until by the outbreak of war in 1914, they have entirely disappeared.

With the translation of James Fordyce to Alloa in October 1753, a new minister required to be appointed to the second charge. **Thomas Mathison (1754 – 1760)** had been a writer in Edinburgh before entering the ministry. Licensed by the Presbytery of Dalkeith in 1748, Mathison was to serve an appointment in England for a time until being ordained to Inverkeilor in September 1750. However, he was presented by George II to the second charge in March 1754 and inducted on 11th July, 1754. His ministry was to be short, for he died in June 1760 leaving a wife and three daughters. Unfortunately, we do not know whether Mathison's relationship with Blair was any better than Fordyce's had been but it seems unlikely, given that Blair was vehemently opposed to ministers, such as Mathison, who were appointed by royal patronage rather than congregational election; as Coats states: "There was probably not much in common between him (Mathison) and Mr Blair."[2]

Two scandals were to occur during the latter part of Blair's ministry. In February, 1757 a dispute arose between William Wilson, doctor at the grammar school, and the schoolmaster (Wilson's senior colleague) John Bruce. Bruce accused Wilson of being

---

[1] Coats, 54
[2] Coats, 54

overfamiliar with his wife, an allegation Wilson strenuously denied. An investigation took place and the accusation was found to have no substance, so Presbytery duly censured both John Bruce and his wife. However, the whiff of scandal remained and, though justice had been done, it did not run smoothly and Wilson demitted office soon after. Bruce himself was demoted to doctor of the school. Perhaps significantly, Bruce was denied the two other jobs that normally went with the doctor of school, namely, precentor and Session Clerk. These went to John Clark, a town merchant. By 1760, it seems that all had been forgiven though and John Bruce becomes Clerk and precentor.

The second scandal occurred in May 1764 and involved none other than Blair's son, Cumberland[3] William Blair. On the night of the 3rd of May a drunken frolic had taken place in the Cathedral in which the "cutty stool"[4] or stool of repentance below the pulpit had been thrown down, having stood there from "time immemorial". This act had occurred when "the sin of uncleanness rages in this place."[5] At first, suspicion fell upon a group of wrights who had been constructing a new loft within the Cathedral and had possession of the key. However, as further investigations took place it came to light that Cumberland Blair and some of his youthful chums had broken in to the Kirk and sawed it away from the pulpit. A fortnight previously, Cumberland had been dared to take it down but stated he would not do so "for a thousand guineas". Alexander Strachan said that he would take it down "for a pint of ale" (a slightly cheaper price!) and David Lyon didn't really care "a farthing whether it were taken down or not." An inspection revealed saw marks, though these in themselves were not enough to cause the resulting damage. Whether it was because Cumberland was the minister's son, or whether it was because he made an impassioned plea that it was time the cutty stool was done away with, in any case, the matter was quietly dropped. The stool was never replaced and an old pew was placed on the south wall next to the pulpit "in the meantime".

Andrew Bruce (1760 – 1798) was to succeed as minister of the second charge on Mathison's untimely death. Born in 1722, Bruce was educated at Marischal College, Aberdeen before being licensed by the Presbytery of Deer in January 1753. He was to be ordained as an assistant at Pitsligo before serving as assistant at Montrose. Presented to the charge by George II in August 1760, it was nevertheless shortly after George III's accession to the throne in October that he was inducted to Brechin on 13th November

---

[3] One can see David Blair's Hanoverian bias in naming his son after the Duke of Cumberland, victor of Culloden. Culloden was fought in April 1746 and Cumberland was born on 9th September of that year.
[4] Although traditionally in Scotland the cutty stool was a three legged round seat, in Church it was a larger piece of furniture upon which sat (or sometimes stood) a penitent as he or she was berated by the minister from the pulpit for their sins.
[5] See Kirk Session minute, 4th May, 1764.

1760. He married one Rebecca Forbes and they had six children, four daughters and two sons; the eldest boy, John, going on to become minister at Forfar in adulthood. We must be grateful to Andrew Bruce for providing us with the very first record of the parish in the 1st Statistical Account published in 1794; though his son, John, was to cross swords with David Blair's successor, John Bisset. Bisset took issue with Bruce's earlier description of the Round Tower "bending like a willow in high winds so as to almost touch the steeple." His son, John, claimed however that his father never uttered such words and that they were put into his late father's mouth by Bisset himself! Amongst other things Bruce records that within the parish "there are neither Jews, Negroes nor Roman Catholics in the parish, but some of these sturdy beggars, called gypsies, occasionally visit."[6] Bruce also records a number of fascinating lesser known historical stories for which I, for one, am indebted to him.

David Blair, who had come to the Cathedral's second charge in 1733 died on 20th April, 1769 aged sixty eight. A controversial but colourful figure, he had lived through some interesting events in Brechin's story and he would be a hard act to follow. Nature abhors a vacuum and in November 1769 **John Bisset (1769 – 97)** was inducted to the first charge, having been presented by George III. Bisset was born in 1725, son of John Bisset, minister of the second charge of Aberdeen. Educated at Marischal College like his colleague Andrew Bruce, he was licensed by the Presbytery of Brechin in August 1749 and ordained to Culsalmond parish as assistant in November 1751. He married Elizabeth Angus, the daughter of the parish minister, and they too had six children of which John, the elder son, eventually became Professor of Rhetoric at Columbia College in the United States.

In 1774 financial issues again reared their head. Arbroath's Kirk Session owed Brechin £1900 Scots, given over in loans in March 1734 and May 1740. Unfortunately, Arbroath had recently become bankrupt and was no longer able to service the interest payments, let alone the repayments. This in turn, combined with a growing population within Brechin, put the Cathedral's Session poor funds under almost intolerable pressure. So in December the seat rents were raised to 2d due to "the considerable increase of people in the town and a great demand for seats in the Kirk."[7] For a few years this alleviated the problem but in 1777 the funds were again running low; this time the Session turned to the heritors to make contributions to the poor fund. Never eager to part with money, the heritors objected on the grounds that funds were being given over to strangers and travellers not in the bounds of Brechin. The Session retorted that the giving

---

[6] Old Statistical Account of Scotland, edt. Sir John Sinclair of Ulbster (1794) 77
[7] Kirk Session minutes, 29th December, 1774

of charity to strangers who came to the town was "common in every parish up and down the kingdom."[8] A further financial dispute arose with the Town Council in 1780 over the ringing of bells. The normal practice hitherto was that the fee for the ringing of the bells[9] at burials had been paid into the Poor Fund. But the "muckle bell" had recently been recast after a night's frolics by young men one Saturday night and the repair expense had been borne by the Town Council. In an effort to recoup their costs, the Council demanded money from the Kirk Officer who reported to the Session. In the September the Session threatened legal action[10] unless Provost Mollison (who seems to have been the main protagonist in this matter) backed down. By the November a compromise was reached:[11] the Magistrates would have custody of the bells and direct the ringing of them in exchange for £10s.4d being paid into the Poor Fund. According to the minute this sum was equivalent to forty years' worth of dues for bell ringing though Rev. Bisset was not convinced it was a satisfactory arrangement and records his dissent to the decision.

The bells will ring again later in our story! In the meantime we must note that this incident was simply the beginning of the secular powers encroaching upon matters previously dealt with by the ecclesiastical authorities. A year later the Town Council passed an Act regulating the mode of sitting in the municipal loft within the Cathedral. In 1783 Provost Mollison (who seems to have been the bane of the Cathedral authorities) called the attention of the Session to the fabric of the Cathedral. The gable walls and aisles were in urgent need of repair and, stated the Provost, minor repairs had always been paid from Session funds. The Session replied that they were not in the habit of using the Poor Fund for fabric repairs but they would consult the heritors upon whom the cost of the repairs ought to fall. That same year the Magistrates decided to appoint a schoolmaster to teach English, writing and arithmetic at a salary of £80 Scots per annum[12] and that the office of doctor of the Grammar school should be abolished. The problem was that by convention the doctor of the school had until now also acted as Session Clerk and precentor, only charging parishioners for making entries in the baptismal and marriage registers. The new arrangement meant the Cathedral would have to now pay a salary for these posts. As a result of these changes John Robb demitted as an elder and the Clerk, John Clark, resigned his office.

---

[8] Kirk Session minutes, 19th June, 1777

[9] A fee of 10 marks was by this time the usual payment.

[10] Kirk Session minutes, 19th September, 1780

[11] Ibid., 17th November, 1780

[12] William Dovertie was also permitted to charge each pupil quarterly 1s.6d for English, 2s for English and writing and 2s.6d for English, writing and arithmetic. Mr. Dovertie seems to have ended up teaching foreign languages, since the Rector taught English and counting.

The period 1794 – 1805 saw various wars being fought with France, yet the citizens of Brechin remained loyal to the Crown. In late May 1798, the Lord Lieutenant of Forfarshire wrote to the Session requesting that they draw up a list of all men in the parish from sixteen to sixty years who are "fit to be enrolled for the defence of the country."[13] Little wonder that a service of thanksgiving was held in November 1798 for the victories at the Battle of the Nile (August 1798) and the battle of Tory island off the coast of Donegal (October 1798)

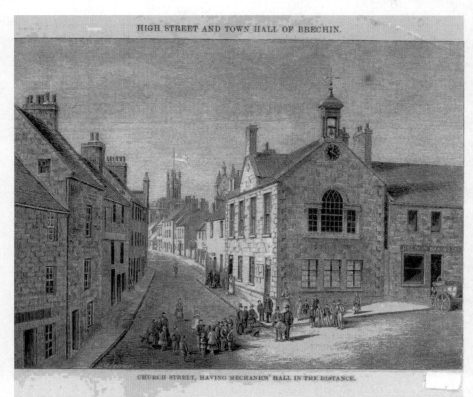

HIGH STREET AND TOWN HALL OF BRECHIN.

CHURCH STREET, HAVING MECHANICS' HALL IN THE DISTANCE.

followed in 1815 by a service of "great thanksgiving", held in the Cathedral, following victory over Napoleon at the battle of Waterloo. The colours from the Forfarshire regiments in the Napoleonic wars are still laid up within the Cathedral and may be seen by visitors as a link to those far off days. In 1789 the old Tolbooth of Brechin was replaced by the new Townhouse.

---

[13] Kirk Session minutes, 28th May, 1798

Despite foreign wars and famine caused by a number of poor harvests, the weaving community grew and the town prospered. During this period too there was great change in the ministers of the Cathedral. John Bisset died on 9th October, 1797 and was succeeded as minister of the first charge by **James Burns (1798 – 1837)**.

Burns was born in Falkirk in 1774, son of John Burns and Grizel Ferrier. Educated at the universities of Glasgow and St. Andrew's, he was licensed by the Presbytery of Linlithgow in November 1795. After presentation by George III, Burns was ordained on 4th October, 1798 and almost immediately became chaplain to the Brechin Volunteers during the wars.

By contrast, **Rev Robert Coutts (1798 – 1804)** who succeeded Andrew Bruce[14] as minister of the second charge was less militarily inclined.

---

[14] Bruce died 23rd September, 1801

The famous story is told of Coutts who came across some soldiers drinking in the Tavern at the time of Tuesday prayers. He duly berated them and took the matter to the Session that they might be further disciplined. However, the elders were less inclined than Coutts to pursue the matter, arguing that these men had fought for King and country and ought to be given some latitude in their behaviour.[15] Coutts was born in Largo in 1772, son of the factor to the Earl of Leven. Educated at St. Andrew's and Edinburgh universities,

Coutts was licensed by the Presbytery of St. Andrew's in 1796. He then spent a few years as assistant to Professor Vilant in the Mathematics department of St. Andrew's university as well as being ministerial assistant within the town. On December 27th 1798 he was ordained assistant and successor to Rev Andrew Bruce.[16] Coutts seems to have had a good working relationship

with James Burns. He stressed a process of disciplined visitation within sections of the parish as well as introducing a February Communion season to compliment the one in July. Communion tokens for Brechin were issued for the first time in February 1799. Both Burns and Coutts began catechizing new folk who wished to receive Communion and strangers to the town were provided with certificates that they might attend the Sacrament. Burns and Coutts also succeeded in doubling the number of elders serving on Session. Coutts himself was well known as a strong evangelical preacher and was not part of the traditional Moderates party of the Kirk. It all promised a bright new beginning to a new century. Sadly, Coutts' ministry was to be a very short one. He seems to have suffered from poor health and died (aged only thirty one) of tuberculosis at Forfar on 18th

---

[15] Adams, *Brechin, the Ancient City*, 78

[16] This was to become common practice for many years where an assistant was ordained to replace a minister on retirement.

June, 1803, on his way back from a tour that had been intended to restore his health. His memorial tablet, erected by the congregation to this relatively young man, can still be seen within today's Cathedral.

Coutts was succeeded into the second charge by **George Whitson of Parkhill (1804 – 1835)** of whom we know comparatively little. Born in 1775 we know he had a younger brother Alexander. Licensed by the Presbytery of St. Andrew's in 1797, he was presented by George III and ordained at Brechin on 15th March, 1804. One of his claims to fame is that he married Mary Molison, daughter of the infamous Provost!

Towards the beginning of the nineteenth century an extraordinary event took place in Brechin that was, to some degree, a prelude to our current National Health Service. One Dr Ogilvie, a surgeon, offered his advice and assistance to the poor gratis for a six month period on condition that "the Session only pay for such medicines as were sent to any of the poor confined at home."[17] As the conditions of the poor seem to have deteriorated further to such an extent that they were "in time of scarcity and dearth"[18] emergency consultations were held between the Magistrates, Session and heritors. Dr Ogilvie's initial offer for six months was later extended to a year. However we find in 1813, ten years later, that it is still going strong when Dr Ogilvie presents his account for the medicines. The Session minute records that "thanks were expressed in most polite terms for his gratuitous attention to the cause of the poor during so long a period…giving attention to the poor without demanding any remuneration."[19] Dr Ogilvie's services were probably in great demand due to poor diet and malnutrition amongst the poor folk, leading to a whole variety of what, today, would be easily treatable conditions. The wars with France, a particularly cold winter in 1794/95 and a series of poor harvests had resulted in a huge spike in the price of wheat. Hunger, famine and death were the consequences for the most vulnerable. Sadly, we know not what became of the surgeon David Ogilvie; he disappears from the Cathedral's story as silently as he appeared.

---

[17] Kirk Session minutes, 29th December, 1799
[18] Ibid. 24th December, 1799
[19] Ibid. 10 February, 1813

Very little meantime had happened regarding the Cathedral's decaying fabric (ruinous is the word used in the documents of the time) since Provost Molison had drawn the issue to the Session's attention in 1783. Meetings with the heritors had been held until finally, in 1806, work had begun to repair the building. During the building work the Cathedral congregation were to meet in the City Road Secession Church[20]. The renovations were duly completed in December 1807, though later generations were to regard them as a disaster!

Dr Coats records the work that was done, clearly not to his tastes:

Instead of seeking simply to restore the building where it was going to decay, those responsible tore down the aisles and built new ones, with walls high enough to carry a wide roof over the whole. There was a plaster ceiling, and although the pillars were left, they were also plastered over. The pulpit stood in the middle of

Brechin Cathedral 1790.

[20] The small church of the anti-Burger Seceders was set up in an old malt barn in City Road in 1764. By contrast, the Brechin Burger Seceders met in Airlie Street then in Maison Dieu lane from 1802. The church was rebuilt in 1864. For an explanation of the complexities of these break away groups see J.H.S. Burleigh *A Church History of Scotland* (Edinburgh, 1983)

the south side of the Church, and there were galleries all round. Tradition has it that the Edinburgh architect wanted to pull down the Round Tower to get materials for building new walls, but Lord Panmure threatened to hang the first man who removed a stone. Even in those days there were some who felt that a great wrong was being done, but protest was useless in the degraded state of the public taste. Doubtless the building as re-opened in 1807 was more comfortable than it had been in its previous state of decay. And in course of time, as new generations grew up, with the associations that cling to a place of worship, however ugly…a certain tender sentiment attached itself to the "auld kirk", and there were some who regretted the work of restoration undertaken in later days.[21]

The question was whether what had been gained was worth that which had been lost? Various trades erected their lofts, complete now with armorial shields. Boxed Georgian style pews became the norm for seating[22] (as opposed to the stools and desks that had been introduced at the Reformation). In fact, the sale of pews within the Church by public auction in January, 1809 resulted in £258.2s.6d being raised, still leaving a deficit of over £200 in the cost of the repairs to the Church[23]. Adams estimates that the post 1806 Cathedral had enough seating capacity for 1600 people. Perhaps as well, for the population of Brechin was growing rapidly. Within the Session minutes it is recorded that the population had grown from 5466 in 1801 to 5559 in 1811.[24] The 2nd Statistical Account of 1833 shows that the town had 1050 weavers plus 200 workers in the spinning mills. There were nine schools, though working class children only attended either morning or afternoon; the rest of the day they too worked in the mill. White collar workers appeared with the arrival of the Dundee Banking Company in 1792 as well as the opening of the distilleries in the 1820s. The railway arrived in 1837 and there were a good nine or ten inns or hotels.

---

[21] Coats, 57; the later restoration he refers to is that of 1902.
[22] It is of note that when the Heritors and Kirk Session met to discuss the allocation of pews in the newly refurbished church, the poor came well down the list of priorities!
[23] Kirk Session minutes, 11th January, 1809
[24] Ibid. 23rd June, 1811

Other changes came too; the deacon, who had acted as Precentor, disappeared with the auld kirk, as too did the deaf widows, who traditionally had sat on the baptismal seats, adjoining the precentor's desk at the pulpit, complete with their bonnets of Scotch plaid. The new pulpit was surmounted by a dove with olive branch, which can still be seen at the north entrance door of today's building.

David Blair of Cookstown, son of the previous minister, gifted to the newly refurbished building a silver baptismal basin with a lid with a sacred dove. At this time also the parish was first divided into districts. Set fees were introduced ranging from everything from proclamation of wedding banns to burials[25]. The hours of tolling the "muckle bell" were regulated by the Town Council from 1809 and from 1820 the tolling of the bells at a private funeral was discontinued, though still permitted in the case of a royal death.[26] It was indeed a time of great change and everything became more regulated as the industrial revolution took off.

Some things did not change, including the great strain on the Cathedral's finances due to poor relief. Bad harvests from 1796-99 resulted in a soup kitchen being opened in

---

[25] The fees were: Proclamation of wedding banns on three different Sabbaths, 5s; proclamation of banns three times in two Sabbaths, 7s. 6d; proclamation of banns three times on one Sabbath 10s 6d
Extract from Session records: 1s for first page and 2d per page thereafter
Extract from Baptismal record 6d
Burials: child's grave, 1s 6d; mid-size grave 2s; large grave 2s. 9d.
[26] It is of note that as late as 1704 the Presbyterian Church were still charging for the "popish ceremony" of ringing the mort bell before the coffin. This was partly to warn of the approach of a funeral cortege and partly to encourage those who heard the bell to pray for the dead person's soul. A practice Knox certainly frowned upon!

1800. These were the "dear years" for Brechin. A very cold winter in 1809/10 resulted in coals being distributed amongst the poor and Cholera was to infect the town on three occasions – 1831/2, 1849 and 1868. Means testing for those on the Pension Roll was introduced in December 1810 with the result that those receiving a pension from the Parish had an inventory taken of their property which remitted to the Kirk upon their death. 1816/17 saw such a severe winter that the poor fund was in danger of being completely depleted by the end of the summer and the Session begged the heritors to assist. November 1818 saw another change: no longer were persons under discipline to be rebuked publicly before the congregation, now it would be done in private.

A prelude to a coming storm arose in April, 1829. A petition, signed by over one hundred members of the congregation, was presented to the Kirk Session desiring to appoint James Adam[27] to the office of Precentor. It was early signs of a growing wave of democracy which would finally engulf the Kirk in the tsunami of the Disruption in 1843. Since the Patronage Act of 1711[28] ministers to parishes had been "presented" to congregations either by local aristocracy, a university or the Crown. The aim of the act had been to restore to patrons the right to appoint clergy which had been lost after the "Glorious Revolution" of 1689/90. The roots of this practice lay in pre-Reformation times when a local landowner would endow a church, abbey or Cathedral with a financial gift but then expect as a consequence to have some say over who served as its clergy. Many churches grew very wealthy in this way and it was easy to see why formerly influential local landowners wanted to re-assert their control of parishes following the Treaty of Union in 1707. However, the system was wide open to abuse. For one thing, the aristocratic patrons were generally Episcopalian or even Roman Catholic in their own adherence with no knowledge (and sometimes no love) of the Kirk. Ministers (though in principle opposing the idea of patronage) were often very reluctant to voice their opposition publically, since they owed their living to their patron. All ministers had to swear allegiance to the Hanoverian monarchs. Congregations technically could object to a presentation on the grounds of unsuitability, and many did, though the General Assembly usually upheld the patron's choice for fear of litigation in the civil courts. In short, the Patronage Act was a measure of control by the nobility over the Kirk and with the rise of an undercurrent of popular democratic feeling it was only a matter of time before turbulence arose. Burns himself had sought to petition the General Assembly in spring 1836 with a view to repealing the Patronage Act, perhaps he foresaw the clash that would come over the issue.

---

[27] Kirk Session minutes, 5th April, 1829. The conduct of said James Adam was called into question in the August of 1829 and he was finally discontinued in his post come the October.

[28] Technically the Act was *An Act to restore the Patrons to their ancient Rights of presenting Ministers to the Churches vacant in that Part of Great Britain called Scotland*

SACRED
TO THE MEMORY OF
THE REV: JAMES BURNS,
FIRST MINISTER OF THIS PARISH, WHO DIED
ON THE 2? OF JAN? 1837, IN THE 62? YEAR OF
HIS AGE, AND THE 38TH OF HIS MINISTRY.
He was a good man, and full of the
Holy Ghost, and of faith.
ACTS. XI, 24.

ALSO, TO THE MEMORY OF
CHRISTINA CHALMERS,
HIS SPOUSE, WHO DIED 6TH OCTOBER 1837,
IN HER 63? YEAR.
Blessed are the dead, who die in the Lord.
REV. XIV, 13.

For Brechin this clash was to come in the early days of 1837. Just into the New Year, Rev. James Burns passed away at the age of 62 years; this left the first charge vacant. The practice hitherto had been for the Home Office to consult the Town Council and the Heritors before issuing a presentation. However, this time events moved somewhat differently. A mere week after Burn's death the Town Council took the initiative declaring in a resolution that "a memorial should be addressed to the Home Secretary, praying him not to grant a presentation…until the wishes of the congregation had been consulted, and a majority, duly ascertained, been found to concur."[29] The Session though did not want the Council to gain the advantage and so they wrote to the two M.P.s, Patrick Chalmers of Aldbar and Lord Douglas Hallyburton, informing them steps were being taken "to secure the congregation the free choice and election of a minister."[30]

First into the frame for the post was James Chalmers Burns, assistant at North Leith and son of the late minister. This seemed to be a popular choice and canvassing began led by his brother, David Burns (later founder of the "Brechin Advertiser"). Yet young Burns peaked too early in the popular minds. For one, many felt he was too young; for another, many saw him as an integral part of the town establishment. Not only was he the late minister's son but he was also nephew of the Provost's wife.[31] In late January a meeting between the Principal Heritors and Session took place at which two resolutions were passed. The first demanded that "an able, experienced and zealous

---

[29] Soc. Of Friends Book 23 (1974), 12
[30] Kirk Session minutes, 13th Jan, 1837
[31] Anne Burns (1784 – 1870) was the younger sister of Rev. James Burns and wife to Provost David Guthrie II (1786 – 1854), commonly known as "sugar Davie". In addition, the Provost's brothers were managers in the "New Church" in City Road, a *quoad sacra* church began in 1836.

Minister be appointed"[32] while the second insisted that whoever was appointed must have been a minister of a Parish or Chapel of Ease for at least two years. Both these measures were designed to rule out young James Burns. The Heads of families struck back declaring the meeting on 26th January illegal and taking measures to appoint a Committee of ten to draw up a short leet of preachers to present to the Presbytery. The lines of battle were drawn, as outlined in the *Montrose Review* of February 1837:

> The Heritors naturally want to have something to say, the Session, with the exception of two or three, seem to be taking the matter very quietly, the Town Council seem to think that because in days of yore the candidate recommended by the Council got the presentation, no other body has the right to approach the patron, and finally, the managers and members of the New Church, though in a way of providing candidates for their own pulpit, think that they are not precluded from taking a hand in filling up the vacancy... the best interest of all parties would be best consulted were the Secretary of State to take the matter into his own hands...[33]

Lord John Russell, the Home Secretary of the day, proposed to send a leet of four from whom the congregation were invited to make a choice. However, the Head of Families Committee led by Colin Rickard, a bank agent, prepared another list of five. Both lists were to contain the name of James Burns,jr., while the Rickard list also had the name of one William Norval, minister at South Church, Kirriemuir. Interestingly, James Burns,jr. was persuaded to withdraw his name from the leet in favour of the Provost's younger brother, one Rev. Thomas Guthrie[34] of Arbirlot. It is fascinating to speculate on what might have happened in Brechin had Guthrie taken the charge, but he was already being considered for Old Greyfriars in Edinburgh.

On 8th March the Presbytery met to receive the petitions. Peter Gordon, in his detailed paper on these proceedings, records that "there were so many Brechin people present that the meeting was transferred from the Session Room to the Town Hall in the High Street."[35] The Heads of Families Committee with five names on their leet was signed by 319, whereas the Heritors' petition was signed by 169. It was clear to the Presbytery that the idea of the congregation hearing preachers from a leet was simply going to divide the community further; a decision would have to be made by the Home

---

[32] S of F, 14
[33] S of F, 15
[34] Guthrie was arguably the greatest preacher of that generation within Scotland. He began the ragged schools, campaigned for temperance and was one of the leaders of the Free Church of Scotland, becoming its Moderator in 1862.
[35] S of F, 16

Secretary. So, on 4th April, 1837, in one of the last acts of William IV, a presentation was made to William Norval, minister of the quoad sacra chapel of Kirriemuir South Church.

William Norval (1809 – 71) was born in Glasgow on 26th June, 1809. The son of James Norval and Grisel Pettigrew, his father was a humble combmaker, so clearly his parents would have had to make sacrifices to send him to Glasgow University where he gained his MA in 1829. Licensed by the Presbytery of Haddington in 1834, he was appointed to the newly created extension charge of Kirriemuir South in 1836, becoming its first minister.[36] With the Crown Presentation being made in his favour, Norval now had to preach before the congregation of Brechin on two succeeding Sundays before Presbytery could induct him. Of course, even with a Crown Presentation, the congregation could exercise a veto; though this was supposed to be out of concern for the spiritual life of the congregation, not simply for malicious intent! But it was clear that many were prepared to veto Norval simply because he was the Crown's choice. Norval duly preached before the congregation on 7th and 14th May, 1837 and seems to have made a favourable impression upon many. The Presbytery met on Tuesday 16th May to purge the Roll and the call to Norval was read which had been signed by Sir James Carnegie, the factor of Lord Panmure, 12 heritors, 8 of the 11 elders and 184 heads of families; even in today's terms this would be a strong call. Yet 81 dissented but as this was only 1/7th of the total Heads of Families, the veto failed. Thomas Maitland, advocate for the dissenters, begged leave of Presbytery to appeal to the higher court and the whole matter was thus referred to the forthcoming General Assembly.

On the same day as Presbytery met a printed handbill appeared on the streets of Brechin addressed to the Male Heads of Families. It alleged that in the sermon Norval preached on 7th May, he had plagiarised directly from Henry Melvill's[37] book of sermons, published in 1836. In early June the Presbytery met at Lochlee for an ordination and received a petition alleging that Norval was a fraud and thus "not morally qualified to be inducted"[38] to Brechin. Norval admitted that Melvill's works were known to him and he had heard him preach but categorically denied the charge of plagiarism. An enquiry began to hear witnesses which dragged on through the summer and early autumn. In the meantime, in July 1837, the old ecclesiastical parish of the medieval Cathedral was finally divided into East and West, with the Cathedral taking the west and

---

[36] I am indebted to Rev. John Orr, Minister of Kirriemuir: St.Andrew's linked with Oathlaw Tannadice, as well as staff of the Gateway to the Glens Museum in Kirriemuir for researching William Norval's life.

[37] Henry Melvill, BD, was an English divine of the University of Cambridge said to be one of the most gifted preachers of the age. He later became one of Queen Victoria's chaplains and canon of St. Paul's Cathedral in London.

[38] S of F, 20

the City Road Chapel of Ease the east. By October Presbytery decided that while the accusation was not proven it was still to be referred to the Synod which met in Brechin on 24th October. This was a long meeting! The Synod met in the Cathedral on Tuesday 24th October until 11.45pm, resumed at 9am the next morning and finally closed at 10pm on Wednesday 25th. Norval's defence agent alleged that the Guthrie family, led by the Provost, had been behind every malicious accusation. Yet after all this long debate the Synod passed the matter on to the General Assembly for decision! Norval was not without local support; 349 males and 541 females signed petitions in his favour, this being well over half the congregation.

In late November of 1837 the evening service at the Cathedral was temporarily discontinued due to the long vacancy; clearly the whole controversy was having an impact upon the spiritual health of the congregation. Finally, the General Assembly gathered at the Tron Kirk in Edinburgh on Thursday 17th May, 1838. When the Assembly met on the Monday, William Norval had by now had enough and resigned the presentation. But Norval was still of course minister of South Church, Kirriemuir, and the charges of plagiarism still stood, so, after some debate on the floor of the Assembly, the matter was referred back, this time to the Presbytery of Forfar to consider further disciplinary proceedings.

Three months on, Norval demitted from Kirriemuir and joined the Church of England. So we find him at Durham University from autumn 1838 – June 1840 taking his LTh. He was briefly a curate at Trimdom, Durham (1840-43) then St.Andrew's, Glasgow (1843/44) before going on to St.James' Bermondsey where he served from 1846-51. In 1851 he gained his own charge at Ickleford in Herfordshire (1851-55) but, rather curiously, resumed as a curate at St.Andrew's, Holborn in London in 1865-70. However, Norval is probably best remembered in the Church of England as the first chaplain to the Fulham workhouse (1863-71). He died on 11th September, 1871 at Fulham. Peter Gordon is, in my view, correct in his analysis of the affair when he describes Norval as more victim than villain.[39]

---

[39] S of F, 25

Meantime, we must retrace our steps towards Brechin! George Whitson, minister of the second charge, had retired on 29th December, 1834 and in so doing gifted two hundred barrels of coal to the poor during an inclement winter (he died in November, 1835). Whitson was succeeded by **Alexander Leith Ross Foote (1835-43)** who had been originally appointed in February, 1834 as Whitson's assistant and successor. Foote was a son of the Manse, born 6th February, 1805 to Robert Foote, minister at Fettercairn.

Educated at Marishal College, Aberdeen where he gained an M.A. in 1821. He was licensed by the Presbytery of Aberdeen in 1827 and went on to gain experience as a probationer assistant in Montrose. Ordained as assistant to Whitson on 18th September, 1834, Foote was to singlehandedly minister to the congregation during the Vacancy crisis of 1837. However, like many young ministers, his ministry began somewhat inauspiciously as two petitions were received in 1835, signed by sixty members in all "complaining of the late alterations that have been introduced into the Church music in the congregation and praying the Session to interfere."[40] This was duly countered by another petition, this time signed by ninety nine members "approving of the alterations introduced by the Rev Mr Foote and requesting the Session to carry forward the improvement of this part of public worship."[41] Leaving aside the fact that worship is still today a matter reserved solely to the minister, under the jurisdiction of the Presbytery rather than Kirk Session, this again reveals the democratic tendencies latent in not just

---

[40] Kirk Session minute, 1835
[41] Ibid.

Brechin, but the wider Church. Unfortunately, we are not told the nature of the musical innovations that Foote brought about. The Session actually supported Foote yet urged him that any attempts at improvements should "meet the approbation of all".[42]

By early summer of 1838 the Cathedral still lacked a minister for the first charge. Shiress, solicitor in Edinburgh wrote to the local M.P. advising him that Act V of George I would mean that since Norval had been presented and resigned (and six months had subsequently elapsed) it would fall to Presbytery under the *ius devolutum*[43] to appoint a minister. Letters passed to and fro to the Home Office. There was a "dread among the people if the power be in the Presbytery that Mr Burns be given the appointment."[44] Professor David Welsh, Professor of Ecclesiastical History at Edinburgh, came to the rescue by putting forward the case for Rev. James McCosh, currently minister of the Abbey Church in Arbroath. This was supported by the Solicitor General, Andrew Rutherfurd, who felt that not only would those who had been opposed to Norval support McCosh, but it was better to have in post a proved minister rather than a licentiate, given the lengthy vacancy and the ensuing controversy. Thus on 7th June, 1838 the new young Queen Victoria, just days away from her coronation, signed the Presentation in favour of *John* McCosh. This misnaming of McCosh in the Royal warrant gave rise to further delay, so Presbytery did not deal with the matter until 4th July. By this time legal advice given to Presbytery suggested that the *ius devolutum* had fallen to them to appoint the new minister.

The meeting of Presbytery on 4th July, 1838 was perhaps the most extraordinary in the long tale of this extended vacancy. After considerable debate, Presbytery resolved not to accept the Crown Presentation and invoked the *ius devolutum* whereupon Dr Paterson moved the Presbytery should present McCosh while Alexander Symmers of Lethnot and Navar moved that Robert Inglis, minister at Lochlee[45] be appointed. Upon a vote being taken nine voted for McCosh and ten for Inglis; the trouble was Inglis had voted for himself! An appeal was entered to Synod. The reaction of the town was perhaps best summed up by Sir David Leighton who wrote: "the Parish may be left without a minister for years. I do not mean to enter any part in the future proceedings, being heartily sick of the question."[46] Foote was apparently in great distress and those who had opposed Norval indignant. Rutherfurd, Solicitor General, was of the view that the Presbytery had exceeded their authority.

---

[42] Ibid.

[43] Literally from the Latin "a right which has devolved"

[44] S of F, 22

[45] Later minister at the Free Church in Edzell (1843-76)

[46] S of F, 23

On Tuesday 23rd October, 1838, the Synod of Angus and Mearns began meeting and continued until 7.30pm on 24th October. After lengthy speeches for both candidates the Synod resolved that "the Rev. James McCosh is the true Presbtyterial presentee, and remit to the Presbytery to settle the Rev. James McCosh with all speed."[47] The decision was met with great cheering by the crowd and it is to Robert Inglis' credit that he withdrew from the case and did not appeal to the General Assembly.

James McCosh duly preached before the congregation on 25th November, 1838 as well as the following Sunday. The call was signed by 5 Heritors, 7 Elders and 69 Male Heads of Families; less than half the number who had signed William Norval's call some nineteen months earlier. So it was that after two years and twenty two days since the death of James Burns, James McCosh was finally inducted to Brechin's first charge on Thursday 24th January, 1839. His ministry was to be a comparatively brief one, for it was soon overtaken by national events.

Born on 1st April, 1811, **James McCosh (1839-43)** was the only son of Andrew McCosh and Jean Carson, farming stock of Straiton in Ayrshire; both families having strong covenanter roots. Educated at both Glasgow and Edinburgh universities, McCosh gained an M.A. in March 1833. Licensed by the Presbytery of Ayr in March 1834, he was ordained and inducted to Arbroath Abbey Church in December 1835 where he was renowned for his stress on visiting and teaching. After leaving the Auld Kirk (as we shall presently see) McCosh went on to have a highly accomplished academic career, appointed as Professor of Logic and Metaphysics at Queen's

[47] Ibid, 24

University, Belfast in 1851 and President of Princeton College, New Jersey in the United States from 1868-88, though continuing as Professor of Philosophy at Princeton. McCosh's publications are far too numerous to mention but include *Method of Divine Government, Physical and Moral* (Edinburgh, 1850, though frequently re-published in New York) and the rather more pointed *Does the Established Church acknowledge Christ as its Head?* (Brechin,1846). McCosh and Charles Hodge became highly involved in the debate about Darwinism, with McCosh (unlike Hodge) seeking to reconcile Darwinism with Christianity in *Christianity and Positivism* (New York, 1871). He died at Princeton in November, 1891 and, though his connection with Brechin was short, did much to restore stability and harmony following the acrimonious Vacancy controversy of 1837-8. It is said that during his time here "he worked laboriously in preaching and teaching not only in the large Cathedral Church, but in barns and kitchens."[48] In many ways, McCosh laid the foundations of a good Bible knowledge amongst the local population.

Amongst the events of McCosh and Foote's joint ministries at the Cathedral was a clear sign of the growth of the industrial age as protest was made "against the conveyance of mail on the Sabbath day, especially by railway coaches."[49] Education for "young paupers" proved one of the hallmarks of this period, as did a drive against the sin of intemperance! Schools had been set up at both little Brechin and Drums and in August, 1842, McCosh himself gifted £50 to augment the schoolmaster's salary. In December, 1840 the parish was divided into districts and the Session met on the last Monday of every month to consider matters of discipline and other ecclesial matters and dealt with administration of relief to the poor on other days. In April, 1842, Alexander Foote suffered personal tragedy when his wife Margaret Fordyce died[50]; the Session minute records "their sincere and deep felt sympathy under the protracted and afflictive dispensation with which it hath pleased God to visit his domestic circle."[51]

In order to chart the next phase in the Cathedral's life we must briefly turn away from the local story to the national stage. We have already seen many of the issues regarding patronage that would lead to the Disruption of 1843 encapsulated within the Norval case. The crux of the whole matter was the question: who governs the Church; State or Church? The *Veto Act* of 1834 was intended to allow congregations to veto the choice of an unpopular minister imposed upon them by the patrons. In actuality, the

---

[48] Brechin Almanac, 1882
[49] Kirk Session minutes, 30th March, 1840
[50] Foote was to remarry twice; Jessie Murray in September, 1847 and Alison Kerr in November, 1859. He had children to both these wives, but not to Margaret Fordyce.
[51] Kirk Session minutes, 10th April, 1842

terms of the *Veto Act* were quite limited; grounds of immorality or poor learning had to be given by Heads of Families if the patron's choice was rejected. In practice, there were abuses of the Act on both sides. In 1838, Robert Young, who had been presented to the Parish of Auchterader but was rejected appealed to the Court of Session. By an 8-5 majority the Court ruled that the Church had exceeded its authority in rejecting the choice of the patron and that, in fact, the Church was a creation of the State by Act of Parliament. The Evangelical party within the Kirk was incensed; this ruling contradicted the very Confession of Faith of the Church which had Christ as the Church's Head. Two further cases added insult; one was the Stewarton case, where the Court of Session ruled that ministers appointed to *quoad sacra* Chapels of Ease[52] could not have membership of Presbyteries. This effectively was saying that there were two classes of minister: ones presented by patrons who had full rights and ones appointed to Church extensions had only limited rights. The second was the Strathbogie case where seven ministers were suspended for disobeying the Assembly and adhering to proceed with an induction sanctioned by the Courts. The outcome of these (and other) cases was the *Claim, Declaration and Protest anent the Encroachments of the Court of Session* otherwise known as "The Claim of Right" adopted by the Assembly of 1842. In stark terms it outlines that the Church's obedience lies with Christ, not the State. Yes, the State may control the endowments, but it makes it impossible to self-govern the Church if the State is constantly interfering in the appointment of ministers. Thus does the Church:

> ...protest against sentences of the Civil Court in contravention of the Church's liberties, which rather than abandon they will relinquish the privileges of establishment; and call on Christian people everywhere to note that it is for loyalty to Christ's Kingdom and Crown that the Church of Scotland is obliged to suffer hardship.[53]

The problem was that the State viewed the growing crisis very differently, Victoria's Whig Prime Minister Lord Melbourne in particular seeing these Scottish churchmen as lawless rebels! It was not just Whigs; Sir James Graham, Tory Home Secretary of Sir Robert Peel's second premiership, also flatly rejected the Claim of Right. The final act came in Parliament in March 1843 when (even though the Scottish MPs voted 25-12 in favour) the House rejected a plea to consider the grievances of the Scottish Church in committee. A predominantly English House, grounded in the establishment practices of the Church of England, failed to grasp the theological basis of the Kirk's Evangelical party.

---

[52] So called because these were new church extensions built near new housing where, generally the working class could more easily attend worship. It was a sign of the growth of urbanization and the diminishing of a rural, agricultural economy.

[53] Burleigh, 349

The General Assembly of 1843 duly gathered in Edinburgh in the May. Dr David Welsh (whom we have already noted entered into the Brechin controversy) preached the opening sermon at St. Giles High Kirk as the outgoing Moderator then on 18th May took the chair at St. Andrew's Church in George St. and, rather than constitute, announced that he could not regard it as a free Assembly. Reading his protest, he handed it to the Clerk and duly departed for Tanfield Hall at Canonmills accompanied by 121 ministers and 73 elders. There, Thomas Chalmers was duly installed as the first Moderator of the Free Church of Scotland. The Disruption had begun.

Eventually, around 450 ministers (just over one third) would leave the Established Kirk. As Burleigh puts it "The willingness of so many to make financial and social sacrifice for the sake of principle created a deep impression and called forth widespread admiration. It also gave them a sense of moral superiority over the 752 ministers who stayed in…"[54]

Sacrifice indeed these men did, losing not only their livings, pulpits and manses but also their status within their communities. Those who remained did so in many cases in order to preserve the peace and unity of the Church but were seen by the "outers" as "worldly minded hirelings"[55] who were only interested in financial security. Congregations were to be divided, losing many of their more active members to the Free Church. Yet, the

---

[54] Burleigh, 352
[55] Ibid.

Free Church too lost out, for it was to become far less tolerant than the Auld Kirk of differing doctrinal viewpoints. Principal Cunningham in his *Church History of Scotland* rather unkindly records that "never perhaps in the history of any Church has so great a voluntary sacrifice been made for so slender a principle – but yet not too slender for the Scottish ecclesiastical conscience to apprehend and exalt into a question of life and death."[56] The body was rent and there would be no going back.

So what happened in Brechin? Both ministers, Foote and McCosh, were to "go out" taking around 825 of 1400 members with them (this was about 2/3rds of the congregation, a considerably higher fraction than in many other places). Only 400 folk remained as the "rump" of the Auld Kirk. The *Montrose Review* of 2nd June, 1843 recorded:

> Sabbath last will long be remembered in Brechin, the doors of the old church having been locked. A portion of the congregation, adhering to their outgoing ministers, remained at home, and improved the solemn occasion in private, others of them repaired to the Secession churches, while the non-adhering portion helped to fill Bishop Moir's chapel, thus showing in plain characters the direction in which the two antagonist principles are working.[57]

It is remarkable how quickly the Free Church in Brechin was to be founded. By late November 1843, Foote, formerly of the second charge, had set up the West Free Church in the Lower Wynd, now Church St. a mere stone's throw from the Cathedral! Foote was to remain minister of the West Free Church until his death on 6th September, 1878. Foote it appears was to grow into a preacher of remarkable oratory, often breaking forth into his native Doric in a sermon, apparently to the astonishment of his congregation! His style of preaching was said to sometimes sound peculiar to modern ears and occasionally he would wander round his subject for some time before, suddenly, unexpectedly, reaching his point! His obituary records that as well as a striking preacher and gifted classical scholar (he was awarded an honorary Doctorate of Divinity by Edinburgh University in April 1870), Foote was "an acceptable visitor in the houses of poverty and sickness."[58] He was said to have a good knowledge of music and a fine voice and ear. On his death one worthy local matron described him as "abody's body" – a rare accolade.

While McCosh was involved for a short time in the West Free Church after the Disruption, his task was to found the East Free Church, ministering there for a few years (1843-51) before going on to excel in the field of academia. The die had been cast

---

[56] As quoted in Burleigh, 352
[57] Black, 217
[58] Brechin Almanac, 1878

however and Church life in Scotland and in Brechin would never quite be the same again. For the Cathedral, it was to be the end of an era.

ADDITIONAL INFORMATION – Section 5

THE ROLE OF THE OLD PRECENTORS

Come raise your voices loud and clear, and keep in proper time

Then you may cast away your fear, and sing to any rhyme

The Church of Scotland has never owned an "official" liturgy and from Reformation times the Psalms of David have been the basis of praise for Presbyterians. The first Scottish Psalter appeared in 1564 and a harmonised edition for congregational use followed later.

Originally, there was simply an "uptaker of the Psalms" but by the mid-1600s the term "Precentor" (literally from Latin: one who sings before) came into vogue. Due to the expense of printing and the illiteracy of congregations, copies of the Psalter were limited. Thus the bulk of the population relied on the Precentor to teach them, by repetition, both words and tunes.

In the pre-1807 Cathedral we would have found the Precentor reading passages from the Psalms before the service and leading the congregation in singing a Psalm as the minister entered. Eventually this reduced to just "reading of the line" prior to the service. In his day though the "full stentorian tones of the Precentor fell on the congregation like a call to arms."[59] He inspired the timid and his swaying of the book marked the accent or emphasis. The Precentor stood in the second platform of the three-tiered pulpit, above the Reader but below the Minister.

When the Psalms began to be set in verses this was the real beginning of concerted singing in the Kirk and choirs, choir training and then the organ came in turn. Ironically, it was the success of the Precentor in teaching music to the population that eventually resulted in his demise.

Perhaps the most famous Precentor of the Cathedral was one **James Adam** (appointed c.1800) who was a man of small stature and thin appearance but with a redoubtable voice and musical gift. He travelled on foot all the way from Dundee to present himself for interview for the vacancy. By profession Adam was a handloom weaver and could not read music. His range of tunes was somewhat limited but his voice, it is said by one who heard him, was "as sweet as a lintie". He married Bell Mitchell (Rev. James Burn's cook) and had seven children, though only son William remained in Brechin. Rumours

---

[59] *Brechin Almanac*

abounded about Adam's background as he was very well spoken, had a keen intellect and he wore clothes that had a faded grandeur. As William Sievwright puts it in *Brechin Faces of the Olden Time* (1903) "there was something about (Adam) that awakened one's interest." He had an air of refinement and quiet dignity. Was he the illegitimate child of some noble family? Or had he somehow gained an education superior to most at that time? Even today the mystery of James Adam, Precentor, continues…He died around 1840.

THE HAND LOOM WEAVERS OF BRECHIN

Brechin has long been associated with the Weaving trade. The trade may have originally come from Flemish shores to Dundee or Montrose as early as the C14th. A country *gude wifie* in the C15th would either buy a mat of flax or grow and dress her own. The servant girls on the farm had to do a fair share of spinning their *stent* of yarn each day. The *gude wifie* would then sell her yarns at market at the Cross with butter and eggs each week.

A typical handloom weaver "factory" of the C17th and C18th.

Gradually the hand-loom weavers came together settling in Bridge Street and Union Street. It was very much a family affair; the weaver's wife filling her husband's pirns while the bairns, after school, had to wind their stent before supper. Along these roads the click of the shuttle and thud of the lay could be heard from early morning to late at night, when they continued spinning by candlelight or cruisy lamp. Sons and daughters were all taught the craft and many a courtship started over a loom! This was the main source of family income during the cold, dark winter days before the farms re-hired in the spring. The last weaving shop of Brechin was owned by Baillie Dakers (famous for his special fabrics) and was just a stone's throw from my own Manse in Chanonry Wynd.

In 1796 the spinning of lint by machinery began in Brechin at a small mill on the Den burn. The works were set up by Thomas Jamieson, a mill-wright and there was great secrecy as to the nature of the machinery in the mill. At its height, Brechin as a mill town had 1400 power looms and 2000 folk employed. As well as two cotton factories and the East mill flax spinning works, there were also two tobacco factories.

CHAPTER EIGHT
The great Work & the Great War

The glory of this present house will be greater than the former house
- *Haggai 2:9*

Too many of the homes in the town had been stricken during those four years of war for any signs of rejoicing at the intimation that hostilities were at length at an end.

- *Brechin and the Great War, vol. 1918*

Given the locked doors of the Cathedral in early June, 1843 (a situation probably last encountered at the Reformation) it is remarkable how quickly the Auld Kirk got back on its feet again! Although Foote and McCosh had taken 800 folk with them, 400 remained requiring a pastor. The State acted fairly quickly with Queen Victoria making presentation of **Alexander Gardner, M.A. (1843 – 93)** to the second charge on 12th July.

A YOUNG REV ALEXANDER GARDNER (1843-93)

Gardner, son of Euphemia Dalziel and Matthew Gardner, a farmer from Cambusnethan, was born in 1810 and already had an accomplished career behind him. Educated at Glasgow University where he gained his M.A. in 1834, he was licensed by the Presbytery of Glasgow the following year and went on to assistantships at Annan, Lanark, Roberton and finally at Brechin. He was already known therefore to the folk at the Cathedral from his assistantship to Rev. Foote and seemed a popular choice. In August 1842 he had been ordained to Lethnot and Navar and was only getting into his stride then when called to Brechin. However, the established Kirk were extremely short of clergy following the Disruption, particularly men of calibre such as Gardner, that it is little wonder he was soon translated to Brechin on 31st August, 1843. Gardner was to prove (as we shall see) something of a mixed blessing for Brechin, though he was to become the longest serving of the Cathedral ministers and was the first to have the vision of restoring the Cathedral to its medieval fabric, a work that he sadly did not live to see.

When a much depleted Session met on 11th September, there were only three elders plus George Alexander, Session Clerk[1] and schoolmaster. It is probably difficult for us in a much more secular age to appreciate how divisive the Disruption had been. Entire families were split down the middle, even to the extent of a wife going to the Auld Kirk (the Cathedral) while husband attended a "secessionist" congregation[2]. The first task of the Session in these difficult days was to admit new elders and this happened in the November of 1843. The parish was also re-divided into districts.

---

[1] Rev. George Alexander, MA, was (to date) the longest serving Session Clerk (1809 – 76). As well as being Master at the Parish School, he was also Rector of the Grammar School. He died on 17th May, 1877.

[2] However, it must be noted that working class men were more likely to attend the Auld Kirk (i.e. the Cathedral) as they were not required to make such a large personal contribution for its upkeep as those in the Secessionist churches.

By this time too **Nathaniel Morren (1843-47)** had been inducted to the first charge on 28th September, 1843. Morren was an Aberdeen man, born in February 1798 and educated at Aberdeen Grammar then Marischal College, where he gained his M.A. in 1814. Morren was a teacher to profession, acting as a tutor to a family at Fort George then teaching at a school in Caen in France. He studied theology both at Aberdeen and Edinburgh universities and was licensed by the Presbytery of Aberdeen on 16th October, 1822. After this in June 1823 he was ordained to Blackhall Church in Greenock, now part of Old West Kirk. At the Disruption he defended the established Kirk's position writing a book called *The National Church, a national blessing* in 1844. He was a prolific author, most especially his two volume work *Annals of the General Assembly*

1739 – 66, which is still a major reference book today. Sadly, Morren's time in Brechin was brief; he died of "apoplexy" (probably a stroke) on 28th March, 1847 aged forty nine, leaving his wife, Mary Shand, but no children.

In December 1843 another new appointment was that of John Scott as Precentor, who also undertook to teach the young folk church music. The autumn of 1844 reveals two matters that arose largely because of the Disruption. Firstly, there was a serious conflict between the Auld Kirk (this was the Cathedral's name at this time) and the dissenting congregations over the date of the autumn celebration of Communion. The "secessionist" churches sought some sort of standardisation of date, but the Auld Kirk Session dismissed this out of hand, restating the practice of holding the sacrament on the Sabbath preceding the Harvest full moon, since it was expected by then that all the harvesting had been completed[3]. Secondly, in October, a special collection was held, notably, not for the Poor Fund as often in the past or some particular charitable case, but rather "for the purpose of defraying the cost of heating the Church during winter"[4] It was clear that the loss of attenders occasioned by the Disruption had also hit hard the financial position of the Auld Kirk. Indeed by early 1845 the way the poor were cared for in Scotland itself changed. The Poor Law (Scotland) Act of 1845 created a Board of Supervision. The provision for the poor now fell to a local superintendent and the Kirk Session (which hitherto had been responsible for the poor) paid a yearly tax of £24. The Session at the Auld Kirk was resistant to the loss of an ancient responsibility, but Victoria's socially progressive governments were determined to standardise practise across the lands of the kingdom. This in turn changed Church practice, as the evening service collection at the door (which before had gone to the Poor Fund) was discontinued in October 1845. By early 1846, six members of the Kirk Session had been invited to serve on the Parochial Board for the relief of the poor, which perhaps sweetened the loss of status the Kirk felt in this matter. Lord Panmure assisted greatly too by donating £20 annually for coals for the poor over the winter months.

The issue of the date of the autumn Communion service had not gone away! In the summer of 1846 it was fixed as the "second Sabbath of November"[5] but complaints were received and by spring, 1848 it reverted to "the Sabbath nearest the full moon after the Harvest has been completed."[6] So bitter grew the argument that it reached the columns of the *Montrose Review*. This serves as a good example of how internal, navel-gazing the focus of the Auld established Kirk became following the Disruption; no

---

[3] Kirk Session minutes, 16th September, 1844
[4] Ibid., 28th Oct, 1844
[5] Ibid., 15th June, 1846
[6] Ibid. 1st May, 1848

longer did it look outwards towards the community and the world, the blow to its prestige was such it felt safer looking inwards at its own affairs. It would remedy, but the healing took time.

With the death of Nathaniel Morren, the first charge was once again vacant. So in late September, 1847, **Rev. Andrew Halkett (1847-1872)** of St. John's Church, New Brunswick, Canada was inducted. Halkett and Gardner were to form an uneasy, at times

turbulent partnership, for many a long year – as we shall observe. Although coming to Brechin from Canada, Andrew Halkett, son of Samuel Halkett (a commission agent) and Euphemia Wallace, was born in Edinburgh on 2nd November, 1810. Educated at Edinburgh High School and the University of Edinburgh, he was licensed by Edinburgh Presbytery in 1836 and went on to have an assistantship at St. George's Church in the city. Ordained to St. John's Church, New Brunswick in September, 1843, Halkett managed to avoid much of the initial rancour following the Disruption. There he founded the new Presbyterian church of St. John's and in 1844 married Frances Ann Taylor. He had ten children in all, though not all lived to maturity. From August 1852 until April 1857, Halkett was to serve as Clerk to the Presbytery of Brechin. He died at St.Andrew's in 1874.

National events again loomed large in 1850 when in September Pope Pius IX issued the Bull *Universalis Ecclesiae* in which the Roman Catholic hierarchy in England and Wales was re-established. The residents of Brechin considered this "popish aggression" and a petition signed by 3027 inhabitants was sent to Queen Victoria, for fear something similar might occur in Scotland. At this time too, the Kirk began to recover financially and special collections were taken up for various national schemes including Foreign mission (£6.10s), Colonial mission (£3.13s.6d) and even Jewish mission (£4.2s.2d).

In November, 1853, we have the first rumblings of a disagreement between Halkett and Gardner over the ordination of new elders. Halkett sent two letters to the Session protesting against the way, in his absence, certain individuals had been nominated. The Session, perhaps duly alarmed, decided not to proceed to ordination. However, five years later, one John Walker, an elder, is caught *in flagrante delicto* with a lady of the night at the North Port Distillery[7]. Walker maintains his innocence but the matter ends up being investigated by the Session. Gardner seeks to pursue a more aggressive questioning of Walker, while Halkett urges caution on the grounds he (Walker) might incriminate himself. The Session votes to support Gardner's approach and Halkett (recently retired as Presbytery Clerk) records his dissent. Walker was to resign his eldership a week later but one is left wondering if something more lies behind this story, given that Walker was of working class stock and Alexander Gardner seemed to want a Session made up solely of middle class businessmen.

1856 sees the first mention of a choir; the new Precentor, Charles Brown was instructed to "hold at least one meeting weekly for the purpose of practicing Church music with all those of the congregation who choose to attend."[8] In 1859 the Hearse (the old brass chandelier gifted by Bishop Lamb in 1615) was converted to gas light and hung in the centre of the Church, directly in front of the Pulpit.

By the 1860s changes were afoot. Repairs were urgently required to the Cathedral and when the Heritors took no action, despite Session's pleas, the matter was referred to Presbytery in February, 1863. Clearly this broke the log jam for some two months later work began. Extraordinarily perhaps, during the period the congregation were unable to use the sanctuary for worship both the East Free Church and the West Free Church, the breakaway churches from the Disruption, offered to accommodate the Cathedral congregation for their own services. Twenty years had passed and some healing had taken place. A letter of thanks was sent to Rev. Alexander Foote, minister at the West Free Church (and formerly of the Cathedral) thanking his congregation for their help. The letter concludes "we may reasonably hope for an abundant increase of brotherly kindness and charity, both here and elsewhere, all redounding to the honour and glory of Him who is all our desire and our salvation, our adorable Redeemer, the Lord Jesus Christ."[9] Two years later in 1865 another dispute arose between Halkett and Gardner, this time over a Presbytery suggestion that the old collegiate charge be abandoned and two new parishes "Brechin East" and "Brechin West Kirk" created. Andrew Halkett was to be given the new East Church, while Alexander Gardner would continue at the

---

[7] Kirk Session minutes, 5th July, 1858
[8] Ibid. 3rd November, 1856
[9] Ibid., 8th June, 1863

Cathedral which would be renamed Brechin West Kirk. Gardner insisted that his parish was by far the larger and so he would require an assistant minister or, at the very least, a missionary helper. Needless to say, Halkett was not best pleased by this idea! The debate rumbled on until in February, 1867, Presbytery abandoned the idea of a disjunction in the parishes. The Kirk Session urged Presbytery to reconsider in the "spiritual interests of the Parish"[10] but Andrew Halkett once more recorded his dissent suggesting Gardner was the main drive behind the idea.

Again, later that same year, division between the two ministers re-surfaced, this time over William Fettis, Elder, being elected to represent the congregation at Presbytery. Halkett complained that this matter had been dealt with during a month when he was scheduled to moderate the Session and that Gardner had effectively snuck the matter through.[11] Session stuck to their original choice, though Halkett and Prain, an elder, dissented. By the March of 1868, regulations were introduced governing the calling of Session meetings so that such a matter might never re-occur!

Also that year Rev. J.Y. Scott, minister at the East Church, requested elders from the Auld Kirk (or "Parish" church) so that they might set up their own Kirk Session[12]. The Kirk Session at the Cathedral meanwhile sought to increase the circulation of the *Missionary Record*[13], perhaps a sign that the focus was again moving away from internal matters to external causes. Another good example of this move was in August 1870 when old table cloths were requested, to be sent to the sick and wounded in the Franco-Prussian war, presumably as bed linen and bandages. It was also recorded that "they (the Session) hereby record their deep and heartfelt sympathy with the many suffering victims of the said unhappy war."[14]

As we enter the 1870s, two matters were to pre-occupy the Auld Kirk. The first was in regard to worship; attempts to move the time of the Sunday service and to discontinue the service on the Saturday afternoon preceding Communion[15] both failed. Although it is not immediately clear from the records, it does seem that there were two parties at work: the revisionists and the traditionalists. The excuse used to stop any

---

[10] Ibid., 25th February, 1867

[11] The two ministers of the collegiate church alternated as Moderator of Session on a monthly basis.

[12] James Young Scott was minister of the East Church from 1867-71. The East Church had begun as a Chapel of Ease and was finally disjoined from the Auld Kirk in July 1874.

[13] Probably referring to the publication of the United Presbyterian Church, began in 1846, though each denomination had its own missionary newsletter from the foreign missions.

[14] Kirk Session minutes, 29th August, 1870

[15] Communion season included a service on the Saturday afternoon before Communion and on the Monday evening following.

alterations in worship was the old one "its aye been done like this"; "regard to existing arrangements which have been of long continuance."[16] Given that several changes occur after Halkett's death in 1874, it would seem that he led the traditionalist party while the more visionary Gardner led the revisionist.

The second matter was raised tension between the Church and civil authorities. For one, the Town Council began interfering in the ringing of the Church bell and there was also dispute over who was to pay for maintaining the Kirk yard. Eventually, it boiled down to a personality, one Charles Low, who had been dismissed as Church officer and was still under discipline and debarred from Church privileges, but whom the Town Council proceeded to employ as a gravedigger! This act was not likely to lead to rapprochement between the two sides. Added to this mix, in 1872, the Education Act came into being which handed responsibility for parish schools from the Church to the State. This was seen by many Church folk as yet another erosion of Church rights, though the Cathedral continued to maintain the "Sessional School" at Little Brechin until it closed in 1880 (when it was temporarily re-used for Mission services.)

Forty years on from the Disruption, the Patronage Act of August 1874 finally got rid of the thorny issue. Repealing the 1711 Act (which had been always considered contrary to the Act of Union of 1707 by the Kirk), the new Act declared:

> The right of electing and appointing ministers to vacant churches and parishes in Scotland is hereby declared to be vested in the congregations of such vacant churches and parishes respectively, subject to such regulations in regard to the mode of naming and proposing such ministers by means of a committee chosen by the congregation, and of conducting the election and of making the appointment by the congregation as may from time to time be framed by the General Assembly of the Church of Scotland.

For the Cathedral, it came at an opportune moment, for Andrew Halkett died at St.Andrew's on 1st September, 1874. Although the Act did not come into force until 1st January, 1875, a letter was received by the Session that November from the Home Secretary of Disraeli's Conservative administration, R.A. Cross, stating that he would not pursue patronage in the vacancy but leave it to the congregation to elect a new minister for the first charge. This brought its own set of problems, as objections began to be received as to who was (or was not) listed on the Communicant (and thus Electoral) Roll of the congregation. For the first time the congregation were to have full authority in the choice of minister and they wanted to get it right, so Brechin being Brechin, various parties appealed the Session's revision of the Roll and this went through both Presbytery

---

[16] Kirk Session minutes, 28th June, 1869

and Synod before reaching the General Assembly! Suddenly the Kirk at large realised they needed more rigorous ways of determining membership of the Church; gone was the Medieval practice where living in the Parish and being baptised was enough.

On 1st July 1874, the great evangelical pair, Ira D. Sankey (gospel singer and composer) and Dwight L. Moody (evangelist and preacher) visited Brechin. This was part of a Scottish tour sponsored by the great Free Church minister, Andrew A. Bonar (younger brother of Horatius, the hymn writer). Moody and Sankey came on a Wednesday forenoon to the West Free Church and to the Cathedral in the afternoon, yet despite it being a working day "many hundreds were unable to gain admittance".[17] It must have been quite an occasion!

James Mackay (1875-91) from Braes of Tough in Aberdeenshire was duly elected as minister of the first charge and inducted on 26th August, 1875. James was born to William Mackay and Elizabeth Herd on 20th January, 1835. Educated at the University of Aberdeen, Mackay first went into the teaching profession before completing his theological education. He served as assistant minister at the West Parish in Aberdeen. He was ordained and inducted to St.Clement's Church, Dundee on 22nd December, 1864 from where he was translated

[17] Brechin Almanac, 1874

to Brechin. During his seventeen years in Brechin he was instrumental in seeking to provide a Parish Hall, completed in 1888. He served on the School Board and was a Bursary examiner. He married Isabella Nicoll, daughter of a mill spinner from Dundee, and had ten children in all, of which three sons died in infancy. Son Robert went on to become minister at Boarhills and son David to be an attorney in Oregon, USA. James himself was to retire by reason of ill health in November, 1891 moving to Edinburgh then St. Andrew's. He died at St.Andrew's on 17th May 1899 after a prolonged period of illness. His wife predeceased him but was survived by two sons and four daughters.

To the Glory of God and in Loving Memory of the Rev. James Mackay M.A. Minister of the 1st Charge 1875 ~ 1891 and Isabella Nicoll his wife "Until the day break and the shadows flee away"

With Mackay's arrival, Alexander Gardner had finally found what he thought was a likeminded fellow. At first it certainly seemed so. They were agreed over the need to introduce an organ to the Cathedral. At first, following the Reformation, choirs and "kists o'whistles"[18] had been anathema to Presbyterians; unaccompanied Psalm singing led by a Precentor[19] was the norm for several generations.

[18] A derogatory name for the organ.

[19] The Precentor was second only to the Minister in the conduct of worship and stood in the second tier of the three tiered pulpit with the Minister above and the Reader below. The word comes from the Latin meaning "to sing before" and of course we have already noted that the office existed in Medieval times. Due to illiteracy, the Precentor's task in the Reformed Church was to teach the congregation the Psalms via repetition. The Reader usually read Scripture passages before the service, while the Precentor would lead the people in singing as the Minister entered to begin the service. Eventually this practice dwindled to the reading of a line and today the Call to Prayer via Scripture is all that is left of this once common feature of worship.

Indeed, the first reformed Psalter had been issued just after the Reformation in 1564. But, in 1870, the Kirk published the Scottish Hymnal[20] (followed in 1898 by a Hymnary for the Established, Free and United Presbyterian churches); this was the catalyst for a renewal in Church music. In July 1877, Mr.Fyffe, the Precentor (perhaps sensing the way the wind was blowing) took a leave of absence. Two weeks later on 23rd July, 1877, the congregation took a vote on introducing an organ for worship; 523 voted for and only 17 against. By the September, subscriptions were being sought for the organ and in the January of 1878, the Session decided the purchase price should not exceed £750. Some controversy arose in the December of 1877 when the Session purchased the East gallery from the Guildry. The Guildry saw the loft more as a piece of historical property than an active link with the Kirk.[21] Nevertheless, the loft produced an annual income of £11 so there was much negotiation before a final purchase price of £200 was agreed. This, it soon became clear, was to be the site of the new organ! A contract was agreed with Messrs. Conacher & Co. of Huddersfield for the erection of the organ at a cost of £800 including carriage. The organ was duly installed in the East gallery on 23rd April, 1878 and Mr. Pearson, assistant organist at Carlisle Cathedral, was appointed the very first organist. The organ was "opened" by Sir Herbert Oakley, Professor of Music at Edinburgh University, on 25th April, 1878, who gave a recital ably assisted by the Brechin Amateur Musical Society.

If the organ at first brought harmony between Gardner and Mackay it was sadly short-lived. By 1879, a dispute arose over who was to provide organ supply during Pearson's summer holiday. Gardner, it seemed, was averse to a woman, Miss Mitchell, playing the organ on the Sabbath. He recorded his dissent along with Mr. Murray, one of the elders. The offer from Miss Mitchell was swiftly withdrawn!

Alexander Gardner was, to be blunt, becoming somewhat irascible in his old age. He forced a number of votes in the Session on what should have been straightforward, non-contentious matters. In the summer of 1881 things were to come to a dramatic and painful climax; once more the Cathedral was convulsed by disunity. The Kirk Session sought that summer to add to the number of elders, including one Charles Anderson[22], a

---

[20] This continued to be used in the Cathedral until the Revised Hymnary was introduced in 1930. The Scottish Hymnal was very much seen as "Auld Kirk".

[21] Only three members of the Guildry exercised the right to sit in it by 1878.

[22] Anderson's solicitors firm was founded in 1849 in St. Mary's Street when he was a young solicitor of only twenty seven years. He was Treasurer of the Burgh School Board (1872-1902) and Chair of the Parochial Board from 1873-95 when the administration of the Poor Law devolved upon the Parish Council. Was his community involvement perhaps the source of the original conflict with Gardner? Anderson went on to become Dean of the Faculty of Procurators for Forfarshire and Sheriff-substitute in

local solicitor. Anderson was approached and wrote expressing acceptance. However, there appears to have been a long-standing personal animosity between the solicitor and Rev. Gardner, so he records his dissent to the choice.

Perhaps Anderson was a popular choice for elder, for a petition was received by the Session, signed by 402 members and adherents of the congregation demanding that following the Patronage Act of 1874, selection of office-bearers be made by the congregation not the Kirk Session itself.[23] It seems it was not enough for the Auld Kirk of Brechin that they had a choice of minister they wanted to choose the elders too! Presbytery it seems became aware of the dispute and wrote to the Session urging them "to seek the peace and wellbeing of the Church."[24] At this point Gardner withdrew his objection.

But the "phony peace" did not last long! When the Session met again in late August they once more sought to make Anderson an elder and Gardner once more lodges an objection. Perhaps Gardner thought that the Session would desist from another attempt to ordain Anderson? In September 1882, a letter from 169 members of the congregation is sent to the Session objecting to the choice of Anderson as elder – Gardner clearly had rallied his troops! It also became clear at this stage why there was such an antipathy between the two men: Gardner wrote "…said Charles Anderson has for several years displayed towards me a spirit of the bitterest hostility, acting in a manner so unbecoming a gentleman and so grossly offensive as to make his conduct a matter of public scandal."[25] Quite why there was such hostility between them we are not told, though we might surmise faults on both sides!

In the November there was a chink of light; Gardner declared he would allow Anderson's ordination as elder if the congregation were allowed to vote on the matter, either in a duly convened meeting (by standing) or by voting papers. He clearly did not believe the congregation would be supportive of the choice. Yet, in a letter objecting to Anderson, only 174 members out of a membership of 1500 signed the text and there were no grounds or objections to Anderson's moral character or doctrine. Gardner's opposition seems to have purely been for personal reasons. Late November of 1882 saw reconciliation take place between the two men as they agreed to put aside their

---

April, 1900. He died on 3rd March, 1905 aged eighty three. It is said that he was "held in high esteem by all who met him."

[23] One of the democratic deficiencies of the Presbyterian system, it seems to me, is that while ministers are elected by the congregation, the eldership is an oligarchy chosen by the Kirk Session itself.
[24] Kirk Session minutes, 28th June, 1882
[25] Ibid. 25th September, 1882

differences. The minute of the meeting of the Session on 27th November is so compelling as to be worth quoting in full:

> Mr Gardner laid on the table and read a statement whereof the tenor follows – Joint Minute for the Reverend Alexander Gardner and Mr. Charles Anderson to the Kirk Session of the Parish of Brechin. The Revd. Alexander Gardner stated that after anxious consideration and with the view of promoting the peace and harmony of the Session and the general welfare of the congregation he now craved permission to withdraw all statements or charges made by him at the Session and in the Presbytery which could in any way be calculated to injure Mr.Anderson's feelings or to reflect upon his character or qualifications for the office of Eldership, and stated his anxious desire that any feelings of animosity which may have arisen in the course of the present controversy should be allowed to pass away and be forgotten, and that relations between them should be such as become a Christian minister and member of his flock.

> The said Charles Anderson also stated that for similar reasons he withdrew all statements made by him in the Session or elsewhere which in any way reflected on Mr. Gardner's position as a Minister of the Gospel or on his private character, and stated that the relations between himself and Mr. Gardner should be such as Mr. Gardner referred to in his crave.

> The said Alexander Gardner and Charles Anderson jointly craved that in order no record of their misunderstanding should be preserved, the Kirk Session will be pleased to delete from their Minutes such portions thereof as relate to the nomination or appointment of Mr. Anderson to the eldership; and should it be considered necessary they agreed to concur in an application to Presbytery for leave to delete or alter their Minutes to the extent stated. ..

> The Session unanimously agreed to accept joint Minute, and to grant the craves therein contained; and further they agreed to apply to the Presbytery for authority to delete from their Minutes those portions referred to…

> Mr. Murray also craved to be allowed to withdraw all his Objections, Protests, Dissents and Complaints; to which request the Session agreed.[26]

Unfortunately we are not told whether Presbytery allowed this radical alteration to previous minutes, though there are whole sections of the Minute book prior to this date that have been scored through. Fortunately, particularly for the historian, they did not make a good job of the deletions and the original statements are still perfectly legible!

---

[26] Kirk Session minutes, 27th November, 1882

160

If the light of reconciliation shone upon Gardner and Anderson in November 1882, light of a different kind arrived in Brechin on 15th December, 1882 when J & J Smart, manufacturers installed the town's first electric lights!

1883 shows there was a false dawn of hope in the Anderson controversy; when the suggestion of Charles Anderson as elder is made once more in spring 1884, Gardner once more dissents. Three years on from the initial proposal, the Session was by now seriously divided. Indeed Mr. Murray, one of the Brechin elders, stated at Presbytery that the Session was utterly incapable of conducting its business (Murray was a Gardner supporter and one of Anderson's detractors).

Finally, on 13th April, 1884 Charles Anderson was ordained to eldership by Rev. James Mackay, Messrs. Murray and Edwards having failed to appear at Session to make objection. This was not the end of the matter though. When Session met on 28th April, Gardner read them a letter stating that they had proceeded illegally in Anderson's ordination. He lists three grounds to his objection:

i)   No notice had been given of Anderson's nomination. (Given that the issue had been an active one for four years, this seems unlikely!)

ii)   The election of Anderson as an elder would be detrimental to Gardner's usefulness as a minister.

iii)   That the election of an elder contrary to the wishes of the minister is contrary to Church Law.

As ever the matter was to go through appeals at Presbytery and Synod (both of whom dismissed Gardner's case) until it finally reached the General Assembly on 24th May 1884. After a long debate and with frequent advice from the Procurator, the Assembly decreed Anderson's ordination as elder to be irregular and invalid by 37 votes to 35! Nevertheless, the Assembly also affirmed that, given the special circumstances, Anderson's *election* as elder ought to be confirmed. The Procurator himself described the case as "a most unfortunate and petty one" that might have easily been settled by the exercise "of a little forbearance and good sense."[27] Normally, at the next diet of the Session intimation would be made of the Assembly's judgement but Gardner even sought to delay that and it was not until January, 1885 that the "Elder's case" (as it became known) finally returned to Session. The minute of the meeting is again so extraordinary it bears recording verbatim:

---

[27] Minutes of the General Assembly, May 1884

161

The Kirk Session having the judgement of the General Assembly in the Elder Case under consideration, in order to promote unanimity in the Session and peace in the congregation, unanimously resolved that all offensive allegations and expressions by whomsoever made in the proceedings which have taken place in this case should be entirely withdrawn and held to be unsaid…"[28]

The unanimity again was not to last long; in March 1885 the Treasurer, Mr. Mitchell, moved that the Session should pay the £48.9s.5d incurred in the "Elder's case". Again, Gardner objected stating that only the members of the Session who were supportive of Anderson should be liable for the costs. It is also noticeable that come the May celebration of Communion that year, Rev. Mackay excused himself from taking any part, leaving Gardner to preside alone. Perhaps Mackay's spirit was broken by all the in-fighting over the "Elder's case"; in any case he resigned the first charge some years later on 5th November, 1891. It was certainly an extraordinary episode in the Cathedral's history in which Christian charity was to surface time and again only to be swamped by petty and personal jealousies and animosities. Sadly, such was to be re-visited anew during Robin Mackenzie's tenure. Charles Anderson, for his part, never was officially recognised as an elder, so it might be argued Gardner won the day.

A number of changes had taken place during this time of great upset and controversy. In September 1884, the Prime Minister, William Gladstone visited Brechin and was given the freedom of the burgh. Following a petition from the town's inhabitants the old Fast days (a residue of the Reformation) were finally abolished in spring 1890 (only the diehard traditionalist Mr. Fettis[29] dissenting!). An attempt in January 1885 to alter the market day from Tuesday to Wednesday proved less popular and failed. Also that year, on Thursday 16th April, 1885, the very first marriage ceremony in a Presbyterian Church in Brechin took place between Alice, younger daughter of Rev. Alexander Foote, and Thomas Branton-Day.[30] Public worship on the Saturday before Communion was moved from 3pm to 7pm; perhaps a sign of folk working on a Saturday or the menfolk being engaged in the sport of football on a Saturday afternoon. The new Scottish Hymnal[31] was introduced from January 1888 and there is the first mention of a Christmas Eve service (once anathema to the Reformers) in winter 1887. There were also changes in personnel. Mr. Pearson, the original organist, resigned in 1883 and was replaced by Alexander Cherry; he in turn went off to Bridge of Allan, replaced by J.C. Murray in 1890. The Parish Church Hall receives its first mention in 1892 having been built by the architect William Fettes and completed in 1888. Fettes (or Fettis, the spelling

---

[28] Kirk Session minutes, 19th January, 1885
[29] This may have been the same Fettes who was the architect behind the Cathedral Hall.
[30] Hitherto marriage ceremonies were often held in homes or local halls.
[31] Published 1870.

varies) was born in Montrose in 1835. He was also the architect who designed the Brechin City Hall (1868) and the Brechin Infirmary (1868). He died in May 1911 at the age of seventy eight. In late May, 1893 a Deed of Trust was drawn up "declaring the purposes for which the Hall and other property should henceforth be held."[32] A weekly 8pm Wednesday service was started in the Cathedral Hall in January, 1894, for those who, by reason of work commitments or distance, could not attend worship on Sunday mornings. It was also in 1894 that Kirk Session meetings moved from the Session House (now the Cathedral Vestry) to the Parish Hall, breaking a centuries old link that went

back to the meetings of the Medieval Chapter. New elders were finally ordained in February, 1894, following years of delay due to the blocking tactics of Rev. Gardner. So too the collection ladles (still displayed in the Vestry) were dispensed with in favour of bags for the offerings.

The late 1880s and early 1890s were to mark a period of great change in Brechin. In the mid-1890s many of the linen factories were put on short-time due to a slump in trade. The prices in the shops rose (a 4lb loaf went up a ha'penny) while wages fell. In June 1895 the end of an era occurred as the last of the hand loom weavers' shops in Bridge Street closed. The Church too saw changes; John Gordon, last of the old Precentors retiring from East Free Church in January 1895. An outbreak of influenza in December 1893 and a severe winter in February 1895 both saw the death rate soar.

---

[32] Kirk Session minutes, 31st May, 1893

Changes too were afoot at the Cathedral. Following James Mackay's resignation in the winter of 1891/2, **John Alexander Clark (1892-1900)** was inducted as minister of the first charge in May 1892. Originally from Glasgow, Clark was born in August 1859 to Laurence Clark and Eliza Kerr Jack. He was educated at Glasgow High School before gaining his M.A. (1880) and B.D. (1883) from Glasgow University. Licensed by the Presbytery of Glasgow in 1883, he went on to become assistant minister at Monigaff and St.Enoch's in Dundee before being ordained to Coltness Parish Church in April 1886. He was then translated to Brechin in 1892 where he had the energy and foresight to seek the restoration of the Cathedral to its medieval origins. Edwards describes Clark as having a "catholicity of mind" and being free from any sense of sectarianism.[33] Clark was certainly a bold and innovative liturgical practitioner, eager to link the worship of the present day Cathedral with the Celtic roots of old. He married Margaret McIntyre in 1890 and had seven daughters, though only one of the twins, Edith (the last of his children) was to survive. Even Clark's arrival was to be overshadowed by Gardner who objected to the gift of a Pulpit Bible, Hymnal and Psalm book being given by the ladies of the congregation to the minister of the first charge. He wanted to know why a similar gift had not been given to him as minister of the second charge. And it is perhaps Gardner's failure to move from second charge to first (as so many of his illustrious predecessors had done) that was the real cause of much of his rancour in later years.

Alexander Gardner himself died, in Brechin, on the morning of 12th April, 1893, aged eighty two after what was described as a "rather protracted illness"[34]. *The Dundee*

---

[33] D.H. Edwards "The restoration of the Cathedral" in the *Brechin Almanac*, 1901
[34] *Brechin Almanac*, 1894

Courier and Advertiser carried notice of his passing the following day and supplied us with some additional details. It appears that Gardner had been housebound for much of the previous winter and had contracted influenza, which the redoubtable old man was unable to overcome. The Session minute's obituary records:

> ...the long period of fifty years, faithfully discharged his duties to the parish and congregation. He was an able preacher, a sound scholar, a diligent student and an earnest pastor. Devotedly attached to the Church of Scotland, as in life he sought her welfare, at his death he left the bulk of his property for Church extension and the welfare of the poor in this parish.[35]

Noticeably, the obituary makes no mention of Gardner as "friend", perhaps a sign of the divided loyalties he provoked. And such was his influence following the "Elder's case" in the 1880s that a long time was to elapse before new elders were finally ordained and admitted. £200 of his legacy was given to the poorer members of the congregation for coals, flannels and underclothing. The interest from another £1000 was to be used to assist the "industrious poor" of Brechin.[36] In addition, Gardner's private library was left to the Brechin Public Library, a full length portrait to the Town Council[37] and his estate at Esbie for the endowment of the new Church and its benefice. £7000 of the legacy went towards the building of Gardner Memorial Church, opened in 1899; for Church extension had been dear to his heart. This new church was built partly in memory of the man himself and part in memory of his son, James, a brilliant advocate who tragically committed suicide in September, 1887, aged only thirty. His fiancée was to be one of the benefactors of the new Church.

Gardner's obituary in the *Brechin Almanac* of 1893, records that his strong evangelical preaching and well-modulated voice drew back many worshippers following the Disruption in 1843. Gardner too had a strong practical ethos; he topped the local poll as chair of the School Board and was very involved in Presbytery work, where his deep knowledge of Church Law often proved an asset. A great preacher and orator, in 1861 he had the honour of preaching at the General Assembly before the Lord High Commissioner. When he celebrated the Jubilee of his ordination in August 1882, Robert Duncan of Montrose preached on II Chronicles 29:12 and this is part of his sermon on that occasion:

> Not many so long bear the burden and heat of the day (as Alexander Gardner). Few, comparatively, are privileged thus so long to labour and to wait. The bulk of

---

[35] Kirk Session minutes, 17th April, 1893
[36] *Brechin Almanac*, 1894
[37] Now situated in the Mechanics Institute

those years he has spent in the service of his church, to which he has been devotedly attached, at whose altar he has faithfully ministered, and whose life and work he has striven uniformly to develop and expand.[38]

In a sense Gardner's fifty year ministry (so far the longest in the Cathedral's history) was his strength and his weakness. He came to the Cathedral just after the Disruption when the congregation was greatly thinned, appearing at worship like "craws in the mist". A very directive style of ministry was called for and cometh the hour, cometh the man. But by the time of his death, the world had shifted; the industrial revolution had changed life in Victorian Britain beyond recognition. Democracy, local decision making, was becoming the norm and Gardner's slightly "presidential" style did not fit that new picture. He started, like many ministers, full of innovative ideas, yet as time went on he became increasingly entrenched in tradition. Possibly too after his son's death in 1887, he became more and more irascible and argumentative. Yet I cannot help wondering whether that, in spite (or maybe because) of his many weaknesses and faults, Alexander Gardner stands out as the most human of all the many clergy to have trod these ancient stones. A portrait of Gardner as an older man now hangs in the Mechanics Hall and was presented by public subscription on the occasion of his 50th jubilee year. (see below)

---

[38] Brechin Almanac, 1893, 51

167

With the death of Alexander Gardner a vacancy arose for the minister of the second charge. The first candidate selected withdrew in September 1893 but by the November **Rev. Adam Duncan Tait Hutchison (1893 – 1942)** was ordained and inducted to the second charge. Tait Hutchison almost brings us into the scope of living memory. When I first arrived in Brechin an old worthy, Meg Napier (who died aged 101 years) had been baptised by him and could remember him. Her memory was not necessarily very complimentary; "like maist meenisters," Meg said "He would greet you at the Kirk door and pass you in the street!" Although Tait Hutchison was not to realise it at the time, he was to be the very last minister of the collegiate second charge. As with John Alexander Clark, the ladies of the congregation presented him with a Pulpit Bible, Psalm Book and Hymnal.

Tait Hutchison was born on 20th May, 1868 at Kirkliston, near Edinburgh. He was the son of Robert Hutchison of Carlowrie and Mary Jemima Tait. Educated at Edinburgh Collegiate School and Edinburgh University, he gained an M.A. in 1888 and was licensed by the Presbytery of Edinburgh in 1891. He was to serve as assistant at the West Parish Church in Aberdeen and the Barony Church in Glasgow before being called to Brechin in 1893. In 1895 he married one Margaret Menzies of Balornock in Lanarkshire and the couple were to have two sons. He retired from Brechin in February 1942, when the first and second charges were united, and died on 8th January, 1949.

Photograph showing the architect John Honeyman examining the Cathedral during the 1901 Restoration

With the arrival of John A. Clark and Tait Hutchison was to begin one of the most fruitful and harmonious partnerships in the Cathedral's story. The great tragedy is that it was so short lived, with Clark dying so suddenly and unexpectedly on 28th October, 1900 aged only forty-one. Clark had left the Manse on Tuesday 23rd to preside at a Synod meeting in Montrose but, en route to the station, had felt unwell and returned home. By the Friday his condition was serious and he died on the Monday, less than a week after his illness first began. Clark was described as having a fine voice with good elocution and his sermons were carefully constructed and well-prepared. He was a member of the School Board, took a keen interest in Freemasonry being a member of St. James' Lodge and was a director of the local Infirmary. Edwards concludes that "Mr

Clark has all along taken a deep interest in every movement calculated to advance the spiritual and material interests of the community."[39]

Almost all were agreed that the reconstruction work carried out on the Cathedral in 1806-07 was of a poor standard. With growing liturgical innovations in the Cathedral's worship (including the first post-Reformation Christmas Day service on 25th December, 1895) and a Victorian obsession with mock gothic, plans were begun to restore the Cathedral to something approaching its original medieval look. To be fair, Alexander Gardner had initially had the notion of restoring something of the Cathedral's former glory. With the opening of Gardner Memorial Church in October, 1898 and an average attendance of over 800 at Communion season, even the cautious Heritors began to realise that the old Cathedral was no longer fit for purpose as a new century approached. A Restoration Committee was formed in December 1897 and the driving force of this was to be the Rt.Hon James A Campbell, M.P.of Stracathro. The architect to be appointed was the renowned Dr. John Honeyman (1831-1914) of Honeyman & Keppie, who had been heavily involved in planning churches in the Glasgow area and was to also be involved in the 1902 restoration of Iona Abbey. The mason's work was carried out by J.H.Whyte & Sons of Glasgow and was of Ardovie stone. The woodwork was by Hutchison & Grant of Glasgow.

In December, 1899, the Heritors agreed that the "great work" could commence and the congregation held their last service in the old Cathedral on Sunday 14th January, 1900. For the next two years, the Cathedral folk would worship in the City Hall at the 11am morning service and 6pm evening service, excepting from 3rd Sunday in May to the 2nd Sunday in October. The 3pm afternoon service was held in the Parish Hall. During the restoration an old Roman coin was discovered as well as traces of the Norman Church that pre-dates the current building of the 1220s.

Sadly, John Clark did not live to see his dream completed. An apocryphal tale tells of how, from his death bed window in the old Manse near Bishop's Close, Clark (being visited by Tait Hutchison) saw the Celtic cross being raised above the restored Chancel. Given that a Memorial Stone was only placed in the Chancel on 22nd September, 1900, and Clark died (aged 41) on 29th October, 1900, this is perhaps unlikely. Nonetheless, at least Clark went to his glory realising that his vision was well on its way to completion. A memorial window to John Clark was installed on 30th November, 1900.

---

[39] *Brechin Almanac*, 1901

Yet the restoration of the ancient Cathedral was not without incident. Tragically, on 25th April, 1900 a young joiner James Watt was to fall to his death from scaffolding while removing the old rafters; a 43 foot drop. Fundraising was key to the Restoration project; when the Heritors approved the project in late November 1897, £3000 of an estimated cost of £10,000 was raised in a few weeks. The Women's Guild (now the Guild) raised nearly £300 for the provision of a new pulpit. By April 1899 collections were so well advanced that it allowed building plans and contracts to be prepared. Following the completion of the Restoration any debts outstanding were virtually wiped out by the Grand Bazaar in the City Hall. This three day event opened by the Earl of Dalhousie on 27th August, 1903, raised £1600. It was described as "one of the most successful bazaars ever held in the town."[40] Any left-over articles were sold at a roup (or auction) in February 1905 raising £40. £12,000 is the cost of the Restoration of which James Campbell donated £1000 and another anonymous benefactor a further £1000.

A new minister for the first charge was needed in the midst of all this building work! An election held on 5th February, 1901 saw Rev. Walter Edward Lee receive 206 votes and Rev. William Veitch 58 votes. However, a huge 283 votes were against either candidate (plus 7 spoiled papers) so Presbytery declared that the congregation had failed to elect. Things went a little better in March: Rev. Walter William Coats, Minister at Girthan in the Presbytery of Kirkcudbright received 621 votes with only 29 against. So, on 16th May, 1901, **W.W. Coats (1901 – 41)** was duly inducted to the first charge.

---

[40] *Brechin Almanac*, 1904

Succeeding John Alexander Clark, who was highly popular and died young, must have been difficult shoes for Coats to fill. Interestingly, Coats had actually been on the short leet for the vacancy when Clark was elected in 1892, and it is entirely possible that in the congregation's grief at losing John Clark they had sought out a well kent face. Walter Coats was born on 18th June, 1856, son of John Coats of Dykehead (a medical doctor) and Jane Jackson. Educated at Glasgow Academy and the University of Glasgow, Coats went on to gain an M.A. (1875) and a B.D. (1878); he was to be awarded an honorary Doctorate in Divinity in 1904 by Glasgow University. According to university records, Coats was a particularly gifted scholar in Biblical criticism. He was licensed by Glasgow Presbytery in 1878 and subsequently became assistant minister at Galashiels and the Barony Church in Glasgow. In July 1880 he was called to Girthon, Kirkcudbright, where he was ordained. He married Margaret Janet Hamilton in January 1888 and the couple had a daughter, Margaret and a son, John, who was to serve as a lieutenant in the Black Watch during the Great War. Coats himself was to serve as Grand Chaplain to the Lodge of Freemasons in Scotland (1911-12) and Chaplain to the Tay defences for several months in 1916. Coats is described as "energetic and faithful in all his duties; his kindness endeared him to all classes." He was to celebrate his Jubilee of ministry in 1930, though the old man wanted no fuss. The

Presbytery of Brechin and Fordoun issued however a congratulatory letter. He died in June, 1941 aged eighty five.

The Cathedral was duly re-dedicated for public worship by Rt. Rev Dr. James Mitchell, Moderator of the General Assembly, on 23rd April, 1902; two services were held, one at 2.30pm and one at 7pm. The original opening date of March was delayed as the Heritors failed to agree with the Session over the allocation of pews, indeed, an action had been raised in Forfar Sheriff Court in February 1902! The changes were very obvious. Not only had the plasterboard been stripped away, the stone pillars made visible again and the old lofts removed but the Chancel had also been restored. Unfortunately, Victorian graves within the area of the Medieval Chancel resulted in only a partial restoration (five lancet windows on each side, as opposed to nine – three for each member of the Trinity – in the original). The Queen's Aisle, dedicated to old Queen Victoria who had died in January, 1901 during the restoration works, did cause some opposition, partly because it was seen by some as a "Papist" side chapel. The north aisle, which had replaced the north transept, had ornamentation under the eaves; a series of masks representing the world, the flesh and the devil, while the south aisle's junction with the Nave saw a boy seizing a fox by the tail! At the west end a dragon'shead forms a gargoyle. The old porch at the north door (which had fallen into dangerous disrepair) was restored and the Hearse (our chandelier) placed centre within the Nave and fitted with electric light fittings. The Chancel seats in the north depicted a Man and a Lion, symbolic of Matthew and Mark, whilst the south had the Bull and Eagle, symbols of Luke and John. There were several memorial tablets in the south aisle and transept including to Rev. David Blair, Rev. Robert Coutts and Rev. James Burns (nothing notably to Alexander Gardner!) But the most poignant memorial was in the east end of the south aisle, a memorial to Rev. John Alexander Clark. Because the Chancel had been restored, the organ was moved from the east loft (now removed) to the west, where unfortunately it obscured somewhat the fine west window. Its original tracker action was replaced too by a tubular-pneumatic system. In analysing the various changes in 1902, Edwards comments: "True there is not that feeling of immensity or ornateness of detail which characterise many of the greater Cathedrals, but the simplicity of construction and somewhat unfinished character of the upper façade of the nave walls have a charm of their own."[41]

There is a wonderful story from August 1902 when Pastor Jacob Primmer, having held an annual conventicle at the Town Cross, went afterwards to inspect the restored Cathedral. His visit was not a success as "he was treated somewhat disrespectfully by

---

[41] *Brechin Almanac*, 1903

someone. Omitting to remove his hat on entering the sacred edifice, he told how someone had come up behind him and removed it for him."[42] Quite right to!

Almost immediately there were problems. Objections had been lodged as early as February 1902 with the seating allocations in the restored Cathedral. These were eventually resolved in the May in a legal determination by Sheriff Lee. The Cathedral's new roof was discovered in December 1902 to be neither wind nor watertight – snagging was a problem even with Cathedral restorations! These problems were to continue until 1907 when it was requested of the Restoration Committee that the balance of their funds be used to secure the Nave roof. There were several complaints from the congregation of draughts (still a problem today!) and of smoke and soot making their way into the Cathedral damaging both organ and furnishings.

Finally in June 1907, at a further cost of £107, the Heritors gave permission for work on the Nave roof to be carried out. In late June too windows were broken in the Cathedral; two young lads appeared in Brechin Police Court for firing stones from their catapults at the windows during divine service. Of course, the restored Cathedral was not appreciated by all, a fact that even Dr. Coats acknowledges in his own history as he speaks of the comparison between 1807 and 1902 works:

> …in the course of time, as a new generation grew up, with the associations that cling to a place of worship, however ugly, that one has attended in childhood along with dear ones who have passed away, a certain tender sentiment attached itself to the "auld kirk" (the 1807 one), and there were some who regretted the work of restoration under taken in later days (in 1902).[43]

In September, the Ministers and Elders gifted a brass collection plate complete with oak stand and brass umbrella stands were placed on each pew. It was not until May 1942 that the two statuettes (gifted by the Women's Guild at the time of the Restoration) were finally placed on the pulpit. Whether Tait Hutchison had considered them "too papist" at the time is a possibility, the minute merely records that "statuettes had for one reason or another been removed from the pulpit and the (Interim) Moderator retrieved them from the office of the Heritor's Clerk after his death."[44]

1906 was to be a notable year in Brechin for a number of reasons. The February saw a large number of unemployed men in the town, largely because severe winter weather had thrown men out of the ordinary, seasonal employment. The Town Council

---

[42] *Brechin Almanac*, 1903
[43] Coats, 57
[44] Kirk Session minutes, 11th May 1942

saw to partly alleviate this by laying new water mains and drains. But it was to mark the beginning of a turbulent year in industrial relations. On 7th June the workers at the Denburn Linen works went on strike in pursuit of a 10% increase in wages and the factory had to close. A week later, the strike was still on and the discontent had spread to both the Caldhame and Valleyfield Works who now closed their gates too. Over 1400 men were now on strike and as the dispute dragged on into July the effects were felt all over the town. Keir Hardie, the Labour M.P., visited the strikers twice. Finally, after a representative from the Board of Trade intervened and offered an inquiry work restarted on 12th July. The final settlement was for 5% and a minimum rate agreed throughout the district. All this occurred in the middle of a long, hot summer with temperatures in September reaching 80F in the shade and 68F at midnight; the hottest for twenty eight years.[45]

1906 was of note for two other reasons. In April the 15th Annual conference of the Women's Guild was held in Brechin with over four hundred delegates from all over Scotland. The Provost and Council staged a civic reception in the City Hall. In September, after a lapse of many years, the senior football club restarted as Brechin City F.C.

In the July of 1907 a Suffragette rally was held at the Cross. In early autumn of 1907, just prior to the October celebration of Communion, it was discovered that several items of the Communion silver had gone missing – so too the Beadle, one William Myles! Myles[46] was duly arrested in Berkshire and appeared at Forfar Sheriff Court on 21st September, 1907 charged with theft. It appears that Myles had fallen into debt and, with six children and a wife to support, had found the temptation to alleviate his cash flow problem too great. He had forwarded two of the Communion cups to a family member in England who had duly sold them on to a Jeweller in Bond Street, London for three hundred guineas. One of the cups was almost sold to a Scottish nobleman for one hundred guineas when their provenance was discovered. What is perhaps most extraordinary is that Rev Dr Coats appeared as a witness for the defence. The *Aberdeen Journal* records: "Rev Dr Coats of the Cathedral Church made an eloquent appeal on behalf of the accused."[47] It is also of note that the details of this case do not appear in the Cathedral minutes – almost as if the Session had closed ranks to hush the matter up and

---

[45] Interestingly, this summer was followed on 26th December, 1906 by the worst snowstorm in living memory. Brechin was cut off for two days and 26 people died as a result of the wintry conditions.
[46] It was rather sad given that Myles had served in India with the 5th Dragoon guards and, on return home, worked in a factory at Kirriemuir where he was apparently highly regarded.
[47] *Aberdeen Journal*, 4th October, 1907

save Myles from further embarrassment. Sadly, Dr Coats' plea did not sway the Sheriff and Myles was sentenced on 3rd October, 1907 to six months in prison.

Coats received his D.D. from Glasgow University in the March of 1904. Also that year, on 5th September, General Booth of the Salvation Army visited Brechin and was greeted with a large audience and enthusiastic reception at the City Hall. The weather in the summer of 1909 was very odd; the hottest day of the year occurred on Saturday 8th May when 98F was recorded yet in July there was a sudden frost that blighted the potato crop followed by serious flooding. Nevertheless, in late August Tait Hutchison celebrated the first recorded Reformed service of Harvest Thanksgiving in the Cathedral.[48] Coronation day in June 1911 was marked by divine service in the Cathedral followed by "sports for the bairns in the Public Park in the afternoon and a dinner for the Guildry in the Mechanics Hall in the evening."[49] The scarcity of water, especially in the summer months, was to plague the town in the first years of the C20th until, in July 1914, the water supply was shut off from 6am – 6pm for over a week.

A few weeks later war broke out on 4th August, 1914. On Monday 3rd August the then Foreign Secretary Sir Edward Grey looked out over Whitehall and remarked to an aid "the lamps are going out all over Europe and we shall not see them lit again in our lifetime." Sadly, Grey's assessment proved all too correct. Within Brechin, as in many communities, there was, initially at least, great excitement. This was tinged though by panic buying in the shops, particularly of sugar and flour, partly in fear of future shortages of certain commodities and partly out of concern for imminent price rises. Added to these initial reactions, the banks (which had been closed for a holiday on the Monday) remained so for a further three days, causing a shortage of ready money and change in the local shops. A special ecumenical evening service of intercessory prayer was held in the Cathedral on Wednesday 12th August conducted by Dr. Coats, Rev. John Fraser of the West United Free Church and Rev. Kenneth Reid from the Episcopal Church. Further prayer services were held on Wednesdays 19th and 26th; these additional prayer services were to continue monthly for the length of the war, alternating in location between the Cathedral and St. Ninian's Church; the offerings from them being gifted to the Red Cross. Collections too were held for the Prince of Wales National Relief Fund and especially the Belgian Relief Fund; the inhabitants of Brechin were particularly touched by the plight of brave, long suffering Belgium. A concert was held in the City Hall by the City Band in October 1914 and Dr. Coat's fundraising efforts alone raised £500 for the sending of clothing to the needy people. The Congregational Ladies

---

[48] This took place on Sunday 31st August. It was followed by a poor honey harvest in September. See *Brechin Almanac*, 1910
[49] *Brechin Almanac*, 1912

Committee collected both money and wool to make warm garments for the soldiers and sailors and thousands upon thousands of pairs of wool socks were knitted and sent via the Red Cross.

Locally, the local company of the 5th Black Watch was immediately mobilized; they left for France in October, 1914 and were soon in the firing line. For a time at least social activities were cancelled, though by Christmas, socials and dances were again being held. In late August, Dr. Coats himself was appointed by the War Office as Military Chaplain to the 4th General Hospital in Glasgow for three months. This hospital was being made ready for "the sick and wounded sailors and soldiers of the Imperial Forces now engaged in war."[50] Pulpit supply was duly arranged during Dr. Coats' absence from the parish. He was Military Chaplain from 26th June, 1915 for a three month period. Tait Hutchison, while remaining at home, accompanied an expedition of Boy Scouts who had been asked to do coastguard duty in the north of Scotland in bleak, wintry weather in early 1915. Later in the war many of the local ministers were asked to do a stint at the YMCA huts.

By January 1915 a Roll of Honour was prepared "of those persons connected with the congregation who are serving in H.M. Imperial forces or who, as members of any other recognised organisation, are actively participating in the defence of our country."[51] The Cathedral Hall began to be used for school classes in autumn 1915, as the High School had been commandeered for military purposes. The first anniversary of war's outbreak in August, 1915 was marked by a large gathering in the Public Park; patriotic speeches were made and rousing selections of tunes played at the bandstand by military and the town bands. It was, as one participant had remarked "a great day oot"[52]. By the following August things were much darker, the war that was supposed to be "finished by Christmas" was dragging on and British and Imperial Forces were engaged in the Battle of the Somme which was consuming huge amounts of lives in its hunger to break the deadlock. 4th August, 1916 had been declared as a day of humble prayer to God on behalf of the nation. This year there were no bands or speeches, just a sombre Intercessory service at the Cathedral attended by the Magistrates, Councillors and representatives of other public bodies.

On 2nd May, 1916 a Zeppelin passed over Brechin, though thankfully no bombs were dropped, but this fear of air attack resulted in the winter months from 1916-18 of the curfew bell being silenced to prevent any enemy aircraft guessing that a civilian

---

[50] Kirk Session minutes, 30th August, 1914
[51] Ibid. 25th January, 1915
[52] Brechin in the Great War, vol. 1916

population lay below. "Darkness and silence," wrote one civil servant, "are essential to public safety."[53] The town, which for centuries had relied on the "aucht o'clock bell" to set its watches, would have to find another means not to be late for work the next day!

The organist, Mr. Gilchrist, offered his resignation in March, 1916 due to his impending conscription. Again in September 1916 Dr Coats was once more called upon as Military Chaplain, this time closer to home in the Tay defence district. By late 1916 the impact of the war was being felt keenly by many families in the town. Of a population of 9836 (1911 census figure) 301 men lost their lives in the Great War[54]. Amongst them were several lads who played for Brechin City F.C., including D. Collie Martin (aged 27, died 26th March, 1917), David Glen (aged 36, died 9th April, 1917) and Frank Forbes (died 20th September, 1917)[55]. Sheriff substitute Taylor, a captain in the Royal Scots who was very much involved in Brechin society before the war (and had already been wounded in 1915), was killed in action in April, 1917. So too James Robertson, a local stationer who ran the Post Office in Montrose Street, and a gifted musician who had a fine bass voice and was organist at Stracathro Church, was killed at Ypres in October, 1917, aged 36. Perhaps the two families who were most tragically affected by the Great War were the Lows and the Sturrocks. Mrs. Charles Low, a widow of 14 Black Bull Close had six sons serving; one was invalided out following a gas attack, two others were injured and two (George and Stewart) both with the Black Watch were killed, one in November, 1916 and one in March 1918. Mrs. Sturrock, a widow of 10 Nursery Lane, saw two of her three sons killed. Patrick, a private in the Black Watch, was seriously wounded in August, 1916 and succumbed to his injuries at the base hospital the following day. His brother, George, also in the Black Watch, died two weeks later, also at the Somme. Indeed, in the September of 1916 no less than four Brechiners died in action on the 3rd with three others seriously wounded. Some, such as Albert Kynoch of 24 Church Street was reported missing in July, 1917 yet it took over a year to establish that he had in fact been killed that day.

It was only in late September, 1916 that the impact of the War began to be felt upon the congregation in terms of its worship. Due to the increasing threat of air raids, regulations were brought into force in the Defence of the Realm Act which restricted the lighting of public buildings after sunset. As it was going to be difficult and prohibitively

---

[53] Ibid.

[54] The names and circumstances of all those Brechin citizens who fell are listed in the Appendix.

[55] Collie Martin played both for Brechin and also Dundee, his abilities as a goal scorer were renowned; David Glen had been a centre forward for Brechin, Dundee and Millwall Clubs and was a great favourite in football circles; Frank Forbes had also been a forward with Brechin and was killed by a shell whilst bringing the wounded back to defensive positions. Hit in the leg by shrapnel, Forbes died later that day. He had been married less than a year.

costly to black out all the Cathedral windows, the Kirk Session "with considerable reluctance" decided to discontinue the evening service.[56] The afternoon service too was moved from 3pm back to 2pm from Sunday 1st October. By late March, 1917, the evening service had been re-introduced but at the earlier time of 6pm. However "in the present critical state of the country when economy in every direction is so necessary and due to low numbers attending"[57] it was decided to dispense with the afternoon service, except on the first Sunday of the month when the Children's Service was held. During that same winter there was a special envelope collection for the National Committee for the relief of Belgium.

When the autumn of 1917 came round it was decided that the evening services that winter would continue, but in the Hall, due to lighting restrictions. And in October 1918, the Chief controller of fuel urgently recommended that all Church services be held during daylight hours. By now there were severe shortages of coal and fuel; the elementary school held classes only in the mornings and even the monthly intercessory services that had been going since war broke out were suspended that autumn of 1918. Sugar was in extremely short supply and milk and bread increased in price, bread by 3d to one shilling! Again, the evening service was discontinued, the morning service held at 11am and the afternoon one at 2.15pm. From the tone of the minutes in the period 1916-18, it is clear that people were considering the real possibility that Britain might actually lose the war. Aside from the variation in service times due to lighting restrictions, there was a very real anxiety of what might happen if Germany prevailed.

Then, on 25th November, 1918 (and one can almost hear a collective gasp of relief) the Kirk Session met:

> Before entering on the ordinary business the Kirk Session resolved to place on record the fact that on the 12th November a Thanksgiving Service was held in the Parish Church for the signing of the Armistice the previous day. It is the earnest hope and prayer of the Kirk Session that a righteous and lasting peace may be speedily concluded.[58]

It was with great relief too that evening services resumed on Sunday 1st December at 6pm and the curfew bell rang out again, even at 10pm on Saturdays! *The Brechin Advertiser* Almanac of 1918 speaks of "heartfelt relief that was too deep for much demonstration." News that the Armistice was signed on 11th November resulted in workers downing tools and flocking on to the streets. Shops and schools closed early and

---

[56] Ibid. 25th September, 1916
[57] Ibid. 26th February, 1917
[58] Ibid. 25th November, 1918

flags were found and hoisted up, the Cathedral bells rang gladly out; it had the air of a festive holiday. And yet these words speak volumes…

> Not all those absent ones will return to take up their former tasks in our midst, for the toll of the war on Brechin was a heavy one. There are very few homes in the town or district that have not been called on to make sacrifice…every man who has fallen has left hearts that ache and lives that are darkened by their loss.[59]

Relief was thus tinged with sympathy for the bereaved and the declaration of peace only deepened the more the sorrow for those who would not come off the train at Brechin to a hero's welcome.

No sooner had the war ended than the Spanish Influenza epidemic hit in November 1919; Brechin was not exempt. Schools closed, entertainments and meetings were severely restricted for fear of "spreading the malady"[60] and factories were put on short-time working. Many small businesses had to close completely. It is estimated that at least 10 – 15 people died.

Almost as a result of the war-time co-operation between the churches, we find a great deal of ecumenical activity in the wake of the Armistice. National Re-dedication services were held in March 1919 and on 23rd March at 3pm there was a joint Communion service amongst the Protestant churches in the Cathedral. This was followed by a Public Peace Thanksgiving Service in the Cathedral in the July. Even into the early 1920s, we find that (due to heating and pipe work being undertaken in the Cathedral – at a cost of £440) a request was made to Gardner Memorial for joint services on Sunday forenoon; the evening service being held in the Hall. A joint missionary campaign was conducted throughout the town in the winter of 1922/23 and at its close the preacher was Rev.Dr. Donald Fraser, Moderator of the United Free Church. Even as late as November 1925 we find joint arrangements being made for a short Armistice Day service and a collection for the Earl Haig Fund. Suddenly, partly because of the Great War, remembering the past was in tune with the popular mood. So, in February 1922, the colours of the Old Volunteer Force from the time of the Napoleonic wars were laid up in the Cathedral "as a memorial of the patriotism of our forefathers in a time of great national peril."[61] In January 1929, the old Roman coin (mentioned in Chapter One and discovered during the Cathedral Restoration in 1902) was sent to Dr. Coats and fixed to the Vestry Wall in a display case.

---

[59] Brechin and the Great War, vol. 1917
[60] *Brechin Almanac*, 1919
[61] Ibid., 20th February, 1922

Women too had found a new confidence and status as a result of the Great War, and not simply as nurses of the wounded servicemen at Brechin Infirmary. There were lady barbers, lady butchers, lady printers, almost lady everythings! Business would have been unable to function without women filling the places of the menfolk at the front. Work had been plentiful in Brechin thanks to government contracts and, though prices had increased, so too had wages.

On Thursday 8th September, 1921, the Cathedral was graced by a Royal visitor when Queen Mary and Princess May (who were staying at Brechin Castle) came to town. They inspected the stained glass windows, viewed the two towers, heard the organist, Mr. Botwood, give a short recital and signed the Visitor's Book. The signature is still visible in a small glass picture case on the wall of the Vestry.

The 1920s were not prosperous years for Brechin. The East Mill (Linen) had closed down at Christmas 1920 and, after several years on short-time, several other factories closed down in early 1921. This, along with the return of ex-servicemen raised the unemployed total to 1527 (nearly 20% of the population). A communal soup kitchen launched at the beginning of March supplying hot soup to 400 households along with 900 half-loaves and coal to 550 houses. The dire poverty was further alleviated by free school dinners to 250 children. The Town Council decided to undertake the repair of some of the town's streets with the object of absorbing as many idle men as possible. An application was submitted for grant aid to re-lay River Street, often the location of severe flooding (e.g. the flood of July 1916 was particularly severe). Although the resumption of out-of-work allowance by the government and the restarting (albeit part-time) of the Caldhame works, the Valley works and the Denburn works by summer eased the problem, Brechin was never to fully recover its industrial past. Around 350 men (and an equal number of women) were still unemployed in October 1921 and a further blow fell in March 1924 when the Paper mill (established in 1851) also closed.

In the autumn of 1925 an interesting pulpit exchange took place; Rev. A.D. Tait Hutchison went to act as chaplain at Simla and Lahore for 12 months while Rev. John Horton McNeil, late of Madras Presidency, acted as locum. In the autumn of 1929 an historical ghost was finally laid to rest. Much of the acrimony caused by the Disruption of 1843 had long since dissipated, yet one thorny issue remained; that of property and endowments. Though the Heritors no longer had any say in the election of the minister of a congregation, they still had a large measure of control over work done on manses, churches and glebes and controlled the teinds. In May 1925, the *Church of Scotland Properties and Endowments Bill* signed into law and the Kirk finally gained full control over all its properties. In 1926 discussions began setting out the agreements between the various Reformed churches in doctrine, worship, government and discipline. What was the trickiest area was amalgamating the various church agencies into one. However, after full and lengthy debate in assemblies and presbyteries the legislation was approved in May 1929 and in October the Auld Kirk and the United Free Church (or at least a majority) re-united into the Church of Scotland as "by law established." There were still misgivings about this phrase (and in the Kirk old rivalries are long lasting) but, as Burleigh puts it:

> …(it had) become meaningless to most people as the controversies it engendered. But the ideal of a national Church both representing and fostering the Christian faith of the whole people, and ideal which in spite of all division was common to all Presbyterians, was in a manner realized. Into the reunited Church in 1929 were gathered the great majority of Presbyterians, forming rather more than four-fifths of the church-going Protestant population of the country.[62]

A special service of re-unification was held on Sunday 6th October, 1929 (though rather cheekily the offering went to the Cathedral's general funds!). There were now seven Church of Scotland congregations (see below) but there were not seven for long. Yes, post War there may have been encouraging signs of renewed co-operation. But another spectre was to arise from the trenches of the Great War to haunt the united Kirk; birth had been given to the spirits of atheism and secularism and they would grow in maturity to disturb the new found status of the Cathedral.

---

[62] Burleigh, 405

THE SEVEN CHURCHES OF SCOTLAND IN 1929

Cathedral	United with Maison Dieu and Stracathro in September 1990
East Parish	United with Gardner Memorial in 1937
Gardner Memorial	United with West and St. Columba's, 1972 to become South Esk; Gardner Memorial name reconstituted, 1999
West Free	United in 1947 to become West and St. Columba's
St. Columba's East Free	United in 1947 to become West and St. Columba's
St. Ninian's	Originally formed from a union of City Road United Free and Bank Street United Free churches in July 1914. Closed 1963. Congregation dispersed. Now used by Roman Catholic congregation.
Maison Dieu	Linked with Stracathro, 1982 Union with Cathedral, 1990

ADDITIONAL INFORMATION – Section 5

THE GUILDRY LOFTS

The trades of Brechin had begun to erect lofts within the Cathedral from 1608.

These were eventually to include:

The Magistrates loft	TEXT – The Decalogue or Ten Commandments
Lord Panmure's loft	Motto & Crest
Scholars' loft	TEXT: "The law was our schoolmaster to bring us to Christ"
Glovers and Skinners' loft	TEXT: "present rams' skins, dyed red, and badger's skins for offering"
Farmers' loft	TEXT: "those who sow in tears shall reap in joy"
Tailors' loft	TEXT: "they sewed fig leaves together and made themselves aprons"
Wrights' loft	TEXT: "the righteous shall flourish like a palm tree"
Weavers' loft	TEXT: "my days are swifter than a weaver's shuttle"
Bakers' loft	TEXT: "man shall not live by bread alone"
Smiths' loft	TEXT: "the Smith drinketh no water and is faint"
Butchers' loft	TEXT: "Rise, slay and eat"
Shoemakers' loft	TEXT: "your feet shod with the gospel of peace"
Believers' loft	By 1872, the pulpit had been moved from the juncture of the Chancel and the South transept to the south wall of the Nave. The result was a gallery or loft *behind* the pulpit, where the preacher's face was not seen. This was called the Believers' loft as one had to live by faith, not sight!

THE CURFEW BELL

D.H. Edwards comments that "the ringing of the curfew (bell) does not emerge from the mists of any doubtful tradition, but from the application of a practical and necessary precaution."[63] The custom arose in the Medieval period when most of the town's houses would have been made of timber. Fire was a constant threat (e.g. in March 1672 a great conflagration destroyed much of the town's homes). So curfew (from the French "couvre feu") was the time at night when fires ought to be doused in the interest of public safety. Remember too that a household fire was usually made in a hole in the middle of the floor under an opening in the roof, through which the smoke escaped – no chimneys then!

In those days, of course, there were no watches or clocks so knowing specific times was difficult. The curfew bell thus became linked to the bell for the last monastic office of the day, Compline, which could vary between 6pm in winter to 10pm in summer. In general at Brechin the bell rang at 8pm on weekdays, 10pm on Saturdays and 6pm on Sundays for a quarter hour. It was also rung to rouse folk from slumber in the morning; 6am in spring-autumn and 7am in winter. People of course rose at daybreak to work and had little leisure time so retiring at 8pm was quite common. Historical records show that a curfew bell was rung in Carfax, Oxford as early as the reign of Alfred the Great.

The ringing of the "muckle bell" of Brechin was often a source of great amusement to the local youth. Indeed, by 1809 the Kirk beadle had so neglected his duty of ringing the bell (leaving the boys to ring it while he sat at the steps and smoked his pipe) that the Magistrates themselves employed someone to do so; this caused some tension with the Cathedral authorities! One young lad rang the bell with such vigour that he was almost choked when it looped round his neck. Fortunately, his chums released him but it is said that he bore the mark of the rope on his neck for the rest of his life. Another lad was locked in the Square tower by his pals as a prank, taking the lantern with them. It was only by tolling the bell in an irregular manner that he found release! The most tragic tale occurred on 7th December, 1895 when the Bell ringer, John Mackay, died as a result of an accident in ringing the bell. He was a great friend of the minister John Clark who was distraught at the awful demise of "the meenister's man".

---

[63] *Brechin Almanac*

CHAPTER NINE
Forties and Fifties – Flourishing and Fading

The Church is finding it necessary to attempt to help classes of people whose distress results largely from the defective Christianity of the community as a whole. It does not lose sight of its main object, which is to save souls and so render people fit to face any conditions…it dare not permit whole classes to slip from its influence.

- **G.D. Henderson, *The Church of Scotland A Short History*, revised 1946**

The failure of the 1950s was the widespread inability to understand how profound was the challenge of the call to mission to the existing culture, power-structures and institutions of the kirks. Yet, for a time, the banner of the multi-faceted Tell Scotland movement brought multitudes of ordinary church members into the streets and to new conceptions of their vocation. Even that level of success was remarkable. Perhaps all idealism ends in this sort of ambiguous mixture of failure and success.

- **Frank D. Bardgett, "The Tell Scotland movement: its failure and success" in Records of the Scottish Church History Society, vol. XXXVIII**

-

Shortly after the re-union of the churches in 1929, the Cathedral adopted the Revised Hymnary (sometimes affectionately known as CH2 or RCH). The original Church Hymnary had appeared in 1898 and in 1922 the Church of Scotland, United Free Church and Presbyterian Church in Ireland began work on a revised hymnary, both in terms of words and music. This was completed in the spring of 1927 and introduced to the Cathedral on 1st January, 1930. In the early 1930s too, in the light of the recent union, there was discussion about possible joint evening services, though it never got off the ground. By 1933 however, the old rivalries once again had re-appeared. In the March there was a major dispute between the Kirk Sessions as to the delineation of parishes. Although agreement was reached locally, one (unnamed) Session then broke ranks and appealed to Presbytery for adjudication; stating that the most populous areas are the ones most coveted by the other churches.

In 1934 we have reference to the Mary Stone: "a sculptured stone (a cross with Madonna and child in centre) which is recorded to have been dug up many years ago in a garden near the Cathedral and is now lying loose on the floor of the Chapel of Aldbar Castle."[1] This, probably Byzantine artefact, is now held in the Cathedral and can been seen above the font.

A number of special services were held in the 1930s too; one on 6th May, 1935 for George V's Silver Jubilee and, more sombrely, on Tuesday 28th January, 1936 at 11am, this being the date and time of the late King's funeral. A planned service to mark the Coronation of Edward VIII on 12th May, 1937 at 10am duly became that for George VI following Edward's abdication in December 1936.

During the late 1930s, the Session also appears to have had a number of "issues" with the organist! In April 1936, a letter was sent instructing him to "make certain improvements in the praise during the service in the Church."[2] This was followed by another letter in autumn 1937 complaining about the Choir whispering during the service and requesting the Organist put a stop to this.[3] Indeed, it may well have been for that very same reason that a proposal had been aired in November, 1926 to remove the organ

---

[1] Kirk Session minutes, 30th April, 1934; See also Chapter One
[2] Ibid., 27th April, 1936
[3] Ibid., 29th Nov, 1937

and choir to the South transept "to make the choir more effective as an instrument of church worship."[4]

By January 1937 we can actually see the clouds of war looming on the horizon even in regards to Brechin. An appeal was launched to take refugees fleeing from Nazi Germany. These were primarily Christians but it seems some Jewish people were amongst the groups arriving in Scotland. By September, 1939, war had again broken out and war time lighting restrictions resulted in changes to worship times. The Sunday evening service was now at 3pm and there was no longer a Preparatory service on Wednesday evening or a Thanksgiving service on Sunday evening during Communion seasons. By late 1941 the afternoon services were themselves discontinued due to small numbers attending.[5] The Cathedral's stained glass windows were also boarded up as a precaution against air raid. By April 1940, the Cathedral Hall had been requisitioned for military purposes. Brechin, briefly, also became caught up in the Battle of Britain! In October, 1940, the afternoon Communion service saw only 83 participants, this was considered well down and was partly due to an air raid siren being sounded at 1.45pm, shortly before the 2pm Communion.[6] Bombs did fall at Edzell on 28th August, 1940 and at Balfour hill on 3rd October, 1941. By May 1941 arrangements were in place that in the event of a Nazi invasion the Church Bell would be rung; a duplicate key to the Square Tower was passed on to the local police office.

In many ways the Second World War had more impact upon the *civilian* population in Brechin. Schools closed on 31st August, 1939 at the outbreak of war and remained so until September 13th. The High School roll was to increase dramatically from 450 to 750, largely due to Harris Academy evacuees. In fact the area received a large number of evacuees from Dundee, both mothers and children that September, and there was scarce a household that did not have either evacuees or soldiers billeted with them. Yet, despite the warm welcome, most drifted back to the big city and by November, 1939 of the 673 children only 240 remained, with 40 of the 133 evacuated adults. Locals reported that many of the city children were extremely rowdy, some scarcely toilet trained, and most totally unfamiliar with rural life. The Polish Infantry, Black Watch, Manchester Regiment and Commandos were all stationed for a time in Brechin. While the troops slept in local halls, families often had them billeted for meals, this had the added advantage of extra rations for the housewife! Fish was not on ration and when the fish van came round on Tuesdays the supplies were often snapped up within a few streets – so the van had to alter his route weekly in the interests of fairness!

[4] Ibid., 29th Nov, 1926
[5] Ibid., 23rd November, 1941
[6] Ibid., 20th October, 1940

Gellatly's the bakers too sometimes had "fine fancies" off the ration, but you had to be quick! Youngsters were sometimes sent to the bakers in Montrose St. then the High St. to see what they could get.

But war, even locally, had a darker side. Brick air raid shelters went up throughout the town, stirrup pumps appeared at larger public buildings, everyone had to carry a gas mask and it was not uncommon to find your bus journey interrupted as soldiers checked the passengers ID cards. Bridges had concrete blocks placed upon them to narrow the road, so that these key roads could be easily defended should the need arise. Windows of homes and shops found themselves criss-crossed with sticky brown paper to prevent shattering and black out curtains were essential at night, unless you wanted the wrath of the ARP warden. All signs bearing "Brechin" were removed (to stop any enemy agents knowing the location) and scrap metal, such as school railings, were removed for the war effort. Even history was not exempt from sacrifice: the bronze cannon from Sevastapol during the Crimean war, which had stood many a long year at Brechin Cemetery, taken for scrap. The churches too played their part with weekly intercessory services taking place at each of the churches in turn.

Certainly, the impact of the Second World War on families was much less deadly (far fewer combatants died) but we only know that with the benefit of hindsight. At the time the threat of invasion was ever present, as well as the fear of the dreaded telegram to tell of a loved one being dead or missing. It was only after D-Day in June 1944, as carriages of wounded men rolled into Brechin station to be transferred to Brechin Infirmary or Stracathro Hospital it looked as if the war was finally turning in the Allies' favour.

It was in the course of the war years that the end of an era came with the death of Rev Walter William Coats at the age of eighty five years on 21st June, 1941. Dr. Coats, we must remember, had served as a Chaplain in the Great War and had been inducted prior to the re-union of the churches in 1929. With Coats' death the question of uniting the first and second charges of the Cathedral was almost immediately raised. By the August Tait Hutchison had indicated that he would be willing to retire for the sake of the union which he duly did in February, 1942, aged seventy four. In March, 1942, the basis of union between the first and second charges was agreed; there were 1342 members on the Electoral Roll (of which 722 had communicated at least once in 1941).

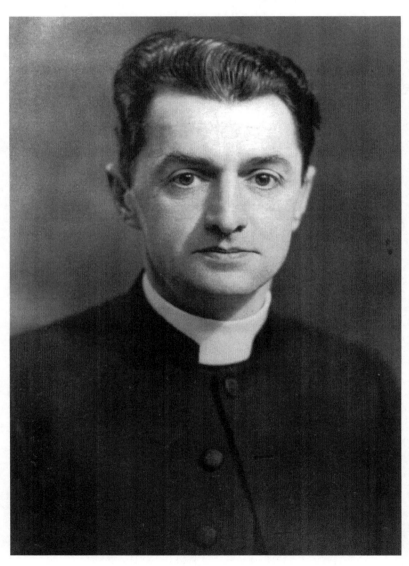

James Anderson (1942 – 1964), the minister at South Leith was duly elected to the one, united charge of Brechin Cathedral on 4th August, 1942 by 215 votes to 27 (one of those voting against being Miss May Coats, daughter of the previous minister. She moved to Farnell Church because she disliked Anderson's style. Later returning to the Cathedral, she died in late summer 1975, aged 85 years.) James Anderson was born at Springburn, Glasgow on 5th August, 1896. Educated at Hanley High School, he went on to study at Glasgow University where he gained an MA in 1922 and a BD in 1926. He was student assistant at Glasgow: Queen's Cross from 1919-24 and then licensed by Glasgow Presbytery in

1924. Following licensing, Anderson became probationary assistant at Langside Parish in Glasgow (1924-26). When his "bishop" Rev. J. McNeil Fraser died suddenly during the latter part of Andersons' assistantship, by popular acclaim, the congregation elected James as the minister. Thus was he ordained at Langside in October 1926. On 5th February, 1936, James married one Catherine Wilson. Translated to South Leith on 17th May, 1938, he was then inducted to Brechin on the 30th September, 1942. He retired in November, 1964 and died in England on 18th September, 1977.

With the arrival of James Anderson, the collegiate charge, largely forged out of the partnership between minister and bishop at the time of the Reformation, ceased to exist. Yet, James Anderson during his twenty two years of ministry was to leave his own historical legacy, most particularly in the field of stained glass. Between 1949 and 1961 no fewer than eight large and eleven small windows saw bequests that allowed them to be adorned with stained glass. No sooner than Anderson had arrived did he seek to replace Communion tokens with cards and the Parish was again divided into elder's districts. With the Session down to around twenty elders, Anderson ordained some sixteen new elders in the midst of the war years in March and April 1943 amongst these was D.B. Thoms, later Session Clerk, and many others who would play leading roles during Peter Gordon's tenure. Also within his first year, he introduced lady visitors to deliver *Life and Work* while also collecting money for Church purposes. Christmas gifts were sent from the congregation to serving members of H.M. Forces; in 1943 this included 8 prisoners of War and 85 members serving in Forces overseas. A collection in Holy week 1943 was sent to the Huts and Canteens Fund of the Kirk.

In April 1943 notification was received from the War Office that Church bells could once again be rung on Sundays, the invasion threat having passed, at least for now. The following month, the Cathedral was first opened daily (except Saturday) to the general public from 11am – 1pm and 2pm – 4pm. A gift of a polished brass cross was, however, declined on the grounds that "members of the congregation might resent the presence of the symbol of the cross in a Presbyterian church."[7] This seems, in a way, rather extraordinary given that the previous May two statuettes (gifted by the Women's Guild at the time of the Restoration) were finally placed on the Pulpit, despite shades of being considered akin to Catholic idols[8]! Yet, the rejection of the brass cross was perhaps a sign that Anderson's pace of liturgical innovations was being deliberately slowed. Clearly, in time, it was accepted – for it currently appears each Sunday on the Chancel niche without any complaint!

---

[7] Ibid., 10th May, 1943
[8] Ibid., 11th May, 1942

In entering what might be considered the modern era, Anderson set up in autumn 1943 a Church Club (a social club with speakers, activities, socials and outings) and began the process of forming Church youth organisations. The "Cathedral Club" as it was to be called was to meet fortnightly on the first and third Tuesdays from October to March and its meetings were to be of a social and literary nature, confined only to congregational members. The subscription fee was one shilling! The records are unclear as to how long the Club ran for but by January, 1948 it seemed to be already running out of steam; a special meeting was called to "re-organise the Club and extend its social and recreational activities."[9]

Rev. J.H. Chisain Smith was appointed the first assistant minister to the newly united charge in May 1944. In December of that year too Anderson re-introduced not only the 11am Christmas Day service[10] but also a Watchnight service on Hogmanay (December 31st) at 11.30pm to theologically and liturgically reflect the Scots practice of seeing out the old year and seeing in the new.[11] A suggestion of a mace for the Cathedral being made from wood from the old pulpit and decorated with the seal of Brechin was made in April, 1945; unusually, despite the idea being left with James Anderson, it was never followed through to completion[12].

Once again in November of 1944, gifts were prepared for those serving in H.M. Forces; there were 212 sent of which 109 were overseas, 9 were POWs and 3 (ominously for the families concerned) were missing. There was more to celebrate at Christmas 1944 than for many a year, for, at last, the war was nearing its end. Special services were held in each local church for Peace in Europe at 7.30pm on Monday 7th May (the day Germany surrendered) and a united service at 11am in the Cathedral on the following day (V.E. Day – Tuesday 8th May, 1945). The Sunday following, Sunday 13th May, a united service of Thanksgiving for Victory was held at 6pm in the West Church. These formal commemorations were followed in early September by a "Welcome Home" social for those returning to Civvy Street from war service.[13] Sadly, of course, not all returned and below are listed those members of the congregation who fell in the course of their duties[14].

---

[9] Cathedral Club Record book

[10] This had originally been initiated by Rev. John A. Clark in December, 1895.

[11] In the 1970s, this practice was abandoned in most Church of Scotland in favour of a Watchnight service on Christmas Eve, though some residue of the Hogmanay service still persists.

[12] Kirk Session minutes, 9th April, 1945.

[13] Ibid., 10th September, 1945

[14] In common with most modern War commemorations the names are listed alphabetically, without rank designation, showing all are equal before God in war. The memorial to the fallen of 1939-45 can be found

George Ballantine	Black Watch Sergeant, BEM	Died 27th September 1945 Buried Brechin
Frank Bruce	Kings Own Scottish Borders Lance Corporal	Died 19th July 1944 Buried Banneville La Campagne War Cemetery
John Christie	Royal Air Force Flight Officer	Died 27th July 1944 Buried Letra Communal Cemetery
James Gourlay	Civil Defence, Fire Guard	Died 11th March 1943 at West Riding Infirmary
Alexander Grant	Reconnaissance Sergeant	Died 15th August 1944 Buried Banneville La Campagne War Cemetery
James Hogg	Gordon Highlanders Private	Died 6th April 1944 Buried Beach Head War Cemetery at Anzio
John W Hogg	Royal Armoured Corps, Trooper	Died 6th June 1944 Buried Bayeux War Cemetery
David Hutcheon	Gordon Highlanders Major	Died 4th February 1944 Buried Anzio War Cemetery
Alfred Mackie	Black Watch Private	Died 10th November 1944 Buried Foli War Cemetery
Albert Malcolm	Merchant Navy Steward	Died 22nd February 1942 No known grave, commemorated Tower Hill Memorial, London
Robert D Malcolm	Merchant Navy Engineer	Died 11th June 1941 Buried Cardiff (Cathays) Cemetery
Robert F Milne	Black Watch Corporal	Died 1st November 1944 Buried Bergen-op-zoom War Cemetery,

in the north aisle of the Cathedral. In this case I have listed only the fallen of the Cathedral, those of Brechin more generally can be found on the War Memorial.

		Netherlands
Charles W Mitchell	Black Watch Private	Died 21st July 1943 Buried Catania War Cemetery, Sicily
Joseph Reid	Royal Navy Stoker	Died 11th December 1944 on board HMS Cassandra after being torpedoed by a U boat U365
Allan Young Aka Alex Menzies Young	Cameron Highlanders Lance Corporal	Died 24th October 1942 Buried El Alamein War Cemetery,

Anderson's innovations appear to have been dealt another setback in November, 1945. Women, having played such a key part in the War effort, were now suggested as Elders. However, on a congregational vote, the idea was well defeated by 15 votes for to 78 against.[15] In April of the following year he was more successful as his idea of *a Society of Friends of Brechin Cathedral* met with general approval. The new Society launched at Trinity 1947 with the following objectives:

- The safeguarding of the amenity of the Cathedral and the beautifying of its surroundings
- The adornment of the Cathedral and its further endowment
- The improvement of the music of the Cathedral
- The encouragement of research into the history of the Cathedral
- The support of any object connected with the Cathedral, as approved by Council

The great liturgist, James Anderson, also prepared a "Prayer of the Society" –

Almighty God, from whom all good things come;

We thank Thee for all thy servants by whose skill and labour

this House of Prayer was built to the glory of Thy holy Name;

Be pleased both to inspire and accept all worship offered here;

---

[15] Kirk Session minutes, 18th November, 1945

Lift up our hearts, we beseech Thee, to worship Thy eternal majesty in spirit and truth;

Through Jesus Christ our Lord,

to whom with Thee and the Holy Ghost be all honour and glory,

world without end; AMEN

Over the last seventy years many gifts have been given by the Society of Friends to the Cathedral, not least the oak tablet with the list of clergy, gifted on 10th May, 1954.

In 1947 too, Anderson introduced a third "non-card" Communion on Sunday 16th February. The comment in the Session minutes was that "there was a fair attendance considering the wintry conditions and the bad state of the roads."[16] A year later another innovation in Communion was proposed, this time in the dress of the Elders. One elder Mr. Birse suggested that the white ties be replaced by black ones in March 1948 but when the matter returned to the Session in April, he withdrew the motion.

In early 1949, the death is recorded of Rev. Adam Duncan Tait Hutchison, Minister Emeritus of the Cathedral who was aged eighty[17]. By June of the following year the Queen's Aisle had become a side chapel and a brass cross (now on the Cathedral wand[18]) and lectern from Duncrub Castle Chapel in Perthshire were dedicated to Tait Hutchison's memory.

---

[16] Ibid., 16th February, 1945

[17] Ibid., 8th January, 1949

[18] In fact the "wand" comprises of the Beadle's staff "selected from the furnishings of the Cathedral before the 1902 restoration" (Kirk Session minute, 11th Sept, 1950) topped by a Maltese Cross in memory of Tait Hutchison.

Just a few months later in November 1950 the family of another former minister, Rev. John Clark, gifted a large standing brass lectern in the shape of an eagle. The era of James Anderson was indeed one of abounding gifts! It was also at this time (June 1949) that an earlier gift from Bishop Lamb, the fine brass hearse, was sent to the Royal Scottish Museum for restoration. Following advice from an architect called Lindsay, the Session (thankfully!) agreed that the hearse should not be wired for electric light but restored to its original state for tallow candles and hung on the Chancel, not the Nave.[19]

The early 1950s saw a number of changes, nationally and locally. King George VI died in February 1952 and the Kirk Session expressed the hope that Queen Elizabeth would have a "long, happy and prosperous reign."[20] The assistant minister, Rev. J.H. Chisaim Smith resigned and was replaced by Alastair Roy.[21] So too George Smith, who had been organist for over twenty five years since 1926, retired on the grounds of ill health in October 1952 and was succeeded by Mr. Bramwell Cook, Music master at Brechin High School. 1953 also saw the departure of Ernest Dawson, the Church Officer, after an unspecified accusation of improper conduct.

We see in this period of the early 1950s signs of growth in the Church. The Youth fellowship grew and took a youth service on the last Sunday of March, 1953. The attendance at Communion hovered continually around the 700 mark (see Appendix) and folk, even today, remember well the packed Kirk of this era. The Children's Talk on Sunday mornings, "dropped from the forenoon services some years ago"[22] was re-introduced on a trial basis with the older children; James Anderson taking them on a journey through Bunyan's *Pilgrim's Progress*. The younger children attending Sunday school continued to meet on Sunday afternoons.

Billy Graham came to Scotland in spring 1955 and many responded to his altar call during the hymn *"Just as I am"*. The late 1940s and early 1950s were therefore certainly a period of rapid growth in Protestant congregations; religious revival was the order of the day. While the numbers attending Billy Graham's crusades were vast (in Glasgow for example in 1955, some 830,670 people attended) there were very few conversions. Callum G Brown in *The Death of Christian Britain*, stresses that we should not overstate the impact of this 50s revival. Much of it Brown claims was simply a

---

[19] Kirk Session minutes, 26th September, 1949
[20] Ibid. 11th February, 1952
[21] Ibid. 8th September, 1952
[22] Ibid. 9th June, 1958

hangover from Victorian values; "the church, Sunday school and family were memorials to their parents' history which the young endured in that decade."[23]

It may have been an exciting, dynamic time in the Kirk, but, sadly, not one destined to last. The 1960s liberation of free love and drugs was already in embryo with Elvis, Rock and Roll and underground cafes. In April 1960 we find these somewhat prophetic words in the Session minutes: "great sympathy was expressed with the youth fellowship leaders who were confronted with very serious problems that beset most of the youth clubs in the country and were tackling their work under rather discouraging conditions."[24] So too in April, 1961, it was noted that only seven boys were attending Sunday School.[25] In the light of what was to follow in the 1990s, the writing, it might be argued, was already evident on the wall as early as the 1960s. For a variety of reasons (well discussed in Bardgett's excellent article Bardgett, "The Tell Scotland movement: its failure and success"[26]) this ecclesiastical momentum of the 1950s was not followed through; partly because the Kirk nationally was not very good at doing mission at home and partly because, frankly, its' dominant historical position had meant it didn't have to. But it was undoubtedly an opportunity missed that we are still dealing with in the 21st century.

Communion once again came under scrutiny in the mid-1950s. With the Queen's Aisle now effectively a side chapel, Anderson began monthly communion services there (a practice later discontinued by Peter Gordon and re-introduced by Scott Rennie!). It was agreed that the afternoon Communion change from 2.15pm to 2pm, though an attempt to increase the number of Communion services to four per annum was departed from after discussion.[27] The idea of a monthly celebration either before or after regular morning worship met with a better reception.[28] In September, 1957, after a year's deliberations, it was agreed to introduce individual Communion cups at the October Communion, though not before Anderson had used common cup at a special Communion service to mark the 400th anniversary of the Lord's Supper in the Reformed Church;[29] perhaps one last hurrah from the liturgist? It was also in February, 1957 that four elders (two for bread, two for wine) served Communion to their fellow elders on the Chancel during the service. It is illuminating to see that many of our so-called long

---

[23] Callum Brown *The Death of Christian Britain* (Routledge, Abingdon, Oxon; 2001) 175
[24] Ibid. 11th April, 1960
[25] Ibid. 10th April, 1961
[26] See Records of the Scottish Church History Society, vol. XXXVIII
[27] Kirk Session minutes, 8th June, 1959
[28] Ibid. 11th June, 1956
[29] Ibid. 16th September, 1957 & 24th June, 1956

standing "traditions" are, in the grand scheme of the Cathedral, relatively recent innovations!

A proposal to remove the organ console to the Queen's Aisle Chapel, thus opening up the west window by removing the organ loft, which was James Anderson's great dream, met with fierce opposition in 1953, when it was discovered that it was to cost £3200 compared to £735 to repair the organ in situ. The measure of the man that Anderson was, is perhaps best reflected when he celebrated his semi-jubilee in October, 1951. During the speeches that enjoyable night[30] at the Mechanics Hall the comment was made that "there were always new schemes issuing from Mr. Anderson's fertile brain, and sometimes the Kirk Session had to put the brake on. But later the brake came off and they went forward."[31] Anderson was a great innovator, sometimes too forward thinking for the conservative Cathedral! Yet, in this period when the collegiate charge had ceased, an era in which war had been replaced by peace, it was an innovator that was most needed. It was said of Anderson that his two key principles were a fitting service of worship each Sunday and that he would be a helper of anyone in need. His semi-jubilee was particularly enjoyed that night in October 1951 as, on the night of his induction in September 1942, there were few visitors in attendance because of wartime restrictions on travel. Rev. A.D. Macleod of Pluscarden preached at Anderson's anniversary service on Sunday 7th October, 1951.

The Cathedral itself *almost* disappeared in the autumn of 1958 when the County of Angus development plan proposed that a 50 ft. roadway from the Castle gates through College yards along Chanonry Wynd to Bishop's Close be built. This would have resulted in the demolition of the Manse, outhouses and Hall and seriously compromised the Cathedral's own foundations. Fortunately, an objection to the Secretary of State for Scotland, John Maclay, proved successful.

Alastair Roy, assistant minister, was elected to Bridge Street Church in Wick in March 1955 and was replaced by Malcolm McLeod, though he had to retire in early 1956 due to his wife's illness. James Campbell from Caithness, a 37 year old who had been wounded in the war, became assistant in November 1956 and, having been called to Andwell-Sandhead in Wigtown was succeeded in May, 1958 by Bruce J.L. Hay of Aberdeen. William Lucy, a second year student at Aberdeen University, was also attached to the congregation over the autumn/winter of 1959-60. There was something of an inter-regnum after Bruce Hay departed in April 1959 for Lochgilphead, as Kenneth Lawson was not due to take up post until April 1960, therefore a retired minister, Rev.

---

[30] Friday 5th October, 1951 was the night of the reception at the Mechanics.
[31] *Brechin Advertiser*, 9th October, 1951

A.G. Paisley from the Presbytery of Shetland, took up post as part-time assistant. As to Anderson himself, he was already showing signs of poor health, having missed Communion services in May 1957 and February 1959. But ultimately it was his wife's illness that resulted in him taking early retirement on 17th November, 1964, nine months prior to his seventieth birthday.

With Anderson's departure, further ecclesiastical alterations were also afoot! The Presbytery of Brechin and Fordoun united with those of Arbroath and Forfar to form the Presbytery ofAngus in March 1961. In late 1963 the congregation of St.Ninian's was dissolved and part of the assets transferred to the Cathedral. The Cathedral had lost its great liturgist and reformer but the pastor was about to arrive.

CHAPTER TEN
Crisis and Controversy

A Church of Scotland minister has been suspended from all duties at Brechin Cathedral over the "unsatisfactory state" of the congregation. The Rev Robin Mackenzie was the subject of a rare committee of inquiry set up by Angus Presbytery. The decision was taken after the presbytery heard evidence from both the committee and Dr Mackenzie.

In a statement yesterday, the presbytery said: "It felt this would be unlikely to be put right if the pastoral tie continued, and the presbytery therefore voted to dissolve the pastoral tie, suspending the minister forthwith from all ministerial duties."

- **Glasgow Herald newspaper, 22nd September, 1997**

If James Anderson had been the Liturgist with a passion for stained glass, Peter was very much the pastor with the common touch, the "people's pastor". Elected on 3rd May, 1965, by 427 votes for to 35 against, Peter moved the Cathedral into a different gear, being the first minister to be born in the twentieth century and was a distinct change from the Victorian gentlemen of Tait Hutchison and Anderson. Peter, given his experience in Church extension charges, was keen to engage with the community; though his lack of experience in a "traditional church" did arouse some opposition locally, at least to begin with! It may seem strange to begin this chapter of controversies and crisis with Peter, for, as he himself admitted, he benefitted from a very stable period of ministry in the Kirk[1]. Yet this is significant in understanding what will occur later in this chapter.

---

[1] DMin interview with Rev Peter Gordon on 9th October, 2013

Peter Mitchell Gordon (1965-85) was born in Aberdeen on 1st July, 1930, the son of Daniel Gordon and Peggy Mitchell. Educated at Ellon then Aberdeen University, Peter gained an M.A. in 1952 and his B.D. in 1957. His studies were interrupted by a period of National Service in the Royal Artillery from 1952-54. Licensed by Aberdeen Presbytery in April 1957, he served as assistant at Aberdeen West of St. Andrews (1955-56) then Holburn Central (1956-57) before doing his probationary assistantship at Glasgow Castlemilk East (1957-59) where he was ordained in 1958. This period in one of the most deprived areas of Glasgow amongst the working class gave Peter a keen sense of social justice that was later to be reflected both in his political leanings and his ministry style. It was not surprising therefore that on 30th August, 1959 Peter was inducted to Dundee Camperdown, a Church extension charge that, as yet, did not have a building. The

Church itself opened for worship on Sunday 12th February, 1961. Also in October, 1961, Peter married a deaconess, Fiona McDonald (daughter of a Procurator of the Church) and the couple were to have three sons.

Peter was translated to Brechin Cathedral on 7th July, 1965, a year after Camperdown had been granted full status as a congregation. He then moved to Airdrie West on 5th September, 1985 and retired in 1995. Peter currently lives just outside Cupar with his wife, Fiona, and might rightly be considered as the "Father" of Brechin Cathedral at the present time, still keeping an active interest in the congregation.

By the time Peter arrived at the Cathedral in the summer of 1965, several assistants had come and gone. Ken Lawson had gone off in May 1961 to become sub-warden at St. Ninian's in Crieff and would very much make his name in Eldership training. Gordon W. Gilmour lasted only a few short summer weeks in 1961 and "felt compelled for health and domestic reasons" to resign at the end of August.[2]

Peter got to work quickly! In the September of 1965 he launched a District Visitation scheme by which folk could get to know the minister and he could get to know them. In the October he sought to re-launch the Youth Fellowship which had declined and finally closed. In the spring of 1966, a Study Group was formed to look at "The broken Church". In early 1966, despite urgings by the General Assembly, the congregation decided not to adopt the Model Constitution but adhere to *Quod Omnia*[3]. It was also agreed that from summer 1966, the evening service would be dispensed with June – August, replaced with an earlier service at 9.15am. That same summer, agreement was reached by the four Church of Scotland congregations to have monthly joint evening services and special joint services; it was to be tried as an experiment for a year. Transport for older members of the congregation was initiated on the 3rd Sunday of each month. In May 1967, a "Prayers at eight" service was begun at 8pm in the Queen's Aisle each Sunday in June. A revolutionary change occurred in January 1968 when "pew rent" was finally abolished in favour of Weekly Freewill Offering; this resulted in a considerable increase in givings of £5503 over 1968, an average of 1s/6d per member.The Cathedral, along with her three sister churches, decided not however to participate in the Stewardship campaign of the Parish development programme. To the chagrin of the then Session Clerk, D.B. Thoms, Peter, in common with most ministers of the Church of Scotland, stopped baptisms after the morning service at 12.30pm and returned to the Reformed practice of the sacrament taking place in the face of the

---

[2] Ibid., 11th September, 1961
[3] In the Model Constitution, the practical affairs such as finance and fabric were administered by a Congregational Board. In *Quod Omnia*, all matters were dealt with by the Kirk Session.

congregation! In Communion too the dress code changed in the late 1960s with the abandonment of tail-coats and "strippit troosers" for the elders serving Communion. For most of Peter's ministry the Sunday school numbers hovered around 100 though dipped towards the latter years.

Perhaps the most notable event in Peter's twenty year ministry was the 75/750 celebrations of 1976-77. These were to mark both the 75th anniversary of the Cathedral's restoration in 1902 and the 750th anniversary of the Cathedral being completed in c.1227. The initial thought behind these celebrations came in 1975 and Lt. Col. W.J. Campbell Adamson (whose great-grandfather had been chair of the Restoration Committee in 1902) was approached to be the Chair. These celebrations also coincided with the onset of local government re-organisation and the winding up of the Brechin Town Council. The celebrations began in August 1976 with a Flower Festival whose theme was "Beautify the place of my sanctuary" with no fewer than twenty-six floral arrangements. In November 1976 a special Songs of Praise "Hymns through the Ages" was held, followed on 23rd January 1977 by a United Service with St. Andrew's Episcopal Church at which Bishop Luscombe preached, the first bishop to preach in the Cathedral since 1689! A Service of Thanksgiving was held on 17th April, 1977, this marking the 75th anniversary of the Cathedral's re-opening after the Restoration works. There were also exhibitions, lectures, music and organ recitals and many fund raising events, perhaps the big fund-raiser being the Grand Bazaar in August 1977 which raised £2320 (the cookery book alone raised £720). One of the exhibitions included a 17th century Communion Cup and the trowel (lent by the Grand Lodge of Freemasons) which had been used to lay the cornerstone of the Chancel in 1902. However, the anniversary event that is best remembered of the 75/750 year is undoubtedly "Round about a Tower", the historical pageant staged in the Cathedral from Tuesday 7th June – Saturday 11th June, 1977. This was an elaborate and costumed retelling of the Cathedral's story from 1237 - 1902 in twelve acts; written by Kenneth Dron, Rector at the High School and produced by Harry Douglas. The production involved the whole community of Brechin ranging from the Brechin Amateur Operatic Society to the U.S. Navy and Marine Corps who were then stationed at the Edzell base. The drama is seen through the eyes of the Beadle of All Time, who acts as interlocutor for the audience. Although all of the 75/750 celebrations were reputedly great fun, they did have a serious purpose: to raise much needed funds to clean the Cathedral stonework and protect it for another 75 years. The 75/750 events were wound up in November 1977 with the erection of a second cross on the Cathedral roof and a commemorative plaque being installed; thereafter the residue of the monies passed to the Society of Friends. At Peter's departure in 1985, the *Brechin Advertiser* commented on the 75/750 celebrations stating they "did much for the community spirit in the area at a time when the city and its surrounds were sorely in need of a boost."[4]

The other major issue during Peter's tenure concerned the Manse; this was perhaps a less successful outcome! Kirk House (25 Church St.) which had been bought in 1967 as additional accommodation for the congregation, particularly for youth groups and meetings, was sold in 1979 for £9135. The Manse, built in 1851, required a good deal of upgrading, not least gas central heating and rewiring. The estimated cost of this was in the region of £20,000 so there was a clear shortfall. The Session considered a variety of options: buying a new Manse in Park Road, building a new Manse on the site of the Old Stables in Bishop's Close or renovating and modernizing the existing building. By March 1978, the Session had decided to accept at least a *partial* modernization, with the East wing of the Manse being retained for congregational use as a kind of mini-Kirk House. During the summer of 1979, Peter and his family took an extended holiday in order for the work on the Manse to proceed a pace – at one stage there were thirty workmen on site! This allowed plumbing, central heating and joinery work to be undertaken; by Christmas 1979 the roof had been completed and redecoration commenced. A Manse Ways and Means Committee engaged in a great deal of varied fundraising to find the necessary funds to complete the project and were finally discharged in June 1982, any balance of monies transferring to the Fabric Fund. Yet, given that a new Manse was finally constructed in 1996 during Robin Mackenzie's ministry, perhaps the Session in the 1970s lacked the vision to address the very relevant issue of an old house. Peter certainly recalls that even after all the work was done, some problems with its fabric still continued. There were problems in the Manse kitchen with condensation and the gas supply[5]; sometimes the Manse doorbell didn't work! Remarkably it took nearly eighteen months to fit a new bell![6] Further re-decoration was required in the Manse in the summer of 1984 at the cost of £230.

Peter's period as Minister of the Cathedral was generally a very stable period (see Communion and Membership Statistics in the Appendix). In many ways (as the reader may by now have gathered) stability at the Cathedral was the aberration rather than the rule! We also get an excellent glimpse of this in the Church Census figures in March 1984, where between 123 – 180 adults and between 40 – 64 children attended worship over the month. Though there were some changes too: individual cups became the norm at forenoon Communion services, with Common cup offered at the afternoon Sacrament. In 1980 an additional Communion service was introduced on the last Sunday in August

---

[4] *Brechin Advertiser*, 29th August, 1985
[5] Kirk Session minutes, 9th March 1982 & 7th February 1983.
[6] Ibid., 7th February 1983 & 12th June 1984

with the Communion in June employing Common cup. In the summers of the early 1980s congregational Picnics (followed by a Songs of Praise style service) were held at both Lochlee and Garvock Hill; it was hardly as if Peter was running out of innovative steam! By the 1980s though, changes were afoot. The great historian and Session Clerk, D.B.Thoms, who had bridged James Anderson and Peter Gordon's ministries died in January, 1980 and in 1981 no less than six long-standing elders passed to glory (many of them ordained by James Anderson in March 1943.) It was as if the end of an era was approaching.

Peter celebrated the semi-jubilee of his ordination on 9th March, 1983 with a social reception in the Mechanics Hall on Friday 11th March and a special service held on Sunday 13th March at which Rev. David T. Reid, BA, BD, of the West Kirk in Helensburgh was guest preacher. David had been the minister at Castlemilk during Peter's assistantship. Everyone who spoke on these occasions mentioned Peter's work as an "encourager". He was presented with a set of new robes by Miss May Bruce, someone whose association with the Cathedral went back to 1915 and whose father had been Session Clerk for many years. Needless to say that with two hundred folk present and Peter being the chatterbox, the event overran its time; the Guild ladies becoming somewhat anxious that they had to clear up from the social and still be fresh and ready for the coffee morning the following day!

Two Moderators of the General Assembly visited the Cathedral in this period: Rt. Rev. Prof. John McIntyre in October, 1982 attended an evening service[7] and two years later in December, 1984, Rt. Rev. Dr. Fraser McLuskey was to visit in the afternoon for a small reception and short service.[8] However, after a long run of ministry by some twenty years, Peter intimated in May, 1985[9] that he had been elected as sole nominee by Airdrie West and would be taking up his new post in the early autumn. Rev. John Becke was asked to be locum and Rev. Alex McKinnon of Careston was appointed by Presbytery as Interim Moderator. The "hallmarks" of Peter's ministry in Brechin were described by the Brechin Advertiser as: faithfulness in the Lord, enthusiasm, kindness, conscientious caring, encouragement and reliability. Fiona, his wife, it was reckoned had to be replaced in no less that thirteen different organisations![10]

Yet, Peter's departure for Airdrie left a number of problems in its wake, several of which would return to haunt the congregation. The Presbytery for one raised the issue

---

[7] 17th October, 1982
[8] 11th December, 1984
[9] Kirk Session minutes, 19th May, 1985
[10] *Brechin Advertiser*, 29th August, 1985

of re-adjustment in the local churches. While, by the July, they had decided to allow the Cathedral to call a minister "without restriction", it was made clear that this issue would be raised at a future date.[11] Several Elders took the opportunity to retire from key convenerships in the light of Peter's going: Mr. Usher (Convener of Music), Mr. West (Secretary of Youth and Education) and Mr. Bruce (Freewill offerings). The Presbytery too highlighted that while Sunday School numbers had increased a little to almost the previous year's level, there was still a very disappointing turnout at Sunday worship and Elders were remiss in failing to attend Session meetings. The future of the Badminton Club was uncertain as there were few leaders and several parents of Sunday School children were failing to attend Church, merely using the facility as free child-minding service. So too the Bible Class reported low numbers. It would be wrong to think that there were no clouds on the horizon as Peter departed and all these issues were to combine into a perfect ecclesiastical storm come the mid-1990s.

So what of the vacancy itself? What is perhaps most striking about the 1985 vacancy is the speed at which the post was filled; Alex McKinnon was an Interim Moderator in a hurry. The 22 person vacancy committee was elected on 1st September, 1985 and by 10th December the committee had its sole nominee, Rev. Dr. Robert (Robin) Mackenzie, who was to preach as sole nominee a mere two weeks later on Sunday 22nd December. McKinnon himself was the Vacancy committee chair and knew well Robin's father, also a minister. There is some corroborated evidence, from those who served on that Vacancy committee, that Alex McKinnon had used his influence as Interim Moderator to secure Robin's appointment. Whatever the circumstances, it cannot be denied that after a twenty year ministry the congregation would have benefitted from a much longer breathing space in which to re-assess their priorities for the future. Three months was hardly long enough to achieve this. Whatever else was to transpire in the future, the speed at which the vacancy was filled and the lack of opportunity for a period of congregational reflection must surely be a contributory factor to the oncoming storm.

---

[11] Kirk Session minutes, 14th July, 1985

A PERFECT ECCLESIAL STORM

Robert (Robin) Mackenzie (1986-98) was born in Madras, India on 13th February, 1950 to Robert Paterson Mackenzie, a minister, and Jessie Ree. Educated at George Watson's College, a private school in Edinburgh, Robin was to gain his M.A. at Edinburgh in 1972 followed by a B.D. (1975) and a PhD (1984). Robin was a very gifted and able classics scholar. He was licensed by the Presbytery of Dunfermline in July 1975. Also that month he married one Susannah Clinton and the couple were to have three daughters, including twins. Appointed as Assistant minister at Hamilton Old and Auchingramont (1975 -77), it was during his time in Hamilton that Robin was ordained on 9th May, 1976. Inducted to his first charge of Creich linked with Rosehall (at Bonar Bridge in Sutherland) on 30th April, 1980, he was then translated to Brechin Cathedral on 20th March 1986.

Robin's call was signed by more members than had signed Peter's in 1965, namely 630 souls, and at first things continued pretty much as they had in the latter days of Peter's ministry. Financial givings were somewhat down at first, but this was to be expected during a vacancy period. There was some discussion in the spring of 1986 over the use of individual glasses versus common cup for Communion, but, after much debate the present practice of that time continued, namely individual cup in the morning and common cup at the afternoon sitting. In December, 1985, just five days after Robin preaching as sole nominee, the glass display cabinet was broken into and several items stolen: 2 pewter flagons (1680), 3 pewter pattens (1660), 2 silver plated common cups (1880), 4 silver plated common cups (1902), a silver baptismal basin (1807) and a silver lid (1967). To date only the 1680 pewter flagons (gifted by Walter Jameson, late Baillie and Kirkmaster) have been returned. Located at an open air stall in London by one of Sotheby's staff, they were brought back into the Cathedral on Christmas morning 1988 by Gordon Smith, Session Clerk, and Jim Pilmer, senior elder on duty[12]. On the lid of one of the flagons is the earliest existing picture of the Cathedral, so it is of great historic significance. Perhaps the 800th anniversary of the Cathedral in 2020 will prompt some other honest citizen to return the remaining items?

---

[12] *Dundee Courier and Advertiser*; Wednesday 28th December, 1988
The Kirk Session minute of November, 17th, 1680 records: "This day in the presence of the Minister, elders and deacons of the Town Session of Brechin, Walter Jameson, late bailie and present Kirkmaster, presented two tin quart stoups, freely gifted by him, they having letters drawn about the bulges of them, with his name engraved on them, showing that they are dedicated by him to serve at the Communion tables, when the sacrament of the Lord's Supper shall be administered."
The three pewter patens of 1660 were gifted by John Mill, Kirk officer.

The second blow came just after Robin's induction in February 1986 when it was estimated that the organ required a major overhaul, at a cost of £10,620. By April, 1987, union and re-adjustment within Brechin had also been raised again by Presbytery after the vacancy at Maison Dieu Church; Presbytery decided at their October meeting to continue this vacancy along with that at Stracathro Church. In February 1988 we glimpse the first of the darker clouds looming during a Session meeting; there was some disgruntlement amongst the Elders over the choice of hymns on a Sunday (a matter actually reserved solely to the Minister under the authority of Presbytery), that there be a wider choice of those doing pulpit supply and that there was little interest or involvement of young people with the Church[13]. At that same meeting the Session agreed also to a different way of addressing the issue of lapsed members; those on the Supplementary Roll would be visited annually by the District Elder, receive a copy of the monthly magazine and still receive an invitation to attend Communion services. The lapsed

---

[13] Kirk Session minutes, 9th February 1988

"would be restored to full membership whenever they resumed an actual interest in the Church."[14] In truth, the cold winds of secularism were being felt at last, even in Brechin! Again in June 1988 the poor attendance at Sunday school and at the afternoon Communion service (30 in May 1988) once again was raised, though few solutions offered. In August of 1989, a proposal was made to discontinue the afternoon Communion service, though Robin was of the view that Common Cup and individual glasses could not be used in the same service so, for the time being, the practice of two diets of Communion (the afternoon service having Common Cup) continued.

By autumn 1989, we see that the then Session Clerk, Gordon Smith, had intimated his resignation having served ten years under two ministers. Also by this stage, two other serious storm clouds appeared on the horizon. Rev. J Perry, minister at Farnell, had decided to retire, raising once more the spectre of Re-adjustment within Brechin (Maison Dieu and Stracathro churches still being vacant). The Cathedral finances had also reached an impasse with expenditure exceeding congregational giving by 15%. Certainly, there was a decrease of giving of £483 in 1989 from the previous year, but the Thatcher government had cut the basic rate of income tax, which in turn impacted upon Deeds of Covenant. A special Kirk Session meeting was convened in December, 1989 at which it was made clear that while previous deficits had been met by utilising reserves, "the reserves were now exhausted, this remedy was no longer available."[15] Furthermore, £125,000 was required to maintain the Cathedral's fabric otherwise "the fabric of the buildings would deteriorate rapidly and would soon be beyond repair."[16] Grant agencies would assist to some degree and one member gave an interest free loan of £2000 to offset the current shortfall. While the Session agreed to review their own level of giving, they baulked somewhat at the suggestion to regularly ask those within their Districts for financial contributions. It is clear from the minutes of this meeting that Robin did not shirk from presenting to the Session a fairly grim but realistic picture; the "sunny days" of Peter Gordon had long passed and some Elders would grow to resent this. A joint Communion service was planned with Fern, Careston and Menmuir, presumably with a view to possible linkage.

In January, 1990, a Quinquennial visit of Presbytery coincided with a visit by the Presbytery of Angus Re-appraisal Committee. The Re-appraisal team of Rev. J, Stevenson and Rev. G. Ramsay raised the prospect of a linkage between Maison Dieu, Stracathro and the Cathedral. The Session passed the following motion at that key meeting:

---

[14] Ibid.
[15] Kirk Session minutes, 3rd December, 1989
[16] Ibid.

That the Kirk Session is pleased to continue negotiations with Maison Dieu and Stracathro with a view to a union, with the understanding that if either of these buildings be kept open for worship it should not be a drain on resources and that the name of Brechin Cathedral continue to be used.[17]

What is of interest is that motion was actually amended at the February meeting and the January minute altered accordingly. Robin himself expressed some disquiet that the Session, as he saw it, attached pre-conditions to the ongoing discussions with the other congregations. An elder thought it "inappropriate" that Robin should have expressed an opinion at all; perhaps forgetting that the Minister of the charge had to agree to the discussions to begin with before any could actually take place! However, we see in this little episode the beginnings of the divisions between Minister and some elders that were to follow. The Basis of Union was agreed fairly quickly and the service of union took place on 21st September 1990. The Cathedral remained as the principal place of worship with weekly services (9am and 11am), Maison Dieu would continue to have fortnightly services for six months (10am) and Stracathro monthly services (11.30am) for a year after the date of union.[18] One other major change was in the governance of the congregation; no longer was Brechin Cathedral *quod omnia*[19], a Congregational Board was introduced on the basis of the Model Constitution. Robin's skill and expertise guided both the united office-bearers and congregation through these confusing early days as they became acquainted not only with each other but with new systems of church governance and changed committee structures. It is easy to forget, given the later difficulties which developed, that the union started harmoniously and that the enormous amount of work Robin and others put into ensuring the union would work effectively. There were, of course, some teething problems; some elders saw the union as an opportunity to retire, while others simply resigned. Christmas 1990 created its own set of issues regarding services, though, in the end, Maison Dieu had a 6.30pm on Christmas Eve, the Cathedral a Watchnight service and Stracathro a Christmas Day service. The complexity of a three church centre worship calendar could not however continue indefinitely.

In December 1990, following a letter received from fifteen former Maison Dieu office-bearers, a special Kirk Session meeting was called with a view to the early cessation of continuation of services at Maison Dieu. The Session unanimously agreed to this on the grounds that it was an "expressed desire to further the unity of the

---

[17] Ibid., 9th January, 1990 as amended 13th February, 1990

[18] Note that the monthly services at Stracathro still continue, twenty seven years on! As I write this, Maison Dieu, long closed and running to derelict, now has planning permission for a series of flats.

[19] That is to say, the Kirk Session dealing with all matters, both spiritual and temporal.

congregation."[20] Regular services at 10am in Maison Dieu would end but occasional ad hoc services might be held there. It soon became clear that despite the goodwill engendered in the union, Robin, as minister was under considerable strain with a congregational Roll of just under two thousand. The sheer size of the newly united congregation meant there were problems supplying adequate pastoral care, the administrational burden was heavy and sufficient communication amongst office-bearers proved challenging. There is also the intriguing comment that the "atmosphere must be changed, to be dominated more by encouragement and less by criticism."[21] It would seem that the expectations of at least part of the congregation towards Robin were highly unrealistic, given this added workload caused by the union. By the early autumn of 1993 the Session were further challenged by a General Assembly directive that ministers have two full days off per week. Discussion ensued and some provision was made for Robin to have free time through the assistance of retired ministers; what is of interest from the minutes is that, despite receiving several generous bequests in this period, and that the pastoral demands of the charge had not in any way decreased, the Congregational Board was still unable to come forward with a funding package for ministerial assistance. Any minister in this situation might begin to have a crisis in morale!

In addition to all this, there was the question of the Manse! Was the Bishop's Close property to be kept and upgraded? Was the Airlie Street Manse (that of Maison Dieu Church) to be utilised? Or was a completely new and purpose built Manse to be the preferred option? Arguments ranged across all these options; cost, historical sentiment and practicality all playing a part. The Session resolved in January 1991 to upgrade the Bishop's Close property but Presbytery (mindful that this had already been attempted in Peter Gordon's time and that the Manse dated from 1850) questioned whether such a historical building was proper for a modern ministry. Had the Session really considered the needs of the Manse family? The debate continued and the decision was reviewed by Session in April 1991 when it became clear that some £80,000 would be required to upgrade the existing Manse. Finally, in late June, an option presented itself to build a new, modern Manse on the site of the garden of the Episcopal Rectory and this won the support of the vast majority of the Session. In June 1993, an attempt was made to review or even rescind this decision which was later withdrawn. It would though take another five years until the new Manse in Chanonry Wynd was ready for occupation in 1996.

During the early 1990s there were a number of elders who resigned from post, largely for health reasons, yet there are clear signs too of poor morale amongst elders. By

---

[20] Kirk Session minutes, 11th December, 1990
[21] Ibid., 8th January, 1991

May 1993 it was noted that several elders were failing to attend either Session or worship. A Rededication service for elders was held on Sunday 5th September at which thirty seven elders attended. This may seem a good total until we recollect that there were sixty two elders![22]

Later that autumn a Quinquennial visitation by Presbytery took place which opened the door to a whole series of issues, some relevant, others less so[23]. The Presbytery Committee's visit had not been due until 1994/95, but was in fact brought forward a year due to concerns over the ministry demands of the newly united charge. The first meeting between Session and Presbytery representatives in November 1993 had proved abortive as only thirteen elders had attended, so a subsequent meeting in December was scheduled. At this meeting there were complaints that Robin was involved in too many Presbytery commitments; worries too over attracting young people, low congregational morale and the poor choice of music on a Sunday morning all featured. As a result an ad-hoc Committee was set up by Presbytery "to offer pastoral care and encouragement and guidance", this committee to report back not later than November 1994.[24] This Committee was to meet with the congregation in September 1994 during a Sunday service. However, at this very same Session meeting on 8th February, 1994 a second crisis arose: Lynda Reid, the Session Clerk, resigned both as Clerk and as an elder. She felt she had come under considerable pressure and that an elder had indicated he did not have a "comfortable relationship" with her. The Session re-convened two days later but since none of the Cathedral Elders were willing to take on the role, one of the Presbytery's ad-hoc Committee, Dr Donald Mowat of Montrose Old Church, agreed to act as Clerk *pro tempore*.[25]

The Presbytery's ad-hoc Committee duly met with both Kirk Session and Congregational Board on 22nd March, 1994. A very large number of issues presented themselves to the Committee; apathy was the defining word. People, it was stated, would contribute financially to the Cathedral, but not attend. Robin himself was criticised for not visiting, having poor social talk skills, and being over-intellectual in his sermons and children's talks, so much so that the High School no longer attended the Cathedral for special services. Some felt Robin's voice was off-putting and his manner over-legalistic. One major complaint was that, as minister, he had little confidence in his office-bearers and ended up doing tasks allocated to them or even re-doing what others had done. An

---

[22] Therefore a turnout of approximately 60%.

[23] The reader will forgive me if I outline these matters in some detail, since they are of such crucial importance to the more recent history of the Cathedral.

[24] Kirk Session minutes, 8th February, 1994, Presbytery of Angus minutes, 1st February, 1994

[25] Kirk Session minutes, 8th March, 1994

advisory group of members to assist with worship had, it was said, been negative rather than positive in outcome as it had put Robin onto the defensive. He was, some said, "a square peg in a round hole" and people came out of Church "empty and angry".[26] All in all, it was not a happy situation for anyone. A day after the meeting, senior Presbytery officials privately expressed the view that unless there were changes in leadership style from the Minister "nothing will be fully remedied under the present Minister."[27] Any change, they insisted, would be too little, too late. This rather damning view would, in my view, rather colour all further discussions and one wonders whether Presbytery officials were wise in so markedly expressing a preferred outcome to the situation at this early stage.

It was not just the members of Session who were now reluctant to be motivated. An attempt to have a Christian Commitment Stewardship Programme was stopped in its tracks as only thirty two office-bearers and five members had agreed to be involved; this was considerably short of the one hundred volunteers needed.[28] In May 1994, rather unexpectedly, Robin raised the issue of a possible vacancy at the Cathedral and the difficulties that might ensue from this. Had Robin applied for another charge? Or was he simply calling the Session's bluff? One can only speculate, though there is just a hint of a threat in the minutes. Robin certainly urged a measure of secrecy around the issue, instructing the elders present not to discuss the matter with anyone outside of the meeting. Elders were urged to attend worship, visit their districts and regularly attend Session meetings. At the June meeting, it becomes clear that divisions are occurring in the Session itself. Two elders had written expressing support for Robin while another elder stated that "Dr Mackenzie had a great deal to answer for" in the present difficulties, all the problems could not be laid at the feet of the Session.[29] The problems were now developing into a full scale conflict situation.

In the Church Magazine of July 1994, Robin wrote of the role of the Moderator of the Kirk Session and his words bear scrutiny:

> …(The Moderator) is not supposed to be merely a disinterested chairman.
> Certainly it is his job to know what the rules are, what the laws and practice of the
> Church of Scotland are, and to see that they are followed. But *it is always also his*
> *job to do what he believes will be in the best Christian interests of his*
> *congregation. Sometimes this will mean that he will remain silent and not let his*
> *personal views be known. Sometimes it will mean that he ought to argue*

---

[26] Minute of Presbytery Ad-Hoc Committee, 22nd March, 1994

[27] Presbytery of Angus records, 23rd March, 1994

[28] Ibid., 10th May, 1994

[29] Ibid., 7th June, 1994

214

vigorously for a particular course of action. I trust that you will ever pray that I will be given the grace, wisdom and courage to make the right choices.[30]

Clearly some in the congregation were unhappy with Robin's more directive style of leadership, and perhaps even with the direction he was taking the Church. As an observer to these events, it might be recalled that as far back as the Medieval period there had been tensions over governance between the Bishop and the Chapter; this may have started as yet another instance of this. Unfortunately this particular crisis would deepen further into a full blown storm.

By November, the Sunday school comprised of just one child and there was still no sign of a new Session Clerk (though Lynda Reid returned as Minute Clerk in December). After six months involving eleven meetings with Robin, three with the office-bearers and eight on their own, the Presbytery's ad-hoc Committee was discharged[31] and now the Superintendence Committee had to decide whether the congregation was in a satisfactory state or not. Robin outlined the serious situation to the Session at their meeting on 8th November and concluded with these extraordinary words: "an experienced Minister in a normal situation simply ignored gossip. This situation was, however, far from normal and those Elders who had joined in the small-town entertainment of gossiping and speculating, had to realise that they might have done the congregation great harm." "Well intentioned promises for the future" were not enough; decisions would be made on past record and present practice. [32] The lines of battle were beginning to be drawn and this was most certainly impacting on the congregation. At the October diet of Communion a mere 280 attended out of a membership of 1569 (18%).[33]

In addition, relations between the Cathedral and South Esk Church had deteriorated. There were no joint services between the Cathedral and South Esk Church at Christmas 1993. In the summer of 1994, a squabble arose between Robin and Rev. James Drysdale (minister at South Esk) over the use of raffles in the Church of Scotland. Robin wrote to the Principal Clerk, Rev. Dr. James Weatherhead for advice and the issue was raised at Presbytery in the September.

In January, 1995 the Presbytery Superintendence Committee met to consider the report by the Visitation Committee. The result of this meeting was Presbytery were unable to find Brechin Cathedral to be in a "satisfactory" state. Two elders of the

---

[30] *Cathedral Magazine*, July 1994; emphasis mine.

[31] Presbytery of Angus minutes, 1st November, 1994

[32] Kirk Session minutes, 8th November, 1994

[33] Even in these more secular times, the average for most congregations is between 30 – 35% of the membership.

Cathedral had made submissions to Presbytery, one suggesting that, while Robin had many intellectual abilities, the best course of action would be his departure. Another elder highlighted the somewhat difficult relationship between elders and minister, though it was suggested that this was characteristic of Brechin, not just the Cathedral. At a special Session meeting on 29th January this decision was communicated to the elders. This resulted in a somewhat confused and acrimonious meeting. Robin faced down his opponents who made several complaints against him, ranging from an inability to engage in "small talk" to worship being in a "19th century time warp" and sermons being too "high brow". The problem with all of this was its subjectivity which, nevertheless, was having an adverse impact upon the morale and direction of the congregation. Some stated that the sermons were thought-provoking while another commended Robin for his courage "in the face of a degree of hostility and gossip over a number of years."[34]

What was the way forward? A committee of enquiry made up of three church folk from outside the Presbytery and three within would take soundings and "endeavour to remedy the situation."[35] Meantime, the Session agreed on its own motion:

> The future of the kirk depends on us getting people over the door of the kirk and for this reason we accept the deliverances of the report and invite Presbytery to act to help us endeavour to remedy the situation.[36]

The new committee of enquiry of six comprised of: Rev Colin Caskie (Convener, Carnoustie), Rev Lawrence Whitley (Montrose Old) and Mrs. Elma Reid (Inverarity) plus Rev Stewart Young (Blairgowrie), Rev Ken Petrie (Stonehaven) and Mr D Anderson (Broughty Ferry).[37] The problem with this new Committee was (as Robin himself stated in a letter to Rev. Graham Norrie, Presbytery Convener of Superintendence) that they *began* from a prior position of the Cathedral being in an unsatisfactory state without specifying *what* was unsatisfactory or *how* they might seek to remedy the situation; it was akin to providing a verdict without a jury hearing first the evidence. In fact, in a joint meeting of Kirk Session and Congregational Board on 31st March, 1995 with the Committee of six, many of the old grievances and complaints were once again aired. It was certainly a frank exchange of views, though these were light on suggested solutions to ingrained issues. These included: poor attendance at worship, tensions between some elders and the minister, a lack of communication with the congregation and worship being too high brow. Of 1600 members, the average congregation on a Sunday was twenty one.

---

[34] Kirk Session minutes, 29th January, 1995
[35] Ibid. Also Presbytery of Angus minutes, 7th February, 1995
[36] Kirk Session minutes, 29th January, 1995
[37] Presbytery of Angus minutes, 7th March, 1995

Meanwhile, to further complicate and confuse an already delicate pastoral situation, the national Parish Re-appraisal Committee decided to look again at Angus. For Brechin, the timing was at best unfortunate and at worst irresponsible. So on April 4th, 1995, Rev Alan Taylor, Convener of the Parish Re-appraisal Committee in the Kirk came to the Cathedral. The Session indicated that if further re-adjustment were to be pursued then the preference would be a linkage with a rural charge, rather than another town union. Yet, one elder made the rather telling comment: "the Church of Scotland was perhaps failing in its duty to ministers by creating bigger charges with the result that pastoral care subsequently suffered."[38] In a sense this was the nub of the issue; a much larger ecclesiastical unit had been created with the union of the Cathedral, Maison Dieu and Stracathro in 1990 but no-one (least of all Presbytery) had sat down to consider how this mammoth beast was to be managed. Whatever other factors were involved in the difficulties during Robin's tenure, we should not lose sight of this one. Indeed, at the Session meeting on 11th April to consider the Committee of six's report, Robin (not normally given to expressing his inner self) comes closest to admitting that he was stressed and in danger of ministerial "burn out". He was certainly conscious by now that his future in the ministry was under scrutiny and that, unlike many of his predecessors, he had no form of private income.[39] The result of the National Re-appraisal Committee's visit was that no suggested changes occur at the Cathedral because of its "distinctive form of worship", yet Oathlaw/Tannadice and Fern, Careston/Menmuir (presented with possible terminable tenure) approached the Cathedral to seek a possible linkage. The benefit for the Cathedral would have been a collegiate ministry with two ministers serving three charges, thus offsetting part of the stress of providing adequate pastoral care that Robin was under.

Yet it was clear that four elders in particular felt that the continued crisis at the Cathedral would really only be resolved by Robin's removal. At the May meeting of Presbytery, Robin moved a motion that would have delayed the matter being brought to a special meeting of Presbytery in late May on the grounds that no real attempt had been made by Superintendence to remedy the situation[40]. This attempt failed; however, when Presbytery re-convened on 30th May *in hunc effectum*[41] to deal specifically with the Cathedral's situation it was clear that in the light of the re-adjustment conversations it was better to allow time and delay. The following motion was thus agreed by Presbytery:

---

[38] Kirk Session minutes, 4th April, 1995
[39] Personal email to the author, 1st November, 2016
[40] Presbytery of Angus minutes, 2nd May, 1995
[41] Latin: for a special purpose

> In the case of Brechin Cathedral the Presbytery grant the Committee's request for time to give further consideration to matters which have arisen, and instruct them to bring forward their report as soon as is appropriate.[42]

Therefore since these adjustment discussions had entered a sensitive stage, any attempts to remove Robin were put on ice over the summer of 1995. If this crisis could be turned around, this was probably the key moment. To add to the more positive tone at this time, in May 1995, nine of the Cathedral's office-bearers had written to the Presbytery Clerk expressing their support for Robin, though it is noticeable that most of these were former Maison Dieu members. One elder expressed disquiet at four elders approaching Presbytery to complain about Robin without Session's knowledge; a more balanced view was needed and, with encouragement, Robin could undoubtedly get on with the duties of ministry in a more peaceful frame of mind. Lynda Reid, the ex-Session Clerk, perhaps had the most perceptive comments. She stated that "Dr Mackenzie is an honest, sensitive, caring pastor who simply cannot meet the high expectations of some of his congregation."[43] Only a few elders were committed to the congregation, resulting in a burden on an already overworked minister. Lynda's view was that Robin was being unfairly persecuted by a small group within the Session, who had little knowledge of the Presbyterian system or the problems facing the Church of Scotland nationally. Allowing for her natural bias towards her friend, Lynda nevertheless touched in this letter on some key elements that had exacerbated the crisis. The summer of 1995 also saw Grampian TV record three services at the Cathedral, partly around the 995 anniversary of King Cinaed Mac Mael Coluim II (r.971-995) dedicating the great monastery of Brechin to the Lord. These were judged to be a success and gave the congregation a much needed lift.

By the start of September, it was clear that the proposal from Presbytery's Church and Ministry Committee for re-adjustment in Brechin was in fact a linkage between the Cathedral and South Esk Church, with one full time and one part-time minister. There was no mention now of the Cathedral having a distinctive worship style, or a linkage with a rural charge. This proposal (for a linked charge of 3000 within a parish population of 6000) would again put additional pressure on ministry and dilute any form of reasonable pastoral care. When Session met again in October it seemed that the re-adjustment discussions were developing into a "free for all" and that a great deal of fear amongst congregations was prevalent.[44] This sense of fear was crippling any attempts at logical decision making. Thus Presbytery considered the Presbytery Plan proposals in a very lengthy *in hunc effectum* meeting on 17th October, 1995. Despite attempts by Robin

---

[42] Presbytery of Angus minutes, 30th May, 1995
[43] Presbytery of Angus records, 20th May, 1995
[44] Kirk Session minutes, 10th October, 1995

to introduce at this meeting a collegiate style ministry of three which would include Brechin Cathedral, Brechin Southesk, Fern/Careston/Menmuir, Oathlaw Tannadice, Edzell/Lethnot and Glenesk, Presbytery decided to stick with the Committee's proposals of 1.5 ministers for Brechin. The General Assembly's Committee on Re-adjustment then approved the Presbytery Plan in December.

Because of these re-adjustment discussions in late 1995 it was not until late March 1996 that the Committee of six returned to meet with the Cathedral office-bearers. This proved to be, once again, a rather fraught meeting and perhaps revealed how deep the divisions between Robin's supporters and detractors had become. One elder stated that Robin had now "lost the confidence of his congregation."[45] Another elder drew attention to the fact that historically the Cathedral had been "dominated by a forceful Session Clerk, who, along with the Kirk Session, were under the impression that the Session controlled the minister and dictated to him." Robin had sought to change that model and been strongly resisted.[46] Following the Committee's visit, the Presbytery met again in May when the issue of the continued situation at the Cathedral was once again taken up. The Presbytery's decision in the light of the Committee's report bears including verbatim:

1. Presbytery is unable to find the congregation of Brechin Cathedral to be in a satisfactory state.
2. Presbytery instructs the Superintendence Committee to seek to implement the following recommendations:

i) Appoint up to 12 Assessor Elders (one of whom should be available to act as Session Clerk) to be loosed from their present duties and to act with the elders of Brechin Cathedral for a period of one year: presbytery to be responsible for the payment of travelling expenses. All Kirk Sessions within the bounds to be asked to consider this matter and to bring forward nominations to the Superintendence Committee.

ii) Ask the Stewardship and Finance Committee of Presbytery to visit the office-bearers of Brechin Cathedral to offer advice.

iii) Arrange a Forward Plan to be drawn up and each member of the Kirk Session to be asked to place his/her name against a positive commitment plan of modest targets for the future. Thereafter offer a similar programme of targets to members of the Congregational Board.

---

[45] Kirk Session minutes, 26th March, 1996

[46] Ibid. Personally, I am not sure that this analysis bears scrutiny. It is certainly true from my D Min interviews that there is a consistent view that D B Thoms dominated the Cathedral landscape for many a long year, but his relationship with Peter Gordon seemed to be more that of fruitful partnership. The reader must judge for him/herself!

iv)   Invite office-bearers to attend a thriving Kirk Session meeting elsewhere in order to see "how it could be done" in Brechin Cathedral.

v)   Explore ways of bringing the minister and disaffected office-bearers into conversation.

3. Presbytery instructs the Superintendence Committee to *review the situation 12 months after the appointment of the first Assessor Elders.*

4.   Presbytery instructs the Clerks to report the current state of the Quinquennial Visitation to Brechin Cathedral to the Board of Practice and Procedure in accordance with Act II 1984.

5. Presbytery thanks the sub-Committee anent Brechin Cathedral for their diligence and discharges the Committee.[47]

I have highlighted a crucial clause in section 3 of the Presbytery's deliverance (or motion) which will be of importance later in our tale.

The Session met again on 14th May, 1996 to consider the Presbytery's decision as well as poor attendance by some elders at meetings and worship. One elder walked out of this meeting, expressing disquiet at the appointment of assessor elders by Presbytery. Another elder subsequently went on to resign his office of Roll-keeper as a result[48]. Once again the Session was without a Clerk, Lynda Reid having signalled her intention to relinquish her elder's duties since one elder had remarked that "(she) did not possess the temperament required."[49] Robin himself now temporarily took on that role. At the August meeting, ostensibly in connection with a discussion on pastoral care, we find this extraordinary statement from Robin in the minutes:

> As it is a widely held view that religion is a major cause of conflict in the world, and this is a commonly given reason for not wanting to have to do with the Church, it is well to remember that conflict keeps and drives people away. Being treated as mere numbers, as the equivalent of posteriors on pews or of collection bag fodder, being sucked dry and spat out, coping with power games, all are things which people get enough of elsewhere. Elsewhere too are plenty of groups which can satisfy an appetite for status. For the Church it should be millstone-round-the-neck stuff to manipulate people through their children. The Church is needed for none of these things. Rather, as the body of Christ it is here to express the humanity of Christ in the world, and, offering the humanity of God, always treat people with humanity as identifiable human beings.[50]

---

[47] Presbytery of Angus minutes, 7th May, 1996. Italics mine.

[48] Kirk Session minutes, 13th August, 1996

[49] Ibid., 14th May, 1996 & 11th June, 1996

[50] Ibid., 13th August, 1996

Whatever was originally behind this outburst of feelings, it certainly begins to show to observers, like ourselves, the level of stress that the whole situation within the Cathedral had put Robin under. So too Robin commented in the Cathedral Magazine that "you will have gathered from the press that some office-bearers seem to have difficulties with me."[51] Robin goes on "any office-bearer airing difficulties with me through gossip or on the street are seriously failing their fellow office-bearers and the congregation as a whole. Should you find any thus speaking you are quite entitled to remind them of that."[52] If the rumours were bad, things were about to get even worse!

On 20th September, 1996, a letter had been hand delivered to the Cathedral Manse by Rev. Martin Fair, the new Convener of Superintendence, citing Robin to appear at Presbytery on 1st October. It appears that the Superintendence Committee, contrary to that which had been decided by Presbytery in May, now intended to review again the situation at the Cathedral (well before the twelve months stated.) Their arguments in support of this decision were as follows:

1. It had proved impossible for Presbytery to get 12 Assessor Elders from other congregations. Only 5 had volunteered, two of which were unsuitable. This left three elders, which the Superintendence Committee deemed were insufficient for its purposes.
2. There had been a fairly negative response from the Cathedral Kirk Session to a suggestion of a Stewardship Campaign.
3. Martin Fair had issued a "Commitment Questionnaire" to Cathedral office-bearers on 22nd August, 1996; again the response had been fairly poor.
4. No-one had volunteered to attend a "thriving Kirk Session" elsewhere.
5. Only three elders from the Session had been prepared to enter into discussions with the Committee over their fraught relationships with Robin.

In short, it was proving impossible for the Superintendence Committee to fulfil the instructions given to them by Presbytery in May, so they now wanted to move things on earlier than intended. Without impugning the reasoning of the Committee, it would have been rather convenient in terms of Presbytery planning for a vacancy to occur at the Cathedral at this juncture. Rev Jim Drysdale at Southesk Church was likely to retire in the next few years[53] and the Cathedral was about to open a new modern, purpose built manse. With a "double vacancy" the plan for 1.5 ministers in Brechin could have been achieved with a new manse as an attractive "carrot" for any applicants. Events however were to take a different turn.

---

[51] *Cathedral Magazine*, July 1996
[52] Ibid.
[53] Rev Jim Drysdale retired on 31st January, 1999, some six months after Robin's departure.

At the meeting of Presbytery on 1ˢᵗ October, Presbytery (despite a motion to the contrary from Robin) decided to receive the Superintendence Committee's report and Robin dissented and sought leave to appeal. The matter was now "sisted" (or put on hold) by Presbytery's Moderator, Rev. Brian Ramsay, until Robin's appeal was duly received and dealt with. However, come the November meeting of Presbytery, Finlay Macdonald, Principal Clerk to the General Assembly, had advised that in fact Presbytery need not delay on a procedural appeal from hearing the report by the Superintendence Committee; Act VII (1996) of the General Assembly stating that "an appeal on part of a case or on a point of procedure does not sist procedure." While Finlay Macdonald was undoubtedly legally correct, can we consider him correct in terms of the morality of natural justice (since part of the basis of Robin's subsequent appeal was based on the fact that Presbytery had proceeded to consider the situation at Brechin *before* the twelve months agreed had elapsed)? Heavy legal waters were now being entered. Consequently, Presbytery resolved that a Committee of Inquiry was now to be set up, comprising Rev W Bruce (retired, Carnoustie), Rev R McCrum (Forfar: Lowson Memorial), Mrs E Adamson (Kirriemuir) and Mr H Jackson (Aberlemno). Effectively, Presbytery was now suggesting that unless the pastoral tie between Robin and Cathedral was dissolved, the unsatisfactory state of affairs would continue.[54] It became apparent however that the advice given by the Principal Clerk on the matter (that the Superintendence report be heard) was at variance from advice given by the Presbytery Clerk! Robin further argued that the congregation had not been cited as an interested party at the November meeting of Presbytery and that the Superintendence Committee was in a total breach of trust having brought the matter forward after five, rather than the twelve months earlier agreed. Procedure was now confusing an already complicated situation. It also seemed to be the case that some in Presbytery wanted a swift end to the ongoing issues and felt that Robin was coming close to prevaricating. Letters in support of Robin once again began to be sent to the Presbytery Clerk. One member wrote that certain elders had disgraced themselves by openly stating on the street "when are we going to get rid of him?" Lynda Reid, former Session Clerk, was again fulsome in praise of Robin. Her feeling was that there was a personal vendetta against him by a few elders who, she stated, had a "scant awareness" of the Presbyterian system. This situation was exacerbated by a general religious decline in the nation and an historic building that was "unviable" in a climate of declining spiritual awareness.[55]

---

[54] Presbytery of Angus minutes, 5ᵗʰ November, 1996 & see also Act I 1988 of the General Assembly for background on the legal situation.
[55] Presbytery of Angus records, October – November 1996

In November 1996, in the midst of all this ecclesiastical wrangling, Robin and his family moved into the new manse in Chanonry Wynd. Finally too in December 1996, Kenneth Allan was appointed as the new Session Clerk. The Committee of Inquiry got to work early in 1997. During this period, while life appears normal from the minutes and the work of the congregation certainly continued, one gains the impression that there is a considerable underlying tension and a haemorrhaging of attendances at meetings. Suddenly, on 16th September, 1997, a *pro re nata*[56] meeting of the Presbytery was called to consider the Committee of Inquiry's report into Brechin Cathedral. The final judgement of Presbytery was as follows:

1. The congregation of Brechin Cathedral is in an unsatisfactory state.
2. The unsatisfactory state will continue unless the pastoral tie between Minister and congregation is dissolved.
3. Dissolves the pastoral tie from 28th September, 1997.
4. Suspends the minister forthwith from all ministerial duties.
5. Declares the charge of Brechin Cathedral vacant from the above date.
6. Calls on the Kirk Session of Brechin Cathedral to examine itself, its recent actions and motives, and to accept the help and support of Presbytery to achieve a more spiritual basis.[57]

Robin, naturally enough, appealed to the Assembly's Judicial Commission and Brian Ramsay was appointed as Interim Moderator.

It must be noted that the dissolving of a pastoral tie only occurs under the most extreme circumstances, when all other possible avenues to remedy a situation have been exhausted. Because only the minute of the final judgement of Presbytery is available (the actual records of the Presbytery meeting of 16th September, 1997, being kept apart and destroyed in 2002) it is impossible to say what arguments were employed to reach this state of affairs. One contributing factor may have been that the Presbytery Clerk (Robert Ramsay) having resigned in June, Malcolm Rooney, the new Clerk wanted to quickly tidy up matters left in abeyance by his predecessor and this included the Cathedral. Of course, we must recall too that the situation began some four years previously with the Presbytery committee's visit in 1993. On news of Presbytery's decision reaching the congregation, two elders who had supported Robin immediately resigned on principle. Others waited to see how the wind would now blow.

Because Robin's suspension from duty took effect immediately upon the Presbytery meeting on 16th September, it fell to a retired minister, Rev. Tom Milroy[58] to

---

[56] Latin, literally "that which has come to birth", used in the event of urgent business that cannot be delayed.
[57] Presbytery of Angus minutes, 16th September, 1997

convey the judgement of Presbytery to the congregation when he arrived to conduct morning service on Sunday 21st September. For many this was the first they knew about it. The *Brechin Advertiser* reported that "after the service, many of the congregation were seen to be leaving the Cathedral in tears. Others left as soon as the announcement had been made."[59] As a result, Anna Don, one of Robin's main supporters, organised a three hundred signature petition in his favour. Letters too began to appear in the newspapers. One from a former Maison Dieu member read: "there were too many snobs at the Cathedral" and complained that Robin had lacked support from elders, yet also acknowledged that Robin's sermons were "sometimes above my head."[60] Another stated: "supporters of Rev. Mackenzie were far more willing to stand up and be counted than his detractors, who preferred to hide behind a cloak of anonymity."[61] In actual fact, given that the matter was now subject to judicial appeal at Commission of Assembly, it was perhaps natural for many to remain silent. Some did put their heads above the parapet in opposition to Robin. Amongst the criticisms were that he did not listen to the opinions of those at odds with him, that he was too formal and his sermons far above the grasp of the majority of the congregation. Perhaps the most vociferous comment in support came from Lynda Reid, former Session Clerk, who commented that "the church appears to be adopting the football adage that if some of the team do not play the game, the manager takes the blame." The *Brechin Advertiser* reported that the Cathedral could be without a minister for some time and the most likely outcome was a linkage with Gardner Memorial Church.[62]

However, Robin was not actually to be absent long! The Judicial Commission met in the Church of Scotland offices in Edinburgh on 12th November, 1997. Robin was accompanied by Rev. Alex McKinnon (whom we recollect had been the Interim Moderator at the Cathedral before Robin arrived) and Rev. Professor Bill Shaw, formerly of St. Andrew's University and a former lawyer. The Judicial Commission unanimously upheld Robin's appeal on the grounds that the Presbytery of Angus had not (as stated in Act I 1988) taken "all reasonable steps of a pastoral nature…to remedy the situation"[63] but in May 1996 had rather prematurely gone down a legal road. But it was not just a clean slate for the Cathedral; Assessors from the Board of Practice and Procedure were to assist Presbytery in the oversight of the congregation. This meant that Robin was immediately re-instated and on Sunday 16th November returned to the Cathedral pulpit,

---

[58] Tom was my own minister in St. Rule's, Monifieth. He retired in 1992. He died on 29th July 2012.
[59] *Brechin Advertiser*, 25th September, 1997
[60] Ibid.
[61] Ibid.
[62] It reverted to Gardner Memorial for its centenary in 1998.
[63] General Assembly Act I (1988) section 2.

preaching a hopeful message of inclusiveness, lack of bitterness to any and the need to recognise that they were a congregation with difficulties and that better communication was needed. Robin's letter in the Cathedral Magazine of December 1997 reflects these themes:

> In speaking to the (Judicial) Commission, I made no generalised attack of any kind on congregation or Kirk Session, nor on any specific individual. If I had wanted a generally negative view of Brechin Cathedral to prevail, I could have left that to the Presbytery. It remains my firm belief that in what we have done together, we have achieved much. More progress is to be made, not by aggravating difficulties, but by expanding upon our strengths. Yes, enormous challenges now face us. Not least, I think, many of us are sensing a profound challenge to our priorities and values. Sometimes in life we need to put aside our own feelings in some matter for the sake of others...[64]

Again, as with the Presbytery's judgement in September, community opinion was greatly divided. George Allan, an Angus Councillor, suggested that all should now unite behind Robin. One elder stated Robin had "absolutely no credibility left" and it was "a hollow victory."[65] Another wrote that "a lot of hard work by a lot of good people has been pushed aside. Too many good people have been forced out of Brechin Cathedral."[66] But the main criticism of Robin in the newspapers was because of his suggestion, during the appeal, that the real problem was the union between the Cathedral and Maison Dieu, which mixed the "Co-opie Kirk" with the establishment, the "tap o' the toon" with "the bottom o' the toon". One correspondent wrote that the problems in the Cathedral were due to far more and were far deeper than any sociological divisions.[67] I, at this point, might put on record that I found no such social divisions indicated either in my interviews or in my research of records, but, of course, these matters are often subjective.

When the Kirk Session met in December 1997, seventeen elders had resigned and three others, including the Session Clerk, Kenneth Allan, had not only resigned but left the congregation. Robin had won his case, but could he continue to minister at the Cathedral? At first, he certainly believed he might: eight new elders were duly appointed in February 1998 and Revs. Maudeen MacDougall and Jean Montgomerie had been duly appointed as Assessors to work with the Presbytery's Superintendence Committee in overseeing the Cathedral. By April it seemed that Robin was about to leave and take up an appointment elsewhere, yet there was little sign of any likely reconciliation with

---

[64] *Cathedral Magazine*, December 1997
[65] *Brechin Advertiser*, 20th November, 1997
[66] Ibid.
[67] Ibid.

Robin's detractors. The Session stated in its April meeting that "the future of former elders was in the hands of the Kirk Session and a clear majority of the Session agreed that former elders would not again be members of Session in the foreseeable future…there being no sign of any apology."[68] It is unlikely that many elders who had resigned saw any need for apologising!

In May, Robin had received a call from Strachur and Strathallan in the Presbytery of Dunoon, his induction to be held on 17th June, 1998. Taking his leave of Presbytery on 5th May, the Moderator Tom Maplesden noted that despite the recent controversies surrounding the Cathedral, Robin had many strengths and talents and showed great wisdom in Presbytery debates. Brechin Cathedral was now ready for a new ministry, but what form would that take?

When Presbytery met on 5th May, the two Assessors, Maudeen MacDougall and Jean Montgomerie suggested that a new form of ministry, *Interim*[69] ministry, be put in place at the Cathedral for a two year period. Further, four assessor elders would be appointed from within Presbytery and that:

> All elders of Brechin Cathedral should be encouraged to attend a refresher course, and, at a special service, be given the opportunity to state that they adhere to their ordination vows; that new elders should undertake a Presbytery training course, and that no former elders be automatically invited to be re-associated with the Kirk Session of Brechin Cathedral.

> Also that an early opportunity should be given for members of the congregation to re-affirm their commitment to the Church of Jesus Christ during an act of morning worship. [70]

When the Kirk Session met on 26th May, 1998, they voted unanimously for an interim minister, so too at a congregational meeting on 14th June, 1998, 101 members to nil voted both for an interim ministry and an unrestricted ministry to follow the interim minister.

---

[68] Kirk Session minutes, 7th April, 1998

[69] Interim ministry was introduced into the Church of Scotland in 1997 and consists of FIVE specific tasks:

    i.   To identify and deal with the hurts, disappointments, anger etc. that exist within the congregation.

    ii.   To help the congregation decide what it means to be the church in their particular parish, and in this light establish their priorities.

    iii.   To ensure that the congregation has appropriate leadership, organisations and resources to achieve these priorities.

    iv.   To enable the congregation to see more clearly their role within the Presbytery and the wider Church.

    v.   To prepare the congregation to find a new minister.

[70] Presbytery of Angus minutes, 5th May, 1998

Again Presbytery (having consulted with Parish Re-appraisal) decided to move the goalposts! At their meeting on 1st September, instead of an unrestricted call, a reviewable tenure appointment (albeit without predetermined length) was agreed following the interim ministry. The meeting of Cathedral office-bearers which heard this on 18th August confessed to "some feeling of disquiet and of having been let down."[71] At a congregational meeting on Sunday 23rd August, 59 voted in favour, 1 against with 3 abstentions. There was a general sense that the whole thing was *a fait accompli*. It was not the best place from which to start to an Interim ministry.

---

[71] Minute of meeting of office-bearers, 18th August, 1998

INTER-REGNUM

Very Rev Dr James A Simpson, former Moderator of the General Assembly (1994-95) and Minister Emeritus of Dornoch Cathedral was introduced as Brechin Cathedral's first (and so far only) Interim minister on 15th September, 1998. Historically, for the first time since the Disruption of 1843, a minister was in Brechin Cathedral who had not been elected by the congregation. A few days later, at his first Session meeting, Jim Simpson (having been saddened and disturbed by recent Session minutes) indicated that he thought that the elders who had resigned should be invited back onto Session. Quoting Mark 3:25 (and perhaps emulating Lincoln's famous speech) Jim Simpson suggested that "a house divided against itself cannot stand". The minute goes on:

> Whilst Dr Simpson accepted that it is never easy to forgive he reminded the elders present that the Kirk Session is a body charged with a responsibility for the spiritual health of the congregation, and by putting into practice the teaching of Jesus must take the initiative in the healing process.[72]

The Session agreed unanimously to extend the hand of friendship to those who had resigned and of the seventeen, thirteen elders were re-admitted at a Communion service in the Queen's Aisle on Sunday 25th October, 1998. One elder who resigned and decided not to return was less effusive about Jim Simpson's attempts at reconciliation commenting "Dr Simpson thought that just by being terribly nice to everyone he could undo the terrible hurt that had been caused."[73] There is also some evidence (recently presented to the author) that Jim Simpson was fairly dismissive of friendly overtures from neighbouring congregations; indeed, that he saw his work as that solely of building up the Cathedral to the exclusion of bridge building elsewhere.[74] The trouble was that Jim Simpson's peace-making efforts did not really do justice to those who had been deeply aggrieved and appalled either at the way Robin had been treated by some elders, or by the way Presbytery had acted judgementally towards him. It must also be recognised that Jim Simpson's eager desire to re-instate the elders who had resigned was in stark contrast to Presbytery's instruction of 5th May 1998 "that no former elders be automatically invited to be re-associated with the Kirk Session of Brechin Cathedral" (presumably because of the fear that a similar situation would arise with a new minister.) To some extent, we are still living with some ghosts from these difficult times; some hurt and wounds remain yet unresolved.

In a further effort to unite the congregation, Jim Simpson decided on one diet of worship at 11am, so that "all attended as one family" and to ensure "all who attended were hearing the same message."[75] Perhaps surprising is how quickly after the turbulent events of the late 1990s the Session and congregation returned to normal business. Yet

---

[72] Kirk Session minutes, 22nd September, 1998
[73] Doctor of Ministry interviews
[74] Private correspondence with the author: 20th March, 2017
[75] Kirk Session minutes, 22nd September, 1998

old problems remained. Early into 1999, the need for a Session Clerk from within the congregation, a new Treasurer (Ian Mackie due to retire in March) and few children in the Sunday School were all highlighted as issues needing addressed.[76] However, attendance at worship had increased to around 150 and financial giving had improved with an emphasis on deeds of covenant. Presbytery noted "there were still many problems, but these were not specific to (Brechin Cathedral's) specific situation."[77]

In March 1999, William Low was elected by the Session as their new Clerk. Ironically, William had been one of Robin's main critics. Jim Simpson (who was due to relinquish his responsibilities as Interim Minister in September) now began to set in motion the necessary requirements for the election of a new minister. A Vacancy Committee of nineteen was elected by the congregation on 23rd May, 1999, the Electoral Roll duly attested and a Parish Profile drawn up. Although Jim Simpson was to conduct his farewell service on Sunday 5th September, 1999, it was clear that he had been one of the key players in securing Scott Rennie as the next minister.

Before moving on to the final section of this chapter, let us pause for a moment to consider Robin's legacy. While it is certainly true that Robin seemed to provoke a number of personality clashes and that his style of governance was too dictatorial for some, we should not be left with an impression that all was negative on his watch. Robin sought (and partly succeeded) to restrain the Cathedral's spending which, for many years had out-paced income by over 15%, particularly in Peter Gordon's latter years. He sought to put the Cathedral fabric too into good repair, working tirelessly to secure grants and raise money. Like James Anderson, he was an imaginative liturgist introducing the Lent Symbol sequence to echo Advent and, in his final year, the Cathedral con-celebrated communion with the Episcopal congregation. He also introduced the Easter Dawn service. Of course, we should not forget either that Robin's expertise and wisdom was vital to the union in 1990.

In many ways though, Robin arrived in the midst of a "perfect ecclesial storm."[78] The Church of Scotland generally in the 1980s-90s was declining in both membership and influence nationally. Commenting on the controversy that later arose in Robin's ministry the *Glasgow Herald* stated "Brechin Cathedral is having the same kind of problems many congregations have, but unfortunately they are all coming together at the same time."[79] The union itself was to add a great strain on Robin with the vastly

---

[76] Kirk Session minutes, 9th February, 1999
[77] Presbytery of Angus minutes, 6th April, 1999
[78] Shards of Hope, 101
[79] *Glasgow Herald*, 5th Oct, 1997

increased pastoral and administrational demands (unlike his predecessors he had no regular assistant and had to rely on retired ministers); congregational expectations definitely exceeded ministerial capacity. Perhaps some in the Session should have been more sympathetic to this? Yet, Robin allowed himself to be drawn into this complex web of events and got dragged down with them. His rather formal personality and intellectual sermons did not help him be endeared to the congregation.

Perhaps we get a glimpse of the inner man of Robin Mackenzie in a very heartfelt farewell letter to the congregation in May 1998:

> …I leave Brechin with a huge feeling of possibilities unfulfilled. There is a feeling of frustration that the absolute necessity of coping with meetings and procedures which could never bring any genuinely positive result has absorbed so much time and energy. Most of all I can think of a great number of people whom I would have liked to meet more often and get to know better…Some have seen me as a pig-headed little man of little use beyond being a master of works and a financial organiser. Others have been kind enough to see more in me than that…Yet who I am begins to fade into insignificance here.[80]

Unfortunately, Jim Simpson's period as Interim minister of a mere year was hardly sufficient to solve all the problems and Scott went on to inherit several unresolved issues. Indeed in one of his final pastoral letters in the magazine, Jim Simpson complains that in his year of ministry nearly 60% of the congregation had failed to attend worship at all[81]. But we should not lay the blame for all the problems either at Robin's door, or indeed at the elders (both pro and anti-Robin). Perhaps had an agency like *Place for Hope* been in existence in the 1990s much angst and heart-ache would have been avoided. Presbytery must certainly shoulder some of the responsibility for the (at times) cack-handed and legalistic way they responded to what was an acute pastoral crisis. What began as a series of upsets developed into a full blown stand-off between minister and some elders; all involved must bear some sense of responsibility for the outcome of events. So have lessons been learned? In my own view, history will I think be kinder to Robin than perhaps was the case at the time; as one of the other Cathedral ministers noted: "it was a most unhappy period but Robin has been resurrected."[82]

---

[80] *Cathedral Magazine*, June 1998
[81] *Cathedral Magazine*, September 1999
[82] DMin Interview

A GAME OF TWO HALVES?

Scott M Rennie (1999 – 2009) was born on 31st March, 1972 into a working class background at Bucksburn in Aberdeen. Having first studied geography to M.A., Scott went on to gain a B.D., also at Aberdeen University. Later he was to gain an S.T.M. (Sacred Theology Masters) from Union Seminary in New York. He was married to Ruth for five years and the couple had one daughter. The couple later separated and divorced and, on coming to terms with his homosexuality, Scott formed a civil partnership (later converted into a same sex marriage in December 2014) with David Smith. He was elected to Brechin Cathedral (his first charge) on 26th September, 1999 by 229 votes to nil (17.2% of the Roll) and was subsequently ordained and inducted to the charge by the Presbytery of Angus on 4th November, 1999.

As a keen fan of the "Dons" (Aberdeen F.C.), I am sure Scott will allow me to compare his period of ministry within Brechin to "a game of two halves". Scott's ministry started with a flourish of good will and a palpable sense of relief that the dark days of controversy were behind. Riding on that optimistic tide, within a few months a number of new elders were ordained and several new initiatives begun. Yet, as soon as the second Session meeting chaired by Scott in January 2000, there was a reminder that Presbytery were monitoring the situation at the Cathedral closely. As well as the four Assessor elders appointed to the congregation by Presbytery (namely, Audrey Greig, Bill Beedie, Jim Gordon and David Scrymgeour), Rev Malcolm Rooney (Presbytery Clerk) gave a presentation to the Session on aims and objectives.[83] It is worth noting that this

---

[83] Kirk Session minutes, 11th January, 2000

was not by instruction of Presbytery itself, but simply a private arrangement between minister and Clerk. One wonders though whether a Presbytery Clerk visiting the Session so soon after Scott's induction did not smack a little of "big brother" watching? The new young minister had scarce had time to settle in. Was there a fear amongst Presbytery officials that what happened with Robin might repeat itself with a minister in his first charge? There is always a fine line between concern and interference.

Meanwhile, Scott's ministry continued to embark upon new ventures; ecumenical picnics, Session BBQ, teams to consider youth work and pastoral care, a stewardship campaign "Count me in" were all begun. There was almost a breathless pace of new initiatives! But as soon as September, 2000, Presbytery also started consideration of Re-appraisal within its bounds once more. There was a general feeling that this would impact upon the Cathedral. Presbytery forum meetings were duly held and the Cathedral Session felt somewhat nonplussed at a formal presentation being given to the Presbytery team by Gardner Memorial without knowing. This was followed in September 2002 by a Presbytery wide meeting at Kirriemuir Old. By late 2002/early 2003, Presbytery mooted the idea of Parish groupings with the Cathedral, Gardner Memorial and Edzell being the main centres and the other rural churches as satellites. In this regard, Gardner Memorial and the Cathedral began discussions for a joint paid youth worker. A few months later there was also talk of a joint office for the two congregations being located within the High Street. In summer 2004 for the first time there were joint services between the Cathedral and Gardner Memorial with Scott and Rev. Moira Herkes of Gardner conducting in each other's churches. While apparently successful, concern was expressed at two services being held by Gardner each Sunday to one at the Cathedral. Further collaborative ventures stalled as various conversations took place between Gardner Memorial and Farnell over a possible linkage[84]. It is noticeable that after this linkage was affected, joint services between the two town congregations more or less ceased. This left the Cathedral out on a limb and in January 2005 Scott suggested that the Cathedral go it alone in appointing a Youth worker. Nevertheless, a successful attempt was made to re-start Brechin Council of churches on the 23rd January, 2005.

Scott organised an animal blessing service in October, 2001 and Elder training sessions on a Sunday evening. The prospect of resuming some form of evening service was also raised and the timing of the Sunday morning service discussed. The problem of such a constant flow of new ideas and programs, particularly with a minister in his first charge, is that ultimately it is unsustainable as the sheer routine of parish life (e.g. funerals, visits, meetings, preparation and study) bears down; the danger is that a minister

---

[84] This eventually took place in 2008.

can easily burn-out. Thus while Robin was unable to have ministerial capacity meet congregational expectation, Scott was unable in some sense to meet *self-expectation*. In many ways there were enough new initiatives proposed in Scott's first few years to sustain a ministry of twenty or so years! If any criticism can be levelled it is perhaps that Scott sought to do too much too soon, consequently proposed plans were not always followed up by concrete actions. Energy and optimism would in due time give way to reality.

The first signs of this "reality check" occurred in November 2001 when, as a result of the "Count me in" stewardship program, 316 people (22% of the Church Roll) expressed no interest in the Cathedral or congregational life. After discussion it was decided to transfer them to the Supplementary Roll, with the proviso that they could resume full membership at a later date; the "overall feeling was that we should concentrate on the other 78% and at the same time not alienate those who are being transferred."[85] One or two supporters of Robin also took the opportunity to leave the congregation.

On a more positive note, the Quinquennial Visitation Report from Presbytery in December 2001 was very different from the 1993/4 one. On this occasion Presbytery commended "the minister, office-bearers and members of Brechin Cathedral for their hard work, enthusiasm, and for the significant progress made during the last three years."[86] Several new members joined the Cathedral, either by profession of faith or by transferring from other nearby congregations. On 28th April 2002 a Centenary service was held marking one hundred years since the Cathedral's restoration. There was an extensive guest list of civic and ecclesiastical dignitaries; Rev Bob Brown of Queen's Cross Church, Aberdeen was the guest preacher (Scott having served there as probationer) and the Presbytery Moderator, Rev. Matthew Bicket led some of the prayers. This was followed by a finger buffet lunch and then in the afternoon at 4p.m. a "Songs of Praise" service with the combined choirs of the Cathedral and Inverbervie churches. In addition to the Centenary celebrations, Dr John Purser rang various Celtic bells from the top of the Round Tower in late March, 2002 and then gave a talk in the Cathedral Hall. These bells would have been used to call the clergy to worship and this was the first time they had been heard for some eight hundred years![87] On 17th November 2002, Rt. Rev Findlay Macdonald, Moderator of the General Assembly visited the Cathedral and preached at a joint service with Gardner Memorial. Several elders were presented with long service certificates and a finger buffet was held afterwards at the

---

[85] Kirk Session minutes, 15th November, 2001
[86] Presbytery of Angus minutes, 4th December, 2001
[87] Kirk Session minutes, 9th May, 2002

Mechanics Institute. Also in 2002 Scott raised a suggestion about pews being removed in the Cathedral though further discussion on this matter quickly went into abeyance.

It was not all plain-sailing however; early in 2003 there was concern expressed that due to other commitments, Scott was not conducting many funeral services and that Rev. Peter Youngson (who was assisting from time to time) was doing the bulk of them. In March 2003 Scott was appointed to the Committee of the Board of Ministry and, in time, this would lead to a criticism that he was spending more time on extra-parochial matters. In September 2004, this criticism was further fuelled within the community of Brechin more widely when Scott decided to stand as a Parliamentary candidate for the Liberal Democrats in the forthcoming General Election. Further, in the latter period of Scott's ministry, much of his time was pre-occupied with Presbytery business, namely attempting a (ultimately abortive) union between Forfar: East and Old and Forfar: St.Margaret's. While the truth of this criticism of "taking your eye off the parish" is entirely subjective, what we do see in the mid-2000s is a series of initiatives being delayed; for example after a couple of years of delay an Elders' outing to St.Giles' and Greyfriars took place in November 2005.

Spring 2003 saw a new secretary take up post and this was followed by a new organist, Ian Robertson, in September. In the summer 2004 a number of choir members complained at being "suspended"[88] from the choir by the Minister and Session Clerk, as they could not accept the authority of the organist. By the end of 2003, and after considerable discussion at Session and a congregational survey,[89] the main Sunday service time moved from 11 am to 10.30 am. Despite Scott himself volunteering to lead the Junior section of the Boys' Brigade (and a continuing demand from the youngsters), at a meeting of parents in late 2003 there was simply not enough committed support for the 4th Brechin Company to continue and it duly folded in early 2004. So too (despite a very successful Going Bananas with 100 children the year previously) a youngsters' event *Seaside Rock* was cancelled at Easter due to work commitments of volunteers and the detrimental effect that Child Protection legislation was having on people volunteering.

---

[88] Kirk Session minutes, 8th July, 2004
[89] The congregational voting had in fact shown 67 in favour of 11am and 54 in favour of 10.30am. However, the 10.30am slot was preferred by parents of Funday Club members and "we have to target the younger members of the congregation." See Kirk Session minutes, 13th November, 2003. The irony is that Funday Club has now ceased and we have inherited the 10.30am time slot today.

In November, 2005 two significant developments occurred. Firstly, a Peace Pole was installed in the Cathedral grounds, the first for any Church in Scotland. The morning service on 27th November reflected that international theme as the Pole was duly dedicated, visitors attended from the World Peace Prayer Society and a lady from Japan read the lesson.[90] Secondly, Ian Gray was appointed as a pastoral assistant whose task would be "to cover Parish funerals and pastoral hospital visits".[91] What is of note is that this was not the appointment of a Youth worker, as had been discussed earlier, but rather a pastoral assistant to the Minister. While, at first, this appointment was funded by the congregation it went on to be centrally funded by the Church of Scotland in 2007. There are also indications that during these years Scott underwent a very difficult time personally; partly caused by struggles with his sexuality and the breakdown of his marriage, partly by having to work through the grief caused by the untimely death of his mother.

By summer 2006, a change in the allocation of ministries to Angus Presbytery[92] resulted in a review of the Presbytery Plan. Locally, both the Cathedral and Gardner Memorial were to be raised from "reviewable" to full status and Gardner was linked with Farnell in early 2008. In addition, the Cathedral, Gardner and the Edzell churches would form a "cluster". Another change in governance occurred in April 2007 when the Session agreed to adopt the Unitary Constitution that did away with the need for a Congregational Board dealing with finance and fabric, but instituted teams within the Session[93]. But, again, there were slight signs of a lack of commitment as the Session

---

[90] Kirk Session minutes, 12th January, 2006
[91] Ibid.
[92] The allocation rose from 24 ministries to 30.
[93] This was formally ratified by the Kirk's Law Department on 10th July, 2007

struggled to appoint a Presbytery elder. Rev. Moira Herkes of Gardner Memorial had in autumn 2007 to demit her post due to ill health. This vacancy was to delay progress in instituting a Parish Grouping which was finally put into place and agreed by the congregation on Sunday 22nd June, 2008[94]. This was followed by a congregational meeting on 21st September, 2008 that officially raised the Cathedral back to full status. At this time also a serious outbreak of Dry Rot was found in the Cathedral which was going to cost in the region of £45,000 for treatment.

As I said earlier, Scott's ministry was a "game of two halves" and the second half really began in earnest on 23rd November, 2008 when (following his mentor, Bob Brown's retiral) Scott was invited to preach as "sole nominee" for the vacancy at Aberdeen: Queen's Cross. In a secret ballot 140 members voted in favour to 28 against; the "Call" itself being signed by 246 members of the congregation. When the matter came before the Presbytery of Aberdeen in January 2009, 60 voted to sustain the call to 24 against. The Kirk Session at the Cathedral proceeded to move into vacancy preparation mode, but all was not to go as smoothly as hoped. As early as spring 2008 there had been speculation locally regarding Scott's sexuality and the fact that a man was living as his partner in the Cathedral Manse. Two verbal complaints had been received by Presbytery from members of the congregation and another two written ones from members of Presbytery[95]. In addition a group of primarily evangelical ministers within Aberdeen Presbytery (led by Rev. Ian Aitken) following the Aberdeen Presbytery meeting in January 2009 now complained about an openly gay minister to Commission of Assembly. While Scott has always correctly stressed that he was perfectly open about his sexuality in terms of his move to Aberdeen, those I have interviewed locally maintain that there was much more an air of secrecy within Brechin; very few of the Cathedral members had been openly told by him and were "left to guess", as one member put it. They would not be left to guess long as the buzzing swarm of the media descended upon Brechin looking for news about this controversially gay minister. Parishioners speak of satellite vans belonging to the principal news channels being parked near the Cathedral and cameramen on hand to record worshippers' reactions on leaving the services. The Cathedral now found itself in the eye of a storm of controversy within the Kirk.

Two questions from this period still lie unanswered. Firstly, did Scott realise in advance the furore that would engulf the Kirk when news of his sexuality broke? Or was he naïve in assuming that his private life would stay private? Having come to terms with his sexuality himself, was he (as some have suggested) a "publicity seeker", out to

---

[94] A Presbytery service to initiate the Parish Grouping was held at Farnell Church on 6th November, 2008

[95] See Kirk Session minutes, 26th February, 2009.

become the first openly gay minister in the Church of Scotland? Did he anticipate that there might be a backlash from the evangelical wing of the Church? The evidence I have managed to unearth actually suggests that, in some ways, contradictory theories may be true. One interviewee, who knew Scott well, was certain that Scott knew what might happen and, while not necessarily embracing the publicity, thought about it and went into the situation with his eyes wide open.[96] But it may have been a case that Scott *found* himself in the situation rather than *actively creating* the storm. However, having got into it, he played for broke and decided to stand his ground on what he believed was a principle of openness and toleration. Others did not quite see it that way, particularly some of his more evangelical colleagues. Many of them felt that recognising your sexuality yourself is one thing, practising it openly is quite another. Criticism was laid at Scott's door for putting self -interest before the interests of the Church at large. It was (and in many ways still is) a hugely divisive issue.

The second question is: how well supported was Scott by the congregation at the Cathedral in being open about his sexuality? One interviewee suggested that (perhaps after all the upsets during Robin's ministry) the congregation closed ranks and did not want the same thing to happen to Scott.Indeed, had there not been such acrimony in Robin's time, the likelihood is that the controversy over Scott's sexuality locally would have been far greater and more damaging. The Session Clerk, William Low, had almost a fatherly protection of the minister. His popularity in town and compassion for him after a family bereavement and a marital breakdown offset any criticism of "gay lifestyles".[97] One elder wrote in Scott's support to the local paper in advance of the General Assembly decision.[98] Others volunteered to stand by Scott when he faced Commission of Assembly. Yet, again, the evidence is contradictory. When Scott eventually did move to Aberdeen, the Session Clerk William Low said that there were no obvious signs that the events had adversely affected the congregation, yet acknowledged that "it had been a very emotive business" and "it was not clear if some members were upset".[99] The Quinquennial report by Presbytery in November 2009 noted that "events surrounding Mr. Rennie's translation were a distraction in the life of the congregation" and that his departure had left mixed feelings with perhaps some "residual disharmony."[100] So too a later visit by Presbytery representatives revealed that "the Session kept a united front to the press (on Scott's sexuality) even if the Session had various thoughts on the

---

[96] D Min interview
[97] Ibid.
[98] *Brechin Advertiser*, Thursday 21st May, 2009
[99] Ibid., Thursday 11th June, 2009
[100] Kirk Session minutes, 8th April, 2010

subject."[101] We do now know that two *verbal* complaints against Scott because of his sexuality had been made locally to Presbytery officials; though, in light of the Assembly's decision, not acted upon in any way.[102]

When Commission of Assembly met on 25th March, 2009, they decided by a very narrow majority of one to refer the whole matter to the General Assembly which met in the May. The issue it was felt was simply too controversial and contentious to be dealt with by the Commission alone. In the interim, *Forward Together* (an evangelical Christian group) were forced into a humiliating apology for claiming that Scott had left his wife and daughter for another man. In fact, it was only a number of years after the marital breakdown (and after Scott had resolved his sexuality struggles) that he went on to meet his male partner.[103] Scott himself stated in the *One Kirk* journal that "It wasn't until after the demise of my marriage, and the pain and grieving that entails, that I finally decided I had to face up to my own issues around sexuality."[104] Given Scott's fairly working class background in Bucksburn, Aberdeen, this would have been something that was not normally part and parcel of the cultural context of his growing up.

An online petition organised by *Forward Together* against Scott's appointment attracted 12,555 signatures, including that of 481 fellow ministers. The strength of Aitken and others' legal case against Scott's appointment was that at the time the Presbytery of Aberdeen processed Scott's translation, the law of the Kirk on same-sex relationships was completely unclear. This meant that perhaps it might have been wise to *sist* (or suspend) the translation until the doctrine of the Church caught up with its practice.[105] However, this could have taken years and meanwhile Scott would be in a kind of "parish limbo", neither at Brechin nor Aberdeen. The weakness of Aitken's argument was that the congregation at Queen's Cross had endorsed Scott's appointment by 86% of members; many of them fondly recalling his time as an assistant there. Who had the right to choose a minister: Presbytery, Assembly or local Christians? In many ways it was a similar issue to that of the Disruption in 1843 when landowners imposed their choice of minister on an unwilling population.

---

[101] Kirk Session minutes, 8th June 2010

[102] Another two written complaints by members of Presbytery that Scott's lifestyle was incompatible with the Christian gospel were dismissed by a Presbytery Committee on the grounds of insufficient evidence on 3rd June, 2009.

[103] *Herald newspaper*, 2nd May 2009

[104] As quoted in *Dundee Courier and Advertiser*, 6th May, 2009

[105] My own view as a Church historian is that very often Church practice on the ground has in fact shaped its doctrine, not necessarily the other way around! The controversy between St Augustine and the Donatists over treatment of apostates is one such ancient example.

When the General Assembly met in May 2009, passions were running high. There were dire claims by some evangelicals that if the Assembly decided in favour of Scott's appointment to Queen's Cross it would provoke a split in the Kirk unequalled since1843. In actual fact, despite protesters shouting outside the Assembly Hall, the debate on Saturday 23rd May was a gracious if somewhat protracted one. After a four hour debate the Assembly decided by 326 votes to 267 to allow Scott's translation to Aberdeen: Queen's Cross, defeating the case of *Aitken and others versus the Presbytery of Aberdeen*. There were 150 abstentions and 121 commissioners at the Assembly lodged their dissent. A further Overture from the Presbytery of Lochcarron and Skye was heard on Monday 25th May which, more generally, sought to prevent anyone entering ministry who had had a sexual relationship outside of marriage. This resulted in a Special Commission on same-sex relationships, though the overture itself was heavily defeated. Another motion that day at the Assembly finally cleared the way of any ambiguity in process and allowed for Scott's unimpeded translation to his new charge.

During these few months between January and May 2009, Scott was in a kind of "parish limbo" with his mind already on Queen's Cross while his person was still in Brechin. Nevertheless, and perhaps rather controversially, he did create a few initiatives and make some personnel appointments, flouting the normal Kirk convention that no changes should be initiated in any impending vacancy (out of fairness to one's successor).

Scott's final service was a month later on 28th June, 2009[106], when a packed congregation of three hundred heard Scott preach on inclusiveness and welcome. He stated that "the main reaction locally has been astonishment and incredulity at the turn of events…(people) find it hard to understand why their minister was put through this."[107] The congregation gave him a standing ovation and he was duly inducted to Queen's Cross Church on Friday 3rd July, 2009. The controversy over same-sex relationships in the Kirk was to rumble on for many further years and some might say is still not fully resolved, despite the decision of the General Assembly of 2015 that congregations might, if they so wished, elect ministers who were in same-sex marriages. This has, to date, yet to be tested in law[108].

The Cathedral now found itself in a vacancy situation with Rev. Carleen Robertson as Interim Moderator and Ian Gray as locum. It was perhaps not the best time

---

[106] Had all gone according to plan, Scott's final service would have been on 25th January, 2009.

[107] *Brechin Advertiser*, 25th June, 2009

[108] Interestingly, the Theological Forum will present a report on Same Sex Marriage to the 2017 General Assembly.

for a vacancy. Scott's case had resulted in a moratorium on all further inductions or ordinations of those in gay partnerships and the setting up of a Special Commission by the General Assembly. Even amongst those who were not gay, there was a certain climate of fear. Fear that the Kirk might be about to haemorrhage with various ministers and congregations leaving over the General Assembly decision; fear too amongst ministers that a witch-hunt had started that would result in sexual peccadillos, even from one's teenage years, being brought to light. It was a period as one wag said to me when "naebody was moving nowhere". Well, as it turned out, not quite!

Two changes were to take place in personnel during the vacancy. Ian Gray was appointed as the new Pastoral Assistant to the Esk Parish Grouping in March 2010 with the result that Bill Beedie (formerly an assessor elder) became the locum. The Session Clerk, William Low, was admitted to hospital in late March and sadly died late in the June 2010. During this time too there were various rumblings about the support (or lack) from Presbytery and exception was taken to some of the wording from the Quinquennial report in November 2009.[109]

Having been invited in early June to meet with the Nominating Committee and consider the vacancy, on Sunday 15th August 2010 I preached as sole nominee for the vacancy at the Cathedral and was duly elected by 173 votes to 1 against (20.7% of the Roll). I was then inducted to the charge on 23rd September, 2010 and that, you might say, was where I came in…

Although I am less than the least of all God's saints, (God's) grace was given to me: to preach to the Gentiles the unsearchable riches of Christ, and to make plain to everyone this mystery, which for ages past was kept hidden in God…

- **St. Paul's letter to the Ephesians 3:8**

---

[109] Having read the report myself, its contents seem to me very balanced. I suspect that some of Scott's supporters took exception to references on the impact of the Assembly case on the congregation. There was, I believe, a tendency amongst some to over exaggerate the positives in Scott's ministry and downplay the negatives. In my view, the Presbytery report *partly* corrects that tendency.

AFTERWORD – A Final Act?

The past may teach us how to act in the living present

and how to turn the future to good account – D.H. Edwards, Brechin Almanac, 1873

When I arrived at Brechin Cathedral in September of 2010 there was a sense in which my congregation were uncertain of their future direction, their Christian identity. Indeéd, this very issue had come out in my discussions with the Nominating committee some months before I was inducted. To me this seemed rather curious. Here was a congregation which could trace its pedigree back into the misty world of the Celtic Church in the seventh century, yet it was not sure where it would go next. Was it exhausted? Had it any future at all? And more important to my ministry amongst these faithful people who seemed stuck in an ecclesiological lay-by, what could I do to help them get back onto the road? My intuition was that it was going to be necessary to go back into the Cathedral's history in order to go forward. I became convinced that part of the answer to my congregation's crisis of identity lay in its extensive past. This was for two reasons: one based on a theological understanding of the narrative of the Cathedral and the other being grounded in a particularly theological view that I have of history.

Following the completion of my Doctor of Ministry degree[1] in summer 2015 (this book being based upon much of the research for my doctoral project) I hope we have, together, a better sense of our future direction and that both the 70th anniversary of the Society of Friends in 2017 and the 800th anniversary of the Cathedral building in 2020 will provide a launch-pad for that new future.

Since my doctoral thesis was based upon a theatrical model of a play with various acts, someone asked me at one of my talks on the Cathedral's history if I was "the final act"? The answer to that question is a resounding NO! The reader will, I hope, by now realise that the Cathedral's narrative shows a waxing and a waning in many ages. As Peter Gordon said to me in interview "some people held the vision, others made it real, while during the times of others the vision achieved a falling away." What we may well be witnessing in our current age is a waning of old, nineteenth century models of Church and the birth pangs of new forms. We are in an era of change, but change brings life as well as pain, opportunities as well as crises. We must mutate in our nature as Church if

---

[1] See Roderick J Grahame *Shards of Hope – an investigation into the history of Brechin Cathedral from an eschatological perspective* (Pittsburgh Theological Seminary, 2015)

we are to survive. As Ian Henderson, one time editor of the Cathedral Magazine observed in an article in the *Scots Magazine* in 1996 that "the story of Christianity is the story of resurrection." This is undoubtedly true of my own congregation's history; each dark period is followed by growth and new beginnings. I wonder, perhaps if we are in the dark hours between Holy Saturday's prolonged waiting and Easter morning's joyous glory? I would like to think that, in some small way, I may have brought that Easter glory a few steps nearer for the folk of Brechin and the Cathedral.

> *Old landmarks change – a shadow still is cast.*
>
> *From this old tower, touched with the light of years,*
>
> *whose fadeless glory all the past endears...*
>
> - *M.E. Leicester Addis, Scottish Cathedrals and Abbeys, 1901*

ABOUT THE AUTHOR

Roderick James Grahame (2010 – present) was born in Dundee in June, 1964 and grew up in the small Angus town of Monifieth, where his year was the first through Monifieth High School. He studied Astrophysics for a time at Dundee University, before changing over to a B.D. degree at St. Andrew's where he gained honours in Ecclesiastical History and the History of Doctrine (1987) and won the Gray essay prize for his paper on St.Augustine. He then had a year out travelling in Europe and Israel, as well as volunteering on Iona before returning to Aberdeen for his Certificate in Pastoral Studies (1989).

He served his probationary period under Rev J. Wilson McLeod at Bellshill: West Church and was ordained and inducted to the recent union of Clydebank: Kilbowie St.Andrew's on 13th March 1991 (the 50th anniversary of the Clydebank Blitz). Roderick was Chair of the 60th anniversary commemorations of the Blitz in 2001, which had international media coverage. In February, 2002, Roderick moved to become minister at Largs: St. Columba's on the Ayrshire coast. He was Moderator of Ardrossan Presbytery in 2007-8. He was then called to Brechin Cathedral and back to his Angus roots in autumn 2010. Roderick has extensive experience in the ecumenical scene and in summer 2015 completed his Doctor of Ministry degree from Pittsburgh Theological Seminary (in conjunction with Aberdeen University) gaining the Richard J Rapp Memorial Prize for that year. Roderick has recently been appointed Depute Clerk to the Presbytery of Angus. Roderick has a passion for labrador dogs, swimming, reading, theatre, gardening, travel and watching Scotland play Rugby Union.

A NOTE ABOUT THE 2020 PROJECT

The publication of this book in June 2017 launches the Cathedral's 2020 project which in three key areas: Celebration, Education and Legacy, will mark the 800th anniversary of the foundation of the current building. Various community events are being planned. Anyone who thinks they would like to be involved in *any* way is invited to contact Roderick by email (RGrahame@churchofscotland.org.uk)

BRECHIN CATHEDRAL
D. H. Edwards

BRECHIN IN ANGUS
With the Antique Tower & Antient Cathedral founded 1150

The spirit of a time is writ
Not in all books; but who hath wit
Shall find in it the arrow head,
The kelt, the barrow for the dead
And stone-groined power
Beneath the massive tower.

O let my due feet never fail
To walk the studious cloisters pale,
And love the high embowed roof,
With antique pillars massy proof,

West View of the Cathedral Kirk of Brechin in Angus Shire Thursday 6th October 1808.

And storied windows
richly dight,
Casting a dim religious
light:
There let the pealing
organ blow
To the full voiced quire
below,
In service high and
anthems clear,
And may with sweetness
in mine ear
Dissolve me into
ecstasies
And bring all heaven
before my eyes.

Where priest 'mid
tapers dim
Breathed the warm
prayer, or tuned the
midnight hymn;
Where trembling
penitents their guilt
confess'd

Where want had succour, and contrition rest;
To scenes like these the fainting soul retired,
Revenge and anger in these cells expired;
By pity soothed, remorse lost half her fears
And soften'd pride dropped penitential tears.

APPENDIX 1
Table of Clergy of Brechin Cathedral, 1156-2015

BISHOPS

T (only initial known)	1156
Samson	1158
Turpin	1178
Rodolph (Abbot of Melrose)	1202
Hugo	1218
Gregory (Archdeacon)	1225
Gilbert	1247
Albin (Precentor)	1248
William de Kilconcath (Rector of Dominicans at Perth)	1260
Edward (Monk at Cupar Angus)	1280
Robert (Archdeacon)	1284
William	1286
John de Kinninmund	1298
Adam	1328
Philip (Dean)	1350
Patrick de Leuchars (Lord Chancellor)	1351
Stephen	1374
Walter Forrester of Garden (Lord Clerk Register)	1400
John Crannoch	1426
George de Shoreswood (Lord Chancellor and confessor to the Royal household)	1454
Patrick Graham (Nephew of King James I)	1463
John Balfour	1466
Walter Meldrum	1488
John Hepburn (arch anti-Reformer)	1517
John Sinclair (President of Court of Session)	1562
Andrew Campbell (titular only)	1566
Andrew Lamb	1607
David Lindsay	1619

Thomas Sydserf (Dean of Edinburgh)	1634
Walter Whiteford (Sub dean of Glasgow)	1635
David Strachan	1662
Robert Laurie (Dean of Edinburgh)	1672
George Halliburton	1678
Robert Douglas (Dean of Glasgow)	1682
Alexander Cairncross	1684
James Drummond	1684

MINISTERS OF THE FIRST CHARGE

John Hepburn (illegitimate son of Bishop Hepburn)	1562
John Merschell	1600
Alexander Bisset	1608
William Rait	1644
Bishop Strachan	1662
Bishop Laurie	1672
Bishop Halliburton	1678
Bishop Douglas	1682
Bishop Cairncross	1684
Laurence Skinner (from second charge)	1689
John Willison	1703
Robert Gray	1717
David Blair (from second charge)	1738
John Bisset	1769
James Burns	1798
James McCosh (demitted at Disruption)	1839
Nathaniel Morrin	1843
Andrew Halkett (from Canada)	1847
James Mackay	1872
John A. Clark (died in office)	1892
Walter W. Coats	1901

MINISTERS OF THE SECOND CHARGE

David Carnegy	1631
William Marshall	1633
Robert Norie	1639
Laurence Skinner (to first charge)	1650
John Skinner (never formally ordained or	1687

inducted)	
John Johnston	1710
David Blair (to first charge)	1733
William Shank	1740
James Fordyce	1745
Thomas Mathison	1754
Andrew Bruce	1760
Robert Coutts (assistant and successor)	1798
George Whitson	1804
Alexander L.R. Foote (demitted at Disruption)	1834
Alexander Gardner	1843
Adam D. Tait Hutchison	1893

MINISTERS OF THE ONE CHARGE

James Anderson	1942
Peter M Gordon	1965
Robert (Robin) W McKenzie	1985
James Simpson (interim minister)	1998
Scott M Rennie	1999
Roderick J Grahame	2010

APPENDIX 2
Table of Chapter Clergy of Brechin Cathedral, 1156-1690

BISHOPS	DATE OF CONS.	DEAN Held Prebendary of Farnell from 1274	PRECENTOR Or **CHANTER** Held Prebendary of Stracathro from 1274	CHANCELLOR Prebendary of Navar from 1274	TREASURER Prebendary of Glenbervie from 1274-1422, when separate preb.
T (only initial known)	1156				
Samson	1158			*ABBOT OF CULDEES John?*	
Turpin	1178	Mattussali 1178-88 Matthew 1189/98-1212/18 *PRIOR OF CULDEES Bricius 1178-87*		*ABBOT OF CULDEES Dovenald*	
Rodolph or Ralph (Abbot of Melrose)	1202	Matthew 1189/98-1212/18 *PRIOR OF CULDEES Mallebryd until 1222?*		*ABBOT OF CULDEES Dovenald* William de Borsho or de Bois, Chancellor from 1211-26 Died 1231 Also	

				Archdeacon of Lothian	
Hugo	1214/15	*PRIOR OF CULDEES Mallebryd until 1222?*		*ABBOT OF CULDEES John from 1219*	Henry 1219-36
Gregory Archdeacon	1218	*PRIOR OF CULDEES Kinnaber 1232?*	Albin		Henry cont… A (only initial) 1236? – 46
Gilbert	1247		Albin – appointed as Bishop 1246		
Albin (Precentor)	1248	William de Crachin 1248-69/75	Thomas de Perth or Bell 1248-59		Robert, Sept. 1248 David de Inverbervie 1256 – 74/76
William de Kilconcath (Rector of Dominicans at Perth)	1275?	William de Crachin 1248-69/75[1]			
Edward (Monk at Cupar Angus)	1280				
Robert (Archdeacon)	1284				
William	1286	Thomas de Dundee (Dono Dei) 1295 Appt. Bp of Ross, Jan 1296	William de Cluny 1296-98		John de Stowe, 1296?

[1] William de Crachin according to some sources had been elected Bishop in 1269 but the Papal legate, Ottobone refused to consecrate him. He died unconsecrated in 1275. William de Kilconcath of Perth refused the see on the grounds the benefice was too small.

		Imbert Aurei 1296, Appt. by Pope Boniface VIII			
John de Kinninmund	1298	Fulco 1323/7-39			Robert de Dundee, 1298
Adam	1328	Fulco cont… Thomas de Fingask Appt. Bp. Of Caithness Dec 1342 Philip Wilde de Brechin 1343-50 Becomes Bishop 17 Feb 1350		Philip Wilde 1342-43 Becomes Dean 8th March 1343 Hugh, 1348 Richard de Mowat,1372[2]	Radulf de Kinninmund 1329 -1339
Philip (former Dean)	1350	Alexander de Kininmund 1350 – 52 when Appt. Archdeacon of Aberdeen			
Patrick de Leuchars (Lord Chancellor)	1351	John de Crail or Carelle 1352-93	Fergus de Tulloch, 1372		Matthew de Arbroath, 1372
Stephen	1374	John de Crail or Carelle cont… 1352-93, resigned Andrew de Kyle 1393-	Salomon Rae 1380-85/89 Alexander Doig or Dog, 1393 Cuthbert de		

[2] Richard de Mowat was to resign the Barony of Fern and Sherrifdom of Forfar in November 1377; King Robert II ratified this and gave him £20 in lieu from the "great customs of Dundee" in January 1378.

		97/99 John de Hawick 1394 Patrick de Spalding 1394-97[3]	Brechin 1393-99, becomes Dean Gilbert Brown 1399-1439		
Walter Forrester of Garden (Lord Clerk Register)	1400	Cuthbert de Brechin de Henrici or de Alanson 1399-1437	Gilbert Brown cont…	Geoffrey or Galfridus of Arbroath 1410-39, Died	John Lyall 1409 – 36
John Crannoch	1426	Cuthbert cont… 1399-1437 Died 28 Apr 1437 Duncan de Lichton 1437-39/40 David de Crannach 1437-1440 John de Lichton 1438-51[4]	Gilbert Brown cont until 1439, Died Robert de Crannoch 1440-53 Andrew Fife 1440-42[5]	Geoffrey of Arbroath cont…until death in 1439 Richard Wylie 1444/46-48 Richard Dot or Doid, 1444 David de Crannach 1444-52 William Gylepsy, 1444	John Lyall cont… until 1436 Patrick Reid, 1438 Thomas Archer 1439-42 David Reid 1440-42, unsuccessful challenge[7]

---

[3] The multiplicity of Deans in this period was due to de Kyle being investigated for fraud. The Archbishop of St. Andrew's, Walter Trail, was given Papal mandate to investigate; he was still in possession in October 1397 and died before 24th June 1399. Patrick Spalding had ambitions to be Dean of Aberdeen, which he was appointed to in October 1397, though was given a prebendary of Brechin which he held until his death in 1422.

[4] Once again we have a multiplicity of Deans! David Crannoch was associated with the Council of Basle and the anti-Pope Pope Felix V, elected by the Council. David was appointed by his brother John, who faced a charge of nepotism. The de Lichton family supported the Forresters (see Chapter 3). John de Lichton was eventually the compromise candidate when charges of schism were dropped against David Crannach. Duncan de Lichton exchanged with brother John, receiving his vicarage.

		Robert Tulloch 1441 (unsuccessful) Richard Cady 1450 David de Crannach 1452-53		Patrick Reid, 1445 Lawrence Wylie, 1448[6] Walter Stewart 1452-54, Becomes Dean 19th April, 1454	Stephen Johannis de Mayr or Angus, 1444 – 77
George de Shoreswood (Lord Chancellor and confessor to the Royal household)	1454	Walter Stewart 1454 William Forbes 1454-55 (resigned in favour of Spalding) John Spalding 1456-87, (Also acted as chaplain and confessor to the King.)	George Seres 1457-80 James Lindsay, 1459[8]	David Ogilvie 1456-57/58; Exchanged with William Ogilvie, Dean of Ross, May 1457; Died Oct 1458 William Ogilvie 1457/58 – 81	Stephen de Angus cont…
Patrick Graham (Nephew of	1463	John Spalding	George Seres cont…	William Ogilvie cont…	Stephen de Angus cont…

---

[5] Andrew Fife contested Robert Crannoch's rights as Precentor on the grounds that he was elected prior to Brown's death. However, Pope Eugene IV ruled against Fife in Sept 1442. He attempted to become Dean at Dunkeld, again unsuccessfully!

[7] David Reid attempted to secure several appointments in Scotland, all unsuccessfully.

[6] There was considerable litigation over the Chancellorship on the death of Geoffrey of Arbroath. Richard Wylie resigned rights in Feb 1448 after loss of position in 1446; Dot resigned Sept 1444 with no position; Reid resigned with a pension, April 1445; Lawrence Wylie's attempts after relative Richard's were unsuccessful; Crannoch was the real winner and was in possession of the appointment by Nov 1446. There is no record of what happened to Gylepsy, though he seems to have been the popular choice.

[8] Lindsay was given dispensation to have some of the benefice of the Precentor along with others.

King James I)					
John Balfour	1466	John Spalding 1456-87 Exchanged with Hugh Douglas (Precentor) having reached 69 yrs John Barry 1477-87[9]	George Seres cont... Died 1480 Hugh Douglas 1485-87, becomes Dean John Spalding 1487, former Dean	William Ogilvie cont... Died 2nd March, 1481 James Balfour 1483-90/92	Stephen de Angus cont... until 1477 David Seton, 1471, unsuccessful challenge Thomas de Camera, 1476-77, unsuccessful challenge
William Meldrum	1488	Hugh Douglas 1487-1512	Henry Meldrum 1489-96, Related to Bishop William William Meldrum 1500-1517/18, Related to Bishop William Exchanged with Ferne to become Archdeacon of Dunkeld	James Balfour cont... Deceased by March 1492 Walter Fenton 1500-1506 Deceased by Feb 1506 William Cadzow, 1506 Thomas Meldrum 1509/10 - 24	Patrick Boyce 1493 – 1526
John Hepburn (arch anti-Reformer)	1517	Hugh Douglas (to 1512)	George Ferne 1518-27, former Archdeacon	Thomas Meldrum cont...	Patrick Boyce cont...until 1526

---

[9] John Barry sought to gain the Dean's position by *commissio privationis*, by which Spalding was accused of irregularities in procedures. The matter went to litigation but eventually Barry withdrew his claim in May 1487 in exchange for a pension.

| | | Alexander Stewart 1523/4-29[10]

Henry White 1534-41/2 Died, 1542

Patrick Stewart 1536-45[11]

John Erskine 1542

James Nasmyth 1545

James Hamilton 1545-54 Exchanges with William Cunningham to become Bishop of Argyll

William Cunningham 1555 – 58/60 Vicar General on death of Bishop | of Dunkeld; Resigned 1521 but retains some of income

James Scrymgeour 1521-41 In position by 1528

Thomas Scrymgeour 1543-62, Died March 1562 | John Colden 1532 – 38/40; Resigned on exchange with Turing for Methven.

Alexander Turing 1540-48; Deceased before Oct 1548

William Cuni, 1541[12]

George Hepburn 1548 – 85; Son of Sir Patrick Hepburn of Waughton. The bishop at first refused the appointment, probably because by 1560 all appointments were made by the Crown, not the Pope. | Arthur Boyce 1527 – 32, Resigns on basis of right of return

Charles Fotheringain 1532 – 36 Bishop refused to appoint but was made to do so by April 1533; Resigns Oct 1536

Robert Monypenny 1536 – 37

Henry Sinclair, 1538

Thomas de Huchesoun or Hugonis, 1539; appt. by Pope Paul III; resigned in favour of David Methven |

[10] AlexanderStewart was appointed to the Bishopric of Moray in Sept 1529. He was given Papal dispensation to remain as Dean of Brechin, though resigned in favour of Henry White in 1534. The holding of multiple benefices was one of the main complaints of the Reformers.

[11] White had given indication to resign in Feb 1536, though did not do so until June 1541, died 31st May 1542.

Thus from 1536-42 Stewart was coadjutor as Dean.

[12] Turing had given indication that he would resign in favour of Cuni in May 1541 but for some reason changed his mind. There is no further record of Cuni.

		Hepburn			1539 James Arnott, June 1541 James Ard 1543-47 James Wawane, 1543 Henry Sinclair 1543 John Hepburn 1552 – 96 Died before 2nd Jan 1598 **First Reformed Minister of Brechin**
John Sinclair (President of Court of Session)	1562	James Thornton 1563/66-77	Robert Fraser 1564 Robert Fraser, son, Appt. 1565 due to Father's sickness	George Hepburn cont…	John Hepburn cont…
Andrew Campbell (titular only)	1566	James Thornton cont… James Nicholson, minister at Farnell 1577-81 Dougal	Paul Fraser 1566-1609 Appt. on resignation of both Robert Frasers, July 1566; Becomes minister at Stracathro, 1583 when Privy Council	George Hepburn cont… until Oct 1585 when demitted in favour of Edward Edward Hepburn 1585 - 96/97; resigned May 1597,	John Hepburn cont… until 1598 Henry Stirling 1598-99, minister

		Campbell, minister at Farnell 1581-1619	makes it one benefice; Died Aug 1609	Vicar of Navar. David Lindsay 1597, presented by Crown but failed to secure appt. later Bishop of Ross, 1600 James Shewan 1597 – 1613	
Andrew Lamb	1607	Dougal Campbell cont…	Paul Fraser cont… Robert Norrie 1611-23	James Shewan cont…	John Norrie 1613 – 23/5
David Lindsay	1619		Robert Norrie cont…to 1623	Laurence Skinner, 1623	John Norrie cont…until death in Nov 1625 Patrick Lindsay 1625 William Ogilvie 1633
Thomas Sydserf (Dean of Edinburgh)	1634	David Carnegie 1633-38			
Walter Whiteford (Sub dean of Glasgow)	1635	David Carnegie cont…			
David Strachan	1662	David Carnegie Resumed after Restoration in 1660 - 68	J Guild, 1667 at Restoration	Hercules Skinner, Appt. 11th April, 1667	David Strachan, Appt. 11th April, 1667
Robert	1672				

Laurie (Dean of Edinburgh)				
George Halliburton	1678			
Robert Douglas (Dean of Glasgow)	1682			
Alexander Cairncross	1684			
James Drummond	1684			

APPENDIX 3
LIST OF SESSION CLERKS OF BRECHIN
CATHEDRAL From 1615

1615-36	**James Watt**, Reader & Precentor
1638-82	**Patrick Brocas**, Reader, Precentor from 1671; Doctor of Grammar School; Appointed Clerk to Presbytery from June 1648; Deceased between May – August 1682
1682	**Alexander Fairweather**; Doctor of Grammar School for one quarter
1682-85	**Laurence Skinner**; Doctor then Master of Grammar School 1685
1685-1701	**Alexander Rires**; Doctor of Grammar School Removed Martinmas 1701
1702-04	**Robert Milne**; authority restricted March 1704; Demits as Precentor May 1704; Session repudiates his appointment made during Vacancy. Milne was clearly supportive of Skinner and opposed Willison.
1704	**Andrew Doig**, Clerk pro tem
1705-09	**William Gray**; Precentor, from Rothes; resigned Whitsun 1709 and moved to Cupar in Fife.
1709-16	**Thomas Paul**; Precentor; Doctor of Grammar School from 1704; Master of Grammar School from 1716; Ordained Elder October 1719 Paul agreed to conform to Church of Scotland
1716-24	**Andrew Knox;** Student of Divinity; Precentor; Doctor of Grammar School; Ordained & inducted as Minister at Kinnaird, 9th April, 1724 Manse invaded by housebreakers 1747 Charged with slander by an elder of the Presbytery; Died Feb 1748
1724-39	**John Weath**; Student of Philosophy; Precentor; Doctor of Grammar School; Clerk to Presbytery 1725-32 Ordained & inducted Minister of Tannadice 31st March 1743 December 1743 Married Jean Dow, widow of John Johnston, minister of second charge of Brechin Died April 1766
1739-43	**Hugh Christie**; Precentor; Master of Grammar School from June 1744; Clerk to Presbytery 1744-51
1743-44	**John Philip;** Schoolmaster at Drum; Precentor; Doctor of Grammar School The "Streaker" Clerk! Dismissed on recommendation of Presbytery following his drunken antics, 10th June, 1744 (He may have been rehabilitated, appearing as a Doctor of Grammar School in November 1746)
1744-46	**Hugh Christie;** Clerk pro tem
1746-49	**Robert Miln;** Schoolmaster at Edzell; Precentor; Doctor of Grammar School

		Died Candlemas 1749
1749-52		**David Lindsay;** Precentor; Doctor of Grammar School Appointed as Presbytery Clerk September 1752 Resigned as Session Clerk 14th November, 1752
1753-55		**William Scott;** Precentor; Doctor of Grammar School Resigned as Session Clerk October 1755, removed elsewhere November 1755
1756-57		**William Wilson;** Precentor; Doctor of Grammar School; Complained against John Bruce, Master of the Grammar School Resigned May 1757
1757-60		**John Clark;** Merchant Resigned January 1760
1760-83		**John Bruce;** Precentor and Doctor of Grammar School; Later employed John Strachan, weaver, as Precentor at 6d per week Died May 1783
1783-1809		**William Dovertie;** Clerk to Poor Fund; English Master at Grammar School; Admitted as Elder 1796 Died 24th August 1809
1809-76		**George Alexander;** Clerk to Poor Fun; Elder February 1815; licensed minister; Master Parish School (1832-65) then Rector at Grammar School (1869-76); £10 annually paid by him to hire Precentor; Resigned June 1876
1876-1908		**Andrew Robertson;** Assistant Clerk 1872-76 Ordained as Elder 1868 Rector of High School 1865-94; Resigned March 1908
1908-25		**Robert McLellan;** ordained as elder 1893 Schoolmaster at High School Resigned due to ill health May 1925 – Andrew Wallace Clerk pro tem from March 1924
1925-29		**Andrew Wallace;** Elder Bank agent
1929-57		**Robert Bruce;** Elder 1922 Chief Constable
1957-1980		**David Boath Thoms;** Elder 1943 Schoolmaster at High School; Died 12th January 1980
1980-90		**Gordon W.B. Smith;** Elder 1974
1990 – 94		**Lynda Reid** Resigned as Clerk and Elder, 8th February, 1994 Resumes as Minute Clerk, 15th December, 1994 *
1994		**Dr Donald Mowat** (of Presbytery's ad-hoc Committee) Clerk *pro tempore* until November

Dec 1994 – June 1996	**VACANT** ***See above**
June - December 1996; **December 1997- June 1998**	**Rev Robin K Mackenzie, Moderator** **Rev Robin K Mackenzie, Moderator**
December 1996 – November 1997	**Kenneth Allan;** ordained elder and appointed Clerk, 1st December, 1996
June 1998 – March 1999	**David Scrymgeour, Assessor Elder, Kirriemuir** **Clerk *pro tempore***
March 1999 – June 2010	**William Low,** Elder Died in office, 19th June, 2010
October 2010 -	**Arthur Douglas Taylor,** Elder 1978 Former Depute Session Clerk to William Low; Appointed as Clerk, 14th October, 2010

APPENDIX 4
LIST OF TREASURERS OF BRECHIN CATHEDRAL
From 1615

1615-20	**Alexander Clerk** Elder 1615
1620-24	**Charles Dempster** Skinner
1624-27	**David Liddell** Elder 1616
1627-42	**Charles Dempster** 2nd period of office
1642-75	**John Liddell** Merchant
1675-90	**Walter Jameson** Bailie
1690-91	**David Young**
1704-16	**James Miller** Elder 1704; Shoemaker & Deacon Convener Dismissed as an Elder for supporting the 1715 Jacobite Rebellion
1716-22	**Robert White** Merchant; Bailie 1716
1722-26	**Henry Coway** Merchant; Elder 1719
1728-40	**Thomas Paul** Master of Grammar School; Elder 1719
1740-52	**Hugh Christie** Master of Grammar School
1752-1800	**George Reid** Elder 1752
1800-12	**William Gourlay** Preacher of the Gospel
1812-31	**John Nichol**
1832-39	**David Simpson**
1839-58	**David Hobb** Elder
1858-64	**Joseph Hendry**
1864-77	**Thomas Nicoll**
1877-89	**John Lindsay** Elder 1868

1889-93	**James Edwards** Elder 1868
1894-1931	**James Scott Lindsay** Elder 1893
1932-34	**William James Bisset** Elder 1893
1934-54	**Alexander Drummond** Bank manager; Elder 1934
1954-70	**Alexander Simpson Third** Bank manager; Elder 1949
1970-79	**Gordon Knight Baxter** Bank manager; Elder 1964
1979-92	**Archibald G. Morgan** Bank agent; Elder 1979; retired as Treasurer June 1992
1993-96	**Agnes Robinson** Retired as Treasurer November 1996
1996- 99	**Ian Mackie** Retired as Treasurer March 1999, moved to Aberdeen
1999 -	**William Christison** Elder

APPENDIX 5
LIST OF ORGANISTS AT BRECHIN CATHEDRAL
From 1878

1878 – 83	**Mr Pearson** (Formerly assistant organist at Carlisle Cathedral); *resigned 1883
1883 - 90	**Alexander Cherry** (from Linlithgow; voted in with 639 votes to Nil) *goes to Bridge of Allan
1890 – 95	**J.C. Murray** (organist at Heatherlie Church in Selkirk) *resigns in February 1895 when the Kirk Session at the Cathedral refused him permission to also play each Sunday at the United Presbyterian Church in City Road. There had also been issues over "the Psalmody of the Church" with a view in December 1894 to give Mr. Murray three months' notice.
1895 – 1901	**J.A. Edlington** (organist at Ladhope Parish Church, Galashiels) *resigned May 1901
1902 – 1909	**Alfred Mann** (organist at High Kirk in Paisley) *resigned April 1909 to take up new appointment at Bridge of Allan.
1909 – 1919	**Marshall M. Gilchrist** (organist at St. Boniface's Church at Frankfurt Am Main in Germany) *resigned March 1916 due to his conscription and subsequent military service in Egypt (Feb 1918). Technically remained officially organist until March 1919 when he went to Holy Trinity Church, Elgin.
1916 – 1921	**Miss Phyllis Anderson**, organist *pro tempore* during the war years
1922 - 25	**Richard Vaughan Bolwood** (organist from Nairn Parish Church; he received 184 votes to 54 votes for Mr. Thornley) * resigned November 1925 after concerns expressed about psalmody of Church
1926 – 1952	**George Smith** (organist from Partick Glasgow appointed on 161 votes in favour to 65 against.) * resigned 13th October, 1952 following several months of ill health
1953 – 1955	**Bramwell Cook** (Music master at Brechin High School.) * resigned on 25th December, 1955 after taking up a new teaching appointment at Stirling.
1956 – 1963	**Raymond Brown** (took up supervisory role in Carlisle, December 1963)
1963- 64	**W.A. Scott** (Temporary organist from December 1963 – April 1964)
1964 – 66	**Richard Galloway** from Peterhead (took up office on 13th April, 1964) *resigned 6th March 1966 on taking up new teaching post at Aberdeen Grammar.
1966 – 71	**John R.W. Calderhead** of Dundee with **Miss Ann D. Gall** as assistant. * resigned 29th August, 1971
1971 – 76	**Miss Elizabeth Bell** of Arbroath appointed from 1st November, 1971 *resigned April 1976 when promoted to Edinburgh.
1976 – 1982	**Arthur G. Balfour**, B.Mus., Assistant Music Teacher at Brechin High School appointed from 2nd May, 1976 *resigned 31st August, 1982
1982-	**Noel Smith** of Cartmel Priory in Cumbria as new organist and choirmaster.

99	*Retired 25th July, 1999 but agreed to assist with Organist rota until new Organist appointed. **Mary Alexander** functioned briefly as deputy in early 1987 due to Noel's illness and at some other times.
1999-2003	ORGANIST ROTA (Organised by Music Committee of Session)
2003 -	**Ian Robertson**; appointed summer 2003

APPENDIX 6
CATHEDRAL STATISTICS 1894 – 2010
STATISTICS OF THOSE RECEIVING COMMUNION

DATE	Number of Communicants
22nd October 1894	759
13th May 1895	802
21st October 1895	811
12th May 1896	875
19th October 1896	789
9th May 1898	872
17th October 1898	778
15th May 1899	859
16th October 1899	747
14th May 1900	715
14th October 1900	721
16th May 1901	779
21st October 1901	710
11th May 1902	839 *Cathedral re-opened after Restoration: Wed 23rd April, 1902
19th October 1902	721
10th May 1903	677
18th October 1903	657
8th May 1904	709
16th October 1904	647
14th May 1905	766
15th October 1905	638
13th May 1906	721
21st October 1906	572
12th May 1907	683
20th October 1907	616
10th May 1908	748
18th October 1908	566
9th May 1909	716
17th October 1909	639
8th May 1910	702
16th October 1910	594
14th May 1911	745
15th October 1911	600
12th May 1912	650

Date	Value
20th October 1912	548
11th May 1913	558
19th October 1913	627
10th May 1914	656
18th October 1914	589
9th May 1915	680
17th October 1915	544
15th October 1916	505
13th May 1917	526
21st October 1917	438
12th May 1918	610
20th October 1918	491
11th May 1919	597
19th October 1919	522
9th May 1920	637
17th October 1920	542
8th May 1921	650
16th October 1921	580
14th May 1922	642
15th October 1922	522
13th May 1923	663
21st October 1923	580
19th October 1924	551
10th May 1925	654
19th October 1925	500
9th May 1926	603
17th October 1926	519
8th May 1927	617
16th October 1927	551
13th May 1928	629
21st October 1928	509
12th May 1929	626
20th October 1929	527
19th October 1930	503
10th May 1931	AM – 435, PM – 128 **TOTAL – 563 ***
18th October 1931	527
8th May 1932	AM – 532, PM – 128 **TOTAL – 660**
13th October 1932	AM – 391, PM – 99 **TOTAL – 490**
14th May 1933	AM – 565, PM – 140 **TOTAL – 705**

15th October 1933	AM – 413, PM - 88 **TOTAL – 501**
13th May 1934	AM – 539, PM - 135 **TOTAL – 674**
21st October 1934	AM – 411, PM - 93 **TOTAL – 504**
19th May 1935	713
20th October 1935	AM – 356, PM - 91 **TOTAL – 447**
10th May 1936	AM – 506, PM – 131 **TOTAL - 637**
18th October 1936	AM – 431, PM – 105 **TOTAL – 536**
9th May 1937	AM – 421, PM – 135 **TOTAL – 556**
17th October 1937	AM – 418, PM – 113 **TOTAL – 531**
8th May 1938	AM – 491, PM – 129 **TOTAL – 620**
16th October 1938	AM – 375, PM – 131 **TOTAL – 506**
14th May 1939	AM – 509, PM – 134 **TOTAL – 643**
15th October 1939	AM – 406, PM – 94 **TOTAL – 500**
12th May 1940	AM – 454, PM – 126 **TOTAL – 580**
20th October 1940	AM – 382, PM – 83 **TOTAL – 500** **Nos. at the afternoon service were reduced due to air raid**
11th May 1941	AM – 370, PM – 114 **TOTAL – 484**
19th October 1941	AM – 330, PM – 113 **TOTAL – 443**
10th May 1942	AM – 306, PM – 109 **TOTAL – 469**
18th October 1942	AM – 407, PM – 117 **TOTAL – 524**
16th May 1943	AM – 692 + 28 visitors, PM – 180 **TOTAL – 872**
17th October 1943	AM – 503 + 16 visitors, PM – 159 + 4 visitors **TOTAL – 662**
21st May 1944	AM – 589 + 15 visitors, PM – 185 +

	9 visitors **TOTAL – 774**
13th October 1944	AM – 538 + 11 visitors, PM – 154 + 4 visitors **TOTAL – 692**
20th May 1945	AM – 593 + 11 visitors, PM – 180 + 3 visitors **TOTAL – 778**
21st October 1945	AM – 509 + 16 visitors, PM – 169 + 3 visitors **TOTAL – 675**
19th May 1946	AM – 608 + 9 visitors, PM – 174 + 5 visitors **TOTAL – 796**
14th October 1946	AM – 522 + 5 visitors, PM – 147 + 8 visitors **TOTAL – 669**
12th May 1947	AM – 564 + 10 visitors, PM – 182 + 6 visitors **TOTAL – 746**
19th October 1947	AM – 538 + 20 visitors, PM – 150 + 1 visitors **TOTAL – 688**
16th May 1948	AM – 652 + 13 visitors, PM – 156 **TOTAL – 808**
17th October 1948	AM – 402 + 11 visitors, PM – 204 + 4 visitors **TOTAL – 606**
16th October 1949	AM – 582 + 7 visitors, PM – 187 + 1 visitor **TOTAL – 711**
21st May 1950	AM – 610 + 9 visitors, PM – 161 + 3 visitors **TOTAL – 771**
15th October 1950	AM – 498 + 11 visitors, PM – 174 + 1 visitor **TOTAL – 672**
20th May 1951	AM – 539 + 13 visitors, PM – 195 **TOTAL – 734**
21st October 1951	AM – 477 + 12 visitors, PM – 181 + 2 visitors, **TOTAL – 672**
18th May 1952	AM – 609 + 12 visitors, PM – 181, **TOTAL – 802**
19th October 1952	AM – 477, PM – 173, **TOTAL – 650**
17th May 1953	AM – 594, PM – 179 + 15 visitors, **TOTAL – 788**
18th October 1953	AM – 487, PM – 182 + 14 visitors, **TOTAL – 669**
16th May 1954	AM – 538 + 4 visitors, 187 + 2 visitors, **TOTAL – 731**
17th October 1954	AM – 458 + 7 visitors, 107 + 5 visitors, **TOTAL – 577**
15th May 1955	AM – 557 + 2 visitors, 197 + 2 visitors, cards forgotten – 16

	TOTAL – 772 *Afternoon Communion reverted to 2.15pm
16th October 1955	AM – 513 + 4 visitors, PM – 182 + 1 visitor, **TOTAL – 695**
20th May 1956	AM – 558 + 7 visitors, PM – 188, cards forgotten – 19 **TOTAL – 782**
21st October 1956	AM – 486 + 3 visitors, PM – 155 + 1 visitor, **TOTAL – 641**
19th May 1957	AM – 558 + 5 visitors, cards forgotten – 4, PM – 147 + 3 visitors, cards forgotten – 2, **TOTAL – 719**
20th October 1957	***From this Communion individual cups were introduced** AM – 530, PM – 161, Visitors – 6, **TOTAL – 691**
18th May 1958	AM – 564, PM – 200 + 5 visitors, **TOTAL 764**
19th October 1958	AM – 531, PM – 135, Visitors 8, **TOTAL – 666**
17th May 1959	AM – 599, PM – 162, Visitors 9, **TOTAL – 761** ***A proposal to increase to four Communions in June 1959 was departed from following discussion at Kirk Session**
18th October 1959	AM – 510, PM – 149, Visitors – 9, **TOTAL – 659**
15th May 1960	AM – 620, PM – 132, Visitors – 5, **TOTAL – 752**
16th October 1960	AM – 467, PM – 140, Visitors – 8, **TOTAL – 607**
21st May 1961	AM – 566, PM – 165, Visitors – 5, **TOTAL – 731**
15th October 1961	AM – 477, PM – 133, Visitors – 7, **TOTAL – 610**
20th May 1962	AM – 560, PM – 162, **TOTAL - 722**
21st October 1962	AM – 488, PM – 148, **TOTAL – 636**
19th May 1963	AM – 562, PM – 150, **TOTAL – 712**

20th October 1963	AM – 533, PM – 138, **TOTAL – 671**
17th May 1964	AM – 576, PM – 158, **TOTAL – 734**
18th October 1964	AM – 479, PM – 114, **TOTAL – 593**
16th May 1965	AM – 604, PM – 151, **TOTAL – 755**
17th October 1965	AM – 510, PM – 128, **TOTAL – 638**
15th May 1966	AM – 628, PM – 142, **TOTAL – 770**
16th October 1966	AM – 470, PM – 149, **TOTAL – 619**
21st May 1967	AM – 599, PM – 134, 13 – Visitors, **TOTAL – 733**
15th October 1967	AM – 570, PM – 163, **TOTAL – 733**
19th May 1968	AM – 640, PM – 152, 8 – visitors, **TOTAL – 792**
27th October 1968	AM – 527, PM – 178, 2 – visitors, **TOTAL – 705**
May 1969	AM – 597, PM – 181, 9 – visitors, **TOTAL – 778**
19th October 1969	AM – 640, PM – 180, 17 – visitors, **TOTAL - 820**
17th May 1970	AM – 621, PM – 204, 5 – Visitors, **TOTAL – 825**
18th October 1970	AM – 529, PM – 205 + 29 at evening Communion on 25th Oct **TOTAL – 763**
16th May 1971	AM – 622, PM – 165, 18 – visitors + 48 (eve: 23rd May) **TOTAL – 835**
17th October 1971	AM – 500, PM – 150, 10 – visitors + 50 with 3 visitors (eve: 24th Oct) **TOTAL – 700**
21st May 1972	AM – 586, PM – 153 + 58 (aft: 28th May) **TOTAL – 797**
15th October 1972	AM – 513, PM – 154 + 57 (eve: 22nd Oct), 12 – visitors **TOTAL – 724**
	There is no extant minute book from Jan 1973 –

	Jan 1977
15th May 1977	AM – 542, PM – 149 + 50 (aft: 22nd May) **TOTAL – 741**
16th October 1977	AM – 442, PM – 139 + 80 (eve: 23rd Oct) **TOTAL – 661**
21st May 1978	AM – 507, PM – 140 + 52 (aft: 28th May) **TOTAL – 699**
21st October 1979	AM – 448, PM – 153 + 61 (eve: 28th Oct) **TOTAL - 662**[13]
19th October 1980	AM – 437, PM – 142 + 99 (eve: 26th Oct) **TOTAL – 678**
May 1983	AM – 423, PM – 135, 3rd table – 75, **TOTAL – 633**
May 1984	**TOTAL – 591**
May 1985	AM – 401, PM – 96, 3rd table – 56, **TOTAL – 553**
October 1985	**TOTAL – 514**
May 1986	**TOTAL – 472**
May 1988	**PM ONLY – 30**
June 12th 1990	AM – 196, PM – 22, other times – 41, **TOTAL – 259**
May 1994	**TOTAL – 296**
October 1994	**TOTAL – 280**
	In March 1998, the practice of issuing Communion cards was departed from. It was re-instated during Scott Rennie's tenure.

- Unless otherwise stated the PM Communion was held in the afternoon

---

[13] From this point onwards the Communion Statistics are not always entered into the Kirk Session minutes, hence the gaps. I suspect that the death of D.B.Thoms, who was Session Clerk, in January 1980 is partly the reason. He was a stickler for accuracy!

CONGREGATIONAL STATISTICS 1934 – 2010

DATE	No on Roll	No Comm Once	Elders	Bapt.	Death	Profess	Cert	Wed
31st Dec 1888[14]	1608	1218 (75.7%)		86				38
31st Dec 1934	1229							
31st Dec 1935	1289	887 (68.8%)	22		14			
31st Dec 1936	1293	878 (67.9%)	22	38	30			
31st Dec 1937	1275	823 (64.5%)	21	31 (2 Adult)	22			
31st Dec 1938	1290	897 (69.5%)	21	26	18			
31st Jan 1939	1282	877 (68.4%)	21	22	26			
31st Dec 1940	1290	819 (63.5%)	21	20	19			
31st Dec 1941	1291	722 (55.9%)	20	23	26			
31st Dec 1942	1356[15]	790 (58.2%)	16	24	[16]			
31st Dec 1943	1375			36				
31st Dec 1944	1415	1051 (74.3%)	33	35	26			
31st Dec 1945	1445	1008 (69.8%)	33	54	22			
31st Dec 1946	1457	1017 (69.8%)		40	29			
31st Dec 1947	1406	1005 (71.5%)	38	49	22			
31st Dec	1516	1048	35	39	26			

[14] These figures are recorded in the 1888 Brechin Almanac; the Summer Communion had the largest attendance since 1843 at the Disruption.

[15] The sudden increase of the Congregational Roll is due to an Electoral Roll being drawn up in March 1942 for the union of the 1st and 2nd charges and the election of a new minister.

[16] The lack of an entry merely indicates that the statistic was not recorded in the Kirk Session minutes – not that there were no deaths!

1948		(69.1%)						
31st Dec 1949	1525	1027 (67.3%)	44	43				
31st Dec 1950	1527	1020 (66.8%)	44	43	22			
31st Dec 1951	1532	1018 (66.4%)	41	48	22			
31st Dec 1952	1517	1008 (66.4%)	46	29				
31st Dec 1953	1519	1004 (66.1%)	44	39				
31st Dec 1954	1491	936 (62.8%)	41	30	34			
31st Dec 1955	1512	993 (65.7%)	46	36	21			
31st Dec 1956	1485	976 (65.7%)	34		30			27
31st Dec 1957	1462							
31st Dec 1958	1490	1008 (67.7%)		42	19			
31st Dec 1959	1468	981 (66.8%)		39	25			
31st Dec 1960	1441	942 (65.4%)		34	26			
31st Dec 1961	1390	940 (67.6%)		28	30			
31st Dec 1962	1363	944 (69.3%)		37	28			
31st Dec 1963	1408	953 (67.7%)		33	30			
31st Dec 1964	1395	925 (66.3%)		27	25			
31st Dec 1965	1382	935 (67.6%)		25	26			
31st Dec 1966	1414	963 (68.1%)		34	20			
31st Dec 1967	1393	1012 (72.6%)		37	31			
31st Dec 1968	1426	1029 (72.2%)		39	15			
31st Dec 1969	1409 Supp Roll – 53	1088 (77.2%)		32	20			

31st Dec 1970	1423	1072 (75.3%)		35	27		
31st Dec 1971	1413	1053 (74.5%)		45 (6 Adult)	21		
31st Dec 1972	1410				23		
31st Dec 1975	1456				30	24	+25 -25
31st Dec 1976	1465	1026 (70%)					
31st Dec 1977	1437	984 (68.5%) Supp – 96			35	28	+19 -38
31st Dec 1978	1425	1035 (72.6%)			36	37	+22
31st Dec 1979	1415	955 (67.5%)			28	26	+22
31st Dec 1980	1385	974 (70.3%)			36	22	+14
31st Dec 1981	1379	937 (67.9%)			39	29	+14
31st Dec 1982	1356	878 (64.7%)			27	22	+9
31st Dec 1983	1353	901 (66.6%)			35	34	+30
31st Dec 1984	1342	859 (64.0%)			30	25	+9
31st Dec 1985	1312	760 (57.9%)			22	11	+8
31st Dec 1986	1293	548 (42.4%)			33	16	+8
31st Dec 1987	1293	523 (40.4%)			29		
31st Dec 1988	1247	546 (43.8%)			31		
31st Dec 1990	1945[17] Incl. 115 (Supp						

[17] The greatly increased figure of membership was caused by the union of the Cathedral, Stracathro and Maison Dieu churches on 21st September, 1990.

	Roll)							
31st Dec 1991	1739 *21 Sun Sch & 43 BB*	551 (31.7%)			107 removed	7	+6	
31st Dec 1992	1684 205 Sup. Roll		65 Elders + 8 Cong Board	24	33	7	+4 -35	
31st Dec 1993	1629 205 SR		62 Elders + 9CB	21 Inc. 2 Adult	27	9	+4 -41	
31st Dec 1994	1571			15	31	1	+1 -31	
31st Dec 1995	1484 Or 1462?[18]			25	42	10	+4 -60	
31st Dec 1996	1431			10	35	5	+9 -10	
31st Dec 1997	1387 *192 SR*		33 Elders + 11CB	14	38	5	+1 -11	
31st Dec 1998	1329				30	0	+6 -34	
31st Dec 2000	1184[19]							
31st Dec 2003	1098							
20th August 2009	854							
31st Dec 2009	839 *230 SR*							

[18] There was some confusion and dispute as to the attestation of the Roll at the end of 1995
[19] There are a number of years in this period where the Roll was not attested at a Session meeting therefore the statistics do not appear in the Session minutes.

APPENDIX 7
VARIOUS RELIGIOUS CENSUS FIGURES

RELIGIOUS CENSUS FIGURES: 1st April 1851 (Population: 8210)

CHURCH	MORN ATTEND	AFT ATTEND	EVE ATTEND
East Free	470	443	
West Free	682	607	965
City Road UP	196	229	
Maison Dieu UP	160	173	380
High St UP	489	548	
Episcopal	150	116	
Free Church Station	45		

RELIGIOUS CENSUS FIGURES: 12th December 1881 (Population: 10,499)

CHURCH	NO. ON CHURCH ROLL	NO. ATTENDING THAT DAY
East Parish	804	503 (62.6%)
East Free	750	368 (49.0%)
West Free	962	526 (54.7%)
Bank St. United Presbyterian	620	316 (51.0%)
Maison Dieu U.P.	400	230 (57.5%)
City Road U.P.	500	270 (54%)
St. Andrew's Episcopal	300	164 (54.6%)
Evangelical Union	300	57 (19%)
Roman Catholic (Mason's Hall)	50	37 (74%)
Brethern	50	9 (18%)
Children's Church/Tenement Schools	100	85 (85%)
Cathedral	1464	905 (61.8%)
TOTAL	6326	3470 (33% of Popn.)

RELIGIOUS CENSUS FIGURES: 31st March 1901

Three Established Churches: 787

5 United Free Churches: 1124

Other Churches: 216

TOTAL: 2127 (20.4%)

RELIGIOUS CENSUS FIGURES: 15th March 1903

Established Churches: 1419

United Free Churches: 2176

Episcopal Church: 416

EU Congregational Church: 145

Salvation Army: 122

Plymouth Brethern: 44

CATHEDRAL CENSUS FIGURES: March 1984

DATE	ADULT	CHILD
4th March	168	55
11th March	148	46
18th March	180	64
25th March	123	40

POPULATION STATISTICS OF BRECHIN

YEAR	POPULATION
1755	3181
1790	5000
1801	5466
1811	5559
1821	5906

1841	7560
1851	8210
1861	8810
1871	9514 4132 male 5382 female
1881	10499 4616 male 5883 female
1891	10453 4537 male 5916 female
1901	10444 4570 male 5874 female
1911	9836 4285 male 5551 female
1921	8781 3804 male 4977 female
1971	6687
1981	7573
1991	7680
2001	7199
2011	7481

ROLL OF HONOUR
OF
BRECHIN
AND
District

Dulce et decorum est pro patria mori

ABERCROMBY, Pte. John D., Welford, Fern—9th Black Watch; killed, Sept. 25, 1915.

ADAM, Corp. Alex.—Black Watch; killed 18th April, 1918..

ADAM, Pte. James, Montrose Street—5th Black Watch; died of wounds, March, 13, 1915.

ADAMS, Pte. Dunbar, Montrose St.—14th Canadian Infantry; killed, July 13, 1916.

ADAMSON, Capt. and Flight-Commander Wm. Campbell, Careston Castle—Royal Flying Corps; killed in action Sept. 5, 1915.

ANDERSON, Lieut. C. Ogilvy,—2nd Royal Scots; died of wounds, October, 1915.

ANDERSON, Pte. D. Lyall, Gladstone Pl.— 'Gordons; died of wounds; 15th September, 1917.

ANDERSON, Driver David, Arrat's Mill—Army Service Corps; drowned, June 1917.

ANDERSON, Cpl. George, Tigerton, Menmuir—Canadians; died of wounds 3rd Sept., 1918.

ANDERSON, Pte. Geo. L., Clearbank, Stracathro—Canadians; died of wounds, 24th May, 1917.

ANDERSON, Pte. Wm., 2 Southesk Ter.—Black Watch; killed, 29th Sept. 1917.

ANGUS, Co.-Sergt.-Major Alex.—South African Scottish; killed, 12th April 1917.

ANGUS, Corpl. Alex., Market Street—Black Watch; killed, 12th Oct. 1917.

ALLISON, Gunner Charles, City Road—Royal Field Artillery; died of wounds, 19th Sept. 1916.

AUCHTERLONIE, Pte. Anderson W., River St.—Gordon Highlanders; killed, 17th June 1917

BAIRNER, Pte. John W., Dalfouper, Edzell—Gordon Highlanders; killed, 3rd April, 1916.

BALNAVES, Corp. Alex. W.—3/4th Gordon Highlanders; killed, 5th May, 1916.

BATCHELOR, David C.—Royal Scots; died of wounds, 11th April 1918.

BATCHELOR, Pte. Jack—London Scottish; killed, 31st Oct. 1917.

BEATTIE, Serg. John, Arrat—2nd Black Watch; killed May 9, 1915.

BEATTIE, Sergt. John, Kincraig—Black Watch; killed July 1918.

BEEDIE, Pte. Charles, Trinity Rd.—Bedford Regiment; killed, 13th August 1917.

BELL, Pte. Wm., Kinnaird Park—Black Watch, died of wounds, 11th April 1917.
BENNET, Pte. D., Montrose St.—Black Watch; died in Mesopotamia, 21st Sept. 1916.
BERN, Pte. Alex., Union St.—1st Black Watch; killed May 9, 1915.
BIRNIE, Pte. Alex., Montrose St.—Royal Scots; killed, 14th July 1916.
BIRSE, Pte. David M. Ledmore—Royal Scots; died of wounds, 16th October, 1917.
BIRSE, Corp. R., Edzell—Royal Engineers; killed 25th April 1918.
BLACK, Corp. Wm., Montrose St.—Black Watch; wounded and missing, Oct. 1916, afterwards reported died of wounds a prisoner in the enemy's hands.
BONAR, Trooper Lawrence M.—Dragoon Guards (att. Leicester Regiment); killed 25th Sept. 1915.
BOWMAN, Pte. Chas., H., 45 Bridge St.—Black Watch; killed, 3rd Sept. 1916.
BRAND, Pte. Alex., Union St.—5th Black Watch; died of wounds, 5th Sept. 1916.
BREMNER, Pte. Stewart, River St.—Canadians (Victoria Rifles); killed, 1st Oct. 1917.
BRODIE, Pte. Cunningham, Panmure St.—London Scottish; killed in action, 9th Sept. 1916.
BROWN, Pte. Alex. B.—Scots Guards; killed, Jan. 25, 1915.
BROWN, Pte. Jas., Fern—Highland Light Infantry; killed, 21st April, 1917.
BROWN, Pte. Robert Fern—Canadians; killed, 9th April 1917.
BRUCE, Pte. Chas., 39 Bridge St.—Black Watch, killed 25th Sept. 1916.
BUCHAN, Pte. Jas., High St.—Royal Scots, att. Yorkshire Light Infantry; killed, 8th June, 1917.
BUICK, Pte. David, Montrose St.—Black Watch; died in Mesopotamia, 11th Jan. 1918.
BURNETT, Corp. James, Kinnaird Place—15th Highland Light Infantry, killed, 3rd July, 1916.
BURNETT, Pte. Wm., Andover Hill—Scots Guards; killed, March 30, 1916.

CALDER, Pte. Andrew, City Road—5th Black Watch; killed, Feb. 8, 1915.
CAMERON, Corp. Stewart G., Lochside, Edzell—Gordon Highlanders; killed 2nd April 1917.
CAMPBELL, Bombr. Neil, 25 High St.—R.F.A.; killed 23rd July 1918.
CAMPBELL, Pte. Robert, 231 Montrose St.—9th Black Watch; killed, 26th Sept. 1915.
CARCARY, Corp. Edward, 113 Montrose St,—Black Watch, killed March 1918.
CHALMERS, Pte. Douglas S., Park Road—Gordon Highlanders; killed 16th April, 1917.
CHRISTIE, Pte. Allan, The Kennels—Canadians; killed 28th Sept. 1918.

CHRISTIE, Pte. Wm., Montrose St.—1st Black Watch; killed, May 9, 1915.
CHRISTISON, Bomb. A. N., Rangoon—Indian Volunteer Artillery; taken prisoner at Kut, and reported dead, 1st May 1916.
CHRISTISON, Pte. Robert, Tarfside—Gordon Highlanders; killed Aug. 1916.
CLARK, Pte. James, Nursery House—2nd Black Watch; killed 22nd April, 1916.
CLARK, Lance-Corpl. J. D., 180 Montrose St.—Gordons; killed 20th Sept. 1917.
CLARK, Sergt. P., Bloomfield—Seaforth Highlanders; killed, 1st May 1917.
CLARK, Pte. Wm., Farmerton, Fern—1st Black Watch; killed, 31st May, 1916.
CLARK, Pte. Wm. M., 5 Albert Pl.—Gordon Highlanders; died of wounds, 16th Oct. 1918.
CLUNESS, Pte. Leslie, Careston—Black Watch; killed 21st March 1918.
CLYNE, Pte. Don Keith, Menmuir—Cameron Highlanders; died from wounds, 4th Sept. 1916.
COATES, Pte. Roy A., Balnamoon—15th Royal Scots; killed, 1st July, 1916.
COBB, Pte. James, 233 Montrose St.—Black Watch; killed 27th Sept. 1917.
COOK, Sapper Geo. M., Albert Pl.—Royal Engineers, died of wounds, 30th Sept. 1916.
CORDINER, 2/Lieut. George G., Southesk St.—Royal Air Force; killed in flight accident, 25th June 1918.
CORDINER, Pte. Harry N., 23 Southesk St.—Royal Scots Fusiliers; killed 1st Oct. 1918.
CORRAL, Pte. Wm., High St.—Black Watch; killed, 31st July 1917.
COROTRIE, Wireless Operator Ernest A.—s.s. Ohio, torpedoed March 1917.
COWIE, Pte. Wm., Stracathro—1st London Scottish; died of wounds, Sept. 28 1915.
COWNIE, Pte. D. Edzell—Highland Light Infantry; killed Sept. 17, 1914.
CRAIK, Pte. Joseph R., 72 Montrose St.—R.G.A., killed at Salonika, 9th May 1917.
CRAM, Pte. George, Hunter's Cottages—Scottish Rifles (M.G.C); killed, 1st May 1917.
CROCKET, Pte. John, 52 Montrose St.—S. African Infantry, killed 26th Sept. 1917.
CROCKET, Pte. W P.—Canadian Black Watch; killed 10th Oct., 1918.
CROLL, Pte. David B.—Scots Guards; killed, Nov. 6, 1914.
CRUICKSHANK, Pte. James, Tarfside—4th Gordon Highlanders; killed, April 14. 1915.
CURRIE, Corp. Matthew, Bothers Close—Gordon High., killed 9th April 1916.

DAVIDSON, Lieut. A. R., Ellenlea—Seaforth High., killed in Mesopotamia, 22nd April 1916.
DAVIDSON, Pte. Alex., Montrose St,—Highland Cyclist Battalion; died in hospital, August 28, 1915.

Continued

DAKERS, Pte. Andrew, Union St.—Machine Gun Corps; killed 25th April 1918.

DAWSON, L-Corpl. Jas. C., Meikle Tullo—Scottish Horse (att. Black Watch); killed, April 1917.

DEAR, Corpl. Wm. F., (7 Kinnaird Pl.)—102nd United States Infantry; killed 23rd Oct. 1918.

DON, Lieut. V. G., Maulesden—8th Royal West Kents; killed, 26th Sept. 1915.

DONALDSON, Pte. Evan A., M.M., Maulesden—Gordon High., killed 9th April 1918.

DORWARD, Pte. Edwin, Albert Place—Royal Irish Fusiliers; killed at Dardanelles, August 16, 1915.

DORWARD, Pte. Peter—Royal Scots; killed 11th Aug. 1918.

DUNBAR, Pte. A., Glenesk—Black Watch; died from wounds, Sept. 1916.

DUNCAN, Sergt. Andrew, Glenesk—1st Gordon Highlanders; killed, Nov. 14, 1914.

DUNCAN, Lance-Corpl. Charles, The Banks—Royal Scots; killed, 20th Sept. 1917.

DUNCAN, Pte. Charles, Montrose St.—Black Watch, M.G.C.; killed Sept. 1917.

DUNCAN, Pte. Gregory H., Lochty—1st Argyll and Sutherland Highlanders; killed May 11, 1915.

DUNCAN, Corpl. John, Lochty—1st Gordon Highlanders; killed, Sept. 13, 1916.

DUNCAN, Pte. John, Lethnot—5th Black Watch; died of wounds, May 10, 1915.

DUNCAN, Lance-Corpl. John, Farnell—Highland Light Infantry; died a prisoner at Angora, Turkey, 10th Sept. 1916.

DUNCAN, Pte. Joseph, Clerk St.—Black Watch; killed March 1918.

DUNCAN, Pte. Thomas, Mayfield—Black Watch; killed 2nd Sept. 1918.

DUNN, Lance-Corporal Wm., Bank St.—5th Black Watch; killed, Jan. 23, 1915.

DURWARD, Pte. T. A.—43rd Cameron Highlanders, Canadian Expeditionary Force; killed 2nd May, 1916.

DUTHIE, Pte. George, Cookston—Cameron Highlanders; killed, 29th December 1917.

DUTHIE, Pte. Harry, 136 Montrose St.—Black Watch; died of wounds, 25th Aug. 1917.

DUTHIE, Sergt. Robert, Broomfield—Black Watch; killed 8th Sept. 1918.

EASTON Pte. Gilbert, East Pittendreich—1st Black Watch; killed Sept. 25, 1915.

EDDIE, Sergt. James—Canadian Mounted Rifles; wounded and reported missing, 2nd June 1916; afterwards died a prisoner of war in Germany.

EDWARD, Pte. James, Westmuir—5th Black Watch; died from wounds, 21st Sept. 1916.

EMSLIE Pte. James—Black Watch; d'ed of wounds 15th May 1918.

FARQUHAR, Pte. David, 171 Montrose St.—Black Watch; killed, 13th Nov. 1916.

FARQUHAR, Trooper Jas. Pitforthie—Fife and Forfar Yeomanry (att. K.O.S.B.); killed, 15th April 1917.

FENTON, Pte. Arthur, Andover Hill—5th Black Watch; killed in action, 23rd July, 1916.

FERRIER, Lieut. John K., Dalladies, Edzell—Rifle Brigade; killed Aug. 1918.

FERRY, Pte. Laurence, River Street—Black Watch; killed Nov 1918.

FETTIES, Pte. John—Seaforth Highlanders; killed, 21st April 1917.

FINDLAY, Pte. David, Scott Street—Gordon Highlanders (M.G.S.); killed, 15th July, 1917.

FINDLAY, Capt. Lorimer—R.F.C.; accidentally killed, 14th June, 1917.

FITCHETT, Pte. James, 23 Church St.—42nd Batt. Canadians; killed 29th Sept. 1918.

FITCHETT, Pte. Joseph, Witchden Road—5th Black Watch; died of fever at Rouen Hospital, April 21, 1915.

FORBES, Pte. Frank A., 34 Montrose St.—R.A.M.C.; died of wounds, 26th Sept. 1917.

FORSYTH, Capt. Wm., T.D., Mountskip—7th Gordon Highlanders; died of wounds, October 20, 1915.

FORREST, Staff-Sergt.-Major George—Transport Division, Indian Army; died in Mesopotamia 3rd August, 1916.

FOWLER. Pte. Walter, Damacre Road—Black Watch; killed, 23rd April 1917.

FRASER, C.S.M. John S.—Gordon High., killed 22nd March 1918.

FREEMAN, Pte. Jas., Luthermuir—78th (Canadian) Cameron Highlanders; died in hospital Feb. 26, 1917.

FYFE, Pte. James, 3 Trinity Rd.—Gordon Highlanders; died of wounds, 17th Oct. 1918.

FYFFE, Pte. Edwin H., Church St.—London Scottish; killed in action, Sept. 1916.

GARDEN, Pte. Norval R. Edzell—Black Watch; killed 18th April 1918.

GARVIE, Trooper Wm., Lumington—Canadian Cavalry; died of wounds 12th Oct. 1918.

GELLATLY, Corpl. Fred, Southesk Ter.—Black Watch; killed, 20th Nov. 1917.

GIBSON, Pte. Edwin W.—South African Infantry; killed 12th April, 1917.

GLEN, Pte. Archie, Montrose St.—Black Watch; died of wounds, 16th Oct. 1916.

GLEN, Sergt. David, 28 Kinnaird Pl.—Royal Scots; killed, April 9, 1917.

GLEN, Pte. Jas. Blibberhill—Black Watch; killed, 9th April 1917.

GOODALL, Pte. Geo., Market St.—Black Watch; killed 23rd April, 1917.

Continued

283

GORDON, L.-Corpl. Allan, 12 Union St.—5th Black Watch ; died of wounds, 15th Oct. 1916.
GORDON, Lieut. James W. N.—5th Black Watch ; killed, Feb. 22, 1915.
GORDON, Pte. James, Bridgend, Lethnot—killed, 24th Jan. 1917.
GORDON, Pte. John S. 135 River St.—Royal Scots ; killed 22nd Aug. 1918.
GORDON, Pte. Wm., 6 Crocket's Buildings—Black Watch ; killed, 14th Oct. 1916.
GORDON, Corpl. Richard, Aldbar—Royal Scots, killed Sept. 1916.
GOVE, Pte. James—Canadian Scottish ; killed, 4th June, 1916.
GOVE, Pte. Wm., East Drums—Black Watch ; killed, 30th July 1916.
GRAHAM, Corp. Chas., 17 Witchden Road—Black Watch ; killed 28th July 1918.
GRAHAM, Pte. John, 17 Union St.—Black Watch ; killed 25th July 1918.
GRAHAM, Pte. Norman, 9 Bridge St.—Seaforth High. ; killed July 1918
GRANT, Pte. Wm. F., 145 Montrose St.—Royal Scots ; killed, 22nd Oct. 1916.
GRAY, Pte. Harry, 65 River Street—Highland Light Infantry ; killed, 18th Nov. 1916.
GRAY, Pte. James, 13 Southesk St.—Black Watch ; killed 21st March. 1918.
GREWAR, Pte. Arthur, Kinnaird—8th Black Watch ; killed, Sept. 25, 1915.
GUILD, Pte. Andrew. 180 Montrose St.—Gordon High. ; died of wounds, 2nd April 1918.

HAGGART, Trooper David K., Balnamoon—Lovat's Scouts, att. A. and S. Highlanders ; died in hospital at Salonika, 13th July 1917.
HAMPTON, Serg. David, M.M., Little Tullo, Edzell—Canadians ; killed 2nd Sept. 1918.
HARDIE, Pte. Andrew, Albert Pl.—5th Black Watch ; killed at Neuve Chapelle, March 14, 1915.
HASTINGS, Pte. George—Royal Engineers ; killed, 2nd Nov. 1917.
HEBENTON, Pte. George, Glenogil—9th Black Watch ; killed, July 1916.
HENDERSON, Pte. Wm., River Street—3rd Seaforth Highlanders ; killed, July 11, 1916.
HENDERSON, Trooper John, Kincraig—Scots Greys (att. Royal Scots), killed April 23, 1917.
HENDRIE, Pte. Andrew, 211 Montrose St.—Gordon Highlanders ; killed, 23rd April 1917.
HENDRY, Pte. Geo., Dubton, Stracathro—1st Black Watch ; killed 21st April, 1916.
HILL, Pte. Charles R., 113 River St.—Scots Guards ; killed, 31st July 1917.
HODGE, Reg.-Quarter-Master-Sergt. John, 35 Park Road—Australian Imperial Force ; killed 10th Aug. 1918.
HOOD, Pte. Allister M., River St.—H.L.I., killed 14th March 1918

HOOD, Gunner Andrew, Kinnaird Pl.—R.G.A. died of wounds, 3rd July 1917.
HOOD, Pte. Sidney. River Street—Black Watch ; killed, 14th Oct. 1916.
HUNTER, Pte. A.—2nd Gordon Highlanders, died of wounds, Nov. 21, 1914.
HUNTER, Pte. Wm., Dalbog, Edzell—Gordon Highlanders ; died Dec. 1916.
HUTCHEON, Corpl. Edwin, 12 St Mary St.—Royal Scots Fusiliers ; died at Salonica, 5th Oct. 1918.
HUTCHINS, Pte. Geo., 85 River St.—Black Watch, killed 10th Oct. 1916.
HUTCHISON, Pte. Harry, Union St.—5th Black Watch ; died of wounds, May 10, 1915.
HUTTON. Pte. Harry, Damacre Road—died of wounds, 9th April 1917
HUTTON. Pte. Stewart, Southesk Terrace—Royal Scots ; killed, July, 1916.
HUTTON. Pte. Walter—Gordon Highlanders ; killed at Loos. 25th Sept. 1915.

INNES, Pte James I., Glenesk ; killed 1914.
IRVINE, Pte. Tom, Nursery Lane—5th Black Watch ; died of wounds, June 12, 1915.

JAPP, Pte. David, Bridge St.— 8th Black Watch ; died 12th July. 1916.
JAFFREY. Pte. John, 249 Montrose St.—Black Watch ; killed 22nd Oct. 1918.
JEFFRAY. Corporal Robert, M.M., 127 River St.— Black Watch ; died of wounds, Nov. 23 1917.
JOE, Pte. David S., 29 Union St.—Black Watch ; died of wounds. 26th March 1918.
JONES. Pte. Geo. R., Montrose St.—Black Watch ; died of wounds. 2nd April 1917.

KEAN, A.M. James S., Montrose St.—Royal Air Force ; killed March 1918.
KEILLOR, Pte. John P.—Scots Guards ; killed, 10th April 1917.
KEMP. Pte. Arthur, 30 Bridge St.—Black Watch ; killed 16th Oct. 1918.
KERR, Pte. A., Poet's Lane—9th Black Watch ; died of wounds, 16th February, 1916.
KIDD, Pte. David, 11 Union St.—Royal Scots ; killed 3rd May 1917.
KINNEAR, Pte. John—killed in action, 13th Aug. 1916.
KINNEAR, Pte. Wm., High St.—Royal High ; killed 3rd May 1917
KNOX, Pte. Wm., Park Road—Black Watch ; died of malaria in Egypt, 21st Nov. 1918.
KYNOCH, Pte. Albert, 15 Albert Pl.—Black Watch ; killed 31st July 1917.
KYNOCH, Signaller Peter, (Whyte's Buildings)—46th Canadian Battalion ; died in hospital, Nov. 30, 1915.
KYNOCH, Pte. Rae, 15 Albert Pl.—Gordon Highlanders ; killed, 20th Feb. 1917.

Continued

284

Continued

LAING, Pte. Bertie C. H., 4 Union St.—Seaforth High.; killed 28th July 1918.

LAW, Gunner Alex., 9 Southesk Terrace.—R.G.A.; killed 1st Oct. 1917.

LAWSON, Seaman James, Nether Careston—Nelson Batt., R.N.D. killed, 13th July, 1915.

LEITCH, Pte. James, Bridge St.—Royal Scots; died of wounds, September 29, 1915.

LINDSAY, Pte. Walter, Market St.—1st Black Watch; killed, Sept. 25. 1915.

LONGMUIR. Pte. John, 50 Montrose St.—Black Watch; killed 3rd May 1917.

LOW, Pte. Charles. Trinity. Park—2nd Black Watch; killed, 22nd April. 1916.

LOW. Pte. George, Black Bull Close—Black Watch; killed 13th Nov. 1916.

LOW, Pte. Jas., Kinnaird Pl.—Black Watch; killed, 23rd April 1917.

LOW, Pte. Stewart, Black Bull Close—Black Watch; killed 23rd March 1918.

LOWE, Pte. David, Montrose St.—Black Watch; died of wounds, 17th Nov 1916.

LYELL. L.-Corpl. Geo. W., 48 Bridge St.—Black Watch; killed, 14th Oct. 1916.

LYON, Pte. John S., Star Hotel—2nd South African Infantry; killed in German East Africa, March, 21, 1916.

MACDONALD, Pte. David—Seaforth Highlanders; died at Salonika 20th Oct. 1916.

MACDONALD, Pte Jack, Market St.—2nd Black Watch; killed, Mar. 10, 1915.

MACDONALD, Lance-Corp. Ronald, Kinnaird—83rd Field Company Royal Engineers; killed, 22nd Feb., 1916.

MACFARLANE, Sergt. G. Y., D.C.M., Glengyle—Black Watch; killed, 31st July, 1917.

MACGREGOR. Pte. James, High St.—Cameron High.; killed 23rd April 1918.

McDONALD, Pte. Edward—1st Black Watch—killed,. 5th Oct. 1914.

M'DOWALL, L.-Corpl. James—New Zealanders; killed 8th Oct. 1918.

McFARLANE, Pte. Francis, Market St.—Royal Engineers; died of wounds, 11th June, 1917.

McGEE, Pte. James 220 Montrose St.—Royal Scots; killed, 23rd April 1917.

McGREGOR. Pte. John, 18 Montrose St.—Black Watch; died of wounds; 30th Dec., 1916.

M'GREGOR. Farrier-Sergeant J., Edzell—Scottish Horse; died October 24, 1915, of wounds received at Dardanelles.

M'HARDY, Lieut. J., Andover Hill—Canadians; killed 26th Aug. 1918.

M'INTOSH, L.-Corp. John, Nether Careston—Highland Light Infantry; killed August 1916.

McINTOSH, Pte. Walter Weir—Royal Scots; killed 28th April 1917.

McKENZIE, Pte. A., Edzell—Royal Scots; died of wounds, April 1917.

McKENZIE, Pte. Alex., Clochie, Lethnot—Royal Scots; died of wounds, April 18, 1917.

M'LAREN, Pte. David, 31 Montrose St.—Gordon Highlanders; died of wounds, 18th June 1918.

M'LEAN, Stoker Chas.—H.M.S. Infefatigable; lost in Jutland battle, 31st May, 1916.

M'LENNAN, Corpl. James, Montrose St.—8th Black Watch; killed, 14th July. 1916.

M'LENNAN, Pte. W., Market St.—9th Black Wach; killed, May 29, 1916.

M'LEOD, Engineer David R., R.N.R., Montrose St; drowned when mine-sweeper Briton was lost, July 21, 1915.

MARR, Pte. Alex., Bridgend—8th Battalion Canadian Contingent; killed at Ypres; April 25, 1915.

MARTIN, Pte. Robert—Scots Guards; killed, May 20th, 1916.

MARTIN, Corp. D. Collie—Black Watch; killed, 26th March 1917.

MASSIE, Pte. Leonard, City Road—Black Watch; died of wounds, 14th Nov. 1916.

MILNE, Pte. George, Eastbank—Scottish Horse (att. Black Watch; killed 17th Oct. 1916.

MILNE, Pte. James, 92 Montrose St.—Black Watch, killed 14th Oct. 1916.

MILNE, Pte. John, Ballownie—Black Watch; killed. 12th Oct., 1916.

MILNE, Pte. Wm.—Durham Light Infantry; killed, 8th June 1917

MILNE, Pte. David, 40 Montrose St.—Scottish Horse, att. B.W.; killed, 29th March 1917.

MITCHELL, Lance-Corporal Geo.—2nd Black Watch; killed in Mesopotamia, February, 1916.

MITCHELL, Pte. Hugh, Aldbar—Canadians; killed, April 1917.

MITCHELL, Sapper Jas., V., 3 Albert Pl.—Royal Engineers; killed 24th Oct., 1918.

MITCHELL, Pte. Thos., Park Road—Gordon Highlanders; killed 28th July 1918.

MELDRUM, Pte. George, 11 River St.—Black Watch; killed 3rd Sept. 1916.

MOIR, Drummer Wm. S.D., 5 Swan St.—23rd London Regt.; killed, 22nd Aug. 1918.

MONRO, FRANK W., Arrat's Mill—Canadians; killed 13th Aug. 1918.

MORRISON, Pte. Frank—Royal Scots; died from wounds, May, 1916.

MORRISON, Pte. James, Limefield—2nd Life Guards; died in hospital, February 7. 1915.

MORRISON, Pte. John—4th Black Watch; died from wounds, May 29, 1915.

MUDIE. Gunner Robert, Menmuir—M.G.C.; died in Mesopotamia, June 1917.

MYLES, Lieut. Wm. W.—10th Cameronians; died from wounds, 20th Sept. 1916.

O'DONALD, Lance-Corp. C., Lethnot—Black Watch; killed in action, May 9, 1915.

PAISLEY, 2nd Lieut. Tom, Careston—10th Scottish Rifles; killed Sept. 22, 1915.
PATERSON, Pte. Chas., Dunlappie Rd., Edzell—F. & F. Yeomanry, att. Black Watch; killed Sept. 1917.
PAUL, Pte. Alex.—Black Watch; died of wounds a prisoner in Germany, 15th Aug. 1916.
PETER, Corp. Alex., Oakbank—Fife and Forfar Yeomanry; died December 5, 1915, from wounds received at Dardanelles.
PETRIE, Corp. Wm., 25 High St.—Royal Scots Fusiliers; died 28th Nov. 1918.
POTTIER, Capt. Robert—Black Watch; killed 14th Oct. 1918.
PYOTT, Serg. James, 113 Montrose St.—Black Watch; died of wounds, 15th Nov. 1916.
PYPER, Pte. J. B.. Damacre Rd.—Canadians; died of wounds 12th Nov. 1918.

RAE, Driver Joseph, Balwyllo—Motor Transport; killed, Feb. 1916.
RATTRAY, Pte. A., Edzell—Black Watch; died of wounds, Nov. 1916.
RATTRAY, Sergt. Alex., Union Street—5th Black Watch; killed, May 9, 1915.
REID, Pte. Archie, The Banks—5th Black Watch (Reserves); died in hospital Oct. 26, 1914.
REID, Lance-Corp. Fergus, Montrose St.—5th Black Watch; killed, March 14 1915.
REID, Pte. James, East Kintrockat—1st Black Watch; died of wounds, Oct. 17, 1915.
REID, Gunner Tom, 7 St Mary St.,—R.G.A.; killed 22nd Sept. 1918.
REID, Pte. Walter, Auchmull—Princess Patricia's Canadian Light Infantry; killed 28th Sept. 1918.
RICHARDSON, Pte. Thos. N.—Tank Corps; killed 29th Sept. 1918.
RILEY, Pte. Robert, 54 Bridge St.—Black Watch; killed 23rd March 1918.
RITCHIE, Pte. Geo. C., Edzell—Canadian Contingent; died of wounds, June 15. 1915.
RITCHIE, Lance-Corp. James, Montrose St.—Black Watch; killed 25th Sept. 1916.
RITCHIE, Lance-Corp. W., Careston—Black Watch; Nov., 1914.
RITCHIE, Engineer Arthur G., R.N.R.—lost with H.M.I. Genista, 23rd Oct. 1916.
RITCHIE, Pte. Frank, 1st Scots Guards; killed, 17th June, 1916.
RITCHIE, Corpl. James W., Edzell—F. & F. Yeomanry (att. B.W.); killed Sept. 1918.
ROBB, Pte. James, 51 River St.—Black Watch; killed March 1918.
ROBERT, Pte. Jas D., 12 Scott St.—5th Scottish Rifles; killed, March 25, 1916.

ROBERTS, Pte. James L., 60 High St.—Black Watch; killed 14th Oct. 1916.
ROBERTSON, A.M. Arthur, Dalhousie St.—R.F.C.; died in hospital, 6th March 1917.
ROBERTSON, Gunner Alex. B.—Canadian Division; killed, 22nd July 1917.
ROBERTSON, Pte. Daniel, River St.—Black Watch; killed in action, Sept. 1916.
ROBERTSON, Pte. Daniel—44th Batt. Australian Force, killed, 2nd April, 1917.
ROBERTSON, Pte. David, Market St.—Black Watch; died of wounds, 16th June 1917.
ROBERTSON, Gunner Jas. E., Montrose St.—R.G.A.; killed, 5th Oct. 1917.
ROSS, Pte. Andrew, 65 River St.—Royal Scots Fusiliers; killed 23rd Sept. 1918.
ROSS, Pte. David Lethnot—Canadians; killed, 10th April 1917.
ROSS, Pte. John. Church St.—London Regiment; killed, 23rd Sept. 1916.

SANDEMAN, Pte. Frank, 4 Victoria Pl.—Black Watch; killed 1st Oct. 1918.
SANDEMAN, Pte. John—Royal Scots Fusiliers; died of wounds, April. 1917.
SCOTT, Pte. D.,—Black Watch; killed, October, 1914.
SCOTT, Pte. Fred, Montrose St.—5th Black Watch; killed, March 1, 1915.
SCOTT, Pte. Lancelot, River Street—Black Watch; killed July 1918.
SILVER, Pte. Frank, Arnhall, Edzell—Gordon Highlanders; died of wounds, 22nd Nov. 1916.
SILVER, Corp. Joseph, New Forebank—2nd Royal Scots Fusiliers killed in action, 16th June, 1915.
SIM, Pte. Edward, Farnell—Royal Scots; killed, 9th April 1917
SIMPSON, 2nd Lieut. Douglas A.—7th Gordon Highlanders; died of wounds, Oct. 15, 1917.
SIMPSON, Pte. James, 2 School Lane—Canadian Mounted Rifles; killed 8th August 1918.
SINCLAIR, Bandsman Frank—49th Batt. Canadian Exp. Force; killed, 29th Oct. 1917.
SKENE, Pte. Robert, Balglassie—Black Watch; killed Oct. 1918.
SMART, Co.-Sergeant-Major James B.—Highland Light Infantry; killed, 18th Nov. 1916.
SMART, Sapper Chas.—Royal Engineers, Australian I.F.; died in France, 1st March 1917.
SMART, Pte. David, Careston—Royal Field Artillery; drowned at Norwich, Sept. 17. 1914.
SMART, Pte. Harry, Southesk St.—Gordon Highlanders; killed, 9th March 1917.
SMITH, Gunner Albert, 8 Bridge St.—Royal Field Artillery; killed, 31st Oct. 1916.

Continued

286

SMITH, Lieut. Alex. W., M.C.—Gordon Highs.; killed 21st March 1918.
SMITH, Pte. Alex.—Canadian Force; died of wounds. 4th Dec. 1917.
SMITH, Pte. Arthur, City Road—5th Black Watch; killed, March 14, 1915.
SMITH, Pte. Jack B.—New Zealand Infantry (Canterbury); killed, April 1917.
SMITH, Pte. James, 130 Montrose St.—Black Watch; died of wounds, 2nd Sept. 1918.
SMITH, Pte. John (Springfield Cottage)—Canadians (Lincoln Regt.), died 26th April 1917.
SMITH, Pte. Norman, Barrelwell—Gordon Highlanders; killed, 13th Nov. 1916.
SMITH, Driver Oliver, 5 St Mary St.—R.F.A., killed 8th Oct., 1918.
SMITH, Pte. Wm., East Mains, Edzell—Scottish Rifles; killed, 3rd May 1917.
SMITH, Pte. Wm. Newtonmill—Canadian Scottish; killed, June 1916.
SMITH, Pte. Wm. L., Forthill—Black Watch; killed, 3rd Sept., 1916.
SPRUNT, Pte. Alex., 106 High St.—Royal Dragoons; died 30th April 1918.
SOUTTER, Pte. David—87th Canadians; died in hospital, Nov. 1918.
SPRUNT, Corporal Harry M., Union St.—American Expeditionary Force; died of wounds, 4th Dec. 1918.
STEWART, Pte. Alfred, 8 Bridge St.—Black Watch; killed 19th July 1918.
STITCHELL, L.-Corp. Erward, Bridge St.—Royal Scots; died of wounds, 28th Oct. 1916.
STEPHEN, Trooper Walter—Canadian Contingent; died of wounds 25th Sept. 1916.
STEWART, Pte. D., Bothers Close—1st Black Watch; died from wounds, Jan. 4, 1915.
STEWART, L.-Corp. Fred, Balnabreich—Black Watch; killed, July 10, 1916.
STORMONTH, Pte. D. P., Glenesk—Black Watch; died of wounds 16th April 1918.
STRACHAN, Pte. David—Scots Guards; killed, 27th Sept. 1915.
STRACHAN, Gunner Jas. H., Wilson's Park—R.F.A., killed 6th June 1918.
STRACHAN, Pte. Jas., Newington House,—Black Watch; died of pneumonia in Palestine, Nov. 1918.
STRACHAN, Lance-Corp. Robert, 22 Southesk Ter.—Black Watch; killed, 14th Oct. 1916.
STURROCK, Pte. George, Nursery Lane—Black Watch; killed, Sept., 1916.
STURROCK, Pte. Patrick, Nursery Lane—Black Watch; died from wounds, 19th Aug., 1916.

TAYLOR, Capt. Alex., Rosehill—Royal Scots; killed, 21st April 1917.
TAYLOR, Lance-Corp. J.—Gordon Highlanders; died of wounds, January 1917.
TAYLOR, Pte. Alex., Menmuir—Gordon Highlanders; killed, 25th Sept., 1915.
TAYLOR, Pte. Geo., Burnside of Balzeordie—Black Watch; killed, 9th Nov. 1916.
THOMSON, Pte. Alfred, 209 Montrose St.—3/5th Black Watch; died in hospital, Jan., 24, 1916.
THOMSON, Pte. C. Randall, Eastbank—Black Watch; killed, 19th July 1918.
THOMSON, Pte. George—Canadians; died of wounds, March 1918.
TRAIL, L.-Corp. Geo., Edzell—H.L.I., killed April 1918.
TODD, Pte. Andrew, Arrat—Black Watch; killed, 23rd Jan. 1917.
TOSH, Pte. James, Farnell—Canadian Division; killed, 10th August 1917.

VALENTINE, Serg. D. W., M.M., 81 River Street—M.G.C.; died of wounds, 26th Oct. 1918.
VALENTINE, Lance-Corp. J., Edzell—1st Black Watch; killed at Ypres, October 27, 1914.

WALKER, Pte. George, Albert Pl.—Machine Gun Corps, killed 28th March 1918.
WALKER, Gunner Wm. W., 88 Montrose Street—Tank Corps; killed, 20th Nov. 1917.
WALKER, Pte. Wm., Southesk Terrace—Black Watch; died of wounds, 11th Sept., 1916.
WATSON, Pte. Jas.—South African Infantry; killed July, 1916.
WATSON, Pte. John, 152 Montrose St.—Canadian Scottish (M.G.S.); killed, 28th Sept. 1916.
WATSON, Pte. Walter, Market St.—Royal Scots; killed, 2nd Sept. 1916.
WEBSTER, Pte. Alex., Dubton Farm—died 6th May 1918.
WHYTE, Pte. James, Albert Place—Black Watch; killed 3rd Sept., 1916.
WINTER, L.-Corp. D. N., Menmuir—Black Watch; died 2nd Nov. 1918.
WINTER, Pte. David, East Muirside, Menmuir—Black Watch; killed 21st April, 1917.
WOOD, Sergt. Chas. Nether Pert—New Zealand Corps; died 19th August, 1916.

YOUNG, Pte. David, Canadian Black Watch; killed Aug. 1918.

Additional names to the above follow below:

287

The following names feature on the Brechin War Memorial but were not included in the original Roll of Honour in November 1918:

James Bell	Lance Corporal, Black Watch 4th/5th Battalion Died 31st July, 1917 (26 yrs) Son of James and Isabella Bell, 257 Montrose Street, Brechin
David Cooper	Private, Black Watch 7th Btn. Died 5th March, 1919 (29 yrs) Husband of Alice, Dall's House, Montrose Street, Brechin
George S. Cooper	Details of death unknown
David Logan Coupar	Lance Corporal, Black Watch (Fife & Forfar Yeomanry 14th Btn) Died 10th September, 1918
William T Davidson	Private, Black Watch 1st/7th Btn. Died 15th April, 1918 (29 yrs) Husband of Jean Brown 135 Murray Street, Montrose
George M.I. Drummond	Lance Corporal, Black Watch 2nd Battalion Died 1st January, 1919 (23 yr) Son of John Drummond, 221 Montrose Street, Brechin
John C. Emslie	Private, Black Watch 8th Battalion Died 15th May, 1918
George Farquharson	Second Lieutenant, West Yorks Regiment (Prince of Wales' Own) 7th Battalion Died 7th October, 1919 (21 years) Son of Frank & Elizabeth Farquharson, Brechin
Alex Garbut	Private, Machine Gun Corps 21st Battalion Died 21st March, 1918 (21 years) Son of Solomon & Jane Garbut, 49 High Street, Brechin
Harry Gaines	Private, Highland Light Infantry 2nd Battalion Died 13th November, 1916

	Son of F Gaines
William M Inglis	Gunner, Royal Field Artillery Died 21st August 1917 (19 yrs) Son of A.M. & Florence Inglis, 26 High Street, Brechin
Fred Laing	Private, Seaforth Highlanders 1st/4th Battalion Died 5th August, 1916
William McGlashan	Details of death unknown
Alex Milne	Private, Black Watch 6th Btn. Died 21st March 1918
Arthur G Milne	Private, Black Watch 6th Battalion Died 21st March, 1918 (21 yrs) Son of Mrs J. Milne Mathers of West Mains of Keithock
Fred Milne	Private, Black Watch 1st/7th Btn. Died 2nd September 1918
James Milne	Lance Corporal, Black Watch 4th/5th Battalion Died 1st April, 1918 (20 yrs) Son of James & Mary Milne, 44 High Street, Brechin
George Mitchell	Private, Cameronians 6th Battalion Died 23rd July, 1918 (19 yrs) Son of James Mitchell, 194 Montrose Street, Brechin
John Sandison	Private, Gordon Highlanders 1st Battalion Died 17th June, 1916
Charles Edward Sim	Private, Royal Scots 15th Btn. Died 9th April, 1917 (22 yrs) Son of Charles & Elizabeth Sim, 8 Crockets Buildings, Montrose St, Brechin
Alfred James Stewart	Private, Black Watch 8th Btn. Died 19th July, 1918 (30 yrs) Son of John Stewart, 17 Union St, Brechin & husband of Jean Walker.
John Wallace	Details of death unknown
William Watson	Private, Durham Light Infantry

	14th Battalion Died 20th April, 1917 (29 yrs) Son of David Watson & the late Elizabeth Colie Watson of 35 Airlie Street. 3 brothers & 2 sisters (nurses) also served.
Alex Whyte	Private, Australian Infantry 17th Btn. Died 9th October, 1917 (25 yrs.) Son of Mrs. Catherine Whyte, 16 Southesk Terrace, Montrose St., Brechin

Where it is indicated "details of death unknown", this means that from the records of the Commonwealth War Graves Commission I have been unable to make a conclusive identification of the deceased either with Brechin or more generally.

APPENDIX 9
VARIOUS MAPS & DOCUMENTS

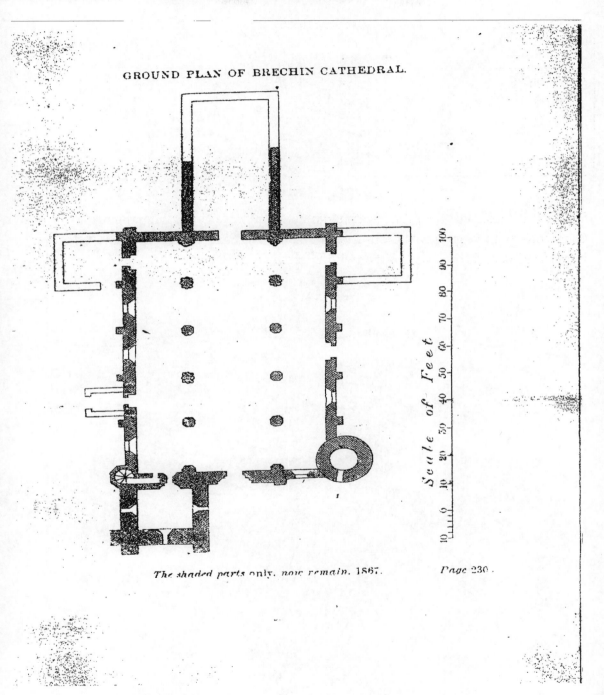

GROUND PLAN OF BRECHIN CATHEDRAL.

The shaded parts only, now remain. 1867.

Page 230.

Scale of Feet

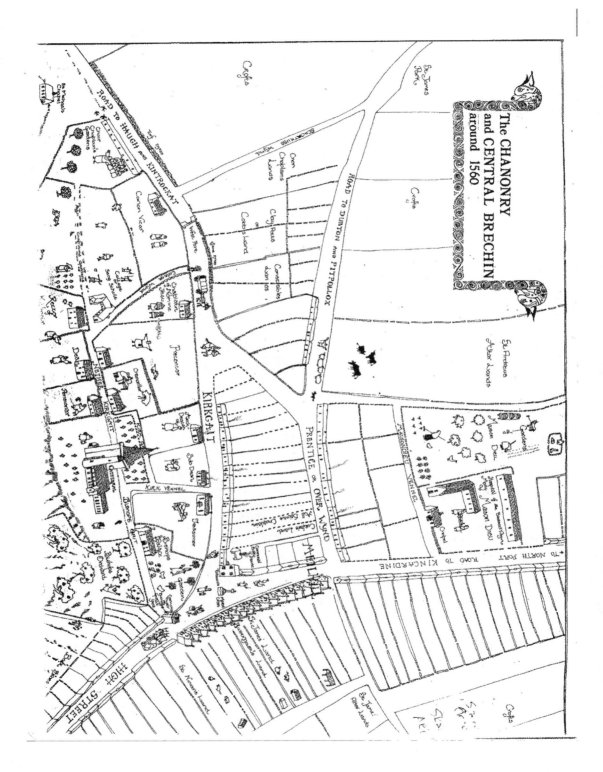

The CHANONRY and CENTRAL BRECHIN around 1560

BRECHIN CATHEDRAL RESTORATION FUND.

FIRST LIST OF SUBSCRIPTIONS.

JANUARY 1898.

Name	£	s	d
J. A. Campbell, M.P., of Stracathro	£1000	0	0
A Native of Brechin	1000	0	0
The Rt. Honble. The Earl of Dalhousie	300	0	0
Wm. M'Nab of Keithock	300	0	0
Mr. and Mrs. Capel Carnegy Arbuthnott of Balnamoon	105	0	0
Rev. J. A. and Mrs. Clark, The Manse	100	0	0
R. Lamb, Ravenscraig, Broughty Ferry	100	0	0
John Coupar, East Bank, as Executor of the late James Scott of East Pittendreich	100	0	0
William Shaw Adamson of Careston	100	0	0
Rev. A. D. and Mrs. Tait Hutchison, The Manse	50	0	0
Miss Webster, Annfield	50	0	0
John Coupar, East Bank	50	0	0
"Anonymous"	50	0	0
Do.	40	0	0
Robert Duke, Bearehill	25	0	0
John Shiell, Solicitor	25	0	0
A. R. Maclean Murray, Grove House	25	0	0
G. S. Lamb, Broughty Ferry	25	0	0
John Lamb, Glencadam	25	0	0
Jas. H. Lamb, The Latch	25	0	0
Provost Scott, Brechin	25	0	0
Miss Baillie, Panmure Street	20	0	0
Misses Smith, Pearsemount	20	0	0
Andrew Robertson, 51 Southesk St.	20	0	0
James Smart, Church Street	20	0	0
Martin M. M. Prain, Edinburgh	15	15	0
Alex. Philip, Solicitor	15	0	0
Wm. Fettis, Rosemount	15	0	0
Alex. Pirie, Commercial Hotel	15	0	0
Charles Anderson, Solicitor	10	10	0
James Craig, Solicitor	10	0	0
David Guthrie Shiell, Solicitor	10	0	0
James S. Lindsay, 17 Clerk Street	10	0	0
Wm. Manson, Panmure Street	10	0	0
Rev. Dr. Mitford Mitchell, Edinburgh	10	0	0
Rev. W. J. Tait, London	10	0	0
Robert M'Lellan, Dalhousie Terrace	10	0	0
Misses Clark, Kippen	10	0	0
Misses Mather, 8 Dalhousie Street	10	0	0
Mrs. Mitchell, Airliesacre	10	0	0
Dr. Leishman, Bearehill Villa	10	0	0
Henry Braid, Clerk Street	10	0	0
Wm. Scott, Kimberley Villa	10	0	0
Charles Richard, Schoolhouse, Little Brechin	10	0	0
Rev. T. A. and Mrs. Cameron, Farnell	10	0	0
Carry forward	**£3821**	**5**	**0**

Name	£	s	d
Brought forward	£3821	5	0
James Grimm, 27 Southesk Street	6	0	0
J. J. Taylor, Southesk Street	5	5	0
Miss M'Intyre, Dowanhill, Glasgow	5	5	0
Fred. M'Leod, High Street	5	0	0
D. C. Milne, Southesk Street	5	0	0
Miss Croal, Park Road	5	0	0
George Anderson, Buenos Ayres	5	0	0
Miss Will, Southesk Street	5	0	0
Rev. R. Paisley, East Manse	5	0	0
James Jenkins, 3 High Street	5	0	0
C. J. Guthrie, Q.C., Edinburgh	5	0	0
John Oswald, Damacre Road	5	0	0
James Mather, 8 Dalhousie Street	5	0	0
David Sherret, 6 Clerk Street	5	0	0
John Bruce, 57 Southesk Street	5	0	0
James Fearn, Montrose	5	0	0
Wm. Mudie, 21 River Street	5	0	0
Mrs. Wm. Clark, 22 Montrose St.	5	0	0
J. C. Robertson, Postmaster	5	0	0
Col. R. G. Lowe, Galveston, Texas	5	0	0
Mrs. D. F. Anderson, Trinity	5	0	0
Mrs. Ford, Infirmary Street	3	0	0
Miss Stuart, St. Andrew's House	3	0	0
J. M. Peddie, 19 High Street	3	0	0
Robert Smith, 1 Bridge Street	3	0	0
W. B. Buchan, 33 Union Street	3	0	0
Mrs. and Miss M'Pherson, Panmure Street	3	0	0
Miss Ewen, St. Ninian Square	3	0	0
Rev. Jas. M. Campbell, Dundee	2	2	0
John Maclachlan, Glasgow	2	2	0
Misses Wylie, 18 Pearse Street	2	2	0
Rev. Jas. Cooper, D.D., Aberdeen	2	2	0
Alex. Macleod, Glencadam	2	2	0
"Two Friends"	2	0	0
Andrew H. Hood, 21 Church St.	2	0	0
Mrs. Robertson, 5 Castle Street	2	0	0
Misses Rickard, Southesk St.	2	0	0
Mrs. Thomson, Union Street	1	0	0
C. R. Shaw, New York	1	0	0
"A Friend"	1	0	0
"Anonymous"	1	0	0
Do.	1	0	0
John Shaw, 19 Union Street	1	0	0
Mrs. Barclay, St. Ninian Sq.	1	0	0
Miss J. Ewen, do.	1	0	0
Mrs. Thomson, Westbank	1	0	0
Mrs. M'Laren, St. James' Place	1	0	0
Mrs. Norrie, Trinity	0	10	0
Mrs. Begg, Banks of Brechin	0	10	0
James Mathewson, Trowbridge	0	5	0
"An Invalid"	0	2	0
	£3978	**12**	**0**

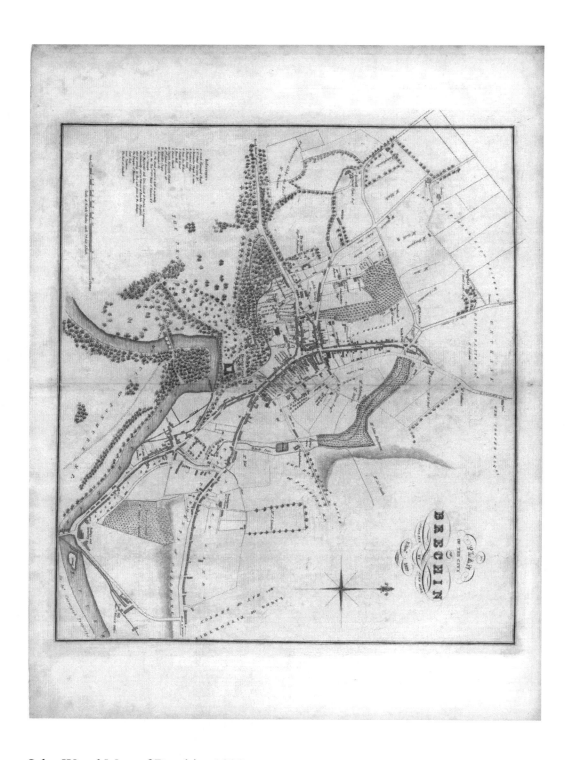

John Wood Map of Brechin, 1822

BIBLIOGRAPHY

PRIMARY SOURCES:

As with any history, the main and best source of material comes from Primary sources; in the case of Brechin Cathedral, we have an abundance! With two exceptions, the Kirk Session Minutes are continuous from May 1615 – Present.

The exceptions are the periods June 1697 – December 1703 (when I suspect John Skinner failed to return a volume) and 13th February 1973 – January 1977 (which are either lost or misplaced.) We had thought that the period February 1973 – March 1987 was lost but, subsequent to the publishing of my D Min Thesis *Shards of Hope*, Elizabeth, our Archivist discovered two missing volumes in a box. There is hope that at least the 1970s lost volume may yet be located.

In addition, I had access to Presbytery of Brechin Selected Minutes from 9th May 1639 – 8th November, 1749. Along with *Extracts from the records of the Presbytery of Brechin 1639 – 1660* W.M. Ogilvie (Dundee, 1877).

The current Presbytery of Angus Minutes 1989 – 2004 and some private papers were also made available to me, courtesy of the Presbytery Clerks.

Shortly before concluding the book a box of papers (being the private research papers of D.B. Thoms, former Session Clerk) was delivered into our custody, from Rev. Dr. Henry Sefton of Aberdeen University. These proved to be both invaluable and enlightening.

In addition, articles and snippets of information in several Brechin Almanacs (accessible at Brechin Library) proved very helpful, especially those dealing with the years of the Great War; so too a number of past copies of the *Brechin Advertiser* newspaper.

Of course, there were too numerous articles in previous Society of Friends' yearbooks and some of the most relevant articles are listed below:

Papers of the Society of Friends of Brechin Cathedral*

*The papers of the Society of Friends are listed chronologically by volume number and relate to the talk to the Society of the previous year.

Simpson, W. Douglas. "Brechin Cathedral" (Vol.1, 1948)

Cant, R.G. "Cathedral Life in Medieval Scotland with special reference to the Cathedral Kirk and Channonry in Brechin" (Vol. 2, 1949)

Thoms, D.B. "The College of Brechin" (Vol.3, 1950)

——. "A Guide to Brechin Cathedral" (Vol.4, 1951)

Dunlop, Annie. "John Crannach: Bishop of Brechin 1426-54 (Vol.6, 1953)

Thoms, D.B. "Bishops and Ministers of Brechin in the Seventeenth Century" (Vol.7, 1954)

——."The Years of Transition: 1691 – 1716" (Vol.8, 1955)

——. "Church and School in Brechin: 1560 – 1872" (Vol.9, 1956)

——."The Cathedral Kirk of Brechin" (Vol.11, 1958)

Gordon, Peter M. "Robert Coutts: Minister at Brechin 1801-03 (Vol.17, 1968)

Watt, Donald. "The organisation of the Medieval diocese of Brechin" (Vol.19, 1970)

Gordon, Peter M. "The Brechin Vacancy: 1837-38" (Vol.22, 1973)

Sefton, Henry R. "John Willison and his times 1680-1750" (Vol.24, 1975)

Gordon, Peter M. "A Pious and Patriotic Duty" (Vol.26, 1977)

Thoms, David B. "The Chanonry of Brechin" (Vol.27, 1978)

Gordon, Peter M. "The Session Clerks: 1615 – 1980" (Vol.29, 1980)

Cargill, David C. "Some recollections of Brechin in the earlier 20th century" (Vol.30, 1981)

Adams, David G. "From Samson to Gregory: Bishops and Clergy 1150-1250" (Vol.34, 1985)

Badgett, Frank. "The Chapter of Brechin and the Reformation" (Vol.39, 1990)

Sefton, Henry R. "Brechin and the Disruption of 1843" (Vol.42, 1993)

Atkinson, Norman. "The coming of Christianity to Angus" (Vol.43, 1994)

Fisher, Ian. "The Saint Mary stone and early Christian Art" (Vol.44, 1997)

Whitley, Lawrence. "The Choosers and the Chosen: Vacancy Filling 1690 – 1745" (Vol.45, 2001)

Murray, C. & H. "Results of Archaeological Dig at Brechin Cathedral" (Vol.52, 2010)

SECONDARY SOURCES:

Adams, David G. *Brechin: the Ancient City.* 1990, unpublished, manuscript available at Brechin Library

——.*Brechin Round Tower: an illustrated guide.* Brechin: Channonry Press, 1986

——. *Celtic and Mediaeval religious houses in Angus.* Brechin: Channonry Press, 1984

Bardgett, Frank D. *Scotland Reformed – The Reformation in Angus and The Mearns.* Edinburgh: John Donald, 1989

Bede. *Ecclesiastical History of England.* trans. A.M. Sellar. London: George Bell & Sons, 1907

Black, David D. *The History of Brechin to 1864.* Brechin: Pinkfoot Press, new edition, 2009

Bradley, Ian. *Celtic Christianity.* Edinburgh University Press, 1999

——. *The Celtic Way.* London: Darton, Longman & Todd, 2003

——. *Colonies of Heaven.* London: Darton, Longman & Todd, 2000

Bulloch, James. *Life of the Celtic Church.* Edinburgh: St. Andrew's Press, 1963

Burleigh, J.H.S. *A Church History of Scotland.* Edinburgh: Hope Trust, 1983

Cameron, Neil; Fraser, Iain; Halliday, Strat. *Early medieval carved stones at Brechin Cathedral.* Edinburgh: RCAHMS, 2007

Coats, Walter W. *A Short History of Brechin Cathedral.* Brechin: Black & Johnston, 1903

Patrick Collinson. "The late Medieval Church and its Reformation 1400-1600" in *The Oxford Illustrated History of Christianity.* edt. John McManners Oxford University Press, 1990

Cruickshank, Graeme *The Battle of Dunnichen.* Brechin: Pinkfoot Press, 2009

Dowden, John. *The Celtic Church in Scotland.* London: SPCK, 1894

--- *The Bishops of Scotland.* Glasgow: James Maclehose & Sons, 1912

Dron, Kenneth W. *Round about a Tower*. Brechin: Society of Friends Publications, 1979

Duke, John A. *The Columban Church*. Oxford University Press, 1932

Edwards, D.H. *A Pocket History and Guide to Brechin*. Brechin: Black & Johnston, 1872

——. "Brechin Cathedral: description of renovated building and fittings" in *Brechin Almanac* 1903

——. "Brechin's patron saint and the cathedral altaries and chaplainries" in *Brechin Almanac* 1908

—— ."Customs and superstitions of Brechin" in *Brechin Almanac* 1936

—— ."The eight o'clock bell" in *Brechin Almanac* 1923

—— ."Life in Brechin long ago" in *Brechin Almanac* 1891

—— ."Local rhymes and lore" in *Brechin Almanac* 1939

—— ."The restoration of the Cathedral: Laying the memorial stone" in *Brechin Almanac* 1901

—— ."Royal visitors to Castle and Cathedral" in *Brechin Almanac* 1922

—— ."The witch's branks and jougs" in *Brechin Almanac* 1922

Fraser, James E. *The Battle of Dunnichen 685*. Stroud: Tempus, 2002

Grahame, Roderick J. *Shards of Hope: an investigation into the history of Brechin Cathedral from an eschatological persepective*. Pittsburgh Theological Seminary, 2015

Henderson, I.A.N. "Bringing the gospel to Brechin" in *Scots Magazine,* 1996

Hudson, Benjamin. *The Picts*. Oxford: Wiley & Sons, 2014

Innes, Cosmo, trans. *Registrum Episcopatus Brechinensis*, Vol.1. Aberdeen: Bannatyne Club, 1856

Jervise, Andrew. *Memorials of Angus and Mearns*. Edinburgh: Adam & Charles Black, 1861

Landreth, James. *Brechin Cathedral: its history, with a survey of the religious bodies that have worshipped on the site*. Brechin, 1883

Leicester Addis, M.E. *Scottish Cathedrals and Abbeys*. London: Elliot Stock, 1901

Low, Leonard *The Weem Witch*. London: Steve Savage, 2006

Maxwell-Stuart, P.G. *An abundance of Witches – The Great Scottish Witch Hunt*.

Stroud: Tempus, 2005

--- *Satan's Conspiracy: Magic and Witchcraft in Sixteenth Century Scotland*. East
Linton: Tuckwell Press, 2001

Meek, Donald E. *The Quest for Celtic Christianity*. Haddington: The Handsel Press,
2000

McHardy, Stuart *A New History of the Picts*. Edinburgh: Luath Press, 2011

O'Dwyer, Peter "Celtic Monks and the Culdee Reforms" in *An Introduction to Celtic
Christianity*, edt. James Mackey. Edinburgh: T&T Clark, 1995

Oram, Richard *Alexander II King of Scots: 1214 – 1249*. Edinburgh: Birlinn, 2013

Reeves, William *The Culdees of the British Islands, with an appendix of evidences*.

Small paper reprint, Llanerch Publications, 1994

Scharlau, Fiona. *Old Brechin in Photographs*. Catrine: Stenlake Publishing, 2006

Scott, Archibald B. *The Pictish Nation – its people and its Church*. Edinburgh: TN
Foulis, 1918

Sievwright, William. *Brechin in olden and modern times*. Brechin: Black & Johnston,
1902

Simpson, W. Douglas. *The Celtic Church in Scotland*. Aberdeen University Press, 1935

Skene, W.F. (edt.) *John of Fordun's Chronicle of the Scottish Nation, Vols. 1 & 2*.

Two volume reprint by Llanerch Publications, 1993

--- *Celtic Scotland: A History of Ancient Alban Vols.I – III*. Paisley: Grian Press, 2014

Smout, T.C. A History of the Scottish People 1560-1830. Glasgow: Fontana Collins,
1969

Thoms, David B. *The Kirk of Brechin in the Seventeenth Century.* Brechin: Society of Friends Publications, 1972

——.*The council of Brechin: a study in local government* Brechin: Society of Friends Publications, 1977

——.*The Guildry of Brechin* Brechin: The Guildry, 1968

Watt, D.E.R. *Fasti Ecclesiae Scoticanae Medii Aevi ad annum 1638.* Dept. of Mediaeval History, St. Andrew's University, 1969 (2nd draft)

--- (edt.) A History Book for Scots – selections from the Scotichronicon by Walter Bower. Edinburgh: Mercat Press, 1998

Woolf, Alex *From Pictland to Alba 789 – 1070.* Edinburgh University Press, 2007.

Wylie, James *History of the Scottish Nation Vol.I – III.* Waxkeep Publishing, e-book

INDEX

D

S

Sabbath evening school · 127
Salvation Army
    General Booth · 187
same-sex debate · 256, 257, 259, 260
Samson, bishop · 18, 19, 268, 272, 321
Sang Schule · 47, 52, 57, 59
Sankey and Moody · 165
Sarum · 49, 56
Scots Confession · 63
Scottish Hymnal, 1870 · 167
Scottish Psalter · 152
Second Book of Discipline · 67
secular canons · 56, 58
secularism · 194, 225
Session Clerk · 128, 131, 157, 204, 219, 223, 225,
    229, 231, 234, 235, 236, 239, 241, 243, 248, 254,
    257, 258, 261, 321
Shanks, William, minister
    also Shank · 119, 120, 121, 271
Shaw, Bill
    Professor · 241
Shemfur · 83
Sievwright, William · 88, 81, 153, 325
Simpson, Douglas · 12, 321, 325
Simpson, James, Interim minister · 247, 248, 249, 271
Sinclair, John, bishop · 68
Skair, Catherine
    witch · 88, 85, 86
Skinner, James · 111, 112
Skinner, John · 97, 98, 99, 100, 102, 103, 104, 108,
    109, 110, 114, 117, 270, 284, 320
Skinner, Laurence, minister · 2, 59, 89, 90, 92, 94, 96,
    97, 112, 270
Skinner's burn · 2, 59
Society of Friends of Brechin Cathedral · 208, 218
Solemn League and Covenant · 82
Somme, Battle of 1916 · 189, 190
South Esk Church · *See* Gardner Memorial Church,
Spanish Influenza · 192
Square Tower · 21, 42, 87, 85, 201
St. Andrew's · 6, 10, 15, 19, 20, 22, 26, 38, 39, 42, 44,
    48, 60, 62, 65, 78, 81, 95, 118, 132, 133, 134, 164,
    166, 241, 264, 276, 325
Stephen de Cellerio, bishop · 43
Stewart, Sir James
    Lord Advocate · 102, 103

Stracathro Church · 1, 2, 37, 57, 99, 190, 195, 196,
    224, 225, 226, 227, 233, 272, 281, 301
Strachan, David, bishop · 20, 33, 48, 49, 58, 92, 93,
    269, 270, 282
Suffragettes · 187
summer · 26, 28, 36, 38, 41, 47, 54, 61, 81, 90, 91, 94,
    108, 110, 138, 142, 144, 160, 167, 168, 186, 187,
    193, 197, 203, 216, 218, 231, 234, 252, 254, 255,
    262, 264, 290
Supplementary Roll · 225, 253
Swan Inn · 124
Sweyn Forkbeard · 14
Sydserf, Thomas, bishop · 79, 80, 269, 282

T

Tait Hutchison, Adam Duncan, minister · 105, 179,
    180, 182, 186, 187, 189, 194, 203, 209, 214, 271
Thoms, D.B. · xi, 18, 19, 43, 89, 94, 95, 99, 100, 102,
    103, 109, 110, 111, 113, 114, 115, 116, 204, 217,
    219, 235, 286, 298, 320, 321, 325
Tolbooth · 65, 91, 132
Town and Landward Sessions · 79
Town Council · 65, 80, 89, 91, 97, 99, 100, 101, 103,
    108, 109, 112, 118, 122, 126, 130, 131, 137, 139,
    140, 164, 176, 186, 193, 217
Townhouse · 132
Treasurer · 57, 272
Turpin, bishop · 19, 21, 268, 272

U

Unitary Constitution · 255
unrestricted call · 244
unsatisfactory state
    of congregation · 214, 232, 239, 240
Urwardus or Edward, monk · 27

V

Veto Act, 1834 · 148
Victoria · 89, 142, 145, 149, 156, 159, 161, 184
Vikings · 9
Virgin Mary · 31, 63

W

Walker, Catherine
  witch · 88, 85, 86, 87
Walter Forrester, bishop · 44, 45, 268, 276
Walter Stewart, Earl of Atholl · 31, 47, 49
war · 28, 36, 51, 77, 87, 82, 110, 127, 156, 163, 188,
  189, 190, 191, 192, 201, 202, 203, 204, 205, 206,
  212, 213, 290
War of the Three Kingdoms · 83, 93
War Wolf · 39
Waterloo, Battle of 1815 · 132
Watt, Donald · 26, 45, 321, 325
weavers · ix, 115, 120, 127, 136, 153, 154, 174
Weekly Freewill Offering · 216
Welsh, David · 149
Western schism (1378-1417) · 44
Whigs · 114, 149
Whiteford, Walter, bishop · 80, 81, 269, 282
Whitson, George, minister · 134, 143, 271
Wilde, Philip · 41, 275
William and Mary · 96, 98, 111
(Glorious Revolution · 78, 89, 96, 97, 138)

William IV · 141
William the Conqueror · 56
William the Lion · 18, 19, 21, 25, 36
William Wallace · 38
William, Bishop of Brechin · 35
Willison, John, minister · 79, 101, 102, 103, 104, 109,
  110, 111, 112, 113, 114, 115, 116, 270, 284, 321
Wilson, William
  Grammar School · 128
winter · 38, 40, 44, 48, 71, 84, 91, 88, 117, 119, 135,
  138, 144, 154, 159, 173, 175, 176, 186, 189, 191,
  192, 197, 213
Wishart, George · 67
witch's branks
  or scold's bridle · 88, 324
witchcraft · 79, 88, 81, 82, 83, 87
Wycliffe, John · 44

Z

Zeppelin · 189